CULTURAL THEORY:
THE KEY THINKERS

in

th

Andrew Edgar and Peter Sedgwick are their posts at the University of Wales, Cardiff. They are the authors of *Key Concepts in Cultural Theory*, also published by Routledge.

ROUTLEDGE KEY GUIDES

You may also be interested in the following Routledge Student Reference titles:

CULTURAL THEORY: THE KEY THINKERS

Andrew Edgar and Peter Sedgwick

Routledge
Taylor & Francis Group

LONDON AND NEW YORK

First published 2002
by Routledge
11 New Fetter Lane, London EC4P 4EE

Simultaneously published in the USA and Canada
by Routledge
29 West 35th Street, New York, NY 10001

Reprinted in 2004

Routledge is an imprint of the Taylor & Francis Group

Typeset in Bembo by RefineCatch Limited, Bungay, Suffolk
Printed and bound in Great Britain by
TJ International Ltd, Padstow, Cornwall

British Library Cataloguing in Publication Data
A catalogue record for this book is available from the British Library

Library of Congress Cataloging in Publication Data
Sedgwick, Peter
Cultural theory : the key thinkers / Peter Sedgwick & Andrew Edgar.
p. cm.—(Routledge key guides)
Includes bibliographical references.
1. Culture.   I. Edgar, Andrew.   II. Title.

HM621 .S43   2001
306 — dc21   2001038716

ISBN 0–415–23281–3 (pbk)
ISBN 0–415–23280–5 (hbk)

CONTENTS

LIST OF CONTRIBUTORS

Gary Day, Andrew Edgar, Stephen Horton, Kevin Mills, Marianna Papastephanou, Mark Patterson, Nadira Regrag, Peter Sedgwick, Shiva Kumar Srininvassan

PREFACE

This volume is intended to complement our earlier volume *Key Concepts in Cultural Theory*. It provides introductions to the work of a range of authors who have contributed to the development of what we now understand as cultural theory. We have selected those whom we regard as the most influential contemporary thinkers, such as Derrida, Habermas and Rorty. We have included major thinkers of the twentieth century, such as Benjamin, Foucault and Heidegger, and have complemented them with thinkers who may have fallen into some neglect, such as Arendt, Benedict and Oakeshott. In addition we have aimed to provide the reader with summaries of the work of crucial pre-twentieth-century figures, such as Aristotle, Hegel, Hume and Plato, whose ideas have served to shape much of Western thought, and thus our understanding of culture. A glossary is included in order to provide the reader with an explanation of some of the terms that recur throughout the text.

AE/PS

ADORNO, THEODOR WIESENGRUND (1903–1969)

German philosopher, sociologist and musicologist who was a leading member (and eventually director) of the Frankfurt Institute for Social Research (the institutional basis of the Frankfurt School of German critical theory).

Adorno's work may be understood as an attempt to develop a Marxist theory of twentieth-century capitalism (Adorno 1987). He follows **Lukács** (1971) in recognising that **Marx**'s account of capitalism is inadequate, for it lacks a theory of bureaucracy. This theory is found in the work of Max **Weber** (1946b). Lukács fused Marx and Weber through his theory of 'reification'. A reified society is one that confronts its members as a quasi-natural object, rather than as a product of human subjective action. Reification is rooted in the all-pervasiveness of the principles of commodity exchange. Commodity exchange entails the comparison of qualitatively distinct goods and processes by reducing them to a common quantitative measure (monetary value). For Lukács this quantification of the qualitatively-unique underpins not just commodity exchange, but all forms of social interaction, including the bureaucratic organisation of workforces and a state's citizens. For Adorno, more radically still, the principles of quantification and exchange infiltrate even thought itself.

While Lukács retained faith in the revolutionary potential of the proletariat, so that he found in the standpoint of the proletariat a supposedly objective point from which to criticise capitalism, Adorno lacks this faith. Traditional class distinctions are no longer relevant, for all human beings are alike integrated into the 'totally administered' capitalist society through commodity exchange, bureaucracy, and through what he calls the culture industry (Adorno 1991a). The culture industry is composed of primarily the advertising and mass media industries, that influence the consumer's judgement of the usefulness (or 'use-value') of commodities. In effect, while in nineteenth-century capitalism consumers chose goods because they found them useful, now our very acts of choice are constructed by the producers. The commodity exists, not to satisfy the needs or desires of consumers, but simply to be exchanged and generate profit (surplus-value) and thus to perpetuate the capitalist system. Criticism of capitalism is hampered because, crucially, the resources that capitalism provides to the intellectual (for example in philosophy or the social and natural sciences) are no longer sufficient to challenge the capitalist order, because these resources are fundamentally coherent with capitalism's basic principles of quantification and exchange. In effect, philosophy and science (like advertising) exist to reproduce capitalism.

Adorno is therefore suspicious of the very possibility of thinking coherently and critically about capitalism in its own terms, and so must seek an approach to social analysis that will break apart the reified or natural appearance of capitalism, and thus open up the possibility of recognising that things could be otherwise.

In part this involves a complex use of language, a refusal to define concepts, and a pursuit of arguments into unresolved contradictions. Contradictions expose the inadequacies of reified thought, and specifically the failure of thought (the order of ideas) to grasp adequately social reality (the order of things). Thus, Adorno's (1973b) approach of 'negative dialectics' (or 'non–identity thinking') proceeds, not, like Lukács', by positing some objective standpoint from which philosophy and criticism could be developed, but rather by recognising only the falsehood of all existing accounts and judgements of society (precisely because they fall into contradiction). Adorno is thus arguing that the thinker or analyst is not autonomous from the reality they seek to analyse. Rather, because the very structure of their thoughts is determined by capitalism, the analyst can only work by recognising the ways in which capitalism has falsified and inhibited thought. The thinker strives for 'exact fantasy' that is at once disciplined by a sensitivity to the object under analysis, and yet is free to take risks, breaking from the control of orthodox systematic thought (1977, p. 131).

Art, and specifically the art of the modernist avant-garde, is for Adorno the principle source of resistance to capitalism. He approaches art through a contradictory thesis: art is at once a social fact and yet autonomous from society. This is to claim that the analysis of art requires both that one recognises that it is determined by society, and yet that it is free of society. Adorno unravels this through a reinterpretation of **Kant**'s definition of 'beauty' as 'purposiveness without a purpose' (Kant 1952a, p. 80). A work of art is purposive, in the sense that it is an intentionally constructed human artefact. It is purposeless in that it does not wholly pursue the dominant purposes of capitalism (which is to say, a work of art is not simply a commodity that exists for exchange and the realisation of surplus-value). Aesthetics – the philosophy of art – presupposes that an art work should be analysed in its own terms. An art work pursues intrinsically artistic problems, such as expression or representation of the natural or emotional world; the organisation of the surface of a painting; the development of a narrative; or the structuring of themes within a piece of music. In contrast, a sociology of art will demonstrate that any given art work is a product of its age. The technology used in the art work will be similar to that used in industry (consider the chemicals in paint or the machinery of the musical instrument), the thought processes of the artist (such as the sense of time, space, narrative and logical development) will be akin to those of their contemporaries, and the art work will be distributed and consumed like other goods. Adorno's claim is that the sociology of art reveals that the autonomous, purely aesthetic, content of the art work is in fact a sedimented social content. By pursuing its aesthetic concerns, the art work is pursuing the concerns of mundane society, albeit crucially stripped of the constraints of the dominant objectives of capitalism. An appropriate reading of a work of art can, potentially, tell us more about society than can an empirical sociology, precisely because the work of art exposes the inner tensions of society, not its reified appearance.

Adorno turns to modernist avant-garde works – such as the music of Schoenberg (Adorno 1973a) or the theatre of Beckett (Adorno 1991c – as the most profound response, not just to aesthetic problems but also, necessarily, to social problems. The shocking, seemingly incomprehensible nature of the avant-garde is important, because the avant-garde is responding to the art of the past, and is recognising that its solutions to aesthetic problems are no longer adequate. Thus, for Schoenberg, the tonal system that governed Western music from the seventeenth to the nineteenth centuries is no longer adequate to express emotions, and its possibilities for organising thematic material is exhausted. In breaking with tonality, Schoenberg exposes as conventional what was previously taken for granted as natural. A reified surface is broken apart, and one realises that things could be otherwise.

While Adorno is a critic of the Enlightenment, he is ultimately a critic of its failure (Adorno and Horkheimer 1973). There has been too little enlightenment, not too much. In avant-garde art, in contrast to the rest of contemporary culture, he still finds the relentless challenging of taken-for-granted foundations and boundaries (myths of givenness or naturalness) that characterise critical, enlightened thought, and a striving for truth, if only in exposing the falsehood of past and present.

[AE]

Further reading: Buck-Morss 1977; D. Cook 1996; Jameson 1990a; Jarvis 1998; Jay 1984; Lunn 1982; O'Connor 2000; O'Neill 1999; Rose 1978.

ALTHUSSER, LOUIS (1918–1990)

Born in Algeria, Althusser studied philosophy at the Ecole Normale Supérior (although he was accepted for *agrégation* in 1939, he did not proceed to it until 1948, having served in the French forces during the Second World War, during which time he was taken as a prisoner by the Germans). He first came to prominence in the 1960s with the publication of a series of articles which expounded his combination of structuralism and **Marx**ism, and presented his criticisms of the humanism of traditional Marxist thought. Althusser's structural Marxism put forward a revised view of the role of economic determinacy with regard to the ideological, political, legislative and cultural structures present within capitalist social orders. Thus, he sought to displace the perceived emphasis in much of Marx's work upon a classical model of political economy which, coupled with an empiricist model for the analysis of social relations, had been taken as providing the basis for the purportedly 'scientific' status of Marx's conclusions. For Althusser, each of these structures (ideological, political, etc.) pertains to a relative autonomy within the larger network of social relations which constitute capitalist society. Thus, capitalist society is a totality, but it is also a structure which does not have a centre of organisation. Hence, rather than advocating a direct determinacy according to which the economic base dictates the superstructure (the model of classical Marxism), Althusser viewed capitalist society as a network of interrelated structures. The autonomy of these structures is, however, seen as relative rather than absolute since, in the last instance, economic factors exert a causal influence over the structure as a whole. In turn, the traditional Marxist conception of 'society', in the sense of an empirically verifiable whole, is replaced within Althusser's account by the concept of the 'mode of production'. The capitalist mode of production is marked by particular features, e.g. the commodification of goods, the notions of exchange and surplus value, the organisation of labour. Modes of production, in turn, evolve through history, and Marxism, on this account, becomes the historical analysis of the development of modes of production in their immanent relationship to the various social, political, cultural, ideological and legislative structures which make up the social totality. Marx is thus credited by Althusser with developing a new theoretical articulation of social relations which, however, due to the economic and scientific paradigms at his disposal, he could not himself fully articulate.

In turn, Althusser proposed replacing the traditional Marxist conception of science as empirical analysis with a model which, instead of grounding itself in procedures of observation and verification, stressed the internal consistency of a theory as providing proof of its validity. Thus, for Althusser, what Marxist theory states need not correspond to an immediately verifiable social reality, for the veracity of its analysis is shown in the internal consistency of the premises that underpin it. The conception of modes of production was then supplemented by Althusser with a reformulation of the meaning and significance of ideology in the shape of his theory if ideological state apparatuses, a conception again developed in order to fill what he contended were gaps in traditional Marxist theory.

Also, Althusser espoused the view that individuals do not in any sense exist independently of the constitution of economic and social structures. This view lay at the heart of Althusser's anti-humanism. Whereas Marxists had traditionally argued that human beings are the authors of their own destinies, Althusser's contention was that individuals are an expression of the relations which inhere within the historically determined structures that make up the capitalist mode of production.

[PS]

Further reading: Kaplan and Sprinker 1993; S. Smith 1984.

ARENDT, HANNAH (1906–1975)

German born (although naturalised American) political philosopher, who contributed significantly to the analysis of totalitarianism, and the fate of Jewry in the twentieth century.

Arendt is perhaps best known for a single utterance, her response to the Nazi Adolf Eichmann standing trial: 'the lesson of the fearsome, word-and-thought-defying *banality of evil*' (1963a). This is not an inappropriate introduction to her thought. Her analysis of Nazism reveals not a psychology of evil, for Eichmann was not the monster of popular mythology, but simply a man without imagination, and yet unquestioningly obedient to the Nazi administration. The evil of Nazism largely lay in its shallowness and ordinariness. This account of Eichmann can be grounded in the arguments of *The Origins of Totalitarianism* (1951b). In its first part, Arendt looks to the historical precedents of totalitarianism, not least in the status of the Jews as a pariah group. The position of the pariah is crucial to the analysis (and indeed to Arendt's life and work as a whole). After an account of the rise of colonial and imperial administrations, with their focus on efficiency at the expense of the real needs of those administered – and it is here that Eichmann finds his place – Arendt turns to the fate of pariah groups as stateless. The pariah is an anomaly in the modern state, for they fall outside the law. The stateless are not deprived of specific rights, but of all rights, and as such are excluded from the community. Arendt notes that even the criminal has rights. Their crime occurs within the law. Pariahs commit no crime, and as such they are the innocent victims of arbitrary violence. Precisely because they have no rights, and as such are not respected by fellow human beings, totalitarianism deprives its victims of their very identity, and their death is anonymous. For Arendt the pariah status is not something that Jews can voluntarily relinquish. Attempts at assimilation led only to new prejudices and to self-denial. She therefore argues for the position of the 'conscious pariah', that can act from a position of strength only by accepting the contingent circumstances of birth and upbringing (or 'natality' as Arendt terms it: 1958b).

In *The Human Condition* (1958a) Arendt turns to a more general analysis of the polity and the weakness of modern political life. Her concern is with the *vita activa*, which she analyses through the categories of 'labour', 'work' and 'action'. 'Labour' concerns the satisfaction of necessary biological needs, and 'work' the production of durable objects. 'Action' concerns the realm of freedom, and thus, for Arendt, the true realm of politics. In freedom individuals act in complete equality with others, capable of pure creativity (the 'beautiful deed'). This realm is, in effect, the community – or republic – from which the pariah is excluded. The problem of contemporary democratic societies lies in the fact that governments have placed the satisfaction of material needs over and above the creation of freedom. In *On Revolution* (1963b), she argues that this failure can be traced to the French Revolution in contrast to the American Revolution. While the former comes to disregard the 'Rights of Man', the latter, with its drafting of a Declaration of Rights and various constitutions, gives higher priority to the creation of a community of free rights holders than to the solution of what Arendt calls 'the social question'. Put otherwise, contemporary societies, in contrast with the ancient Greek polity, fail to recognise that the private realm of the household (*oikia*) was the site of labour and thus necessity, and as such should serve the public realm of freedom (and not vice versa). For Arendt, thanks to technological advance, the material problems that are the focus of the social question have now been solved. The conditions for the possibility of a free republic have then been achieved. Yet contemporary democracies continue to make politics banal (again echoing Eichmann's Nazism), where a narrow focus on utilitarian concerns inhibits the possibility of addressing the genuine political issues of freedom and creativity.

[AE]

Further reading: Canovan 1974; Hill 1979; Kaplan and Kessler 1989; Kateb 1984; May 1986; Whitfield 1980.

ARISTOTLE (384–322 BC)

Ancient Greek philosopher. Aristotle was born in Macedonia, northern Greece. When he was 17 Aristotle made the journey to Athens, where he entered **Plato**'s Academy. Aristotle remained at the Academy for the next twenty years. Upon Plato's death in 347 Aristotle moved to the city of Assos (an area now on the northern Turkish coast). Assos was ruled by Hermias, an ex-pupil of the Academy. During the period he spent there Aristotle married and had a daughter (he was to marry a second time and have a son around fifteen years later). While in Assos Aristotle carried out a large amount of research into the anatomical, dietary and reproductive features of a wide range of animals. Upon Hermias' death (he was executed in 341 by the king of Persia) Aristotle moved to Lesbos and from there to the capital of Macedonia. Here he was invited by the monarch Philip II to be tutor to his son, who was to become Alexander the Great. During Alexander's reign Aristotle returned to Athens. Here he opened a school, the Lyceum. Whereas Plato's Academy was an institution closed to the public, the Lyceum offered many free lectures to anyone who cared to attend. Following Alexander's death in 323 there was an outbreak of anti-Macedonian feeling that prompted Aristotle to leave Athens for Chalcis, where he died the following year.

Many of Aristotle's writings have survived in the form of unpublished lecture notes or student texts. It is common scholarly practice to group Aristotle's work into five categories. In the first are those works concerned with issues in logic, which primarily analyse it as an instrument of thought (e.g. the *Categories, On Interpretation and Topics*). Second, there are the texts concerned with natural philosophy (e.g. *Physics, On the Soul and Generation of Animals*). Third, the *Metaphysics* is a work that considers the problem of 'first causes', i.e. locating first principles. Fourth, those works that deal with practical issues or 'action' (e.g. the *Nicomachean Ethics, Eudemian Ethics and Politics*).

Finally, there are the *Poetics* and the *Rhetoric*, texts concerned with issues of 'production', i.e. a form of action with a purpose external to the act itself. Thus, for example, the activity of using persuasive language is not to be confused with its purpose, i.e. persuading someone of something.

Although a pupil of Plato and indebted to him in many ways, significant aspects of Aristotle's thought differ from that of his teacher. Thus, the *Metaphysics* contains critical references to Plato's Theory of Ideas. Among other things, Aristotle argues that Plato's theory does not have any genuine explanatory power when it comes to the problem of change. Against Plato, Aristotle argues for a theory of substances in which individual entities (e.g. 'this human being', 'that tree') can be understood as being primary. A primary substance (*ousia*), therefore, can be pointed to, it is something specific. Equally, substances can have different properties at different times without losing their identity (e.g. a tree can be a different colour at various times, but is still the same tree). A substance can also change into another substance: the tree can burn down and become a mound of ashes. When such a change takes place what remains constant is the same 'matter' or stuff out of which the tree was, and the ashes are now, made. Without the existence of substances, however, there would be nothing at all (matter must always take some form or other). In turn, Aristotle distinguishes between substances and universals. Universals include secondary substances of species and genus: an individual person is a human (species) and an animal (genus). They also include quantities and qualities (e.g. size and colour) and relations ('*X* is three times bigger than *Y*'). In effect, Aristotle's argument that individual entities are primary and hence ground reality inverts Platonic metaphysics (according to which, particulars encountered by way of the senses are flawed copies of the absolute reality of the realm of Ideas). Equally, in the *Posterior Analytics* Aristotle argues against the view that disciplines of inquiry can be unified by way of common principles. He therefore disagrees with Plato's view, expressed in the *Republic*, that it is possible to provide a general account (dialectic) of the principles on which all forms of knowledge rest. That said, Aristotle agrees with Plato in so far as he holds that ultimate knowledge must be secured by way of definitions, and that such knowledge must be concerned with what is eternal. Also, a variant on the Platonic Theory of Ideas appears to be argued for when Aristotle asserts that substance is form. Thus, primary substance 'is the form present in the thing, and the compound of substance is spoken of as composed of the form and the matter' (*Metaphysics*, Book 7, Chapter 11).

Aristotle's moral philosophy is generally regarded as being stated most fully in the *Nicomachean Ethics*. Ethics, he argues, is a practical form of knowledge that concerns the sphere of human action. When we inquire into human actions we ask why someone did what they did. In other words, we ask about the purposes of action. Again, Aristotle argues against Plato, in that he holds what is good ought not to be accounted for in the Platonic sense of the Idea of the Good. However, Aristotle and Plato alike hold there to be an intrinsic link between virtue and happiness. Happiness is therefore the highest good. 'Happiness' here does not mean the same thing as 'pleasure' or 'being content', however. Rather, being happy in Aristotle's sense means both living and behaving in a manner that is virtuous. This view is derived from Aristotle's claim that humans are different from plants and animals in that they are capable of pursuing a rational existence directed towards action. The highest form of such an existence is one that is directed morally. People, Aristotle argues, acquire good ways of living and they can acquire bad ones. Moral virtues, therefore, are learned. In this regard one might say that, for Aristotle, practice makes perfect. To be an ethical being, in turn, means to be a certain kind of person. What kind of person this is can be approached by way of a sketch of Aristotle's notion of the soul. The soul, he argues, is composed of three elements. The first of these concerns bodily sustenance and development (nutritional needs). The second is a desiring element and the third a rational element. Of these, the first is of no importance for ethics. The second element, though, is under rational control and is a source of emotional virtues, e.g. bravery or generosity. The third is the source of understanding, on the one hand, and wisdom on the other. Of these, the first concerns our conceptual abilities with regard to forms of knowledge, while wisdom consists in our ability to make judgements. For Aristotle, being a moral being means being the kind of person who will live wisely. Such a person lives carefully, in the sense that they avoid indulgence to excess. Avoiding taking too much alcohol or conducting oneself with care in the company of others (neither behaving too boldly or too meekly) are examples of such a form of living. The key point for Aristotle is that such a person attains a balance in their style of living: they indulge in neither too much (excess) nor too little (asceticism). This balance is known as 'the golden mean'. The golden mean does not take the form of a prescriptive rule regarding, for example, how much or how little exercise every individual ought to take daily. Rather, it is a principle that advocates the right kind of behaviour for an individual appropriate to their circumstances. If you live an active life you will not need to exercise as often as someone who spends much of the day inactive. Above all, the principle of the golden mean advocates achieving a balance between various forms of behaviour. Thus, to attain the golden mean means that an individual is not dominated by drives beyond their control. To be mean or profligate with money, for example, is unhealthy. Getting the right balance, in this instance, means knowing when one ought to be careful with one's resources and when one ought to be generous. By the same token, a person ought to know how to speak well in the company of others and how to listen well, too. To be virtuous, it follows, is about knowing how to behave appropriately (which also, for Aristotle, involves not doing or feeling certain things: one cannot, in his view, be jealous or resentful to a degree that is 'appropriate' under any circumstances).

Virtue, then, on an Aristotelian view is about knowing how to act, and such knowledge requires wisdom. To be wise means that one possesses moral virtue and vice versa. Given that Aristotle divides the soul into three elements, it is natural that he locates wisdom as residing in the rational part of the soul along with understanding. Where understanding is concerned with comprehending conceptual knowledge and wisdom with comprehending moral virtue, both are characterised by way of their concern with truth (the spheres of intellectual and ethical excellence). The highest possible achievement one can aim for is to attain 'happiness' in the sense mentioned above and this, for Aristotle, involves engaging in the practice of philosophy, i.e. a life of critical reflection devoted to the pursuit of knowledge and truth.

The other aspect of Aristotle's practical philosophy is found in the *Politics*. This text is concerned with the notion of the city-state and its purpose. The human being is defined by Aristotle as the 'political animal'. By this he means that our daily existence involves living together in communities. Any state is a community that is defined by way of its being composed of people with shared values and ways of living. The function of such communities is to offer those who live within them a worthwhile life. Thus, there is for Aristotle a direct link between human nature and ethics, since individual happiness necessarily involves concern with those with whom one lives in a community. According to Aristotle there are three forms of worthwhile government: monarchy, aristocracy and polity (the latter is a constitutional form of representative government which seeks to balance the interests of the higher and lower orders in a community). These forms are all prone to degeneration into tyranny, oligarchy and democracy (by 'democracy' he means anarchic mob-rule). Aristotle advocates polity as the best form of government (a view that is endorsed by later thinkers such as Machiavelli).

Aristotle's theory of aesthetics is presented in the first book of the *Poetics* (the second book on comedy has not survived). The *Poetics* not only is primarily concerned with the formal nature of tragic drama, but also considers the ethical issues that such art forms raise. Aristotle offers a definition of the tragic form, stating that tragic drama involves a combination of necessary elements. Primary among these are plot and character. A good writer of tragedy, says Aristotle, ensures that the central protagonist is a person of high social status who suffers a fall from grace as a consequence of some act they have made. Thus, in Sophocles' *Oedipus*, Oedipus unwittingly kills his father and marries his mother. Plot should determine the presence of characters in a play (only plot justifies the introduction of characters). Equally, plot must consist of a beginning, middle and end. Hence, a tragedy needs to arrive at some kind of resolution of the tensions built up in the course of the unfolding narrative: it is guided by the unity of purpose given to it by the narrative. At a key moment in tragic drama the main protagonist suffers a disaster, which is usually the result of some hitherto unknown event coming to light. Oedipus' kingdom is blighted and he discovers that he is the cause of it because of what he has unwittingly done to his father, and because of his unnatural relationship with his mother, which has resulted in his children being his siblings. The resolution of plot is achieved when Oedipus leaves the city in disgrace, stripped of his status and blinded by his own hand. The point of tragedy, Aristotle argues, is to generate feelings of pity and terror in the mind of the spectator. Thus, good tragedy achieves a cathartic effect wherein the viewer of the play experiences an emotional cleansing as a result of witnessing the events portrayed.

Aristotle's influence upon European culture, like that of his teacher Plato, has been profound. In the medieval period his writings exerted an extensive influence upon theological doctrine by way of the writings of St Thomas Aquinas (*c.*1225–1274). Aquinas' reading of Aristotle still stands as one of the most challenging interpretations of his thought. Equally, Aristotle's work in the areas of natural science and logic in effect formed the basis for these disciplines. In the twentieth century his work exerted an important influence upon the thought of Martin **Heidegger**, whose *Being and Time* (1927) takes Aristotle's discussion of Being (see *Metaphysics*, Book 4) as an invitation to engage in the project of phenomenological ontology.

[PS]

Further reading: Ackrill 1981; Barnes 1982, 1984; Gerson 1999; Irwin and Fine 1995; Kenny 1992; Moravcsik 1968; Sherman 1999.

ARNOLD, MATTHEW (1822–1888)

Matthew Arnold, English poet, literary critic, and essayist, perceived reformative tendencies accompanying the burgeoning development of industrial society in nineteenth-century England that threatened the wavering hegemonic apparatus of secular and ecclesiastical order, and hindered the appreciation and expression of cultural ideals that would access a smoother course for personal and social advancement in troubled times. As an antidote to the rapid transmission, and easy acceptance, of values advocating industrial progress, individual liberty, Protestant ethic and Puritan bias, Arnold sought civilised unity through a shared cultural identity. Looking to the past to illuminate an age lost in disillusionment, division and menacing anarchy, he advocates the reclamation of ideas capable of nourishing a common need for harmony and growth. From his critical vantage-point he surveys the barren ground of contemporary thought, with its blinkered deference to progress, action and duty, and sees a land incapable of propogating true culture. Arnold's clarion call for the reassessment of commonly accepted values, and the routing of intellectual complacency, is delivered in *Culture and Anarchy: An Essay in Political and Social Criticism* (1867–1869). Here culture is defined as 'the best which has been tought and said in the world', and presented as an ameliorative, subtilising and instructive force with the potential to transform society's attritional habits. In an age where the routes of liberty and progress are waymarked by the pandering desires of the 'ordinary self', Arnold looks forward to the release, through the catalytic medium of 'best' literature, poetry and Christian eisegesis from the past, of 'a stream of fresh and free thought upon our stock notions'.

Lack of faith in church and state's capacity to carry the momentum of transitional development is seen to result in halted progress and cul-de-sac confusion. Arnold sees his countrymen distrusting existing political and religious apparatus, while refusing to let go of their belief in the efficacy of the 'machinery' of external systems as a ladder out of crisis. For Arnold future hopes revolve around a change in perspective, where the individual develops an intrinsic response to culture's untramelling truths. Regeneration at a personal level must prefigure any attempts to rearrange the weak, though workable, organs of state.

'The culture we recommend is above all an inward operation.' As well as being encouraged to question the value of political remonstrance, one is also alerted against placing too much hope in an immediate social recovery. Culture posits 'immortality' and endurance against the evanescent political platform and the unrealistic promises of salvation of new religious leaders. Arnold's belief in the slow maturation of the human spirit through culture carries a resignation to stasis. Culture, we are told, may save the future 'from being vulgarised' even if it cannot 'save the present'.

Wary of the ascendancy of Puritan values, the remote ceremony of Catholicism and the crowd-inciting rhetoric of the 'fanatical Protestant', Arnold sets the task of reclaiming the self-empowering language of Christian religion. Whereas organised religion presents a model of 'incomplete perfection', an intrinsic response to Christian teaching reveals a language of 'Sweetness and Light', attuned to the personal quest for integration and perfect harmony. The writings of St Paul are held up as proof of religion's self-regulating, interiorised potential, declaring to the individual that 'The Kingdom of God is within you'. Poetry, with its capacity to 'resolutely test' imperfect values, and aspirations towards beauty and harmony, becomes religion's ally within culture. Unlike religion, however, poetry has not been wrested from the individual, although its function has been weakened as its cultural bed of source and inspiration runs dry. The classical writings of Greece and Rome, and the literature of sixteenth-century England are championed as exemplary junctures, where poetry and religion meet and flourish. In nineteenth-century England poetry has a special place in culture's agenda; as a force capable of unleashing a generative religious sensibility. Popular literature is denigrated as an imperfect partisan shadow of the classical ideal.

Arnold establishes the 'disinterested' role of the critic as an objective cultural commentator, giving him the power to discern, represent and rank neglected works. From his vantage point, above society's nascent redeemers, he can categorise the opponents of true internal culture. The aristocracy, exhibitors of an ornamental 'exterior' culture, can no longer be looked to as exemplars of aestheticism and inspirational values. As a type he refers to them as 'Barbarians'. The middle classes, towards whom Arnold's attention is almost wholly drawn as a possible spawning ground for the perception and dissemination of true culture, misguidedly revere principles of action and utility, earning them their classification as 'Philistines'. Society's base rests uneasily on the inchoate working classes, the 'Populace', given to moments of foment and anarchy, in the absence of any guiding cultural light.

As an undertow to society's transient dissatisfactions runs a perennial pattern of ascendance, dominance, and usurpation between the vying dualistic forces of 'Hebraism' and 'Hellenism'. Their alternative rise and fall determines the status of culture at any given time in history. Hellenism is humanity's primary expression of 'spontaneity of consciousness', evincing the reflective traits that aspire to the truest representations in literature, poetry and religion. Hebraism advocates 'strictness of consciousness' and manifests laws of conduct, control, duty and action, providing a necessary corollary to the premature excesses of Hellenism. Arnold perceived a series of 'checks' and countercurrents within nineteenth-century society that hindered the re-emergence of a refined Hellenic perspective, gone to ground for the duration of Hebraisms prolonged rule. Culture reclaimed, recognised and acted upon is the key to betterment. A Hellenised future will be characterised by democratic harmony and the pursuit of perfection within a traditional social hegemony. The tutors in this evolutionary venture, the civilising voice of culture, so to speak, will come from a culturally empowered middle class.

[Mark Patterson]

Further reading: Collini 1988; Johnson 1979; Mulhern 1995.

BAKHTIN, MIKHAIL (1895–1975)

Russian writer concerned with the spheres of language, culture, philosophy, and literature. Born in Orel, a town south of Moscow, Bakhtin studied at St Petersburg University, and went on to teach at Nevel and Vitebsk. In texts such as the essays collected together in *The Dialogic Imagination* (1981), Bakhtin argued for the view that there is a vital connection between novelistic language and genre, and emphasised the liberating insights that the consideration of genre brings to the closed perspective implicit in purely stylistic analysis. Thus, he argued for viewing the novel as a dialogic generic form, i.e. as a form that contains within it a multiplicity of voices and perspectives. In turn, the novel exists in a constant process of change and renewal, and is contrasted with other fixed and complete literary forms. As a unique form in this constant state of flux, Bakhtin argued, the novel absorbs into itself other, less flexible forms which it parodies, travesties or reaccentuates.

Bakhtin also famously provided an analysis of the 'carnivalesque' through his reading of the works of François Rabelais. For Bakhtin, the folk tradition of carnival undermines the seriousness of official culture, and does so largely through the debasing effect of carnival laughter which, in the carnival setting, is freed from the dogmatism of religious and ecclesiastical forms of social domination. Shaped by this laughter, carnival challenges the closed world of social laws and restraints and, in turn, offers a world which exists in a realm that is independent of officialdom. As long as the carnival lasts there is no world beyond it, and those who participate in the carnival thereby enter, for a time, into a social domain of utopian freedom, community and equality. Carnival is thus identified by Bakhtin as an alternative and temporary cultural practice with an ambivalent relationship to dominant culture, since its challenge to official culture is a contained rather than a dangerous one. Instead of arguing for a polarised conception of authority and subversion through the juxtaposition of carnival and officialdom, Bakhtin seems to emphasise their ambiguous proximity, for carnival is a contained subversion of the dominant forces underlying social order which is nevertheless endowed with the potential to invert conventional discourse and thought. Thus, carnival undermines dominant culture not in a directly practical sense, but in the sense that it invades and inverts conventional structures of language and thought. It is, it follows, an ambivalent phenomenon which is closely affiliated with the world of officialdom, from which it offers temporary release.

In his essay 'Speech Genres', Bakhtin (1986) examines the interaction and the boundaries between different areas of communication, and provides a framework for discussing the systematic restraints and controls which condition the development of any specific domain of oral or written communication. In this way, his essay problematises a straightforward notion of the interaction between different language modes. He begins by pointing out the different restrictions that a given culture imposes on any utterance. The first restriction, the 'semantic exhaustiveness' of the utterance, is relative to more complex spheres of communication, so that a second restriction is activated in the 'speech plan' whereby a speaker narrows down his or her choice of subject. However, the element of individual choice suggested by the notion of a speech plan serves only to activate a third restriction on utterances. The speech plan determines the form of genre for the utterance, which is relatively stable, but although more flexible in terms of the possibility they offer for variation, genres nevertheless delimit the domain of utterances. A single utterance, in other words, in spite of its individual and creative nature, can never be regarded as a completely free combination of language forms. Genre, therefore, imposes a constraining effect upon the generation of utterances, and thereby undermines the extent to which an individual speaker is free to choose and manipulate language forms in the communicative process. Thus, the speaker cannot plunder and appropriate diverse areas of communication for the purpose of unfettered self-expression. In turn, it is possible on this view to question any contention that language can assume an openness that is interdisciplinary. Rather, any utterance will assume the imprints of its generic form, which endows it with a certain self-contained relative autonomy.

However, when Bakhtin turns to analyse the process of interaction between utterances, this concept of their relative autonomy is further problematised. All utterances exist in a state of an inter-animating tension with other utterances. The sphere of speech is always filled with the words of others, and its manifestations are thereby denied self-sufficiency. Instead, they necessarily have awareness of and so reflect one another. Whatever the conditions of their production, when utterances intermingle with one another they cease to retain their original expressiveness in any pure form, and thereby become vulnerable to the speech genre of an appropriating speaker. In the process of appropriation and assimilation an utterance is transformed: it is endowed with an alien expression which means that it also is reinterpreted. In turn, for Bakhtin, the interaction between utterances becomes an antagonistic process, fought out across the boundaries between one's own and another's words. An utterance thus becomes riven, marked with the traces of its own embattled formation. Hence, during the communicative process an appropriated speech act or text is necessarily realigned or transformed. In terms of this theory, therefore, there can be no simple level at which the exchange of ideas or dialogue takes place, nor can any constant thematic characterisation be transported between the boundaries which separate speech genres and utterances. Bakhtin's thesis thereby indicate some of the processes which may lie behind the interaction between different speech forms (or different genres of discourse).

[PS]

Further reading: Holquist 1990; Lodge 1990.

BARTHES, ROLAND (1915–1980)

French literary critic who was a key figure both in the development of structuralism – in particular in the application of techniques derived from semiology to the analysis of everyday life and popular (as well as high) culture – and in the post-structuralist criticism of structuralism. His work covers an enormous range of issues and topics, including the nature of writing, authorship and reading; myth and ideology; fashion; photography; narrative; the work of diverse writers (including Sade, Michelet, Proust and Balzac) and composers; and subjectivity and sexuality.

Barthes' early works, published in the 1950s, including *Writing Degree Zero* (1967a) and *Mythologies* (1973), are centrally concerned with the illusions of contemporary bourgeois culture, and particularly the bourgeois denial of the 'opacity' of language. Within contemporary culture, it is assumed generally that language is a neutral medium that the writer may use, without restriction, to express and communicate his or her ideas. This culture is concerned with verisimilitude, or the faithful and unbiased reproduction of an independent reality (both in visual representation and is verbal description). Barthes challenges these assumptions, arguing rather that language (or more properly writing – *écriture*) is already bound up within particular social forms, and as such does not report an independent reality, but creates a reality. Different forms of writing bring with them 'realities', and crucially, realities that fuse together accounts of the sort of facts that exist in the world and evaluations of those facts. Because bourgeois culture denies this opacity (i.e. the fact that language creates or presupposes a reality), the value-laden and selective realities that are offered in language appear to be natural, and thus the way in which the world really is. It may be noted that Barthes' work on narrative, similarly, is concerned with the structural conventions that a story must obey, if, paradoxically, it is to appear to the reader as if it was unfolding, not according to a convention, but rather naturally (Barthes 1977b).

In *Mythologies*, in particular, Barthes analyses the way in which a second, 'mythological', level of meaning is added onto signs. The signs under investigation are not only linguistic signs, but also any carriers of meaning, including photographs and other visual images. Myth, for Barthes, works by allowing a particular image to reinforce our prejudices, making them appear to have universal validity. A particular image (or signifier) is fused with a value system (which, at this mythological level, is what is signified). Thus, for example, in Barthes' most famous example, the photograph of a French Negro soldier comes to reinforce the positive value and legitimacy of French imperialism. Myth works through the way in which the soldier is photographed (in this case, loyally saluting the French flag). Mythology hides nothing, but presents everything with a certain inflexion. Precisely because signifier and signified are fused, the value associations of the image are taken as self-evident and indeed natural.

Barthes' *Elements of Semiology* (1967b), written in the early 1960s, on the one hand begins to draw together the methodology of such semiological approaches, but on the other hand, and more importantly, begins to question the basis of semiology itself. He finds in semiological research a 'dream of scientificity'. That is to say, semiology, while allowing the critical approach to bourgeois culture described, still presupposes that it is capable of achieving some fixed point from which it can gain an objective, unbiased and undistorted view of reality. In orthodox semiology, that which is signified is assumed to pre-exist the act of signification (so that a signifier simply refers to some pre-existing reality). For Barthes, the signifier is now seen as creating the signified (just as writing creates reality). There is no access to reality independently of language, and because there is no neutral language, there can never be an account of how reality 'really' is. For literary criticism, as explored in *Criticism and Truth* (1987), this entails that there can be no objective or definitive interpretation of a work, nor can one assume that there is some author, as the originator of meaning, behind the text. Hence, Barthes posits 'The Death of the Author' (1977c) and also a shift 'From Work to Text' (1977d).

This shift, which in effect marks a shift from structuralism to post-structuralism, is exemplified in *S/Z* (1974). Barthes offers a close reading of Balzac's novella *Sarrasine*, in order to explicit the conventions (or codes) that govern its apparently naturalistic narrative. The crucial distinction that is posed is between a 'readerly' (or realist) text, that conforms to the conventions that a reader expects from a well-made narrative, and a 'writerly' text. The latter disrupts the realist narrative codes, and therefore makes the position of reader insecure. (Joyce's *Finnegans Wake* is the model of such texts.) The reader cannot passively consume the text with pleasure. In *The Pleasure of the Text* (1975) and in his final, more autobiographical and novelistic texts of the 1970s (1977e, 1978, 1981), Barthes explores the difference between readerly and writerly in terms of the difference between pleasure (*plaisir*) and *jouissance*. If the readerly text gives pleasure in the comfort and security of reading, then the writerly text gives ecstatic 'enjoyment' (akin to the enjoyment of sexual orgasm). It is an enjoyment in the loss of subjectivity, and in the transgression of academic forms and conventions.

[AE]

Further reading: Culler 1983; Lavers 1982; Moriarty 1991; Sontag 1982b.

BATAILLE, GEORGES (1897–1962)

French philosopher, novelist, poet and essayist. Bataille's work is anti-systematic and hence defies summary, but a number of important themes predominate within it. These themes include an obsessive concern with the erotic, myth, sacrifice, the nature of excess, profanity, heterogeneity and social transgression. Bataille's writings are also marked by an engagement with the thought of such figures as De Sade, **Nietzsche**, **Hegel**, **Freud**, the poetry of Blake, and the writings of Jean Genet. Bataille studied at Epernay College (1913–1915) and then at the Ecole des Chartes in Paris (graduating as a medievalist in 1922). He then occupied a post in the Cabinet des Médales, Bibliothèque Nationale, Paris until 1942, when he retired due to ill health. During the 1920s and 1930s Bataille forged links with the surrealist movement in Paris and also espoused Marxism. From the mid-1930s his attachment to Marxism waned, largely as a result of his increasing interest in Nietzsche's philosophy. His commitment to surrealism also lessened, not least because of his dispute with leading French surrealist André Breton. The latter's conception of surrealism as invoking the 'lower', bodily aspects of life as a means of indicating the fundamental truths attainable by way of art repelled Bataille. It is not, however, surrealism's exploration of bodily excess that Bataille abhorred but its aim of subordinating this element to a 'higher', abstract realm. For Bataille, the 'lower' (the bodily and what is associated with it: carnality, excrement, parts of the body generally excluded from acknowledgement in daily social life) is of interest on its own terms. As such, the body and materiality generally is not, for him, a mere appendage to reality but is constitutive of it.

Nietzsche is significant for Bataille as a thinker whose writings explore the nature of values in the context of the crisis of modernity. Nietzsche's famous pronouncement of the 'death of God' in *The Gay Science* (1974) is a theme taken up in Bataille's work. Bataille is also interested in Nietzsche because he sees him as rejecting various dichotomies. Thus, the collapse between fictional and philosophical discourse that Nietzsche's work enacts is also admired by Bataille. Nietzsche's attempts to conflate the domains of value and the body – in the opening sections of *Human, All-Too-Human* (1878) or in the first part of *Beyond Good and Evil* (1886) – and thereby question the metaphysical opposition between conceptual thought and materiality are also mirrored in Bataille's work. Equally, Nietzsche's claim in *The Birth of Tragedy* (1872) that the high cultural achievements of Ancient Greece are the expression of a sublimated form of violence has its parallels in Bataille's explorations of excess and his interest in the nature of violence. In De Sade, too, it is the conjunction and interplay of erotic, sacrificial and physically violent elements that fascinates Bataille. With regard to Hegel, it is the latter's conception of the Absolute as equivalent to pure rationality that is the object of Bataille's critical attention, and against which he emphasises the bodily conditions of existence. Bataille's reading of Hegel highlights the interconnection between what he conceives to be the realm of bodily affects (e.g. plant life, the play of chance, organic functions) and the realm of rational, abstract thought. Against this, Bataille seeks to show how these two realms are conjoined. However 'spiritual' and rational some aspects of human existence may appear to be, they are underwritten by a material or bodily component that is capable of overrunning them. Freud's influence upon Bataille is evident in texts such as *The Story of the Eye* (1928), a pornographic fantasy that has a psychoanalytic analysis appended to it.

Much of Bataille's thinking aims to illuminate socially imposed limits enshrined in the modern conception of rationality in this way (see *The Accursed Share*, 1949). Humans, he argues in an essay on De Sade, are composed of two contending drives: the drive to excretion and the drive to appropriation. In cultural terms, this is presented in terms of an opposition between collective, orgiastic impulses and social institutions (legal, economic and political structures). Humans conceive of their world as being composed of homogeneous unities in order to facilitate appropriation (science, for instance, thinks in related concepts, in terms of parts and their role within the whole). Philosophy is an intellectual expression of the urge to appropriate. **Kant**'s philosophy, we could note in this context, envisages the world as being conceivable only as a consequence of a legalistic conceptual order that has legitimacy independently of experiences provided by way of the senses (the a priori conditions of experience). But the intellectual desire to appropriate produces its specific kind of own waste products. Nothingness, the infinite, concepts of the Absolute are all, for Bataille, notions that resist recuperation within an homogeneous conceptual order.

He conceives of the body as being opposed to the normative constraints that serve to constitute subjectivity within social formations. The body thereby resists absorption by social forces. For example, in the modern era, which is dominated by the capitalist mode of production and hence by the values of prudence and usefulness, the body serves as a reminder of the limitations of the notion of exchange-value. The body cannot be recuperated within the logic of the market place, since bodily functions do not accord with dominant notions of exchange and profit. The body, rather, is prodigal: its basic constitution is determined by way of an alternative logic of excess (again, Nietzsche's comments to the effect that nature proceeds 'wastefully' in the notes contained in *The Will to Power* spring to mind here). Likewise, Bataille also alludes to the existence of practices that enact excess as a means of stating his case, for example human sacrifice is an act of gross expenditure, a total wastefulness that horrifies modern consciousness because of its violence, senselessness and irrationality. The point for Bataille is not that we should be tolerant of human sacrifice, but that this kind of practice throws into relief dominant practices within modern societies and shows their limits. Exchange-value, for instance, cannot be reconciled with notions of the sacred and profane that are given homage in sacrifice, which is an act of gross materiality. Nor can it be incorporated within the logic of the Hegelian dialectic, which seeks to recuperate all resistances by accommodating them within the dialectical unfolding of Reason. Practices that cannot be subject to the notions of equivalence and exchange are, in other words, heterogeneous. What this implies for Bataille is that, however systematically one would like to conceptualise life, the imposition of a limit that this desire necessitates will always be overcome. Bodily and social systems will always produce waste products (excrement in the one instance, rubbish in the other) which in their very nature resist reintegration into systematic structures. The heterogeneity of the body, it follows, is marked by resistance. This points, among other things, to the limitations of scientific discourse. Where science deals with homogeneous elements, with wholes and the parts that fit harmoniously into them, the heterogeneous is in its very nature profoundly unsystematic.

Bataille's work has exerted a wide influence within the sphere of French intellectual life. The writings of figures such as **Barthes**, **Baudrillard**, **Foucault**, **Derrida** and **Lyotard** all manifest engagements with aspects of Bataille's thought. Most especially, Bataille's intellectual development, marked as it is by a preliminary adherence to Marxism and a subsequent turn to Nietzsche, prefigures a general trend within French intellectual thought of the post-war era.

[PS]

Further reading: Noys 2000; Pefanis 1991; M. Richardson 1994.

BAUDRILLARD, JEAN (1929–)

The most extreme (or uncompromising – depending on your point of view) of the thinkers whose name has come to be associated with the term postmodernism. Baudrillard began as a sociologist, but his later espousal of a postmodernism which rejects all notions of a mind- or language-independent reality, as well as his earlier criticisms of **Marx**ism – cf. *For a Critique of the Political Economy of the Sign* (Baudrillard 1981b) and *The Mirror of Production* (1975) – demonstrate that he has, over the years, moved far away from an acceptance of the basic postulates which underlie social theory. Baudrillard's most influential writings date from the 1980s, and engage in an analysis of the increasing importance, and indeed dominance, in contemporary life of modes of representation and signification. The present, according to Baudrillard's account – cf. *Simulacra* (1981a) and *Simulations* (1983) – is an era marked by the ascendancy of modes of signification, which have in effect obliterated any meanings that might once have been attributed to such notions as objectivity, reference and truth. In the contemporary world signs bear no relation to 'reality' (that is, a mind–independent reality – see realism) in any shape or form. Indeed, the sign is now to be regarded as nothing more than a simulacrum of itself, i.e. signs refer only to other signs, not to any reality external to representation. What Baudrillard means by this is that we do not possess any criteria by which to distinguish between appearance and reality. This view led Baudrillard to make the notorious claim, in articles published in the *Guardian* newspaper in 1991, that the 'Gulf War' was a simulation produced by the representational capabilities of modern technology, rather than an event to be taken in the substantive sense attributable to previous wars.

[PS]

Further reading: Baudrillard 1981a, 1988.

BENEDICT, RUTH (1887–1948)

American cultural anthropologist who developed what is known as the configurational approach to anthropology, exploring the way in which the diverse institutions, activities and traits of a given culture are integrated into a patterned whole (or *Gestalt*).

Patterns of Culture (1935) is Benedict's best known work, and indeed one of the most widely read books in cultural anthropology. Its core is a comparative study of three small scale, pre-industrial cultures: the Pueblo Zuni Indians of New Mexico, the Dobu of Melanesia and the Kwakiutl of Vancouver Island. The inspiration for this comparison came from Benedict's own fieldwork in 1927. She was struck by the difference in culture between the generally reserved and ordered Pueblo Indians and their more ecstatic neighbours. In *Patterns of Culture* Benedict classifies the distinction by borrowing from **Nietzsche**'s *Birth of Tragedy* (1872). The (Pueblo) Zuni are Apollonian. As such, they distrust disorder and excess, keeping to the middle of the road, and not meddling with disruptive psychological states. Individualism is suppressed, as is it suspected of being disruptive to tradition and precedent (Benedict 1935 pp. 56–57). This is in marked contrast to Dionysian cultures, represented in *Patterns* by the Dobu and the Kwakiutl. Here the disruption of boundaries is sought, not least in the pursuit of supernatural visions through extreme forms of behaviour, such as self-mutilation and deprivation (p. 58). In Kwakiutl religious ceremonies the 'chief dancer . . . should lose normal control of himself and be rapt into another state of existence. He should froth at the mouth, tremble violently and abnormally, do deeds which would be terrible in a normal state' (pp. 126–127). The highly competitive Dobu are characterised as having 'the simplicity of mania. All existence is cut-throat competition, and every advantage is gained at the expense of a defeated rival' (p. 102).

It may be noted that Benedict is not offering a detailed commentary upon Nietzsche. However, she implies that she understands Nietzsche as having analysed, in the Dionysian and Apollonian, the two competing themes of ancient Greek society, just as she has identified the themes of the Zuni, Dobu and Kwakiutl societies. Benedict's core point in identifying such themes is that all the institutions and activities within the society will express the theme of the society. In effect, it is the theme that serves to integrate the different elements of a society into a whole that is greater than the sum of its parts (and that also entails that the task of the anthropologist is not merely to document and compare different cultural traits in diverse societies, but rather to interpret those traits within the cultural *Gestalt* within which they occur) (pp. 33–37).

Benedict seeks to explain the emergence and perseverance of a theme within a culture in terms of the selection of certain potentialities of human psychology and behaviour from the gamut of all those that are possible. She draws an analogy with phonology, to argue that just as a human language can only work if it selects a few of all the possible sounds that a human voice can make, so a culture can only work if it too is selective (pp. 16–17). In this way a culture will encourage certain psychological traits and repress others, but perhaps more importantly, the culture is then the source of all meaning and purpose in human life. Benedict notes, for example, that puberty is not a biological phenomenon. Rather, each culture will select a different age upon which to focus puberty rights, and will give puberty, and thus adulthood, different meanings (celebrating or otherwise marking puberty differently). As she notes, '[a]dulthood in central North America means warfare. Honour in it is the great goal of all men. . . . In Australia . . . adulthood means participation in an exclusively male cult. . . . Any woman is put to death if she so much as hears the sound of the bull-roarer at ceremonies' (p. 18).

This approach to anthropology raises a number of major issues. First, Benedict is aware that not all cultures will be fully integrated about a single theme. She identifies societies in British Columbia that are characterised by their cultural borrowings from their neighbours, and thus by the ultimate poverty of the culture, as it fails to elaborate or explore any element in depth or with consistency (p. 161). Second, she is aware that while most people 'are plastic to the moulding force of the society in which they are born', not all the members of a society will fit in equally well (p. 183). There may still be Dionysians within Zuni society and Apollonians within Dobu society. What for Benedict is then of interest is the fact that the labelling of character traits as 'abnormal' is necessarily a cultural event, so that was it is to be abnormal will vary between cultures, and the treatment of the abnormal will vary. She notes how homosexuality is handled in many American Indian cultures, through the role of the man-woman. While the player of such a role may evoke embarrassment and scorn, he will have a place within society, and may flourish (p. 189–190).

Finally, Benedict's work was among the first to raise fundamental questions about cultural relativism. Her work focuses upon the diversity and incommensurability of moral and political values, and she claims in her conclusion that all patterns of human life are 'equally valid' (p. 201). In practice she does judge some societies as better or worse than others (for example, by commenting upon the impoverishment of British Columbian cultures), but more importantly, she sees the founding moral values of anthropology to be strongly anti-discriminatory. Her emphasis upon the cultural malleability of human beings leads to an unconditional rejection of racism, an imperative to understand others – see, for example, her wartime work on Japan

(Benedict1946) – and a recognition that one's own cultural values are in no sense natural or absolute.

[AE]

Further reading: Geertz 1988; Mead 1959, 1974; Mintz 1984; Modell 1983.

BENJAMIN, WALTER (1892–1940)

The German literary theorist Walter Benjamin was associated with what is known as the Frankfurt School of German critical theory (although he was never a member of its institutional body, the Frankfurt Institute for Social Research). His work is diverse in both its content (ranging from studies of Romantic and contemporary literature, through photography and cinema, to the nature of language and translation) and its theoretical approaches (and presentation, as aphorism, autobiographical reflection, essay and fragment). His career can be broken up into (at least) three parts. His early essays on literature and language are at once densely textured, and show the influence of Jewish mysticism (Gershom Scholem being a close friend). After the First World War, Benjamin adopts a form of Marxism, not least under the influence of Bertolt **Brecht** (Benjamin 1973b). At the same time he begins work on a complex and many layered study of nineteenth-century Paris, centring on the work of Baudelaire (Benjamin 1973a, 1999c). His last essays indicate something of a return to an interest in Jewish mysticism, and the potential that Jewish imagery has for articulating a Marxist philosophy of history and revolution. Benjamin committed suicide, on the French–Spanish border, while attempting to escape the Nazi occupation.

Benjamin's early essays include studies of romanticism and Goethe's novel *Elective Affinities* (Benjamin 1996a: 297–360). The earliest of Benjamin's works to have a significant impact in English is his study of *Trauerspiel* (1977). This immensely difficult essay – so difficult that when submitted for a higher degree in Germany, it was failed – focuses upon the 'play of mourning' that developed in Germany after the Reformation, but has its supreme example in *Hamlet* and other Shakespearean tragedies. The *Trauerspiel* is distinguished from the ancient Greek tragedy not only in that it lacks a true hero, but also in the articulation of a fundamentally different conception of time. Tragedy culminated in human protest against fate and the gods. As the Reformation undermines the Christian sense of historical movement towards the Last Judgement, historical time is drained of any sense of direction or movement. *Trauerspiel* expresses this empty time through its use of allegory, and through such stock characters as the prince and intriguer. The prince is both tyrant (responsible for controlling the crisis of the state) and a martyr (unable to deal with the crisis in his own soul – consider Hamlet). The prince's melancholy indecision leaves his action under the control of an intriguer (such as Iago or Lady Macbeth) who choreographs the action of the play. The drama is thus deployed in space, rather than in time. Allegory similarly disrupts notions of developmental time. The allegory has meaning only through a wholly conventional relationship to another object or idea. Yet the allegory can stand for any object. It is thus a medium of exchange, allowing thought to move between, accumulate and also fragment and rearrange ideas and images. The allegory is opposed by Benjamin to the symbol. The symbol expresses true knowledge of the object. Elsewhere Benjamin (1996a pp. 62–74) reflects upon the Jewish creation story of Adam naming creation. The symbol, unlike the allegory, strives to recover the primal Adamite name of things. The allegory is thus a form of communication in a Fallen, post-paradisiacal and ultimately meaningless world. As an art form the *Trauerspiel* is thus a failure, for its allegory can never become symbolic. But precisely in its failure it expresses the tyrannical politics and theology of its age. This culminates in the image of the ruin – which is as important to the Baroque as to the Romantics. In a ruin, history and nature have merged. History has become natural, fixed in the physical decay of the ruin, and yet the eternal transience (and thus meaninglessness) of nature is also revealed to be the essence of what history now is.

The most cited essay by Benjamin comes from his Marxist period: 'The Work of Art in the Age of Mechanical Reproduction' (1970b). This essay is an analysis of the impact that photography and cinema have upon the consumption of art, not least in so far as the reproducibility of the photograph undermines traditional ideas of the originality or authenticity of the work (and thus its 'aura'), and allows mass distribution and possession of the art work. As such it provides a series of provocative insights into the nature of photography and cinema, such as his comparison of film to psychoanalysis (whereby both bring to consciousness that which would otherwise pass as insignificant) or the characterisation of Atget's late-nineteenth-century photographs of Paris as crime scenes. On the other hand, the essay also attempts to generate aesthetic concepts that cannot be of use to Fascism. It is therefore striving towards a genuinely Marxist aesthetics, but as such an aesthetics that is deeply influenced by Dada and Surrealism. While the contemplation of traditional works of art leads to one's absorption by the art work, the shock effect of cinema, grounded in the continual change of images, allows one to absorb the work, albeit in a state of distraction. As with architecture, the audience's response is at once tactile and absent-minded. Benjamin thus proposes the formation of a politically active and critical audience through the disruption and shock of a montage of cinematic images.

The *Arcades Project* is Benjamin's impressionistic and fragmentary study of nineteenth-century Paris (Benjamin 1973a, 1999c). Benjamin is concerned with ephemeral nature of modernism, and particularly with the modern city. The Parisian arcades transform experience of space and social relationships. Again, while more accessible in its written style than the early study of baroque drama, it is perhaps again best approached, at least initially, as a series of brilliant insights. The most celebrated of these is Benjamin's account of the *flâneur*. Edgar Alan Poe's 'The Man of the Crowd' represents an observer of the crowd in a London street. While Baudelaire translated this story, Benjamin suggests that a subtly different figure underpins Baudelaire's own work. The *flâneur* wanders the streets, but remains aloof from the crowds that would surround and jostle him, always remaining the man of leisure, and yet, again, shocked by this contact with the urban world.

Benjamin's last essay, 'Theses on the Philosophy of History' (1970c), presents a Marxist materialist account of history in a strangely appropriate theological language. The most pressing image which Benjamin offers is borrowed from a painting by Paul Klee. The angel of history is represented being blown through time, its back to the future so that it sees only the detritus of the past unfold, and never the destination to which it travels. Again, Benjamin is concerned with the problem of articulating and challenging the emptiness of time in a capitalist society. The language of Messianic theology gives him tools to articulate the possibility (but also perhaps the incomprehensibility) of revolution. The demand is to see history not as unfolding against empty time, but as 'time filled by the presence of the now'. This, as with the interpretation of allegory, requires the revolutionary to make an interpretative leap, to see through what history has become under the commands of the ruling class.

[AE]

Further reading: Buck-Morss 1977, 1991; Caygill 1998; Lunn 1982; Roberts 1982; Scholem 1981; G. Smith 1988; Wiggershaus 1994; Wolin 1994.

BLOCH, ERNST (1885–1977)

German Marxist philosopher, whose interest in utopian thought has perhaps had as much, if not more, influence on theology (Moltmann 1967) than on philosophy or cultural theory.

It is perhaps only a slight exaggeration to suggest that Bloch's substantial and diverse output may best be understood as a gloss upon **Marx**'s observation that 'religion is the opium of the masses' (Marx 1975, p. 244). Marx may be interpreted as saying, not that religion is a mere narcotic that inures the oppressed to their oppression, but rather that religion is also the source of images (akin to opium dreams) of a better life. While such images should not be taken literally (so that the Christian 'heaven upon earth', for example, may never be realised), they can be taken seriously, for if read critically they express much of what is wrong with contemporary society, in a yearning for something better. Bloch's most distinctive works, and especially his magnum opus, *The Principle of Hope* (1986b), explore in great scholarly detail the expressions of the human aspiration to a better, more just life, found throughout human culture (in religion, high and popular art, geography and exploration, and science and technology).

While Bloch's philosophy is overwhelmingly concerned with the historical and political struggle towards a just society, unlike many more orthodox Marxists – and not least his sometime friend and contemporary **Lukács** – he refuses to offer any concrete account of a just communist society. He has, as it were, no absolute account of the good, and thus no Archimedean point from which he can condemn the wrongs of existing societies. Bloch turns rather to culture as an expression of discontent. Ordinary people feel that something is wrong, that life could be better, and their cultural achievements express this yearning. The theoretical apparatus that Bloch develops to interpret this culture thus focuses upon the unfinished nature of humanity and human history. Concepts such as the 'open system', 'non-synchronicity', 'preappearance' and his key logical operator, the 'not yet', all serve to challenge any presupposition of determinacy or completeness in the analysis of human affairs. 'Open system' confronts the closure of the **Hegel**ian system (Hegel 1970, 1971, 1975a). While Bloch wishes to employ Hegelian dialectical logic, he is critical of the way in which Hegel closes off the dynamics of his thinking by the premature declaration of the attainment of absolute knowledge. (This is echoed in Lukács's equally premature declaration of knowledge of the nature of communism.) Bloch's open system is not simply open to new material, but rather recognises that new material, occurring as human history unfolds and reflection upon it develops, can transform the very structure of the system itself, so that the system's most basic categories may have to be rethought. Marxism as an open system must, therefore, be constantly revising itself. The utopian future that justifies Marxist thought and practice is only glimpsed obscurely, in its 'preappearance'. We are 'not yet' conscious of the future, in the sense that our conscious of the present contains, albeit problematically, an awareness of future possibilities and the means to their achievement. To realise that our consciousness is at once an obscure consciousness of the future serves to open the world to new interpretations and to new political practices.

Already Bloch's first book, *The Spirit of Utopia* (1918), is critical of Marxism's over-emphasis on economic analysis. The book is influenced by German expressionism, and its style is often characterised by opaque montages of clipped, gnomic utterances. Its subject matter embraces death (1970), the ornament – 'We are down and out and no longer know how to play' (1988, p. 78) – and a rhapsodic history of music (1985), as well as Marxist philosophy. Yet Bloch worries that economic determinism fails to leave room for the 'the soul and the faith' (1970, p. 39). Religion, in contrast, captures not simply the human motivation to struggle for a better world, but the pain at injustice that should give Marxism its content and purpose. In a remarkable passage he requires Marxism 'to give every man not just a job but his own distress, boredom, wretchedness, misery and darkness; to give everyone's life a Dostoevskyan touch' (Bloch 1970, p. 60).

In *Heritage of our Times* (1991), the concept of non-synchronicity is developed by Bloch, not least again as a response to Lukács' defence of orthodox Marxism. While Lukács understands contemporary capitalism as a totality, characterised by a clear conflict between the progressive proletarian class and the reactionary bourgeois class, for Bloch society is a fractured complex with many subtly anachronistic and progressive elements. He argues that the transition from one historical epoch to the next does not necessarily resolve all the tensions of the old epoch. Thus, there survive into the new age, not mere historical relics of the past, but politically significant forces and possibilities. Expressionist art is thus, for Bloch, an important source for understanding contemporary society, while for Lukács it is merely a symptom of bourgeois reaction, and indeed decadence (Bloch *et al.* 1977). The use of montage and fragmentation, not least in the juxtaposition of radically new and archaic artistic techniques (borrowing for example from medieval and folk art), responds to the real non-synchronicity of capitalist society. In effect, while Lukács relies upon his confidence in the completeness of his political theory, in order to use that theory as the standard by which to judge art as progressive or reactionary, Bloch looks to art (and culture in general) to reveal to theory the real nature and experience of society.

[AE]

Further reading: Daniel and Moylan 1997; Geoghegan 1996; Hudson 1982.

BOURDIEU, PIERRE (1930–)

French cultural anthropologist and sociologist, whose work, character-ised as it is by an equal commitment to empirical as well as theoretical research, has embraced the ethnography of Algerian peasant com-munities (Bourdieu 1979), the sociology of culture (1977b, 1990) and education (1977a) (including the social position of university intel-lectuals (1984)). At the core of Bourdieu's project is the attempt to avoid what he perceives as the problematic extremes of objectivist and subjectivist approaches to sociology. The objectivist (represented by, for example, **Althusser** or **Lévi-Strauss**) presupposes that society is to be understood purely as an external force that constrains or determines the action of the human subject. This approach has no satisfactory way of explaining how human agents may be involved in the producing and sustaining of society. In contrast, the subjectivist (such as Jean-Paul **Sartre**) places too great an emphasis upon the power of the agent to create, voluntarily, meaningful social action (independently of the constraining force that society actually does impose upon the subject).

The concepts of 'habitus' and 'field' serve to articulate the basic outlines of Bourdieu's (1985) approach to sociology. 'Habitus' refers to the dispositions that human agents acquire, through life-long processes of learning and socialisation, that give them the competence to respond in certain ways to given social situations. While these disposi-tions are realised in social practice they are not readily reducible to a set of rules governing social behaviour. They are rather the agent's 'feel' for how to proceed in the situation. As such they have a flexibility that at once serves to explain the stability of the social order and its trans-formation. If 'habitus' therefore allows Bourdieu to theorise the agent, 'field' theorises the objectivity of the social situation. Society is under-stood as a structured hierarchy of relatively autonomous fields (such as the fields of politics, economics literature, and education). A field may be characterised in terms of the political and cultural relationships that exist between the positions occupied by agents within it. However, it is not then to be understood as a fixed structure that exists independently of human agents. Rather these relationships are maintained (or reproduced), and to a greater or lesser degree transformed, by the actions of agents within the field. A dramatic example is the way in which Manet, first of the great modernist painters, transforms the field of French high culture in the 1860s, through the exhibition of such paintings as *The Absinthe Drinker* that in both content and style challenged the then dominant norms of academic excellence in painting (Bourdieu 1993b). Agents within a field may therefore be seen to be in competition over the resources that are characteristic to that field. Such resources may be material (such as income and wealth), but may equally be symbolic power (for example, political power, recognition and status). Manet therefore struggles not for economic gain but for recognition, and does so through an attempt to transform the values of high culture. The gaining of control over resources depends upon agents' capital and the skill (or fortune) with which they invest it. Again, 'capital' is not to be understood as an exclusively material resource (such as financial wealth), but can also be symbolic (one's degree of prestige or honour) and cultural (one's cultural knowledge and competence, such as the socially acquired ability to appreciate works of art). The distribution of all forms of capital is unequal, grounded as it is in the class structure.

One important implication of Bourdieu's sociology, and an implication that he explores in depth in *Distinction* (1984) and other works, is that there are no purely autonomous aesthetic values. As the example of Manet begins to suggest, the values that determine the greatness and endurance of a work of art are not, for Bourdieu, inherent properties of the work, but are rather the result of social processes and in particular struggles to control resources. Bourdieu is thus critical of **Kant**ian aesthetics (which seeks to defend universal and thus ahistorical criteria of artistic value) and of formalist approaches to literature (that focus upon the art work in isolation from the historical and political situation of its production and consumption). Bourdieu does not seek to reduce the aesthetic, simplistically, to its determination by social forces. A work of art cannot be understood straightforwardly as the reflection or expression of the class interests of its producer. Such an account, at the very least, fails to acknowledge the inherent logic of the field of artistic creation and consumption, and thus its degree of autonomy from the economic and political. However, Bourdieu still seeks to explain 'taste', and crucially the generation of distinctions between good and bad (or refined and vulgar) taste, in terms of the reproduction of social differences and inequalities of power. Art and aesthetic value are understood to be produced within a field of power. Works are produced and consumed according to the complex manner in which agents classify themselves and others. Consumption thus serves to express one's difference from others through the refinements and nuances of what one constructs and (perhaps unwittingly) accepts as good taste.

[AE]

Further reading: Brubaker 1985, Fowler 1997; Harker et al. 1990; Jenkins 1992; Nordquist 1997; Robbins 1991; Swartz 1997; Various 1993.

BRECHT, BERTOLT (1898–1956)

German playwright, poet and **Marx**ist theorist. After entering Munich University to read medicine, he served as a medical orderly during the First World War. He became an opponent, not only of the war, but also of the nationalist ideology that supported it, and the capitalism that he saw as its ground. His mature work is influenced by his association with the 'political theatre' of Erwin Piscator, and his study of Marxism in the 1920s. Piscator used novel stage techniques, such as projectors, placards, loudspeakers and the spatial division of the stage explicitly in order to promulgate a revolutionary Marxist attitude in the audience (and thus the wider society). The resultant 'epic theatre' is now primarily associated with Brecht. As a didactic form of drama, epic theatre may be characterised by narrative structures that avoid complex plot construction in favour of a succession of episodes, typically interspersed by songs or commentaries by a narrator. Characters are simplified and remote settings are favoured. All 'culinary', or sensuously attractive, effects are to be eliminated. The impersonality or detachment of the presentation is intended to stimulate the audience's curiosity and critical reflection upon the issues presented, at the expense of emotional engagement or enjoyment. (In his later works, Brecht acknowledged that enjoyment will aid the audience's learning.) Brecht coined the term 'alienation technique' (*Verfremdungseffekt*), as the dramaturgical process that serves to make familiar reality appear strange, in order to distinguish his own drama, not merely from the **Aristotelian** tradition, but also from other forms of dictatic drama. During this pre-war period he collaborated with the composer Kurt Weill on the operas *The Threepenny Opera* (1928) (on the model of

John Gay's eighteenth-century *Beggar's Opera*) and *The Rise and Fall of the City of Mahagonny* (1927–1929). Weill's music is significantly influenced by contemporary cabaret music.

Brecht went into exile in Switzerland in 1933, moving to Denmark, Finland and the Soviet Union, before settling in California between 1941 and 1947. He returned to East Berlin in 1949, where he founded his own theatre company, the Berliner Ensemble. In this period he produced what are regarded as his finest works, including *Mother Courage and her Children* (1941), *The Good Woman of Setzuan* (1943), *The Life of Galileo* (1943) and *The Caucasian Chalk Circle* (1948). In his principal (although unfinished) theoretical work, *Der Messingkauf* (1937–1951), Brecht discusses the techniques and purposes of epic theatre through a dialogue, over four nights, between the philosopher, the producer and the actor. Fifteen volumes of his essays (or *Versuche*, the term being indicative of his belief that a work is incomplete without extensive rehearsal, performance and responsiveness to the audiences' reactions) appeared from 1930 onwards.

[AE]

Further reading: Benjamin 1973b; Thomson and Sacks 1993; Willett 1984.

CASTORIADIS, CORNELIUS (1922–1997)

Economist, psychoanalyst, philosopher and social thinker, a founding and leading member of the French revolutionary journal *Socialisme ou Barbarie*, and author of numerous books and articles. In his *The Imaginary Institution of Society*, Castoriadis (1987) puts forward a highly original theory of history as society's self-creation through institutionalised imaginary significations and emancipation as individual and public autonomy. Throughout his multidimensional intellectual biography, one discerns as his major themes the issues of culture, art, education and democracy, the psychoanalytic significance of the tension between the self and society, and the false dilemmas posed by capitalism and bureaucratic socialism. He has also studied the Greek *polis* and modern public sphere, philosophy of science and chaos theory, and epistemological problems related to validity, truth and identitary logic.

Castoriadis' political thought is characterised by his unrelenting critique of Stalinism (which he called 'bureaucratic capitalism'), Western capitalism (or private capitalism in his own terms) and socialist reformism. Some critics' emphasis on the growing anti-Marxist tone of his writings often obscures his commitment to socialism and his innovative attempts to reformulate it into an ideal of a self-reflective institution*ing* society and free subjectivity. For Castoriadis, socialism should aim to organise a collective, socialised management of production and administration, and as such, it should be the continuing and conscious self-managerial activity of the working classes. This presupposes that the distribution of power will be directly democratic, accessed by all, that the public sphere (termed *ekklesia*) will be empowered, and that a massive simplification of social organisation will be achieved. Like the early Frankfurt School, Castoriadis relates alienation and reification to modern complexity.

As he departs all the more markedly from Marxism, his account of socialism becomes increasingly attached to democracy. The proletariat ceases to be seen as the subject of history and revolution, while the old binary opposition between worker and employer gives way to the thematisation of the division of society in directors and executants. Hence, in political-economic terms, socialism means the collectivisation and socialisation of the functions of direction. In socio-theoretical terms, socialism must promote the autonomy and self-direction of people's; lives that capitalism negates, it must eliminate externally imposed forms of life. It must realise democracy for the first time in history. Democracy – not representative but only in its direct, decentralised form – establishes a genuine public sphere. Together with philosophy, democracy is the antidote to social heteronomy. A truly democratic society does not immunise its institutions from critical consideration, and unlike mythic and religious traditional societies, it does not occlude the perpetual *vis formandi* of thought, its desire to search for new meanings and give new shape to reality. Truly autonomous subjectivity signifies a rare being in history: reflective and deliberative subjectivity. What makes it possible, however?

It is *praxis* that assists the subject in the effort to accede autonomy. As a modality of human action, it combines voluntarism and reason and transforms the self critically. To Castoriadis, critical reflection has not been an omnipresent given of all cultures. He traces two moments in history where reflection was allocated social space: ancient Greece and modernity. But once reason is created and enlarges the rupture in social heteronomy, it acquires a potential universality, since 'every human being can reimagine what another human being has imagined'. Reflective and deliberative subjectivity is also possible due to the psyche's centrifugal relation to society. Institutions guarantee the preservation of humanity as a living species. In their network, those significations that are constitutive of a social 'being-with' can be found consolidated. In a society, however, there is a 'magma' of social imaginary significations that includes not only those embodied in institutions but also a surplus that can be reduced to neither consciousness nor natural/biological functionality. What it is given as *physis* for humans is the psyche's radical imagination at the individual level and the social instituting imaginary at the collective level. Psyche is *physei* meaning-seeking. Now, society forces it through socialisation to limit its search for meaning in the socially available imaginary significations and norms. But society never succeeds completely in this. The surplus of imaginary significations that do not become institutionalised at the collective level, and the surplus of subjectivity that cannot be canalised through socialisation at the individual level, both in their conflicting relation to the settled and fixed world-interpretations, create the potential for autonomy, philosophy and democracy.

Be that as it may, can autonomy and philosophy be meaningful without some account of validity? What is the position of truth (epistemologically and ontologically) in a universe where the imaginary element and representational pleasure are granted primacy over the functional element and organ pleasure and the encounter with reality is never unmediated? Castoriadis distinguishes between de facto validity and *de jure* validity. The former refers to social currency, the latter to truth. But this does not amount to a concession to a correspondence theory of truth that would cause an internal and serious contradiction in his philosophy, which as we have seen, relies heavily on the mediated and imaginary character of the construction of meaning and knowledge, be it descriptive or normative. Ontologically, Castoriadis connects the being of each society with its modes of creating a world of its own. The world created by the social actor is called 'the proper world of the for-itself' while the outside one is named 'world *tout court*'. There is no direct access to the outside world, because for the psyche the external reality is the social world. But that does not mean that the ensemblistic-identitary (ensidic in Castoriadis's terminology) action of the psyche is always arbitrary or illusory. There is in both, i.e. the 'real' world and the human symbolic reconstruction of it, an ensidic dimension and it is that one that allows the latter to create the former in a replica of sufficiently analogous traits to the original. Here lies the ultimate ontological justification of Castoriadis's non-relativist epistemology: the world *tout court* not only lends itself (a dimension of it) to ensidic organisation but also corresponds to it.

Despite his political pessimism about the future and the type of person conditioned by contemporary societies, Castoriadis's anthropology together with his philosophical emphasis on the potential of autonomy, democracy and creation of reflective/deliberative subjectivity has added a new meaning to emancipation and hope.

[Marianna Papastephanou]

Further reading:. D. Curtis 1997.

CHOMSKY, NOAM (1928–)

American linguist, whose work was fundamental to the development of modern approaches to the study of language. In addition to his research in linguistics he has a sustained role in political activism and reflection, and has written copiously from an anarcho-socialist perspective on American and global issues, particularly focusing on the oppressive nature of capitalist governments and businesses (Chomsky 1969, 1973, 1983, 1989, 1991).

At the core of Chomsky's approach to linguistics is the thesis that certain aspects of language use and acquisition must be innate to the human mind, and not the product of individual learning. Chomsky reacted against the empiricist approaches that were dominant in linguistics in the 1950s. Behaviourists argued that stimulus–response models could explain how language was acquired. Chomsky (1964a) replies by observing that such accounts of language learning cannot take account of the potentially infinite number of utterances that the language user will create and encounter (so that competent language users must be able to understand sentences that they have never before encountered). Further, empirical accounts of language acquisition do not adequately account for the uniformity of individuals' knowledge and use of language. Structuralists, such as Chomsky's teacher Zellig Harris, treated any given language as the collection of utterances made by speakers. Linguists sought to explicate the grammar of such languages, with 'grammar' being understood as the set of mathematical formulae that structure the collection of utterances. While Chomsky holds to the mathematical notion of grammar generating language (akin to mathematical equations generating infinite sets of values), he goes beyond Harris's structuralism by abandoning an empirical concern with diverse natural languages, each with a distinct grammar, to focus instead upon a core grammar that is common to all languages (Chomsky 1964b). This core grammar is the essence of language; competence in the core grammar provides the conditions for the possibility of language, and it is this core grammar that is innate to the human mind. Humans, from the Chomskian perspective, come pre-programmed, as it were, to acquire language – they always already know how language works. It may be noted that Chomsky does not require competent language users to be consciously aware of their competence, thus allowing the general point that much that contributes to human competence is in some sense unconscious.

Chomsky's linguistics abstracts from the content of language, including its meaning or semantics, in order to access a formal 'deep structure'. Hence, he famously observes that the sentence, 'Colourless green ideas sleep furiously' is grammatically correct, albeit that it is as meaningless as its reverse, 'Furiously sleep ideas green colourless' (Chomsky 1957). It is this grammatical correctness that interests Chomsky. His research programme (a so-called 'generative grammar') may be characterised in terms of four steps. First, the linguist identifies the 'transformational grammar' of a particular language (where transformational grammar encapsulates the smallest number of basic rules that an ideal native speaker would require to generate all and only the grammatical utterances of that language). Prior to Chomsky's (1957) *Syntactic Structures*, linguistics had concentrated only on what he calls 'finite state' grammar (governing the choices that are made within a sentence as the uttered proceed) and 'phrase structure' grammar (that governed the separation of multiple meanings in a phrase). Second, those rules that could have not been learnt are identified within the transformational grammar. Third, this allows the construction of a Universal Grammar (or Language Acquisition Device), which is to say, the linguistic competence that is given in the human mind. Finally, this model of Universal Grammar can be tested against other natural languages.

Chomsky's general approach, in defending rationalism against empiricism, explicitly echoes **Descartes**'s (1999) philosophy. The grounding of linguistic competence in the human mind commits Chomsky, not merely to a form of innatism, but to a universal and highly formalistic conception of reason (where reasoning is understood in terms of the manipulation of mental symbols, typified by logic and mathematics), and also to a doctrine of the universality of human nature (as opposed to seeing human nature as historically and culturally achieved). The universality of human nature grounds Chomsky's politics, in a demand for a recognition of the equal worth of all human beings.

[AE]

Further reading: Barsky 1997; V. Cook 1988; Hiorth 1974; Huck 1995; Lyons 1991.

CIXOUS, HÉLÈNE (1937–)

The French feminist Hélène Cixous is one of a number of French theorists responsible for developing the idea and practice of an *écriture féminine*, a form of writing and reading that resists being appropriated by the dominant patriarchal *culture*. Patriarchal culture, thought and language are theorised by appeal to the psychoanalyst **Lacan**'s notion of the symbolic, and thus to the process by which the male child is separated from his mother, and brought into the adult world, under the law of the father. The dominant culture therefore privileges a hierarchical way of thinking, grounded in a series of oppositions (such as male/female; culture/nature; intelligible/sensitive; active/passive). The male is dominant over the female. The male is active and looks, in comparison to the passive female who is merely observed. Femininity is therefore only present as it is observed by the male, and crucially, while the feminine is the other to the masculine, for Cixous, the male is interested in this other only in order to return to itself – that is to say that the masculine desire for woman is ultimately a self-love. The woman is therefore excluded from patriarchal culture, not least in that she is a non-presence even to herself. The woman is separated from her own body and her own desires. The woman simply cannot make sense of herself in a language that is designed to articulate and conceptualise masculinity. *Écriture féminine* appeals back to the bodily experience that is prior to the separation of the child from the mother, and thus to that which is prior to the imposition of the father's law.

Cixous seeks to recover the feminine in terms of its plurality. The relationship of maternity (the 'm/other relation') serves to subvert the masculine conception of subjectivity. While the male subject is unified and autonomous, the experience of childbirth and nurturing, for Cixous, suggests a disruption of the self and genuine encounter with the other. The relation is a 'gift' economy, where everything is given, but nothing is expected in return. A similar relationship is uncovered in bisexuality (which in turn highlights the masculine denial of its own femininity). Bisexuality, that is seen to be characteristic of women, offers a *jouissance* (or ecstasy) that is distinct from male desire and pleasure, for it entails an interplay of difference and the other. This *jouissance* cannot be described in masculine language. Similarly, *écriture féminine* cannot be theorised, for it attempts to facilitate the return of that which has been repressed by the imposition of the symbolic and its patriarchal law. In Cixous's own writing, this is expressed in the use of pun and wordplay, and a disruption of traditional oppositions, such as those of theory/fiction; or theory/ autobiography.

[AE]

Further reading: Cixous 1981, 1987; Shiach 1991; Wilcox 1990.

DELEUZE, GILLES (1925–1995) **AND GUATTARI, FÉLIX** (1936–1992)

The French philosopher Gilles Deleuze is often associated with post-structuralism. However, his work, a great deal of which was produced with co-author Félix Guattari, encompasses a wide range of influences and deals with an equally diverse range of areas from epistemology and ontology, to criticisms of Freudian psychoanalysis and semiotics, and questions of meaning. Deleuze has also written on cinema, Lewis Carroll and **Kant**. Deleuze's (1983) famous reading of Nietzsche (*Nietzsche and Philosophy*, 1962) offered an approach which strongly contrasted with that of Anglo-American and German commentators. From Nietzsche, Deleuze developed, in conjunction with Guattari, an approach which advocates an ontology of 'becoming' and a 'poly-morphous perverse' conception of subjectivity. For them, history and culture are understandable in terms of competing forces that fight out their struggles in contending regimes of signs. In *A Thousand Plateaus* (1980), for example, they provide an account of language in terms of different 'semiotic regimes'. This text serves well as a way of providing some overview of their work; also, it is of importance to cultural theory in that it provides a good example of an attempt to link systems of language with particular cultural traditions.

In *A Thousand Plateaus* Deleuze and Guattari (1987) renounce any straightforward mode of logical analysis, and instead favour a viewpoint which envisages the phenomenal world in terms of 'rhizomatic' struc-tures: it is a quasi-organic machine without origin, 'a stream without beginning or end' (p. 25) whose internal structure can only be delineated in terms of relative relationships of force. Phenomena are thus open to being analysed as non-purposive 'assemblages' (p. 4) cap-able of joining or connecting in an infinite number of possible ways. Any machinic assemblage, as 'a kind of organism', thereby constitutes a series of power relations. In turn, Deleuze and Guattari consider these relationships of force in terms of a pure plenitude of positively charged elements, which interact in such a manner as to produce 'phenomena of relative slowness and viscosity, or, on the contrary, of acceleration and rupture' (p. 4). Meaning, too, is reinterpreted within the framework of this line of thought: 'There is no ideal speaker-listener [. . .] There is no mother tongue, only a power takeover by a dominant language within a political multiplicity' (p. 7). For Deleuze and Guattari, texts, likewise, have no originating subjects. Books, too, are machines which produce meaning only through a process of intersection and subsequent interaction with other forces. Thus, literature is taken as a form of 'assemblage', and its meaning cannot be reduced to questions of ideology. Indeed, 'There is no ideology and never has been' (p. 4). This is because there are, on their ontology, only lines of force which join and break to form stratified 'rhizomatic' wholes, or 'haeccities', devoid of permanence.

It may be best to understand Deleuze and Guattari's position in terms of a rejection of both ideological analysis and dialectical thinking which, for them, are opposed to any affirmation of rhizomatic multiplicities. The language of mediation through dialectics is therefore abandoned in favour of an approach which concentrates on the thematics of struggle, seizure and take-over. In turn, they reject transcendental critique (see **Kant**), which is replaced by a viewpoint which concentrates upon 'lines of flight' as constituting the only means of escape from the enclosed and stratified systems of authoritarian thought which map out social and cultural 'reality'.

How, according to Deleuze and Guattari, is the world mapped and stratified? Their answer is: by semiotic systems which invoke transcendence, 'a specifically European disease' (p. 18). Such semiotic systems can be identified in such a way that their meaning may be read in terms of specific sets of characteristics. There are, Deleuze and Guattari argue, a number of signifying regimes: (i) the 'presignifying semiotic', which is pluralistic, polyvocal (i.e. many-voiced) and wards off the tyranny of universality; (ii) the 'countersignifying semiotic', which is 'nomadic' in character; (iii) and the 'postsignifying semiotic', which embodies the process of 'subjectification', i.e. the constitution of modes of subjectivity (pp. 117–119). These semiotics may be mixed together. But, since they are necessarily connected with assemblages which 'determine a given people, period, or language, and even a given style, fashion, [or] pathology [. . .] the predominance of one semiotic or another [is assured]' (p. 119).

In the first instance, Deleuze and Guattari draw a distinction between 'paranoid interpretative' regimes and passional or 'postsignifying subjective regimes' (p. 120). Both embody forms of delusion, in spite of the fact that it is accepted that they differ in terms of their respective force and direction of movement. The paranoid form arises from the development of forces 'organized around an idea'. It is the result of an internalisation of forces. In contrast, the passional-subjective semiotic is the consequence of external forces – a reaction to an event – which is expressed emotionally rather than conceptually (p. 120). As delusions, both can be characterised as types of madness. In the first case (the paranoid form), the madness takes the form of a radiating, despotic paranoia, which functions to extend the paranoiac nature of the regime's *ideé fixe* outwards from itself – its madness is overt. The subjective semiotic, on the other hand, includes characteristics which 'do not seem mad in any way but are' (p. 120). The latter fact is borne out, Deleuze and Guattari maintain, by the passional-subjective semiotic's historical connection with 'monomanias' and authoritarian hierarchies. This distinction, then, forms the basis for what follows in Deleuze and Guattari's argument.

The passional semiotic regime is, in fact, linked to the historical heritage of Judaism: 'There is a Jewish specificity immediately affirmed in a semiotic system' (p. 122). In other words, on Deleuze and Guattari's view of language, different systems for the organisation of signs are linked to different cultural forms. Above all, the significance of the Judaic semiotic is its contrast with nomadic regimes. The nomadic constitutes a part of the Judaic past (the escape from Egypt into the wilderness described in the Old Testament) which has subsequently been elided by way of the authoritarianism of the passional-semiotic. The latter reaches its height of authoritarian expression in the notion of the transcendent subjectivity of God. In turn, Deleuze and Guattari read the Christian tradition as a mixed form of semiotic which combines the passional-subjective and the paranoid-despotic forms – one consequence of which is the Reformation. Above all, it is linked to the Cartesian *cogito* (see **Descartes**) (pp. 128–130), which signifies a form of slavery to the rational self. In line with Deleuze's 1962 reading of Nietzsche, reason is construed as an essentially 'reactive' force, in contrast to the affirmative pluralism of the nomadic.

The Judaic model is contrasted directly with the nomadic semiotic. This is a 'countersignifying' semiotic, which resists the authoritarian regime of Hebraism, and other apparatuses of control, like the state. Nomadism epitomises becoming, and ist effect is a 'line of flight' from the confines of restrictive semiotic systems. Likewise, its rhizomatic nature is a reflection of the cosmic 'order' of chaos which embodies becoming. Thus, nomadism is by definition opposed to 'universality' in the sense of the universal *cogito* of God. Instead, it is found in expressions of specificity: 'It does not ally itself with a universal thinking subject, but on the contrary, with a singular race' (p. 379). This, in fact, is a somewhat contradictory statement in light of the fact that elsewhere (p. 119) Deleuze and Guattari argue against identifying any single regime or semiotic with particular races of historical epochs. But this latter view seems to run counter to the general thesis concerning semiotic regimes in *A Thousand Plateaus*. Deleuze and Guattari's rejection of universalism, and of any general theory, along with their explicit association of particular semiotic forms with particular races (e.g. the passional-subjective semiotic with Jewish 'specificity') appears directly contrary to such a claim. It is perhaps sufficient to recall that the *cogito* and universality are directly linked to the Hebraic tradition, and thus to a specific racial and historical context: 'the authoritarian process of subjectification appears most purely in the destiny of the Jewish people' (p. 182). Nomadism, too, may be monotheistic and pertain to a 'sense of the absolute' (p. 385), but the nomad's is an atheistic monotheism resistant to the universalised subjectivity of authoritarianism. Ironically, then, Deleuze and Guattari construct a model of signification which, behind a supposed 'polyvocality', conceals an essentialism of '*nomadic essences*' (pp. 407, 411, 507). Their semiotics, therefore, relies upon a form of vitalism. But this vitalism is not to be found in the codified annals of history; nomads 'have no history', for history is the product of authoritarianism (p. 393) from which the nomadic 'line of flight' seeks to escape.

Deleuze and Guattari thus construct, on the basis of their semiotics and ontology, a culturally oriented narrative of relations of power. What is, perhaps, most unsettling within this account is their identification of the phenomenon of fascism as a line of flight which, in the form of a 'realized nihilism' (p. 230), abandoned the creativity of nomadism through being dragged back down to earth by the force of the semiotic it was attempting to escape from (p. 506). The danger in this account is of linking the passional semiotic of the Ancient Jews to the fate of those who became victims of fascism in the twentieth century: only because the passional semiotic prevents a nomadic line of flight from taking leave from its confines, does that nomadic form return in the form of fascistic nihilism and death (p. 506). Given this reasoning, in the end Deleuze and Guattari are faced with a stark choice: their affirmation of the nomadic must collapse under its own weight into the nihilism they dread (fascism) or they must impose limiting formulations (i.e. in their terms, 'passional-subjective' 'Thou shalt nots'), namely 'Concrete Rules (pp. 501–514). These rules take the form of definitions concerning their own terminology, and embrace a pragmatic response to the fascistic dangers inherent in the nomadic form.

[PS]

Further reading: Bogue 1989; Boundas and Olkowski 1994.

DE MAN, PAUL (1919–1983)

Belgian-born American literary critic and deconstructionist. De Man's writings, including *Blindness and Insight* (1971) and *Allegories of Reading* (1979), contain insights that exhibit a strong kinship with **Derrida**'s work. De Man is interested in a variety of textual fields. In *Blindness and Insight* he engages with the 1950s literary criticism of the 'New Critics' (see **Leavis**) with a view to identifying the metaphors that govern their critical discourse. New Criticism, de Man argues, was a tradition that displayed a commitment to viewing the literary work as an organic unity. However, the urge to impose an organic order of meaning on the literary work is frustrated by the New Critic's own critical language. Rather than elucidating the 'genuine' meaning of a literary text, the New Critics' use of organic metaphors to envisage the nature of a work's meaning is compromised by metaphorical plays present in their writings. In effect, de Man claims, the metaphor of organic unity serves to undo the very aim it is supposed to achieve. This is because the organic metaphor itself is revealed to be limited by the very ambiguities of meaning it serves to uncover. Thus, the greatest insights of the New Critics, which are the product of a close textual engagement, are achieved at the cost of an essential 'blindness' with regard to the implications and limitations of their own critical discourse. This exhibits a general feature of meaning for de Man since, he argues, all texts are dominated by figural forces that serve to undo the very logic they are supposed to serve. There is a continual tension, in literary and philosophical texts alike, between rationality and rhetorical language. For de Man, there is an implicit tendency within language and textuality that frustrates any attempt to attain an unmediated and transparent truth.

De Man's reading strategy is exemplified by *Allegories of Reading*. This book contains interpretations of figures such as **Rousseau**, Proust and **Nietzsche** which seek to show how the figural language present in their writings creates tensions that cannot be resolved by way of conventional logical assumptions. Central to de Man's ideas about figural language is the view that it is self-deconstructing. In other words, de Man does not view deconstruction as a 'method' that can be applied to texts with a view to extracting their meaning. Instead, it is regarded as an approach to textual analysis that is sensitive to the ambiguities, tensions and paradoxes that constitute an essential element in the generation of meaning. This element ensures that the conceptual order advocated in texts (for example, in the poetry of Romantics like Wordsworth or Coleridge, the poetry of Rilke, or the writings of Nietzsche) is always overturned by their own language. In Nietzsche's case, for instance, his criticism of metaphysics is read by de Man as an enactment of the limits of philosophical language. Where, traditionally, philosophy thinks itself immune from the effects of persuasive language, in so far as it is a purely 'conceptual' discipline, Nietzsche's works reveal the limits of this claim by showing that persuasive language is essential to the 'text' of philosophy. Yet, de Man notes, Nietzsche himself cannot overcome this very dimension of language. He, too, must use both persuasive and conceptual language to communicate his case and hence ends up by enacting the very paradoxes that, he claims, haunt philosophy generally. For de Man, the paradoxical nature of elements within Nietzsche's writings is a sign of the highest conceptual rigour. This is because Nietzsche has, in effect, taken philosophical language to its limits, to the point where it must of necessity find itself enmeshed in inconsistency and paradox. So, according to de Man, Nietzsche himself is a deconstructive thinker in that he uses rigorous methods with a view to engaging in critical reflection about the nature of those very methods. Nietzsche, in other words, epitomises the highest form of self-reflexivity: his claims about the force of rhetorical language are so powerful that they are able to undermine themselves. Thus, Nietzsche questions the law of non-contradiction in philosophy by attacking the primacy of logic (he claims, for instance that logic is an 'either–or' way of thinking that we are unable to throw off, not a law governing a mind-independent 'reality'). In order to stake this kind of claim, however, Nietzsche must assert it. But in asserting it he necessarily invokes the very logic that he is rejecting by excluding the possibility of taking the opposite view. Nietzsche, too, in other words must present us with a choice that takes the form of 'either–or', even though this very choice is what he wishes to place in question. So, de Man notes, in order to attack logic Nietzsche must deny it, but this means being driven by the assertive and persuasive elements of language into arguing by way of an opposition that is unable to free itself from logic.

De Man's influence on deconstruction and literary theory has been extensive. However, a shadow has been cast over his reputation since

1987 when the *New York Times* revealed that he had written for a pro-Nazi Belguim newspaper, *Le Soir*, in the early 1940s.

[PS]

Further reading: Hartmann 1979; Norris 1988.

DERRIDA, JACQUES (1930–)

Philosopher. Derrida was born an Algerian Jew. He settled in France in the late 1950s. He was educated at the Ecole Normale Supérieure (rue d'Ulm) in Paris and came to prominence in the late 1960s and early 1970s with the publication of *Of Grammatology* (1967), *Writing and Difference* (1967) and *Margins of Philosophy* (1972). Derrida's name is inextricably linked with the term 'deconstruction'. Largely because of this, or rather because of some interpretations of what deconstruction is, he must be counted as one of the most controversial of contemporary European thinkers. The controversy surrounding Derrida can be traced back at least as far as the late 1970s, when he was engaged in a dispute with the American analytic philosopher, John Searle. The dispute concerned one of Derrida's essays, 'Signature Event Context' (in Derrida 1982). In this essay Derrida offered a reading of the English philosopher J.L. Austin's (1911–1960) theory of 'speech acts' (see, Austin, 1975). According to Derrida, Austin makes great play upon the role that intentions and literal meaning have in securing meaning. But, Derrida points out, neither intentionality nor literal language alone are sufficient conditions for the generation of meaning. What also needs to be attended to, Derrida argues, is the issue of 'iterability'. Iterability is the possibility of repetition. A word can be repeated many times and must be susceptible to being repeated in order to be a word and hence be meaningful. However, this repetition is never the 'same' in as far as all utterances of necessity occur in specific and ever changing contexts. Due to these contextual factors the possibility of repetition cannot be governed solely by a speaker's intentions or by way of reference to literal language. In 'Reiterating the Differences' Searle criticised this argument by seeking, among other things, to reaffirm the role of intention in meaning in a manner that he thought was true to the spirit of Austin's work. Derrida's response, 'Limited Inc.' (1988b), sought to point out that Searle had not really grasped his argument. However, Derrida made this point by comprehensively citing and at one and the same time (at least as far as Searle was concerned) distorting the arguments in Searle's text by situating them in a different context. Whatever the merits or otherwise of Derrida's and Searle's positions, one effect of the dispute was to contribute to the already marked divisions that characterise the relationship between continental and analytic philosophy. At its worst, this has led some analytical philosophers to deny Derrida the title of 'philosopher' at all.

Derrida is a controversial figure for other reasons more worthy of consideration. Foremost among these is that he is a thinker who has sought to challenge a number of what he argues to be deeply rooted presuppositions that dominate philosophical practice. This challenge, or more accurately the perception of its importance on the part of some readers, led to Derrida's popularity in the late 1970s and early 1980s with an audience that one would not readily define as 'philosophical' in the institutional sense of the word. Many English readers of Derrida came from university literature departments in the USA and UK. Perhaps this readership perceived in Derrida's approach a means of challenging the importance that philosophers sometimes claimed for their subject within the university system. Whereas studying literature, for example, in the end depends upon the existence of fictional works that the critic then analyses, philosophers have generally thought their subject to be free of any 'literary' aspect and have got on with inquiring into the nature of knowledge, truth, metaphysics, morality and so forth. Thus, they have tended to view literal language as the principal tool for arriving at precise and reliable accounts of these issues and metaphor as a secondary issue, susceptible to literal paraphrase or conceptual analysis. Derrida's emphasis of the stylistic and literary aspects of philosophical discourse could therefore be seen as having an instrumental value for those with an interest in challenging philosophy within the university system. Derrida's writings are also marked by an engagement with structuralism, a field familiar to literature scholars due to its increasing importance in the literary criticism of the 1970s. In spite of this, Derrida's work situates itself within the context of philosophy, and demonstrates an especial interest in the work of canonical philosophers, such as **Plato**, **Aristotle**, **Hegel**, **Kant**, **Nietzsche**, **Husserl** and **Heidegger**.

Derrida's engagement with structuralism in some ways allows him to be counted among those who are called 'post-structuralist', although this is not necessarily a helpful term for understanding Derrida's work. Primarily, Derrida mounts an attack upon the purported 'objectivity' of structuralist methodology. Thus, in the essay 'Force and Signification' (1967: published in Derrida 1978), he seeks to decode the significance of the structuralist movement and at the same time question its key presuppositions. The structuralist project seeks to present meaning as a totality that can be easily comprehended, in the sense in which one can overlook the structure of a building while ignoring those who might live or work in it. But in order to do this, Derrida argues, structuralism must negate those elements of meaning that are not susceptible to being analysed in terms of form. To put it another way, structuralism is indebted to something that cannot be accounted for within the structuralist paradigm of meaning. In 'Force and Signification', Derrida refers to this 'something' as the 'living force' of meaning. This living force is linked to the metaphorical substitution that occurs when structuralist analysis thinks of the nature of meaning by way of the metaphor of structure. For Derrida, meaning is at work in the 'movement' of metaphor itself, i.e. when the substitution of one word for another occurs. But this metaphoric process of substitution is not something inherently structural, for, necessarily, it is fluid, and what is fluid cannot be fixed or frozen in form. In turn, Derrida holds the structuralist view to be characteristic of the Western metaphysical tradition. This tradition, Derrida contends, thinks in a manner that privileges structure. By way of support for this argument we need, perhaps, only to think of the work that the foundational metaphor does for **Descartes**' epistemology, or likewise of the formalised conception of the transcendental subject that Kant (1964) presents in the first *Critique* (or *Critique of Pure Reason*, 1781).

Privileging structure is for Derrida a key characteristic of the Western metaphysical tradition not merely in so far as it allows for talk about the 'foundations' of knowledge, etc., but also because the structural metaphor foregrounds the role of the image in thought. The Western tradition, he argues, thereby cleaves to the view that thought is first and foremost 'representational' in nature. Truth, in consequence, is taken to be a matter that concerns the literal and hence formally correct representation of 'things' by way of concepts. On this conception, concepts are by their very nature endowed with the power to 'illuminate' the world. In order to conceptualise reality Western metaphysics hence resorts to a metaphorical opposition between 'darkness and light'. It is this opposition, Derrida argues, which is 'the founding metaphor of Western philosophy as metaphysics' (Derrida 1978 p. 27). Derrida also refers to this mode of thought as embodying a 'heliocentric metaphysics'. This is a metaphysics in which force is regarded as being secondary to the power of the representational image, in which intensity gives way to the primacy of representation.

For Derrida, metaphor is necessary to all philosophical discourse. Derrida argues that a series of oppositions have been constructed by philosophers that in equal measure depend upon and suppress the role that metaphor plays in philosophical language. The tendency to suppress metaphor is evident when philosophers engage in the analysis of truth and meaning. Philosophers, Derrida claims, traditionally display a tendency to separate the metaphorical language that pervades everyday language from the literal or fact-stating language that they rely upon for elucidating concepts of truth and meaning (a case in point being speech act theory, mentioned above). On the traditional view, literal meaning is taken to embody the proper or 'true' meaning of a word. This propriety signifies the consonance between a word and what it refers to. However, for Derrida, privileging literal language in this way ultimately depends upon the metaphorical propensities inherent in everyday language (it is, after all, necessary to define 'literal' language negatively: it is *not* metaphorical). A philosophy that privileges the literal must therefore suppress metaphor as a prelude to equating the literal with the true. Western philosophy, Derrida argues, does just this. It has generally regarded metaphor to be a secondary phenomenon susceptible to being conceptualised within the stable structure or 'economy' of literal language.

For Derrida, however, metaphor is no mere 'accident' within 'the text of philosophy' (Derrida, 1978, p.209). Metaphor is, rather, essential to this 'text'. What is at stake when philosophers assert the opposition between literal and metaphorical language is the relationship between philosophical talk and everyday language and the extent to which philosophers would like to distance their utterances from the ambiguities inherent in such language. But, if philosophers are already caught up in everyday language as a precondition of their being able to philosophise at all, then one ought to consider whether philosophical concepts are essentially 'contaminated' by everyday speech. This issue has cultural and historical implications since, although metaphor as such does not have a history (simply because it is a feature common to all languages and cultures) the conceptual understanding of metaphor is culturally specific and hence has a history. This history is exemplified by Western philosophical thought, the heliocentric discourse that equates universal Reason with 'natural light'. Derrida notes that this discourse has tended to regard other cultures and their languages as being primarily metaphorical rather than literal/rational. Hence, philosophy has exhibited a propensity to view other cultures as being divorced from the very discourse of the true which it claims to epitomise (see, Derrida, 1978, pp. 266–267). In making this claim, Derrida's reading of heliocentric metaphysics enacts a shift of emphasis away from the purely 'philosophical' domain into that of historical, cultural and political relations. To put it another way, engaging in a critical analysis of heliocentric thinking necessitates a critical engagement with the historical and cultural dimension of philosophical language and concepts.

Western metaphysics, Derrida argues, does not merely prioritise form over force and light (reason) over darkness (unreason). It also emphasises the role of the speaker in the generation and securing of meaning. Thus, this metaphysics also understands meaning as arising from the living presence of a speaker who 'uses' language intentionally. In this way, it effectively endorses the view that a timeless conception of the self is the origin of meaning. Western metaphysics, therefore, is also a 'metaphysics of presence': it holds that the meaning of words is ultimately linked to the intentions, and hence living presence, of a speaker/subject. For this reason, Derrida also refers to heliocentrism as embodying a 'logocentrism', in other words, it holds meaning to reside in 'living' speech (*logos*) rather than 'dead' writing. One could again turn to Derrida's treatment of structuralism to illustrate this point, especially to the account of Saussurean linguistics offered in *Of Grammatology* (1967). Here Derrida seeks to show that by conceptualising meaning in terms of the structural paradigm Saussure privileges not only form over force and literal over metaphorical language but also 'speech' over 'writing'. In other words, writing is conceived as a mere adjunct of living speech when it comes to the analysis of meaning. Speech, in contrast to writing, is taken to exhibit all the defining features characteristic of authenticity and originality. As such, speech is taken to ground the concept of truth. On such a model, language is taken to be a 'vehicle' of thought that can be manipulated by the living speaker in order to communicate his or her beliefs, intentions, etc.

For Derrida, as we have noted, the stakes of the metaphysical tradition are essentially linked to the question of culture, since this tradition expresses a belief in its own superiority when it comes to establishing the nature of meaning and truth. The 'phoneticization of writing', that is, the rendering of the significance of writing in terms of the priority of living speech, marks this cultural epoch. It is an epoch with a lineage that can be traced from **Plato** to **Heidegger**. Derrida's criticism of this tradition is mounted by way of the claim that what has hitherto been designated as 'writing' is not secondary. Writing, as he redefines it in *Of Grammatology* and elsewhere, is given an equal or even primoridal role both in the production of meaning and philosophical discourse. *Of Grammatology* announces the 'death of speech' as it has been traditionally understood (i.e. as the source of meaning). Against the traditional view, Derrida argues, we need to acknowledge the fact that 'the concept of writing exceeds and comprehends that of language', since language is already, in a very specific sense, 'writing' (p. 37). In making this claim, Derrida uses the term 'writing' in a very precise way, namely to designate the condition of the possibility of meaning. Derrida's introduction of writing the precondition of speech questions the purportedly 'natural' status of the relation that is assumed to inhere between thought and language. Language, when it is no longer considered merely as 'speech', does not find its essential precondition in the intentions of a speaker – in their presence – but in the possibility of 'inscription'. This condition of possibility is in turn discussed by Derrida in terms of what he variously refers to as the 'trace', the logic of the 'supplement', or 'differance'. *Of Grammatology* offers this observation concerning the trace: it is '*the absolute origin of sense in general. The trace is the differance* which opens appearance and signification [. . .] *no concept of metaphysics can describe it*' (p. 65). Discussing the trace, therefore, takes us to the limit of metaphysical discourse, although not beyond it. Meaning, Derrida argues, is founded upon a 'movement' of difference. To put matters more simply, meaning for Derrida emerges out of ambiguity and 'undecidability', not from clearly definable conditions (See Derrida, 1978, pp. 3–27). Meaning, it follows, is not reducible to so-called 'literal' language, since inherent in its production is a process of simultaneous differing and deferring akin to the process of substitution that typifies metaphorical language. Derrida's notion of the 'trace' represents an attempt to signify this condition. The trace, Derrida argues, is what provides the condition of possibility of meaning, signification, speech, speakers, and even thought. But the trace is none of these. Rather, the term indicates a fundamental possibility of repetition ('iterability') inherent in the production of meaning. Such a possibility cannot be derived from notions of consciousness or presence, or from their purported opposites (unconsciousness or absence), for what it designates is 'irreducible' (p. 70). What Derrida is discussing here can perhaps best be grasped in terms analogous to what he discusses under the name of 'force' in the essay 'Force and Signification'. The trace is not 'opposed' to anything, since it is a term that does not signify a determinate concept, still less something structural. Rather, the trace is what 'must be thought before the opposition of nature and culture, animality and humanity, etc., [and] belongs to the very movement of signification' (p. 70). The trace, in other words, is what allows us to speak of the human and the non-human, of what is 'inside' (the self-reflexive moment in which we assert our consciousness or our own culturally specific identity) and what is 'outside' (the world of empirical experience and also other cultures). In other words, if language involves the giving of names to 'things', then the trace is the *process* of signification that makes this giving possible. The trace thus indicates that meaning itself is, in Derrida's very specific sense, always already 'written' before it can be spoken.

Derrida's conception of deconstruction can be seen at work in his reading of Western metaphysics. Deconstruction is a form of critical engagement that aims to reveal the underlying presuppositions upon which structures of meaning depend. Importantly, Derrida stresses that such an engagement is not to be confused with a form of relativism, since it does not entail the abandonment of a concern with the notions of truth and value. What deconstruction does do, however, is question the kind of metaphysical absolutism that is exemplified by the metaphysical tradition. Thus, Derrida notes, it operates 'without claiming any absolute overview' of reality. As such, deconstruction does not espouse a universal 'method' that can then be applied indiscriminately to any text or argument. In other words, it would be wrong to merely invoke terms like 'differance' or the 'trace' and use these as if they were instruments that of themselves enable one to 'deconstruct' a text. This is because it is the very adequacy of an instrumental view of concepts and terms that is questioned by Derrida's work. From this it follows that 'no one, single deconstruction' exists (p. 141). Deconstruction thus enacts a form of pluralism with regard to meaning and politics alike. Indeed, deconstruction is not inherently 'political', if 'political' implies the advocacy of one specific political agenda above another. There is, Derrida argues, a political aspect to deconstruction, but only in so far as the politics of any interpretation will depend upon the context in which it is formulated.

The notion of context is fundamental to Derrida's view of deconstruction. Deconstruction attempts to show that all concepts are context dependent. Yet it is, at the same time, committed to the view that concepts are governed by conditions that render any determination of meaning according to a universal rule (and hence any single, privileged context) impossible. Derrida's discussion of his attitude toward Western philosophy is significant in this regard. We should not, he argues, undervalue the importance of tradition, which should be regarded as worthy of 'jealous conservation' (p. 141). Derridean deconstruction, it follows, does not entail an abandonment of the values that pertain to the philosophical tradition. On the contrary, deconstruction itself, Derrida claims, both acknowledges and cleaves to the value of truth, the conventions that justify notions such as 'good' and 'bad' interpretation, the importance of conceptual clarity, etc. In this sense, Derrida's writings are not merely of necessity situated within the conventions and norms that constitute Western discourse; they also remain faithful to that discourse. In so far as Derrida's works acknowledge this compulsion they effectively endorse an ethical imperative. Thus, we must, he claims, regard the conventions that determine the value of truth as having value precisely because they constitute the inescapable terrain of our own speech, writing and reading. In this, at least, Derrida remains a self-avowedly 'classical philosopher' (p. 125).

[PS]

Further reading: Ferraris 1990; Norris 1987; Rorty 1978.

DESCARTES, RENÉ (1596–1650)

French philosopher, scientific theorist and mathematician. Descartes was a student at the Jesuit College in La Flèche and then studied law at Poitiers, graduating in 1616. Shortly afterwards he became a member of the Duke of Bavaria's army, and travelled to Holland and Germany. It was in 1619 in Bavaria that Descartes first wrote down some of his thoughts on philosophy. These thoughts, subsequently presented in the *Discourse on Method* (1637) and *Meditations on First Philosophy* (1641), were to exert a profound influence on modern philosophy, effectively determining many of its central concerns for over two hundred years. Descartes's first major completed work was *Le Monde* (1632) which presented a theory of the origins and functioning of the solar system. A central feature of this work is its adherence to the Copernican theory, which holds the earth to orbit the sun. In the wake of Galileo's condemnation by the Catholic Church, Descartes decided against publication. In 1637 he published a work that sought to present his scientific theories, the *Dioptric, Meteors, and Geometry*; the *Discourse on Method* formed the theoretical introduction to this work.

In the *Discourse* and the *Meditations* Descartes set out to offer a theory of knowledge immune to the criticism of scepticism. A sceptic is someone who argues that nothing can be known for certain, a view espoused in the writings of Descartes's near contemporary Michel de Montaigne (1533–1592). Against this view, Descartes aims to illustrate that there is at least one piece of knowledge that all humans have and cannot doubt. In order to show this he employs the 'sceptical method'. This method begins by doubting everything that it is possible to doubt and seeing if there is anything that remains immune to such doubt. Starting in this way, Descartes argues, will thus enable us to discover the foundations of knowledge. Once we have done this we will be in a position to articulate the structure upon which a lasting science can rest. It would, of course, be unfeasible to sift through all of one's beliefs and show each of them in turn to be false. So, Descartes begins bringing into question the beliefs that form the 'foundation' for all the rest (Descartes 1999, p. 60). So, he begins by casting doubt on the veracity of the evidence given to us by our senses. In turn, we can also doubt other beliefs: for example, how is it possible to distinguish with certainty between being awake and dreaming? Likewise, Descartes also questions his own belief in 'corporeal nature in general', e.g. notions of extension, quantity, shape, size, time, place, number and so forth. All these notions, he concludes, can be doubted and hence cannot serve as a means for providing us with a form of knowledge that is immune to the corrosive power of doubt. Famously, Descartes envisages a scenario in which he is under the control of an omnipotent 'evil genius' who is deceiving him about both his experiences and judgements. Such a being could even mislead him into believing that $2 + 2 = 4$, when in reality it equals 5. In spite of this, Descartes argues, one thing remains certain '[A]fter everything has been most carefully weighed, it must finally be established that this pronouncement "I am, I exist" is necessarily true every time I utter it or conceive it in my mind' (p. 64). Thus, however deceived he may be, Descartes is now in a position to assert one truth that cannot be doubted. Whatever else may be the case, it is always true that he exists. In turn, Descartes attempts to define what this existing being is. Above all, he concludes, he is a being who thinks, i.e. he is one who doubts, has understanding, is capable of affirming and denying things, and so forth. Thus, Descartes arrives at the conclusion that he himself can be characterised in one manner above all others: his existence is defined by thought. This view is famously expressed in Part Four of the *Discourse on Method* by the sentence '*I think, therefore I am*' (p. 19).

According to Descartes, the 'I' that thinks can be defined by way of drawing a distinction between the mechanical structure of the human body and the fact that human activities are always exhibitions of intelligence. Because of this, he argues, all human actions are manifestations of a soul or mind. The properties of bodies are physical, in that they can be seen, touched, occupy a particular space, etc. But the veracity of the body can always be doubted. The self that thinks, however, cannot be doubted, for it is the self that is engaged in the act of doubting. In this way Descartes formulates the basis for his dualistic account of the relationship between mind and body. According to this view, mind is a substance that is essentially different from bodily substance. This distinction, in turn, forms the basis for Descartes's conception of knowledge. Certainty emanates from the 'I think', that is, from the self conceived of as a mental substance that is different in kind from that other substance we call 'matter'.

The metaphor of a building is a key element within Descartes's account of knowledge in both the *Discourse* and the *Meditations*. Knowledge, he claims, is like an edifice, and any edifice must be erected upon a secure foundation. The *cogito* (the 'I think') is that foundation. In this sense, Descartes, like any builder of a house, is building his account of knowledge by starting with the foundation and working his way up from there. What is special about the mind, he then argues, is that it has the ability to act and reflect in a spontaneous manner. Humans are endowed with independent will and reflective ability and it is 'reason or good sense [. . .] alone makes us men and distinguishes us from animals' (p. 2). We are above all for Descartes rational beings, and our ability to use our reason implies that we are endowed with 'intellect'. It is our intellect rather than our senses, he contends, which actually reveals the physical world to us (p. 69). Because human beings are rational they are able to think of the world about them in manner that is meaningful. In turn, since we are definable as the possessors of intellect, it follows that we think of the physical world by using ideas (i.e. concepts) to make 'representations' of the things in it. The truest ideas, Descartes contends, will be those of such 'clarity and distinctness' that we cannot find good cause to doubt them (p. 11).

Rationality, for Descartes, is a 'universal instrument' that provides us with the means of evaluating what counts as 'knowledge'. This conception of reason's universality and instrumental value is a central feature of Descartes's philosophy. Equally important is the fact that Descartes derives his theory solely from the act of rational introspection. For him, merely contemplating what he is in isolation from his environment is sufficient for securing a foundation for knowledge. A number of problems attend Descartes's approach. Even if we were to be convinced that we are rational beings made of a substance called 'mind', Descartes has not shown how knowledge of the external world is possible. Descartes's answer to this problem is hardly convincing, since he argues that God must be the sole guarantor of a reality external to the mind. The kind of argument he uses to assert the existence of God is referred to as an 'ontological argument'. According to this argument, if I am able to have a clear and distinct conception of God in my mind then the cause of this conception cannot be attributed to me. This is because I am finite, and it is impossible that a finite being should be the source of the attribute of infinite perfection that characterises God (see *Meditation* 3). To this is added the claim that existence is a necessary attribute of God's perfection because it is more perfect to exist than not to exist (see *Meditation* 5). This being the case, God must exist. In turn, God's existence allows Descartes to argue for knowledge of the external world. Essential to God's perfection, Descartes claims, is the fact that he is truthful. If God is truthful then he would not allow us to be deceived with regard to the perceptions that we have by way of our senses. An obvious objection to Descartes's argument would be to hold that it does not make much sense to claim existence is a perfection. Just because for something to be perfect it must necessarily exist does not imply that there is something that exists that is perfect.

Leaving the above issue to one side, however, one can note that Descartes' major achievement resides in his arguing that the self (the *cogito*) constitutes the core of any theory of knowledge. Descartes thinks of subjectivity in a manner that has been extremely influential. A subject, on his view, is an entity that, because it has self-consciousness, has an immediate sense of what it is. A subject, in other words, can be defined by way of its self-awareness. In turn, it is the sense of certainty that accompanies this self-awareness that character-ises knowledge in general. If a claim is to count as 'knowledge' then it must be *certain*, i.e. immune to doubt. Equally, the claim is, therefore, that simply by first examining the 'contents' of your own mind you will be able to construct a 'theory of knowledge' worthy of the title. This view implies an attitude of individualism with regard to issues of knowledge. For Descartes, the individual is taken to be something *given*. Hence, our sense of individual identity and what accompanies it (rationality, will, our ability to have clear and distinct ideas of things, and so forth) are of such self-evidence that no grounds could be offered for questioning them. Descartes therefore presupposes that an immediate sense of who and what we are constitutes a kind of com-plete and certain knowledge. In this way, Descartes takes human iden-tity to be in essence rational and conscious and hence immune to the possibility that it may have unconscious and irrational dimensions (his philosophy, in other words, is a 'philosophy of consciousness'). More-over, he conceives of the self in essentially a-social and a-historical terms. Thus, from a Cartesian point of view, there cannot be a cultural dimension to either the self or knowledge. Many subsequent thinkers have reacted against this in various ways. Thus, for example, **Hume** argued that the quest for certainty is a fruitless one, while **Hegel** argued that human life is in its very nature historical and cannot be comprehended adequately unless the fact of change is accounted for.

Other thinkers, such as **Nietzsche**, **Heidegger**, **Lévinas**, **Foucault** and **Derrida**, have all in various ways challenged the kind of approach that Descartes's work exemplifies.

[PS]

Further reading: Cottingham 1986, 1997; Rée 1974; Sorell 1987.

DEWEY, JOHN (1859–1952)

American philosopher, educationalist and psychologist. Dewey was educated at the University of Vermont and Johns Hopkins University. He was a lecturer at the University of Michigan (1884–1894) and then Professor of Pedagogy at the University of Chicago. From 1904 Dewey was Professor of Philosophy at Columbia University. Dewey is probably best known for his writings on education and for his attempt to combine elements of the philosophies of C. S. **Peirce** and William James into his own distinctive version of pragmatism. Dewey regards education as the sphere in which all the central elements of philosophical inquiry meet. Thus, education, he argues, involves a concern with the following kinds of issue: what kind of knowledge is to be learned (epistemology), the question of who the possessor of knowledge is (the nature of the self), instruction in right and wrong (ethics), etc. Education is linked by Dewey to social development, principally the rise of modern democracy, the advancement of methods in the experimental sciences and modern modes of industrial organisation (see Dewey 1916). Thus, the ultimate educational institution is society itself, which is regarded by Dewey not as an end but a means of engaging in the pursuits of life. All the key philosophical problems, Dewey argues, can be resolved by way of 'instrumentalism' (to use a phrase from his later writings). According to this view, all of our concepts and ideas are best comprehended as instruments for coping with situations. In turn, it does not make sense to say that any claim we may make about the world pertains to any ultimate truth. A proposition is neither true nor false, it is merely appropriate for a given purpose or it is not. In effect, this is an argument for abandoning many traditional (and Dewey would say unanswerable) philosophical questions in favour of addressing practical issues that can be solved.

In a paper written in 1909, Dewey defines pragmatism as holding the view that ideas [. . .] are attitudes of response taken toward extra-ideal, extra-mental things [. . .] The origin of an idea is thus in some empirical, extra-mental situation which provokes ideas as modes of response, while their meaning is to be found in the modifications – the 'differences' – they make to this extra-mental situation.

(Dewey 1997 p. 155)

In turn, the validity of any idea is assessed by way of its ability to transform the extra-mental situation that provokes it. An idea's validity, it follows, is a matter that concerns its concrete ability to produce a sense of satisfaction in us. 'Satisfaction' Dewey defines as simply being a matter of 'the better adjustment of living beings to their environment effected by transformations of the environment through forming and applying ideas'. This view, Dewey argues, entails rejecting all doctrines that argue for the existence of 'things in themselves' (i.e. the **Kant**ian *noumena*). Human experience is understood wrongly if it is taken to be a matter of the relationship between an independently existing, self-conscious 'mind' and an extra-mental realm that lies 'outside' it (as typified by **Descartes**'s approach). Against this view, Dewey holds that pragmatism starts with a rather different conception of the nature of 'experience': 'experience is a matter of the functions and habits, of active adjustments and re-adjustments, of co-ordinations and activities, rather than states of consciousness' (p. 157). In turn, and against fellow pragmatist William James's argument for a 'coherence' theory of truth (i.e. the view that a proposition is true if it is coherent with other propositions that are known to be true), Dewey argues for a correspondence theory. However, Dewey's theory is a correspondence theory with a difference. According to Dewey, even when thinking we are responding to our experiences in a practical manner. Hence, any experience presents us with a situation that 'calls out thinking as a method of handling it'. Human thought, it follows, is a form of practical response to environmental demands. Our responses, in turn, also have consequences. 'The kind of interlocking, of interadjustment that then occurs between these two sorts of consequences constitutes the correspondence that makes truth, just as failure to respond to each other, to work together, constitutes mistake and error' (pp. 158–159). This means that 'correspondence', as Dewey understands the term, does not involve thinking the relation between thought and a mind-independent existence, but rather the relations between those specific experiences that provoke thought and the ideas that arise as a result of this provocation. Such an account involves stressing the reciprocal

57

relationship between human ideas and their environment: 'what the pragmatist does is to insist that the human factor must work itself out in *co-operation* with the environmental factor, and that their co-adaptation *is* both "correspondence" and "satisfaction" ' (p. 166).

Dewey's view derives from his interpretation of the significance of Darwinian theory for philosophy (Darwin's *Origin of Species* was published in the year of Dewey's birth). The significance of Darwin, he argues, does not really concern the 'theological clamor' that accompanied its publication. In philosophical terms, the importance of the *Origin* concerns its overturning of a view of philosophy that held sway from the time of the Ancient Greeks. This was the view that change is to be accounted for in 'transcendent' terms. Darwin, though, offered the possibility of accounting for the fact of change without the need to refer to a transcendent realm. Before Darwin, philosophy cleaved to the vision of a world that is organised according to purposes that are extrinsic to it. For example, the notions of an Absolute Reason governing the nature of reality or of a spiritual force governing the course of natural developments (the view that the universe is the product of an intentional designer) are characteristic of this way of thinking. After Darwin, Dewey argues, we have to embrace a 'new logic'. This logic 'outlaws, flanks, dismisses – what you will – one type of problems and substitutes for it another type'. Whereas philosophers once sought to enquire into the absolute origin and purpose of ideas and values they must now turn their attention toward 'the specific conditions that generate them' (p. 13). In effect, therefore, Dewey takes the Darwinian theme of the evolution and development of life and applies it to ideas. We can attain 'intellectual progress', says Dewey, but this will not be achieved by seeking to answer all the imponderable questions that philosophers are inclined to ask about the nature of reality and truth. Rather, genuine intellectual progress occurs when we abandon the old unanswerable questions of philosophical tradition and begin to ask new ones that can, at least in principle, be solved: 'We do not solve them: we get over them. Old questions are solved by disappearing, evaporating, while new questions corresponding to the changed attitude of endeavor and preference take their place' (p. 19). This kind of approach is also evident in Dewey's essay 'The Practical Character of Reality' (see Thayer 1989).

Another feature of Dewey's pragmatism is his rejection of mind–body dualism. see 'The Unit of Behaviour' (Thayer 1989). Here, Dewey argues that the assumed relation between 'stimulus', mental states and 'response' in traditional psychology is mistaken. Against a theory that assumes separate spheres of stimulus and response, Dewey argues for a 'circuit' theory, i.e. one that holds the relation between stimulus and response to be reciprocal and to constitute a unity of subject and its environment. Thus, Dewey holds, 'we *begin* not with a sensory stimulus, but with a sensory-motor coordination'. When, for instance, a child reacts to seeing the light from a burning candle, 'it is the movement which is primary, and the sensation which is secondary, the movement of body, head, and eye muscles determining the quality of what is experienced [. . .] [the real beginning is with the *act* of seeing; it is looking and not a sensation of light'. An act of seeing can give rise to another act – it can stimulate 'reaching', for example. In such a case, the act of seeing now takes on a new significance within the context of the larger whole of action: it is 'seeing-for reaching-purposes' (1989, p. 264). If the act of reaching has an outcome (we touch something hot and it burns us) this is not a new stimulus but part of the overall process: the significance of the seeing and reaching are now modified in turn by pain. Thus, the feeling of burning is not a new experience but a reinterpretation of the original seeing within an ever-changing context. Depending upon the context, the acts of seeing and touching will have different significances, since one will be disposed to react in different ways. A motor response, it follows, is no mere passive reaction to an experience, it is an action that is oriented towards 'interpreting it', i.e. determining what kind of stimulus it is. Therefore, what is at stake here is an issue of *meaning*.

Dewey's view implies a monistic conception of the relation between bodily response and environment. Thus, the act of withdrawing one's hand from a flame is also a kind of 'sensory experience' in the same way as seeing a candle flame or the feeling of being burnt are. This does not mean that there is no difference between stimulus and response. But, Dewey argues, we are wrong if we think that such distinctions are to be grasped in terms of ontological 'distinctions of existence'. They are not. What they are is 'teleological distinctions'. By this, Dewey means that the difference between stimulus and response is functionally dependent upon purposes.

A later essay, 'The Pattern of Inquiry' (see Thayer 1989), spells out Dewey's teleological account of meaning. Here, inquiry is defined by Dewey as '*the controlled or directed transformation of an indeterminate situation into one that is so determinate in its constituent distinctions and relations as to convert the elements of the situation into a unified whole*' (pp. 319–320). Inquiry, in other words, has as its purpose the rendering of an indeterminate situation, one that is 'open' in the sense that the parts that make it up 'do not hang together', into a determinate or 'closed' situation. Such a situation is 'a universe of experience', i.e. a unity.

Thus, inquiry involves seeking to move from a state of doubt towards one of satisfaction, wherein one is no longer troubled by a problem. In keeping with Dewey's approach, the word 'doubt' does not relate purely to a subjective state of mind but to our environment. The environment we live in is not determined in advance, since all environments are what they are because an organism interacts with them and this interaction is always open-ended. Doubt stimulates the search for a solution to the problem. A possible solution to the problem Dewey calls an '*Idea*': 'Ideas are anticipated consequences (forecasts) of what will happen when certain operations are executed under and with respect to observed conditions' (p. 324). In other words, we formulate ideas in order to solve problems, ideas are teleological. The validity of an idea is a matter of its 'functional fitness', i.e. of its suitability for resolving the problematic situation. '*Reasoning*' is then required. This involves analysing the meaning of the 'contents' of ideas, and of their relation to one another. Thus, we ask whether the solution we are proposing accords with our other ideas, whether its meaning is truly relevant to the problem at hand, etc. This implies a move away from the earlier correspondence theory (noted above) to a coherence one, since Dewey now contends that a 'constellation of meanings' (p. 327) is required to see if an idea is acceptable: we ask how our new idea fits into the 'constellation'.

Dewey's thought has exerted an obvious influence on the work of Richard **Rorty**. The latter's neo-pragmatist theories exhibit similar anti-essentialist and anti-foundationalist tendencies while at the same time seeking to extend the concerns of pragmatist theory into the sphere of cultural analysis.

[PS]

Further reading: Bernstein 1967; Boydston 1972; Schilpp 1943; Thayer 1981, 1989.

DURKHEIM, EMILE (1858–1917)

French sociologist, regarded as one of the 'founding fathers' of sociology. His early work developed a theory of society as a transcendent reality that constrained individuals, and proposed the methodology necessary to study that reality. His work was influenced by **Kant**, by the French tradition of **Rousseau**, Saint-Simon and Comte, and stood in opposition to the individualism inherent in British moral and social philosophy. In 1898 he founded the journal *Année Sociologique*, which was crucial to the institutionalisation of sociology as an academic discipline in France. His later work showed an increasing interest in small-scale, pre-industrial societies and religions, and thus contributed to the development of cultural anthropology.

Durkheim's first major publication, *The Division of Labour in Society* (1893), offers an account of what holds a society together, and thereby seeks to demonstrate that social order and stability cannot be explained by a reduction to the actions of individuals, and particularly not in terms of Herbert Spencer's appeal to free social contracts between individuals. Durkheim compares modern industrial society to small-scale, pre-industrial society, initially suggesting a sharp distinction between the two. Modern societies have an extensive division of labour. It is this phenomenon that makes social contract theories plausible, for no one individual can master all the skills necessary to survive in the society. Each individual is dependent upon all others to provide those satisfactions which he or she is unable to provide for him or herself. The individual is thereby inhibited, practically, from leaving society. Durkheim calls this 'organic solidarity', drawing on the organic analogy, in which the various parts or institutions within a society are compared to the organs of an animal body, with each organ contributing a specialist function that is necessary to the survival of the whole.

In contrast, pre-industrial societies are characterised by a minimal division of labour. The stability of society is thereby made more perplexing, for, all other things being equal, individuals (or small units, such as the family) have all the skills necessary to survive independently from the rest of society. In effect, all individuals are competent in all the skills necessary to survival, and are thus not practically dependent upon other humans. Nothing appears to inhibit the fragmentation of society into many isolated individuals or small units. Such societies have 'mechanical solidarity'. Each individual is socialised into a common culture, the *conscience collective* (that may be translated as either 'collective consciousness' or 'collective conscience', which is to say that it entails both a cosmology, which structures the way in which individuals perceive the facts of their world, and a morality, through which the world is evaluated). Thus, while modern society allows great individuality, and indeed a cult of the individual that may threaten social solidarity, in pre-industrial society all members of the society are alike. They believe the same things, and share the same opinions and values. Social fragmentation is, however, ultimately inhibited by the rule of law. While law in modern society is perceived to be typically restitutive, compensating the victim for any material loss suffered, in pre-industrial society, law is repressive. To violate the moral or legal code that is inherent in the *conscience collective* is not to injure another individual, but to offend society itself. A crime thus transgresses sentiments that are approved of by all members of society, and the criminal thereby effectively places him or herself outside of the social order (which may be literally enforced through expulsion or execution). Greater force is given to the law in so far as it is given a sacred quality. Durkheim may thus hypothesise that religious imagery (such as god, and the soul) in fact give substance to more abstract social concepts. To worship god is, in practice, to worship society.

This bold distinction between mechanical and organic solidarity is compromised when Durkheim observes that in an economic contract 'not everything is contractual' (1984, p. 158). He thereby suggests that purely contractual relationships are insufficient to explain social relationships even within organic solidarity. A taken-for-granted morality, and thus a *conscience collective*, sets boundaries and the framework within which contractual relations are pursued and observed. The loss of such a *conscience collective*, with the increasing individualism of modern society, is seen by Durkheim as a problem that requires remedy, for example, through the encouragement of moral links with other members of society, in a revival of something akin to medieval guilds. (These ideas have recently been revived in political philosophy, in the communitarian response to liberalism.)

In *The Rules of the Sociological Method* (1895), Durkheim outlined a methodology for sociology. At the core of this is the notion that society is an independent level of reality, and may be studied as such. The regularities that may be identified in society, for example in social statistics, which Durkheim calls 'social facts', may thus be treated as 'things', which is to say that they have an objectivity that must be taken seriously on their own terms, rather than being reduced to the aggregate subjective intentions and actions of individuals. Durkheim thereby encourages a positivistic approach to sociology, encouraging both causal explanations (such that one social fact may be identified as the cause of another) and functionalist explanations, analogous to that used in biology. His approach is, however, more subtle than some commentators and followers have suggested. His substantive research suggests three levels of social objectivity: a morphology, of population densities and distribution, of territorial organisation, of levels of technology, of architecture and other material resources; institutions, of formal and informal rules; and collective symbolism, including values, ideals, opinions, mythologies and religions. The final level indicates Durkheim's sensitivity to the meaning that social facts have for individuals, and thus to something akin to interpretative approaches within sociology.

In *Suicide* (1897), Durkheim further explores the transcendence of society over the individual. He attempts to explain why, for any given country, suicide statistics (and indeed other 'moral statistics', covering murder, prostitution and alcoholism) are highly stable from one year to the next. His explanation works, initially, by relating a particular society's suicide statistics to other social facts, such as religion, military cultures and family structures. (It may be noted that Durkheim was aware of the imprecision of official suicide statistics, and that social factors, such as the stigma associated with suicide, might influence the recording of a particular death as suicide.) From apparently causal links between social facts, so that for example highly militaristic cultures and Protestant cultures have higher suicide rates, Durkheim generates a more abstract explanation in terms of underlying social forces. Suicide is thereby seen to depend upon social integration (i.e. the power of society to give the individual member legitimate goals) and moral regulation (i.e. the power of society to moderate the potentially infinite desires of the individual). Low social integration leads to egoistic suicide, where an individual identifies few of his or her goals with those of a group. Suicide is thus higher among the Protestants and the unmarried. Suicide may fall at times of war, when a common purpose is identified. Conversely, high social integration may lead to altruistic suicide, where an individual is prepared to sacrifice his or her personal goals to those of the collective, either positively, in acts of heroism, or negatively, when failure to achieve collective goals leads to shame. Anomie – the condition of living in the absence of recognised norms and values – occurs due to there being a lack of appropriate means to the achievement of acknowledged goals. Both economic crisis and unprecedented economic success can generate anomic suicide, as old rules of conduct cease to be relevant.

The Elementary Forms of Religious Life (1912), developing certain themes and interests found in his and **Mauss**'s (1963) *Primitive Classification*, is Durkheim's last major work. This may be seen to offer a sociological answer to Kant's *Critique of Pure Reason* (1781) (as indeed *The Division of Labour* responded to Kant's *Critique of Practical Reason*, 1790). Durkheim superficially agrees with Kant's argument that time and space are not objective, in the sense of being part of a world that is independent of the human subject, but rather are imposed upon the perceived world by the human observer. However, where Kant argued that the structures of time and space are universal, being common to all human subjects, Durkheim suggests, using ethnographic data from

Australian aboriginal societies, that different cultures embed different understandings of space and time in their members. An individual's understanding and experience of time and space therefore reflect the structure of his or her society, and the discipline necessary to act competently in that society. Durkheim's argument proceeds further, in order to explore totemism. In totemism, a natural image is bestowed with a sacred quality, and becomes the focus of group identification. A system of totems within a culture thereby serves, on the one hand, to articulate the relationship between groups (such as clans) and thus the social structure itself, for the members of the society, and on the other, through religious ceremonies, to reinforce individuals' identification with the society, their clan, and the values inherent in the culture. Thus, again, religious images are understood as encoding social reality. While Durkheim studies only what he regards as the simplest form of society (and religion), his contention is that parallel relationships hold between the cultures and structures of complex societies. This hypothesis may be seen to have a considerable influence on structuralism (and especially the work of **Lévi-Strauss**).

[AE]

Further reading: Allen *et al.* 1998; Cladis 1992; Giddens 1971, 1978; Hamilton 1995; Lehmann 1994; Lukes 1973; Pearce 1989; Pickering 2000.

ECO, UMBERTO (1932–)

Semiotician and novelist. Eco was trained as a philosopher, specialising in scholastic medieval philosophy. His interests, however, cover a wide range of areas, for example aesthetics, music, theory of the modern novel and modern scientific theories. To the wider general public Eco is best known for his novelistic writings *The Name of the Rose* (1980) and *Foucault's Pendulum* (1988). These works contain many references to his work in semiotics (the theory of signs) as well as to his interest in the philosophical writings of **Aristotle** (the lost second part of Aristotle's *Poetics* is central to *The Name of the Rose*) or the crime fiction of figures like Sir Arthur Conan Doyle. Primarily, Eco's theories are concerned with the role that the reader of a text plays in the activity of interpretation. In this connection, he draws a distinction between 'open' and 'closed' forms of text. Eco characterises modern forms of writing as being 'open' texts, by which he means that they are generally formulated in such a manner as to preclude the possibility of their being interpreted in unified terms. Thus, the meaning of an open text cannot be reduced to issues of, for example, an author's intentions. This does not, however, imply that such works are susceptible to an infinite number of possible interpretations. They are not. In a manner akin to **Derrida**, Eco argues that the meaning of texts is obviously in part determined by intentionality, but that intentions do not constitute the sole criterion for understanding issues of meaning. Interpretation, Eco argues, is an engagement with a work with a view to developing a coherent and justifiable reading of it. Such justification is offered in the first instance by way of the text itself and a sensitive reader will be someone who is aware that any text will be open to being interpreted in more than one way.

Eco's works on semiotics, *A Theory of Semiotics* (1976) and *Semiotics and the Philosophy of Language* (1984), represent attempts to engage with the question of the limits of interpretation. In *A Theory of Semiotics* the central concern is to address the American pragmatist philosopher C. S. **Peirce**'s notion of 'unlimited semiosis'. This is the contention that any sign requires an idea (what Peirce calls the sign's 'interpretant') in order for it to be taken as referring to something. However, every interpretant is in its own turn susceptible to being seized upon by another interpretant and thereby reinterpreted. This is, in principle, an infinite process, in so far as there is no interpretation of a sign that cannot itself become the object of a subsequent interpretation. On Eco's view, the possibility of infinite semiosis is not to be taken as some aberrant feature haunting the generation of meaning. Rather, infinite semiosis is an essential condition of possibility for the act of interpretation in general. That texts are always in principle open to an infinite number of possible interpretations is what makes any single interpretation possible. In turn, Eco's work concentrates upon elucidating the nature of codes as a means of broaching this issue. There are, he contends, two kinds of code. There are codes that contain signals that refer to specific sets of signs. Such codes are epitomised by the cipher. If the elements of a cipher (e.g. numbers) correspond to the letters of the alphabet, then a direct correspondence exists between the two (e.g. $1 = A$, $2 = B$, $26 = Z$). On this basis one can construct a code for a word like 'dog' (4, 15, 7). Eco, however, is more interested in the notion of a code in the sense that refers to the structure of language. Primarily, he is concerned with the implications of **Saussure**'s view of language as consisting of the two axes of *parole* and *langue*, where the term *langue* corresponds to the notion of a code. On the Saussurean view, *langue* is the structural component of language, i.e. it consists of a system of systematically organised grammatical and syntactical elements. *Parole*, in contrast, refers to the activity of using language (in Saussurean terms it is equivalent to speech). Eco refers to the correlation between the structural and spoken elements of language as an 's-code'. An s-code allows for a speaker to utter words. By way of an s-code a speaker selects the appropriate elements from the structural axis of meaning in order to make an utterance. Thus, the structural axis provides the speaker with the grammatical and syntactical elements necessary for a sentence to be constructed. Because of this, Eco argues, s-codes endow sentences with meaning.

There are two kinds of s-code: denotative and connotative. The first of these involves the literal understanding of a proposition. The second, however, involves something more ambiguous and hence difficult to grasp in literal terms. This is because the second kind of s-code can be found within the same utterance that conveys a literal meaning but implies at the same time another kind of meaning (e.g. irony). Words, on Eco's account, do not gain meaning by referring to specific 'things' in the world. In this regard, he follows Saussure. Hence, a word like 'dog' does not mean what it does because it refers to a specific animal but because it invokes the notion of dogs in general. In this way, a word's meaning emerges from the fact that it is produced by a code. All codes, Eco argues, are socially and culturally specific. All human beings live in culture and society and it is this context that endows language with meaning. How people behave in relation to utterances and gestures, it follows, provides the context for them. A model of this kind does not preclude errors: a language user can be incompetent and such incompetence can provoke laughter. But, says Eco, all language presupposes a certain minimal degree of competence with regard to codes.

Eco argues that codes, in so far as they presuppose a speaker's competence, are not fixed in the way that Saussure's theory implies. Rather, codes are continually undergoing modification due to their being used by a range of speakers with constantly changing competences. Against the view that *langue* determines the possibilities of meaning available to a speaker at any one time, Eco argues that *langue* itself will be subject to constant alteration due to the constantly changing requirements of speakers. Because of this fact, the notion that *langue* and *parole* are mediated by way of a structural code must be contested. Language, Eco argues, cannot be grasped as a code because it is a network or web of 'subcodes'. Such subcodes do not have a 'centre' that determines the nature of meaning since they are all altering in different ways relative to one another, subject to use. The production of signs, it follows, does not emanate from an overall structure but from the force of conventions that are at play whenever signs are in use. New signs, it follows are always assimilated within the web of dominant practices that go to make up a culture and society. A similar argument is deployed by Eco in *Semiotics and the Philosophy of Language*, where he argues that traditional approaches to the philosophy of language exhibit a tendency to view it as a closed system and hence do not take the fact of change into account when it comes to questions of meaning.

[PS]

Further reading: Caesar 1999; Capozzi 1997.

ELIAS, NORBERT (1897–1990)

German-born sociologist, who held academic posts in Germany, the United Kingdom, Ghana and the Netherlands. His approach to socio-logical inquiry is characterised by the use of highly detailed historical study, so that even theoretical questions are addressed in a highly con-crete manner. His work covers such diverse issues as death (Elias 1985), time (Elias 1992), sport (Elias and Dunning 1986) and art (Elias 1993). His first major works, *The Court Society* and *The Civilising Process*, both dating from the 1930s, already contain much that is distinctive to his sociology.

The two volumes of *The Civilising Process* (1939) ultimately address the problem of the relationship between the individual human being, and particularly the formation of individual personality, and the broader structures of society. The first volume develops a detailed account of the historical development of manners, etiquette and civil-ised behaviour from the early Middle Ages to the nineteenth century. Elias focuses upon the way in which the biological functions that are common to all human beings, such as eating, urination and defecation, spitting and sleeping, are managed, and how that which is embarrassing or shameful changes. He identifies a trend towards the greater man-agement of their emotional lives on the part of adults. The second volume deals with the development of the European state during the same period. Elias's underlying theoretical point, albeit one supported by a mass of historical evidence, is that the changes in the individual occur within a complex interweaving of processes within the structure of society. These include not merely the extension of state power (over the legitimate use of violence and monopolistic control of taxation), but also the increase in the division of labour, the expansion of urban living and trade, increased bureaucracy, and increasing populations. The individual is thus forced to live peaceably with ever larger numbers of other people. The process of civilisation may then be understood as the internalisation of what were originally external constraints, and that this internalisation leads to the constitution of modern individuality and individualism.

By the nineteenth century, European culture had forgotten the historical process that went into its formation. European standards of civilisation could therefore be presented as being of universal and ahistorical legitimacy, and be imposed upon others (both in colonies and in the subordinate classes within European societies). An important implication that Elias draws from this analysis entails a criticism of philosophy. He argues that the image of humanity drawn in Enlightenment philosophy (such as that of **Descartes** and **Kant**) is merely a product of its age, although it presents itself as universal. The rationalism and individuality of the Cartesian (or indeed Kantian) self is a reflection of the human mode of experience in post-Renaissance Europe. Elias terms this image *homo clausus* (closed man) and pits it against the *homines aperti* (open people) that informs sociological inquiry. Elias is arguing that even philosophical questions cannot be answered, or even properly addressed, through abstract reflection, because such reflection too readily takes as given much in the intellectual and emotional life of human beings that is actually historically constructed. Elias's essay on time illustrates this. Time is not seen as an objective entity (as it is by physicists), nor yet as a metaphysical condition of human existence (as it might be by Kantians), but rather a social phenomenon. Time is a symbol that facilitates the co-ordination of distinct sequences of change (including sequences of social activities), and thus the experience of time will vary according to the complexity of society, and the individual's internalisation of that complexity.

Elias's later works take these themes further, by engaging with the theory of science (1972, 1974) and by examining the relationship of human evolutionary and social change (in the context of a theory of communication) (1991a). Elias's account of science stresses the greater 'detachment' that is achieved in the natural sciences (1987). The results of the sciences acquire greater relative autonomy from the conditions and historical traditions within which they are produced. These results can be more readily formulated as laws. In contrast, the social sciences are more emotionally charged. In part *The Symbol Theory* is an attempt to give greater detachment to the social sciences, as it makes an initial attempt to synthesise the sciences, by embedding symbols (tangible physical patterns) and the development of the use of symbols by humans in an evolutionary context. Elias is not a reductionist, and one of the implicit targets of *Symbol Theory* (1991a) is socio-biology (with its assumption that human social processes can be explained through the principles of population biology), but nor does he wish to see culture interpreted as a realm that is wholly autonomous from nature or the rest of society.

[AE]

Further reading: Featherstone 1987; Goudsblom 1987; Goudsblom and Mennell 1998; van Krieken 1998; Mennell 1989; Mennell and Goudsblom 1998.

FANON, FRANTZ (1925–1961)

Considered as the founding father of postcolonial theory, and most famous for his dictum that colonisation was achieved by violence and must therefore be overcome with it, Fanon's name has become inextricably linked with anti-colonial theories of resistance. Though the course of his life was typically colonial (he enlisted for military service during the Second World War, then studied medicine in France, after which he moved to Algeria to work for the French authorities) Fanon, who was repelled by the excesses of the colonial regime in Algeria, joined the Algerian resistance and became a participant in the armed struggle against them. Fanon was involved with the National Liberation Front (FLN) and was later ambassador to Ghana for the Algerian provisional government.

Using the work of **Marx**, **Sartre** and **Freud** against the West in order to argue for a decolonisation by Europe and thereby effect a change in the world order, Fanon's criticism does not stop at an attack on the dominant history of colonial appropriation. He also criticises the values of Western humanism where, paradoxically, the dehumanisation of colonised subjects found its justification. In his best known works, *Black Skin, White Masks* (1952) and *The Wretched of the Earth* (1961), Fanon voices the numerous ways to resist imperialist domination. He accentuated the general importance of culture, whether black or white, and highlights the role of national culture in the process of liberation; hence, the necessity for the natives to assert their cultural traditions and to retrieve their histories. Fanon also maintains that since, historically, colonialism did not attempt to differentiate between people and cultures, which it all categorised as 'Negroes', cultural resistance should in turn adopt another wide approach, and be achieved in the name of the whole continent so as to defeat colonialist subjugation which led ultimately to the 'black' peoples' self-division and self-alienation.

Fanon sought to articulate the oppressed consciousness of the colonised subject. He argued that imperialism initiated a process of 'internalisation' in which those subjected to it experienced economic, political and social inferiority not merely in 'external' terms, but in a manner that affected their sense of their own identity. Hence, material inferiority creates a sense of racial and cultural inferiority. In turn, Fanon attempted to show the role of language within this process. Colonisation, he argues, also took place through language: under French domination the Creole language is rendered 'inferior' to French, and the colonised subject is impelled to speak the tongue of his or her imperial rulers, thereby experiencing their subjugation in terms of their own linguistic abilities and identity (an experience, it might be added, not uncommon within the context of Europe itself, e.g. the colonial experiences of Irish and Welsh cultures under the dominion of English expansion since the sixteenth century).

Fanon further articulates his desire to transcend historically determined influences; for him, the readiness for acceptance and assimilation, as well as feelings of inadequacy, are the unequivocal outcome of the cultural and ideological processes and constraints of imperialism. Fanon also opposes the hierarchical ideas of the 'white' world (notably notions of progress, racism, rationality and universality) in the light of their enthnocentricity and proposes, instead, a differential view of history which resists a return to the power of the 'same'. Such views as these, coupled with his attention to the role of language in the construction of identity, have led to Fanon being regarded as a poststructuralist *avant la lettre*. Thus, Fanon disturbs the constructed authority of colonial discourse through arguing that both polarities of the colonial enterprise undergo a common experience of enslavement: if the 'Negro' is enslaved by his purported inferiority, the 'White' man, too, in enslaved by his supposed superiority. Such a strategic displacement of the White/Negro hierarchy is also echoed in Fanon's rejection of the 'belatedness' of the Black man, for it is no more than the constructed opposite of the white man's being identified as superior, universal and normative.

The works of Fanon have inspired activists, theorists and writers alike. His theories of resistance to imperialist domination have been of crucial importance in generating a variety of arguments which have enriched the field of postcolonial studies.

[Nadira Regrag]

Further reading: Bhabha 1991, 1994; Childs and Williams 1997; Young 1990, 1995.

FOUCAULT, MICHEL (1926–1984)

The French thinker Foucault has been described as, among other things, a social theorist, a historian and a philosopher, although none of these terms quite sums up the variety of interests and approaches to be found in his writings. Foucault's work is the result of his engagement with approaches and concerns unearthed within these disciplines. The philosophy of Friedrich **Nietzsche**, the writings of Georges **Bataille**, of Maurice Blanchot, and Martin **Heidegger**, and in his later period the thought of Theodor **Adorno** are all of importance to Foucault in various ways. Foucault, like many of the French intellectuals of his generation, finds traditional perspectives and methods of inquiry (epitomised by the humanism of French existentialism, Marxism and phenomenology) lacking. Instead, Foucault turns to thinkers like Nietzsche, employing especially his own reading of the latter's conceptions of genealogy and power, in order to develop his own approach. Nevertheless, it should be noted that Foucault numbers **Marx**, alongside Nietzsche and Freud, as one of the 'masters of suspicion'. Such thinkers, Foucault claims, sowed seeds of doubt about the validity of forms of humanistic discourses prevalent within modern European culture, especially the ideal of a value-free objective methodology of scientific investigation and its accompanying faith in the emancipatory possibilities of reason in the political and moral spheres.

Foucault's writings traverse a wide range of fields and topics. Thus, he is interested at various times in analysing the social construction of concepts of mental illness, systems of discipline and punishment, sexuality and subjectivity, and, more generally, the relationship between discourses of knowledge and power. Often, Foucault's inquiries adopt the methodology of providing a detailed analysis of the historical development of these notions. Such meticulous historical accounts, for Foucault, provide the means of revealing the interests and hidden pre-suppositions that underlie disciplines dealing with these topics. It is because of this that it is difficult to characterise Foucault's work as belonging to any particular discipline of academic inquiry. He has, to be sure, philosophical concerns (primarily in relation to examining epistemological issues, i.e. questions about the nature of knowledge), but Foucault does not seek to construct an epistemology so much as to question what is inherent within the very notion of a 'theory of knowledge'. It is more accurate to describe his approach as 'interdisciplinary', in that his work crosses the boundaries that generally demarcate different forms of analytical inquiry according to the subject-matter at hand. Overall, his concerns might be more correctly understood as falling within the realm of politics.

In rough terms, Foucault's intellectual development can be summarised as occurring in two stages. On the one hand, the work he produced in the late 1960s develops an 'archaeological' and historical mode of investigation. The aim of such an approach is to uncover the genesis of the human sciences, the development of notions of reason and unreason, and the historical development of the modern 'episteme' (a phrase Foucault uses to allude to the dominant mode of understanding knowledge in the modern period). On the other hand, Foucault's later writings turn towards a Nietzschean-inspired 'genealogical' form of investigation. In effect, such an approach supplements the earlier historical analyses by revealing the underlying power relations inherent in discourses of knowledge.

Foucault believes that the subject (i.e. the self) is primarily a political notion that must be subjected to rigorous criticism. From this it is clear that Foucault is no humanist. He holds, rather, that an elucidation of the dominant practices within any form of social organisation (including notions of the self that are produced within it) is essential to that form's being subjected to critique. However, in contrast to a thinker like **Althusser**, who cleaves to the dual strands of structuralism and Marxism in an attempt to resolve the apparent inconsistencies of capitalist society by rendering them within the meta-narrative of dialectical materialism, Foucault rejects any project that would seek to provide a harmonious resolution of social antagonism by way of reference to a meta-narrative. Foucault's turn to Nietzsche, therefore, is at the same time a turn away from more traditional forms of analysis. In their place Foucault offers an account of the political ramifications of discourses of knowledge that takes all knowledge forms to be definable in terms of power relations. Indeed, for Foucault, the terms 'power' and 'knowledge' are closely related, in that they necessarily invoke one another. Hence, within the parameters of Foucault's identification of the convergence of power and knowledge, even the possibility, offered by Marxism, of mounting a meta-critique of capitalist ideology is delusory. In order to offer an account of the nature of ideology it would be necessary to posit at least the possibility of an objective perspective emancipated from the power relations implicit within ideology. For Foucault, this is simply not a possibility. Since power permeates societies, even the notion of ideology becomes questionable. 'The notion of ideology', Foucault tells us, 'appears to me to be difficult to make use of, for three reasons'. First, ideology 'always stands in virtual opposition to something else which is supposed to count as truth'. Second, ideology is a concept that always refers us back to 'something of the order of a subject' – and Foucault (as already noted) argues for the view that the notion of the subject must be criticised. Third, 'ideology stands in a secondary position relative to something which functions as its infrastructure, as its material, economic determinant, etc.' (Foucault 1980, p. 118). Of the reasons offered here, the first is probably the most telling. Ideology-talk presupposes truth-talk and, like Nietzsche, Foucault has little time for disinterested, objective conceptions of 'truth'. Foucault's suspicion of truth stems from his view that all social relations are relations of power. In so far as all knowledge claims have power relations inherent within them, so, too, truth-talk must partake of the same relation to power. In other words, in Foucault's view 'knowledge' is something that occurs and hence has meaning only in the nexus of power relations. 'Knowledge', in this sense, is a relative term. Since there is no external standpoint beyond society and history from which one could envisage viewing the totality of human relations and interests with a view to judging them objectively, all knowledge must, in its very nature, be situated and hence permeated with interests.

Given all this, it should come as no surprise that Foucault also rejects any pretensions to offering an all-encompassing account of history, society and human nature. In the place of such a project he proposes a series of specific analyses of particular knowledge forms. Hence, Foucault's work on madness and psychiatry, medicine, punishment, and sexuality all concentrate upon elucidating the particular power relations involved in different knowledge by way of an analysis of their respective histories (see Foucault 1965, 1973, 1978, 1979, 1985, 1986). This is not to say that all Foucault's works were written with this goal in mind. As Foucault himself tells us, it is only with the benefit of hindsight that he himself realised what he was doing his earlier work is inextricably linked to questions of power:

> When I think back now, I ask myself what else was it that I was talking about in *Madness and Civilization* or *The Birth of the Clinic*, but power? Yet I'm perfectly aware that I scarcely

ever used the word and never had such a field of analyses at my disposal.

(Foucault 1980, p. 115)

We might ask why is it that Foucault did not have the requisite field of analysis ready to hand? One answer Foucault offers is that he was prevented from achieving an insight into the nature of power by his own early adherence to Marxist thought. To concentrate, as Marxists do, exclusively upon issues of class domination entails adopting a perspective that prevents one from appreciating the 'concrete nature of power' (Foucault 1980, p. 116). Foucault's overcoming of the limitations of the Marxist approach arose, he tells us, from the student uprisings in Paris in 1968. At this time the struggle with power revealed power itself in its concrete light by highlighting the fact that all political struggle takes place 'in the fine meshes of the web of power', not in the context of an all-embracing narrative of historical development.

It is worth noting the significance of this last metaphor. Power is analogous to a 'web': it captures and entraps individuated subjects by defining them as such. The genuine nature of subjectivity (that it is historically constituted within relations of power) is thrown into relief only in the very act of resisting power. In this way, power reveals itself to be constitutive both of social relations and subjectivity alike. By the same token, power creates its own resistances by constituting subject positions antithetical to it in the very activity of one party seeking to dominate another. We can also note from this why politics is central to Foucault's thematisation of power. On Foucault's view, power is a matter of the constitution and differentiation of competing interests, and this occurs as a socio–political phenomenon. Power is intrinsic to social life and manifests itself in forms of struggle at the political level. These struggles make subjects what they are. Yet, since power is constitutive of subjectivity, by the same token it also creates modes of resistance in the form of the subjects constituted within its web.

Foucault's conception of politics, it follows, concentrates upon the notion of resistance to power. But this cannot be articulated at the level of a meta-critique, for resistance and theories alike only occur within specific contexts. As such, politics is always a form of practical engagement within particular social relations. The word 'politics', therefore, neither signifies nor refers back to a unified totality, but is always a 'micropolitics'. Again, one can contrast this view with the Marxist conception of politics as a global political struggle against ruling-class ideologies. Whereas the latter holds that power is revealed by way of a general and abstract thesis (the theory of ideology), Foucault contends that power can be disclosed only by way of meticulous historical analysis that focuses upon particular forms of discourse in their specific contexts. Such histories are analysed by Foucault as domains of practices. The concrete exercise of power over subjects, and hence the definition of them as such, is regarded by him as the primary goal of such practices. To take the example of punishment, Foucault argues that the prison can be understood as a means of policing the behaviour of individuals, and by way of that process constituting them as subjects. Thus, power is exercised in order to 'subject' the criminal, in all senses of the word. The criminal is subjected to the power of the prison's regime, and in being defined as such he or she is rendered an individuated subject or self. Likewise, in so far as its function is to reform the criminal type the prison is already located within the framework of a kind of 'knowledge' of them. In this respect the act of definition is itself an expression of power, whether it be the definition of the 'criminal type', the 'insane', of 'sexuality' and so forth. All such instances reveal that exerting power over the body functions as a means of defining subjectivity and thereby shaping and policing social order. The most overt and bloody example is that of the public execution of the criminal (see Foucault 1979). Such an execution demonstrates power over the criminal's body and the expression of this power over the body determines their identity as such.

However, power does not show itself simply by way of such explicit power over the body as is found in the case of public execution. The increasing abandonment of public executions in Western society from the eighteenth century does not, for Foucault, point to a lessening of power. Rather, it shows us that modern society is not policed so much by force as by increasingly hidden forms of coercion. The development of purportedly 'humane' practices of punishment in fact pays testimony to the fact that inflicting pain is no longer a prerequisite of control, not that we have become more humane. Power over the body can be attained more efficiently if a subject is constituted in such a way that he or she is the subject of knowledge. This, Foucault argues, is the aim of the kinds of knowledge that he details in his histories of criminality and sexuality. Thus, the criminal psychologist's knowledge of the offender's mental condition plays its part in determining their sentence so, in practical terms, knowledge of the criminal expresses power over them by submitting their body to the political mastery of power expressed as knowledge.

Nevertheless, it should be noted that, for Foucault, power 'as such' does not exist. For one thing, power is multiple and ubiquitous. In other words, power cannot be 'described' in terms of characteristics that exist independently of the context in which struggles occur. All expressions of power are particularised and local in their nature. Modern society cannot be accounted for in terms of a unified theoretical conception of power. Rather, to return to Foucault's own metaphor, power is to be comprehended as a 'web' of localised relations and practical engagements (i.e. at the 'micro-' rather than the 'macro-' level). In place of the Marxist vision of society, therefore, we are offered a localised politics of resistance, one that seeks to liberate the body from dominant discourses of subjectivity. Equally, the term 'power' does not for Foucault simply denote something negative. Power is also something 'productive', since its very multiplicity implies that its productivity is not to be comprehended solely in terms of repression and domination. Thus, by way of example, power is productive of discourses of truth. Yet, such discourses are open to being questioned and re-thought in alternative forms. What is at stake when this is done is not so much truth itself, 'but the political, economic, institutional regime of the production of truth'. Foucault thus advocates a politics that aims at 'constituting a new politics of truth'. In this regard, for Foucault our key political and cultural concern should not be exposing the illusory power of ideology by constructing meta-theories, but the issue of truth itself understood as a site of contention and struggle.

[PS]

Further reading: Carroll 1987; Dreyfus and Rabinow 1982; Hoy 1986; Lecourt 1975; Mahon 1992; Merquior 1991; Miguel-Alphonso and Caporale-Bizzini 1994; Sheridan 1980; Smart 1983.

FREUD, SIGMUND (1856–1939)

Founder of psychoanalysis. Though born in Freiburg, a small town in the Austro-Hungarian empire, Freud lived almost all his life in Vienna, Austria, before dying in exile in London during the traumatic aftermath of the Nazi *Anschluss*. The son of a wool merchant, the young Sigmund gained admission to the *Gymnasium* at an early age despite his father's financial difficulties. Later, he entered medical school in the University of Vienna from which he graduated in 1885. Here began his lifelong passion for research with early stints in comparative anatomy, physiology and neurology under a distinguished list of mentors. His research career was, however, cut short by economic necessity:

he had become engaged to Martha Bernays of Hamburg and was compelled to find a way to earn a living.

Freud's first break was a travel bursary that took him to study with the celebrated Jean-Martin Charcot in Paris (1885–1886). Charcot had made the study of hysteria and hypnotism respectable in medical circles, and, under his influence, Freud was eventually to revolutionise our understanding of these concepts in relation to a theory of the mind. It also gave him the confidence to set up a practice in neurological disorders on his return to Vienna. It was in the course of this practice that he met Dr Josef Breuer with whom he collaborated on his first 'psychoanalytic' work, *Studies on Hysteria* (1895). Breuer, however, withdrew from the psychoanalytic project because of what he believed to be Freud's overemphasis on the sexual aetiology of hysteria. Freud's formal statement on the role of sexuality in relation to the symptomatology of the subject was set out in *Three Essays on the Theory of Sexuality* (Freud 1977a). Here Freud extends the scope of the term 'sexuality' from the genital model of nineteenth-century medicine to include the perversions, infantile sexuality, and the transformations of the libido in relation to a developmental model of the subject.

Apart from Breuer, the only other witness to the early formulation of psychoanalytic theories was the Berlin physician Wilhelm Fliess, with whom Freud carried on a vigorous correspondence (1887–1902). This correspondence, which has luckily survived, included Freud's first major foray into metapsychology, the *Project for a Scientific Psychology* (1895). The Fliess years also marked the epochal 'discovery' of the Oedipus complex from Freud's own self-analysis. Freud concluded that the love for the parent of the opposite sex and rivalry with the one of the same sex is a 'universal' event of childhood. The fruit of these years is the seminal text *The Interpretation of Dreams* (1900), which initially went unnoticed. In this text and *The Psychopathology of Everyday Life* (1901), and *Jokes and their Relation to the Unconscious* (1901), Freud attempted to work out a comprehensive grammar of the unconscious to encompass not merely the neurotic mind but the structure of the psyche as such. Later he would refer to this opposition between the conscious and the unconscious as the 'two principles of mental functioning' (Freud 1911).

Within the next ten years, psychoanalysis moved from being a local therapeutic innovation to a theoretical movement of international stature. Early recruits included the Swiss psychiatrists Eugen Bleuler and Carl **Jung** and the Viennese physician, Alfred Adler. An international congress of psychoanalysis was held at Salzburg in 1908. Freud and Jung were invited to lecture at Clark University in the United

States in 1909. The movement however suffered from doctrinal splits when Adler and Jung broke away to set up their own schools. Freud also suffered from personal tragedies at this time: the death of family members and the onset of oral cancer which would necessitate several operations in his last years. Recognition (which Freud craved for as a youth) finally came in the form of the Goethe Prize, election to the Royal Society, the institutionalisation of the psychoanalytic movement, his correspondence with Einstein, etc., making it difficult for the Nazis to detain him in Vienna. Assisted by the efforts of the Roosevelt administration and Princess Marie Bonaparte, Freud made his way to London, where he lived in the ministering company of his daughter, Anna, until his death on 23 September 1939.

[Shiva Kumar Srininvassan]

Further reading: Ellenberger 1970; Gay 1988; Jones 1964.

GADAMER, HANS-GEORG (1900–)

One of the most famous pupils of the philosopher Martin **Heidegger**, Gadamer is probably best known in the English-speaking world for his book *Truth and Method* (1960). In this work Gadamer presents his theory of 'philosophical hermeneutics'. Hermeneutics, the theory of textual interpretation and analysis, has its origins in the interpretation of legal and biblical texts. In its modern form, hermeneutic theory is generally traced back to the writings of figures such as Friedrich Schleiermacher (1768–1834) and Wilhelm Dilthey (1833–1911). In general terms, hermeneutics seeks to offer an analysis of the nature of textual interpretation and, in relation to this, the nature of understanding. In line with this, Gadamer's philosophical hermeneutics attempts to elucidate the conditions that are essential to any act of understanding. In other words, Gadamer is not interested in providing us with a 'methodology' that can be applied rigidly to a variety of texts (e.g. literary or philosophical) in order to decode their meaning. Indeed, the concept of 'method', according to Gadamer, hinders a proper understanding the nature of truth: truth, in effect, is opposed to method. Against the claims of method, Gadamer's aim is to articulate the nature of understanding in general. The starting point for Gadamer's project is Heidegger's claim that understanding is an abiding and universal condition of human existence . To be human, for Gadamer, is thus to be a being who is endowed with understanding. We necessarily engage in interpretation simply in virtue of our being the kind of entity that we are.

In Gadamer's view, any act of understanding can be ascribed two features. On the one hand, all understanding is historical in nature. By this, Gadamer means that all understanding is bound by context. There is, according to this view, no interpretation that does not emerge in virtue of the historical and cultural traditions specific to it. Because of this, Gadamer argues, any act of understanding necessarily begins with *prejudice*. Whenever we read and interpret a text we bring to bear on it certain presuppositions, and these presuppositions form the basis not only of any interpretation that we are likely to make, but also of our being able to interpret it at all. Gadamer's approach thereby rejects the Enlightenment view, which held that genuine knowledge is to be defined by way of its being free from prejudice, as aspiring to objectivity by way of recourse to universal and rational principles. Gadamer points out that even the Enlightenment had presuppositions specific to it: for one thing, in its search for value-free, objective criteria for knowledge the Enlightenment exhibited a prejudice against prejudice. Nevertheless, although all interpretation begins with prejudice, it does not follow that it remains trapped within the set of presuppositions that render it possible. For, Gadamer argues, we must understand interpretation as a self-reflexive activity wherein the prejudices that accompany an interpretation can be subsequently subjected to criticism through active engagement and dialogue with a text. A text, in other words, is not on Gadamer's view a passive receiver of a meaning that is actively imposed upon it by a reader. Rather, any text is capable of resisting and thereby challenging the presuppositions of its readers.

Gadamer's claim that all interpretation is historical develops Heidegger's argument that the nature of human being (*Dasein*) cannot be adequately grasped in 'ontical' terms. By way of illustration, one can say that the existence of entities in the world (stones, chairs, non-human life forms, etc.) is a matter that can (in principle, at least) be comprehended at an ontical level. We can think of a stone, for example, as an entity that is simply 'there' nearby, as something that is 'present-at-hand' in the world of our daily experience. Human being, in contrast, cannot, for Heidegger, be glossed in such terms. Being human is distinctive in so far as it involves thinking about and thereby attempting to grasp one's own world by way of one's understanding. Such understanding is not a matter that can be reduced to an ontical mode of existence but is an 'existential' issue. The mode of existence that we, as human beings have involves 'historicity': we are historical beings, and our self-understanding presupposes this. However, whereas

Heidegger, in *Being and Time* (1927), sought to outline his view with the aim of developing a fundamental *ontology* of human being, Gadamer is interested in developing a hermeneutics that can 'do justice to the historicity of understanding' (Gadamer 1975, p. 265). In order to do this, Gadamer begins with Heidegger's discussion of the nature of the 'hermeneutic circle'. The hermeneutic circle, as Schleiermacher discusses it, concerns of the interrelationship of the parts and the whole. So, the single word (the part), we can say, belongs to the sentence (the whole) and gains its meaning from its place within the sentence. Yet, the fact that the sentence is nevertheless composed of individual words makes it what it is. Thus, one cannot understand the part without making reference to the whole, nor vice versa. Understanding is circular in the same manner. We seek to grasp the meaning of the parts of a sentence but already presuppose the whole in order to do so. By the same token, we find that our understanding of the whole is constantly modified by the parts whenever we engage in interpretation. In this way, 'the movement of understanding is constantly from the whole to the part and back to the whole' (p. 291). Heidegger, Gadamer argues, developed this view one stage further by pointing out that the relation between part and whole is not a formal relation that is dissolved when perfect understanding of a text has been attained. Thus, according to Schleiermacher, such understanding is realised when readers position themselves in the writer's mind and, by discovering their true intentions, overcome what is alien about the text. What Heidegger tells us is that the hermeneutic circle cannot be resolved in this way because what it does in fact is to describe the nature of understanding as constituting an 'interplay of the movement of tradition and the movement of the interpreter' (p. 293). The anticipation of meaning which allows us to approach a text is not derived from our own subjectivity, but

> from the commonality that binds us to the tradition. But this commonality is constantly being transformed in our relation to tradition. Tradition is not simply a permanent [and formal] precondition; rather, we produce it ourselves inasmuch as we understand, participate in the evolution of tradition, and hence further determine it ourselves.
>
> (p. 293)

The significance of the hermeneutic circle, it follows, is correctly grasped only in so far as we realise that its movement is a fundamental condition of all acts of understanding. In other words, the hermeneutic circle denotes the *structure* of understanding and this structure is historical.

The other essential feature of all understanding, Gadamer argues, is its relation to language. We have seen that all understanding proceeds from tradition, and it is also the case that it is of 'the essence of tradition to exist in the medium of language' (p. 389). Language and understanding, it follows, are intimately connected. That we are linguistic beings is what makes it possible for us to interpret anything at all. Indeed, even the notion of 'experience', for Gadamer, can be most adequately grasped on a linguistic level (pp. 438ff). Indeed, Gadamer argues, the world we have an understanding of is *constituted by language*.

> What is true of understanding is just as true of language. Neither is to be grasped simply as a fact that can be empirically investigated. Neither is ever simply an object but instead comprehends everything that can ever be an object.
>
> (p. 404)

The 'world' cannot be said to exist in-itself, i.e. independently of language. Yet, it does not follow from this that the world such as it is always exists relative to some *particular* language. Rather, it is our having language at all that makes humans the particular kinds of being that they are. We do not exist 'in' language in the way animals exist in a habitat. We are not, in other words, confined or imprisoned by language. One can learn another language, and thereby enrich one's understanding. But this does not involve the same kind of change of relation to the world that an aquatic animal would have to undergo in order to dwell on the land. Rather, humans dwell in the world precisely to the extent that they have language. We are beings who live within tradition because we are linguistic, and the mode of being appropriate to an understanding of tradition 'is language' (p. 463).

In line with Gadamer's stressing the importance of language, all understanding, he argues, involves dialogue. Dialogue, for Gadamer, can involve conversation between interlocuters. Conversation involves having a common ground with the other speaker, not in the sense of sharing common ideas but in the sense of recognising that their viewpoint, too, needs to be heard. As we have seen, the same point holds for the written text – which is capable of challenging its interpreter's presuppositions concerning it. Dialogue, in other words, is a situation in which ideas are rendered open to being challenged by alternative perspectives. Dialogue is a shared experience and goes to make us what we are.

Gadamer's view implies that there is no objective vantage point from which to judge the past or tradition. All interpretation is always a *reinterpretation*. Gadamer is thus an anti-foundationalist, i.e. he believes that there are no objective truths to be found outside of the realms of history and tradition. At the same time, however, he remains committed to the view that any act of interpretation can pertain to objectivity to the extent that (1) it aspires to self-critical rigour, and (2) it can be justified by way of recourse to the specific historical period in which it is formulated. For this reason, Gadamer cleaves to the notion of truth. 'Truth', in this sense, is not a matter of uttering statements that correspond with a world consisting of states of affairs that exist independently of language. Rather, truth consists in the insights handed down to us by past traditions and cultures. Such insights have their own peculiar power, for they announce themselves in such a way that we are obligated to them.

[PS]

Further reading: Coltman 1998; Hahn 1997; Silverman 1991; Warnke 1987; Weinsheimer 1985.

GEERTZ, CLIFFORD (1926–)

American cultural anthropologist, who has championed interpretative approaches to the study of cultures. His central, and surprisingly bold, claim is that anthropology concerns the description of the activities and events of small social groups. Yet description cannot be of mere physical behaviour. That, following the philosopher Gilbert Ryle, he terms 'thin description'. Anthropology requires 'thick description', which is to say, the anthropologist strives to express his or her understanding of cultural activity as something meaningful (Geertz 1973, p. 6). He illustrates this distinction with the difference between a wink and a twitch. Physically the two may be identical (so that they would be indistinguishable in a photograph). Yet the wink is a meaningful and public act of communication. It is a 'construable sign' (which does entail that it can be misconstrued, and indeed, twitches can embarrassingly be mistaken for winks and vice versa). Geertz therefore defines 'culture' as 'a context . . . within which [social events, behaviours, institutions, or processes] can be intelligibly . . . described' (1973, p. 14); which is to say that a culture allows flecks of physical behaviour, such as the movements of an eyelid, to be turned into significant acts of communication. 'Culture' is summed up as being a 'semiotic' concept, although Geertz does not propose a systematic theory of signs, as found in the linguistics of **Saussure** or **Jakobson**. Rather, in developing their descriptions, anthropologists struggle to 'find their feet'; coming to terms with the alien context that gives meaning to the initially chaotic and baffling events happening around them.

The task of the anthropologist is akin to that of the literary critic, in so far as cultural behaviour can be treated as a text that requires interpretation. This raises important questions about the accuracy (or objectivity) of any ethnographic description. Geertz suggests that these anthropological interpretations are 'fictions', but not in the sense that the events they describe did not happen. Rather, the interpretations are made or fashioned, and as such are second – or even third – order accounts based upon the first order communications of the 'native'. As such they are never definitive, and can always be contested. Anthropology advances only as new studies plunge more deeply into the material opened up by their predecessors, bringing the reader into ever closer touch with the world of strangers.

This gives cultural theory a peculiarly delicate position within Geertz's account. He rejects those approaches to anthropology that try to avoid or remove this incompleteness (or contestability), for example by 'turning culture into folklore and collecting it, turning it into traits and counting it, turning it into institutions and classifying it, turning it into structures and toying with it' (1973, p. 29). (The last transformation attacks the 'alchemy' of **Lévi-Strauss**'s structuralism: see Geertz 1973, pp. 345–359.) Cultural theory is not, then, for Geertz a systematic account of how culture as such works. Theory cannot be imposed upon ethnographic data. Rather theory consists of a vocabulary – integration, rationalisation, symbol, ideology, conflict, charisma, ritual, worldview and so on: (Geertz 1973, pp. 23, 28) – which facilitates the anthropologists' articulation of the construable signs which they encounter. Renouncing grand sociological theories in favour of fine-grained interpretative explorations of the rich content of everyday life, Geertz seeks to explicate the 'native' actors' understanding of their action, and what this understanding tells us about how that particular society works, and perhaps about social life in general.

Ultimately, the anthropologist must write (fashioning their fictions). Interpretations are inscribed (typically in essays, but also in photographs, diagrams, films and museum collections). In more recent writings Geertz has suggested that the power of the anthropologist to convince the reader of the accuracy of their ethnographic accounts comes not simply (or at all) from the rigor or plausibility of their findings, but rather from the rhetorical style within which that account is constructed, and of the personality of the author created in the texts. In this vein, *Works and Lives* explores in detail the way in which four key figures in the development of anthropology write.

[AE]

Further reading: Inglis 2000; Ortner 1999.

GIDDENS, ANTHONY (1938–)

British social theorist, and currently director of the London School of Economics. A broad-ranging body of work, which engages particularly with the problem of modernism (Giddens 1973, 1990, 1991), is grounded in the development of the theory of structuration.

Structuration is offered as an explanation of the relationship between individual human agency and the stable and patterned properties of society as a whole. On the one hand, orthodox social theories such as functionalism or structuralism tended exclusively to emphasise the organised nature of society, so that society was presented as existing independently of the agents who composed it (and indeed, as a force that constrained and determined their actions, much as natural forces do). On the other hand, another strand of social theory (including symbolic interactionism and hermeneutics) emphasised the skills of social agents in creating and managing the social world in which they lived. Giddens recognises a partial truth in both extremes, for society is patterned, so that the isolated and self-interested actions of its individual members do take on the appearance of having been planned or co-ordinated. Annual social statistics, for example, show remarkable stability for the occurrence of many everyday events and activities. Further, precisely because this stability and order are outside the control of individual agents, society does appear to constrain and control them. However, agents are highly competent, with a vast stock of knowledge and range of skills that allows them to make sense of complex and often unique situations, and to manage their relationships with others.

Giddens therefore talks of the 'duality of structure'. Social structure, which is to say, the organised and enduring character of social life, is dual in that it is at once external to the society's members, and internal (constituting the agent as a competent member of society). As Giddens rather cryptically puts it, 'the structural properties of social systems are both medium and outcome of the practices they recursively organise'

84

(1984, p. 25). The social structure exists primarily as the competence that the society's members have to organise their own social life. Social structure is thus a set of rules and resources available to the competent agent. It exists in agents' memories. The crucial point that Giddens makes, though, is that agents do not have to be consciously aware of this. A great deal of their competence is non-discursive, which is to say, that agents would not be able to give a verbal account of what they know. They do, however, know how to 'go on' in a given situation. They have 'practical consciousness'. In practice, the social structure is then realised as something external to the agents. The consequences of the agents' actions in a particular situation are likely to go beyond anything that is simply intended by them. Giddens draws on geography as well as sociology to analyse the external stability of social structures as institutional relations that are articulated across time and space. It is important to the agent that social structure does confront him or her as something external. Giddens's concept of 'ontological security' captures this. Competent social agents are confident that the social and natural worlds (and indeed their own self-identity in relation to those worlds) are stable and secure. The world is made a matter of routine. Anything that disrupts this expectation of the routine is highly disturbing (and a feature exploited in **Goffman**'s analysis of embarrassment).

In recent years Giddens has been more directly involved in political theory, and in particular in the attempt to generate an account of the 'Third Way' (1994, 1998b) as a renewal of social democratic politics. This work draws significantly on his early criticism of **Marx**ism (1981) and accounts of globalisation and the relationship of the individual to the community.

[AE]

Further reading: Bryant and Jary 1991, 1996; I. Cohen 1989; Craib 1992; Held and Thompson 1990; Kaspersen 2000.

GOFFMAN, ERVING (1922–1982)

American sociologist, who developed a distinctive form of study of the meaningful social relationships that exist between individual agents, and how those relationships are created and maintained. He focuses on what he calls the 'interaction order'.

Essentially, Goffman's work looks at face-to-face interaction, or 'encounters' as he calls them, and draws on a dramaturgical model (and thus the metaphor of the social actor), in order to explore the ways in which humans present themselves to others in particular contexts (Goffman 1959). He was therefore concerned with the ways in which encounters are managed, and the skills that actors bring to encounters. These skills are those required not only to present ourselves to others, but also to maintain the coherence and meaningfulness of the encounter, and to repair or to exploit ruptures in the encounter. His well-known example of the social behaviour of waiters illustrates much about encounters. The waiter presents a polite and deferential 'self' to customers in the restaurant. In the kitchen, encountering other members of staff, the waiter swaps deference for cynicism or disdain. Goffman's point is that agents are not simply the co-operative producers of 'encounters', but rather that encounters serve to define a particular social context and in turn determine the 'selves' (or person-alities) that inhabit it. The waiter is two different persons in the dining room and in the kitchen.

The phenomenon of embarrassment (Goffman 1956) – where the actor acts incompetently, and is thus unable to sustain expected or anticipated social action and interaction, however briefly – and stigma (Goffman 1963) – where physical or other abnormalities may be used to disrupt a person's presentation of his or her self, and thereby exclude them from full participation in society – demonstrate the importance of maintaining the appearance of being a competent social actor. Goffman's analyses of psychiatric hospitals, prisons and monasteries as 'total institutions' (where residents spend sustained portions of their lives, cut off from others, in a strictly administered routine) examine the way in which inmates adapt to these environments, and thus highlight the way in which superficially natural behavioural patterns, such as those caused by psychiatric illness, come to be learnt, through continuing socialisation and learning of new identities, that occurs within the insti-tution (Goffman 1961). Among his later work, Goffman's (1974) essay on framing explored the way in which social knowledge is organised.

[AE]

Further reading: Burns 1992; Drew and Wootton 1988; G. Smith 1999.

GRAMSCI, ANTONIO (1891–1937)

Italian **Marx**ist, best known for his elaboration of the concept of 'hegemony'. A founder of the Italian communist party (in 1921), he was imprisoned by the Fascists in 1926, and spent the remainder of his life under arrest. While in prison, and despite poor health, he continued to study and write. The *Prison Notebooks* (1929–1935), published only after the fall of Fascism, represent the core of his considerable contribution to Marxist theory.

Gramsci's Marxism is characterised by a questioning of economic determinism and a rejection of the idea of laws of history. This is perhaps most famously expressed by his observations on the Russian revolution to the effect that the occurrence of revolution in a largely feudal state disproved Marx's theory, despite the fact that the revolutionaries had drawn important inspiration and guidance from Marx. What matters for Gramsci are not quasi-natural laws that determine human development, but rather humanity's consciousness of itself, its society and its place in history. Humans are understood as thoroughly historical beings, who are capable, through their social practice, not just of making their history, but also of continually remaking human nature.

These claims have at least two important implications for Gramsci's theory. First, the economy cannot determine the rest of the society in any simple or straightforward way. The revolution is not an inevitability, simply brought about by the contradiction of forces and relations of production, but must rather be prepared through a development in the consciousness of the oppressed classes. A belief in economic determinism and the inevitability of revolution is, for Gramsci, akin to a religious belief in salvation or predestination. It is a 'common sense' that expresses the discontent of the oppressed with their conditions, but as common sense, it has not yet been subject to critical reflection. Revolution requires a spiritual emancipation of the oppressed class, that transforms it from a mere object of historical and political powers in to a genuine agent of history. In addition, the revolution cannot be predicted or understood in advance of its achievement. Precisely because it involves a radical change in social practice as well as in thought or consciousness, the revolution (and indeed the future of history in general) is 'foreseen' only in its realisation.

Second, Gramsci questions the grounds of Marxist theory, and especially the claims that are made for a Marxist 'science'. He rejects the possibility of attaining any 'objective' ahistorical position from which human society can be viewed. A theory that passes for 'truth' does so, not because it corresponds to the way in which the world really is (for example by representing the iron laws of history), stripped of the values and biases of class interest, but because it responds most effectively to the particular social and political demands of that moment in history.

Theory is itself inevitably a historical and cultural product, and thus there is no Marxist 'science' that has universal validity independently of its place within the superstructure of a particular society. Crucially, Gramsci therefore challenges the claims of the Community Party to have an objective or scientific position that is superior to, and politically in advance of, the consciousness of the proletariat (in marked contrast to Leninism, and **Lukács**'s defence of the Party) and according to which the proletariat could be manipulated into revolutionary action. Marxism is rather a 'philosophy of praxis', that fuses the intellectual and practical moments of the struggle for a renewed self-consciousness and self-understanding on the part of the oppressed. In opposition to the Leninist Party theorist, Gramsci advocates 'organic intellectuals'. All classes, in coming to power, develop a body of intellectuals who express the actual experience of that class (in both philosophy and art) and who are thereby able to combat the ideas and values propagated by the intelligentsia of other classes. For Gramsci, Marxism has neglected this imperative.

It is in this context that Gramsci explores the concept of 'hegemony'. The dominant capitalist class rules, not purely through the threat of violence (in its control of the police and armed forces), but through the persuasive and coherent presentation of its ideas and experiences as normal and valid. This work is carried out through such institutions of civil society as the mass media, the church, schools and the family. However, precisely because this hegemonic account of political control entails consent, ideas cannot simply be imposed upon the subordinate classes. The oppressed class will not passively accept whatever ideas are thrust upon them. The dominant class must tailor its ideas to the experiences and needs of the subordinate classes. Further, the subordinate classes will negotiate and reinterpret those ideas in order to make them fit their very different mundane experiences. The Marxist intellectual can challenge this dominant hegemony, precisely in exposing the tensions that arise between ideas and experience, and thus between what people say they believe and the practical social behaviour that, for Gramsci, expresses their real consciousness. A philosophy of praxis is therefore grounded, not in grand historical narratives, but in a sensitivity to the concrete experience of the oppressed.

[AE]

Further reading: Boggs 1984; Davidson 1977; Holub 1992; Ransome 1992; Sassoon 1987.

GUATTARI, FÉLIX

See Deleuze, Gilles and Guattari, Félix

HABERMAS, JÜRGEN (1929–)

Habermas is the most influential and widely cited German philosopher and social theorist of his generation. His work is controversial as a defence of what he calls the 'project of modernity', and thus the Enlightenment goal of political emancipation (Habermas 1983, 1988a). Apart from offering a grand social theory that is grounded in a rereading and integration of the tradition of sociological theorising (1984, 1987), Habermas's prolific output covers the theory of language (1970a, 1970b, 1979), cognitive and developmental psychology (1979), **Marx**ist accounts of the state and history (1976b, 1979), ethics (1990) and the law (1996), as well as commentary on the contemporary political developments in Europe and Germany (1989b).

The first of Habermas's writings to come to the attention of the English reading public concerned his attempt to provide an account of an emancipatory social science (or critical theory) that is grounded in accounts of labour, linguistic communication and power as the three sources of human action and knowledge (1971a). Labour leads to natural science and technology; language is studied by the hermeneutic disciplines of interpretation; and political power raises issues of the emancipation of humanity from oppression. Critical theory takes Marxism and psychoanalysis as its models. These are understood as synthesising natural scientific explanation with hermeneutic interpretation. Thus, psychoanalysis treats neuroses. These neuroses confront the patient as causal (and therefore natural) forces that spoil their autonomous behaviour. The analysis overcomes this causal force by revealing the meaning of the neurosis (by relating it back to an original traumatic experience) and by restoring the patient's memory of this meaning, thereby returning control of the action to the autonomous will of the patient. An emancipatory social science therefore strives, similarly, to dispel the causal force that social structures appear to have over social actors, and thereby to return society to the control of its members.

In the 1970s and 1980s, Habermas began to develop the theory of communicative action, which is now the basis of all his theorising. Humans are presented as fundamentally communicative beings.

Habermas analyses the structure of communication. He suggests that in making any utterances (be they statements, questions, accusations or whatever), the speaker raises four 'validity claims' – that is to say that there are four levels at which the speaker can be challenged by any listener. First, the speaker can be challenged as to the meaningfulness of what he or she says. Second, the truth of the utterance can be questioned. Any utterance will assume certain facts about the world, and these assumptions may be mistaken. Third, the speaker's right to say what he or she says (or to speak at all) may be challenged. (For example, one may question a person's authority to make a particular assertion, or his or her right to make a request or issue an order.) Finally, the sincerity of the speaker may be questioned (so that the speaker may be accused of lying, being ironic or teasing, for example). From this model, Habermas suggests that, as underpinning actual discourse, there is the presupposition of an 'ideal speech situation', in which every participant in a conversation is free to challenge what is said by any other speaker. In practice, real conversation falls short of this ideal (and is thus 'systematically distorted', not least by the differentials of power between conversationalists: 1970a). One consequence of this model is the development of a 'discourse ethics'. If any utterance can be challenged, then ethics must focus upon the collective validation, through challenges and rational responses, of moral values and principles. This crucially entails that all competent language users should be free to enter the debate. Exclusion, for whatever reason, is a mark of injustice. Another consequence of Habermas's theory of communication was to spur new interest in his earliest work (from the 1960s) on the 'public sphere' (1989a). The public sphere is the realm of social life in which public opinion is formed. It emerges, historically, among the eighteenth-century bourgeoisie, not least in the development of journals and a free press. The public sphere thus aspires to form a general will and thus inform and control the activities of the state. Conflict is resolved through open and free communication.

Communicative rationality, for Habermas, is therefore this process of problem solving and conflict resolution through open discussion. In contemporary society, this rationality is threatened. In order to analyse this threat, Habermas distinguishes between life-world and system as two complementary accounts of social existence. The life-world (a term borrowed from the phenomenology of **Husserl** and **Schutz**) is the social world as it is constructed and maintained through the taken-for-granted social skills and stocks of knowledge of its members. The life-world is therefore maintained through the intersubjective recognition of the world as meaningful. Other people's actions can be responded to because they make sense – they are part of the process of communication. The life-world carries the traditions of the community and is the source of individual socialisation. In contrast, system refers to society when it confronts the individual as a meaningless, seemingly natural force. Social systems are governed by instrumental rationality (not communicative rationality). The rules of social systems are determined by the need for efficiency in realising given objectives. For Habermas, the most important social systems are those that distribute power and money about the society. The workings of such systems still depend upon the social skills of individual agents (derived from the life-world) and the relationship between life-world and system can be beneficial. The rationality of systems thinking can be used to question and revise the taken-for-granted practices of the life-world (and indeed, the difference between a modern society and a traditional one is that this rational self-reflection is part of modern life). However, the system can also 'colonise' the life-world. In colonisation, the rules of the system displace communicative rationality, so that social agents can no longer question (or even understand) the rules that govern their actions. The model of psychoanalysis is still helpful in understanding this. With the colonisation of the life-world, what should be meaningful action, under the autonomous control of competent social agents, become split off, akin to neurotic behaviour or parapraxis (i.e. 'Freudian slips'). Subjective action therefore comes to appear to be objective, and causally constraining. Habermas's theory of communicative action therefore retains the emancipatory impetus of his early critical theory.

[AE]

Further reading: Berstein 1985; Calhoun 1992; Deflem 1996; Dews 1999; Held 1980; How 1995; McCarthy 1978; Outhwaite 1994; Passerin d'Entreves and Benhabib 1996; Rosenfeld and Arato 1998; White 1988.

HALL, STUART (1932–)

Stuart Hall has been one of the principal figures in the development of cultural studies in the UK, not least through his directorship of the Birmingham Centre for Contemporary Cultural Studies between 1968 and 1979. While Hall had been an editor of the *New Left Review* between 1957 and 1961, his first important publication, edited with Paddy Whannel, emerged from the 1960 National Union of Teachers' conference on 'Popular Culture and Personal Responsibility' (1964). (Hall himself was a school teacher at the time.) This early work marks a serious attempt to identify what was distinctive and important in popular culture, and to break away from the **Leavis**ite dismissal of post-war popular culture that characterises even Richard **Hoggart**'s work. Hall's work matures over the 1960s, not only building on the socialist humanist tradition of Hoggart, Raymond **Williams** and the historian E. P. Thompson, but also drawing in contemporary European developments, including **Althusser**ian structuralism and a recovery of the work of the Italian Marxist Antonio **Gramsci** (so that theories of ideology and hegemony became central to his work) (see Hall 1982). At the centre of Hall's work is the analysis of the way in which culture organises everyday life. While Hall has not published a book-length study, he has written and edited a significant number of essays and collections, which have marked key points of development in cultural studies. These include *Television as a Medium and its Relation to Culture* (1971) which theorised the centrality of television to popular culture, and *Encoding and Decoding in Television Discourse* (1973), opened up semiotic approaches to the consumption and production of media messages, recognising the complex social influences that are present in the audience's understanding of a text. Crucially Hall's work also explores the intersections of race and imperialism in contemporary culture, and thus more or less explicitly to his own experience as black British (Hall and Jefferson 1976). In the late 1970s and 1980s he looked to engage with the ideological and political implications of a succession of Conservative governments in Britain and Thatcher's 'authoritarian populism' (Hall *et al.* 1978; Hall 1985). He was Professor of Sociology at the Open University until his retirement in 1997.

[AE]

Further reading: Turner 1996.

HEGEL, GEORG WILHELM FRIEDRICH (1770–1831)

G. W. F. Hegel was the most influential German philosopher of his generation. He provided a comprehensive response to his major predecessor Immanuel **Kant**, and was in turn one of the main sources upon which Karl **Marx** drew in developing his social and political theory. In the twentieth century, his work remains significant, as a major source for Marxists (such as **Lukács** and **Adorno**) and psychoanalysts, including most notably **Lacan**.

Hegel's (1948) early writings are largely theological in tone. He was deeply influenced by Kant's ethics, which he expresses in explicitly Christian terms. Yet, even in the early writings, a key and distinctive aspect of Hegelian philosophy is already made clear. Hegel thinks historically, and links philosophy and history intimately together. Thus, the early writings interpret the myths of the Book of Genesis (including the expulsion from Eden, and the stories of Noah and of Abraham) as allegorical accounts of humanity being forced out of an initial condition of security and complacency, into history. The naive creatures in Eden are well fed and cared for, but ignorant of themselves and their potential. As historical beings, humans must make their own, painful way in the world. But through that struggle, they will learn about themselves. Hegel therefore effectively sees in history the imperative for human beings to overcome the contingency of their existence, and by coming to understand the world, and their place in it, and thereby to take control of their own destiny, and thus to return to Eden. The creatures that return to Eden, however, will be creatures that are rich with self-knowledge and the experience of history.

It may be noted that these early arguments and interpretations already indicate a three-part structure. This is the structure of Hegel's dialectic. There is a naive and complacent opening stage. In the above story, it is Eden. In the mature writings, and especially in the *Encyclopaedia* (Hegel 1970, 1971, 1975a), it is a stage of pure subjectivity, or universality. Hegel's metaphysics is perhaps best approached as being underpinned by a sort of creation myth. So, in the beginning there is spirit (or mind – the German *Geist*) and not a lot of harm is done if this is equated with god. Everything is a pure mental state, but, precisely because there is nothing else, the spirit has no real self-knowledge. There is nothing to which it can compare itself. The second stage is the expulsion into history. Humanity comes up against an external objective world that resists, rather than panders to it. So, the universal subject breaks up, sundering or particularising itself, most fundamentally into subject and object. The subject runs up against something that is its other, and that is alien to it. This particularisation is the unfolding of the natural, social and psychological worlds. Both the subject and the object manifest themselves in a vast range of different forms (for example, as the many forms that consciousness, self-consciousness and the acquisition of knowledge and science take, and the many forms of the physical, chemical and biological realms). These forms are not arbitrary. They have an underlying logical order. For Hegel, nature is therefore organised in a logical hierarchy. Some parts of nature are logically more elementary than others (for example, geological structures, being the manifestation of simple, mechanical forces, are logically simpler than the subtle organisation of botanical structures.) Specifically, over human history, the forms of knowledge gradually grow more adequate to the objects that they are attempting to understand. In effect, human history (and human knowledge) culminates in the recognition that the logical structures that govern our thought are the same structures that govern the physical world. They are alike manifestations of the universal spirit encountered in the first stage of the argument. The third and last stage (the return to Eden) is therefore this recovery of unity, where subject and object are again one, but now blessed with a complex knowledge of that unity.

This may appear to be a bizarre metaphysics, and certainly in the twentieth century such grand accounts of everything fell out of favour (culminating, for example, in **Lyotard**'s criticisms of Hegelian philosophy as a 'grand narrative'). It is, however, full of rich suggestions, and Hegel explores his metaphysics through studies of history (1988a), politics (1942), religion (1988b) and art (1975d). In the *Encyclopaedia* (first published in 1817), Hegel does not attempt to provide a separate comment on everything that exists (in the manner, say of the *Encyclopaedia Britannica*), but rather to uncover the structure that gives unity to everything. Hegel's *Encyclopaedia* is therefore in three sections, following in the dialectical logic already sketched above. The first section is a logic. But, unlike a conventional logic, it has a strict developmental order. Hegel begins with the most primitive logical concept he can conceive of: 'Being'. The argument rapidly reveals that 'Being' (i.e. to say that things are) tells us very little about the world. The logic then begins to move, striving for ever more adequate concepts to explain the world, and at each stage engaging in a self-criticism that reveals inadequacies and contradictions that demand a more profound and subtle resolution in a higher stage of logical thought. The logic is the structure of pure thought. It is therefore akin to pure spirit (or, in our creation myth, the way god thinks). The logic must therefore conclude, so Hegel claims, by going over into, or being manifest in, the physical world. (That is to say that for Hegel, logic can be complete only if there is a physical world. The creation is a logical necessity.) The second part of the *Encyclopaedia* is a philosophy of nature, in which concepts and categories of that logic are seen to be manifest in natural forms. Finally, the last part covers human psychology and political and cultural history. It culminates in what for Hegel are the three most profound forms of human knowledge: art, religion and philosophy. (Note that by ending in philosophy, the *Encyclopaedia* closes on itself. It has returned to logic, and justified itself as a closed and, for Hegel, comprehensive system.)

In his aesthetics, that is sketched in the *Encyclopaedia* but elaborated in enormous detail in a lecture series, Hegel is one of the first thinkers to treat art historically. He defines artistic beauty as the sensuous illusion of truth (1975d, p. 55). That is to say, that the form – or medium – of art is sensuous material (such as the stone of architecture and sculpture, the colour and texture of painting, the sounds of music and the images of poetry). In addition, the content – or subject-matter – of art is, ultimately, absolute knowledge. Art is striving to express the unity of subject and knowledge found in the final stage of the dialectic. Art does not therefore merely imitate reality. Rather it is a creative part of our culture (and thus is seen by Hegel to contribute to theology and philosophy). Through their arts, a people strive to articulate their understanding of the divine, of the cosmos and of their place within it. Put otherwise, before human beings can grasp ideas in the abstract conceptual medium of philosophy, they will be able to gain some understanding through artistic images. Such an understanding will be achieved gradually, over history. Hegel thus identifies three stages in the history of art (the symbolic, classical and romantic). Each has distinct criteria of success. In effect, Hegel may therefore be credited with introducing ideas that are fundamental to the sociology of culture, in that he recognises a structural unity between a culture and the society in which it is created. Further, he credits art with a cognitive role (that in the hands of twentieth-century Hegelians, such as Adorno, becomes art's ability to question and resist the taken-for-granted, politically repressive ways of thinking and perceiving that predominate in contemporary society). The final 'romantic' (or Christian) stage of art is also the stage which sees the death of art. Hegel understands himself as writing the obituary of art. By the nineteenth century, art has become aware of the limitations of its medium, and thus that its medium is no longer adequate to its subject-matter. Art can therefore no longer contribute actively to the development of human understanding, and graciously leaves the field free for philosophy. In this superficially inaccurate thesis (for there has obviously been a good deal of art since Hegel's obituary was written), commentators have found a shrewd anticipation of modernism. Modern art does become increasingly concerned with its medium rather than its subject-matter, and for twentieth-century philosophers as diverse as Adorno and Arthur C.

Danto (1981), twentieth-century art does begin to pose philosophical questions.

[AE]

Further reading: Adorno 1993; Beiser 1993; H. Harris 1972; Inwood 1983, 1985, 1992; Kojeve 1969; R. Norman 1980; Pippin 1989; Rose 1981; Taylor 1975, 1979; A. Wood 1990.

HEIDEGGER, MARTIN (1889–1976)

A philosopher whose thought has exerted an important influence on a wide range of subsequent writers and movements (e.g. Jean-Paul **Sartre**, Jacques **Derrida**, existentialism, hermeneutics, post-structuralism) as well as, in recent years, some influence on analytic philosophy. Heidegger was professor of philosophy at the University of Freiburg from 1928. In the 1930s he publicly declared some sympathy for the Nazi movement, and the question of his involvement with Nazism remains a matter of controversy to this day – not least because of his often vague responses to questions about this involvement posed to him after the Second World War. It is often claimed that Heidegger's thought can be divided into two distinct stages, the transition being marked by a 'turn' (*Kehre*) during the 1930s away from the project outlined in his most influential work, *Being and Time* (1927). Whether this is the case is not entirely clear, since many of the fundamental problems with which Heidegger deals in *Being and Time* (the question of Being, the nature of human existence, and the shortcomings of the metaphysical tradition of the West), as well as the work's articulation of an attitude which is sceptical toward the tradition of humanism, are also persistent concerns of his later work.

Although a theme in the earliest works of the philosophical tradition as far back as the Ancient Greeks, the question of the significance of Being has, Heidegger claims in *Being and Time*, been buried by the preconceptions that have underlain the Western metaphysical tradition since the time of Plato. According to Heidegger, the question of 'Being' is neither an empty question, nor one with a self-evident solution. Further, he claims, Being should not be understood in the manner in which the being of particular entities is understood, but is rather the condition of possibility for the existence of any entity whatsoever. Heidegger concentrates on elucidating this question by way of an analysis of Dasein, a term which he uses to signify a particular kind of entity. 'Dasein' refers to that entity whose Being is an issue for it (namely, us – though humans need not be the only instances of Dasein, they are the only ones we know of). Dasein is the only entity that not only can ask questions about existence and the nature of entities, but also is that entity which must therefore already have an understanding of its Being in order even to pose such questions (even though this understanding need not be regarded as anything more than vague, and certainly need not be articulated theoretically). The question of Being is thus essentially tied to the existence of Dasein when it comes to locating a point of departure for Heidegger's investigation. It is hence only through an interrogation of the constitution of Dasein that one can approach the possibility of formulating the 'question of the meaning of Being'.

In order to formulate the basis of this question Heidegger draws a key distinction between the ontological and the ontical realms. The latter is the domain of the sciences (e.g. physics, chemistry, history, etc.). These disciplines deal in categorising and describing the behaviour of entities, and hence presuppose them (e.g. in biology the notion of an entity that lives, an 'organism', is presupposed and analysed, but not investigated with regard to what it is *qua* entity). Ontology, in contrast, is concerned with the conditions of possibility of all entities, not with elucidating the characteristics of particular entities. Heidegger's project thus stakes a claim for the primacy of a mode of enquiry that is radically different from that of scientific investigation. In turn, Dasein is characterised as an ontico-ontological entity (ontical because it is instantiated in the world, ontological because it is the only kind of entity that can ask questions about its own existence) which already possess an, albeit ill-defined and non-theoretical, understanding of Being. Dasein is thus a necessary condition for the question of the meaning of Being to be raised, and it is also what must be examined in order to elucidate the basis and nature of fundamental ontology. For Heidegger, it follows that without Dasein there is no sense that can be attributed to the question of Being. Hence, if Dasein were not, then it could not meaningfully be said that entities 'are'. All talk of the *meaning* of Being, therefore, is dependent on the presence of an understanding of it, though entities themselves are not: 'Being (not entities) is dependent upon the understanding of Being' (Heidegger 1962, p. 255).

In turn, Heidegger's project concentrates on elucidating a number of key features with regard to Dasein as a means of creating the necessary prologue to posing the fundamental question of ontology. There is space here to mention only two of them. First, there is the formulation of the notion of 'authentic' existence which exerted such an influence on the existentialism of **Sartre** and others. Dasein is an entity which can make choices – each of us has individuality. In making choices, individuals are in effect creating themselves through the activity of living. What any individual Dasein is, therefore, is not determined in the way in which the existence of any individual instance of an animal species is. An individual cat conforms to the basic characteristics and forms of behaviour common to its species and is determined by this fact. Dasein, in contrast, has the capacity for individual identity, and can thus attain a mode of existence which goes beyond that of mere species-existence. This does *not* mean that humans are entirely free to choose any mode of existence, since choices are necessarily limited by the constraints of society and history. Indeed, a central feature of Dasein's existence is inauthenticity – manifest in the 'average-everydayness' of social life in the form of traditions, norms and standardised practices. The unquestioning acceptance of such normative constraints Heidegger deems a paradigmatic example of 'inauthentic' existence (which, in fact, is how he characterises most of human social life). Importantly, however, Heidegger argues that inauthenticity does not signify any 'less' Being (any more than authenticity would signify 'more' Being). Both are merely particular modes of Being – indeed, the average and everday is used by Heidegger as a central means of analysing the basic existential (i.e. ontological) structure of Dasein. Second, temporality is a key notion in *Being and Time*. The question of the meaning of Being is in fact, for Heidegger, a matter of temporality. Since Dasein is that entity which realises itself in the process of existing, it follows that this process is one of a temporal unfolding: Dasein exists as an entity situated in both the past, present and future. But these three terms should not be taken to signify three coordinates within a given realm of 'time'. Rather, they signify a unity (that of Dasein) engaged in a self-transcending process. It is plain from this that Heidegger does not regard time as an independent structure into which Dasein is somehow fitted after the fact. Instead, temporality is the constitutive structure of Dasein itself. In other words, Dasein's Being is temporality.

Heidegger's later thought departs from the approach of *Being and Time* in at least two ways. First, the project of elucidating the Being of Dasein in terms of temporality did not, for him, ultimately serve its purpose, in so far as providing an account of the temporality of Dasein does not ultimately reveal the temporality of Being in the exhastive manner that the text of *Being and Time* seems to have intended. Second, the very notion of a 'fundamental ontology' which underpins *Being and Time* is regarded by the later Heidegger as itself too much a part of the metaphysical tradition to go unquestioned. Heidegger's later thought might thus be described as being less 'systematic' to the extent

that it does away with the notion of elucidating the fundamental ontological structure of Being. However, the question of Being remains a
persistent concern in much of Heidegger's later work, as does his
commitment to a form of realism (in *Being and Time* he expresses the
view that the real (entities) is simply 'there'; the term 'reality', however,
expresses a relationship between Dasein and the real).

The essay 'The Question Concerning Technology' (1953) is as
good an example as any of the later Heidegger's approach. In this piece
he seeks to investigate technology by way of an unearthing of its
essence, a form of analysis also adopted in the essays 'What is Metaphysics?' (1929) and 'On the Essence of Truth' (1949). Heidegger
argues that this essence is in fact a mode of encountering entities that
has a history predating the modern 'technological' era. In short, the
essence of technology is what has made the development of modern
technology possible (it is its condition of possibility) and is not 'technological'. In its essence, technology is in fact both bound up with the
cultural history of the West, and is also fundamental to that history as
one of its preconditions. The essence of technology is a way of revealing and thereby 'enframing' entities within a framework of manipulation. As such, it continually threatens to lead us into delusion; for
example, into the views that the world is merely understandable in
terms of its use-structure, or that humanity encounters only its own
constructs when it encounters entities (hence Heidegger's realism, for
he holds that it is a delusion to believe that everywhere we encounter
only ourselves). The danger of technology, therefore, does not lie with
the technological itself, but rather with its essence; for this mode of
revealing can delude us into believing that it is *the* only means of
revealing entities when it is in fact merely one such mode. In fact, the
essence of technology denies us access to our own essence by trans-
forming humanity into its object; for it is, Heidegger contends, of the
essence of humanity that it is an entity that *cannot* encounter only itself
in its existence. An important aspect of Heidegger's argument in this
essay is that, on the basis of his analysis, that the mode of revealing
which defines the essence of technology is also, and simultaneously, a
covering-up. In short, every revealing is also a disguising (a view that is
echoed in the writings of some post-structuralist thinkers).

[PS]

Further reading: Dreyfus and Hall 1992; Mulhall 1996.

HOGGART, RICHARD (1918–)

The English analyst and historian of working-class culture, the mass media and education, is one of the formative influences in the development of cultural studies in Britain, both through his book *Uses of Literature* (1957), and through his role as the first director of the Birmingham Centre for Contemporary Cultural Studies. Hoggart was born into a working-class family in Leeds. After war service, he taught English literature to adult education classes at the University of Hull. It has been suggested that this experience is vital, not merely for Hoggart's own career, but also for the development of cultural studies as such. A number of key early figures in cultural studies (including **Williams**) were adult education tutors, and as such engaged with those who, for economic or other reasons, had been excluded from the more orthodox educational institutions. Cultural studies therefore emerges, in part, in the attempt to relate literary criticism (and social and political science) to those standing outside the typical academic audience. *Uses of Literature* is addressed to these readers. The book is a documentation and analysis of the culture of pre-war working-class life. Hoggart brings to this culture the techniques of literary studies, but applies them to the cultural products and artefacts of everyday life (such as newspapers and magazines, popular music and popular fiction). Working-class life is revealed through the complex interrelations of its parts (the pub, the working man's club, sports, family roles, gender and language, and even the apparently regressive or negative elements of this life, such as violence). Hoggart thus helps to turn the understanding of culture away from an exclusive interest in high culture. However, his analysis of post-war working-class culture reveals that he is still, in certain respects, under the influence of **Leavis** and even **Arnold**. Where Arnold had lamented the rise of a 'philistine' urban culture in the mid-nineteenth century, Hoggart sees a decline in working-class culture with the impact of commercial and North American culture, after the war. He is dismissive, for example, of the culture of the 1950s coffee-bar, and the life of the young working-class men and women that focus on it. *Uses of Literature* did turn Hoggart into a public authority on popular culture and the media (and included his appearing as a defence witness in the *Lady Chatterley* trial). None of his later work has had the impact of *Uses of Literacy*, although institutionally, apart from directing the Birmingham Centre (from 1964 to 1968), Hoggart has since been assistant director-general at UNESCO, and Warden of Goldsmith's College London.

[AE]

HORKHEIMER, MAX (1895–1973)

German **Marx**ist philosopher, who from 1930 was the Director of the Frankfurt Institute for Social Research (the institutional focus of the Frankfurt School), and as such did much to shape German critical theory (1989).

In the essay 'Traditional and Critical Theory' (1937), Horkheimer (1972a) opposes modern philosophy – broadly from **Descartes** in the seventeenth century through to present-day positivists – with his own **Hegel**ian-**Marx**ism. The distinguishing trait of traditional philosophy is its assumption that it is possible, and indeed necessary, to develop a method of rational inquiry that is valid ahistorically, and autonomously of either the subject-matter to which it might be applied, or the human subject that is using it. The object of philosophical and scientific inquiry is therefore such that it is knowable through the application of reason, and the human who carries out the inquiry is characterised purely in terms of its ability to reason. Inquiry aspires to objective truth by the application of a rigorous methodology. Horkheimer condemns such an approach for ignoring the thorough-going historical nature of perception and understanding. A materialist philosophy – critical theory – must therefore recognise that both the inquiring human subject and the object of inquiry are social and cultural entities, and as such change over history. An ahistorical methodology would not merely be insensitive to a historically changing object, but further, the formulation of such a methodology would require the human subject to rid itself of the very cultural conditions that gives it substance. Both the possibilities and limitations of human thought and understanding are historically constituted. There can therefore be no objective knowledge in the sense intended by the traditional philosopher, for the very categories that philosophers use to organise and express their knowledge are shaped by the political and cultural tensions of the society within which they are formulated. Knowledge is therefore always value-laden.

The formulation of a critical theory poses a major problem for Horkheimer. He explicitly rejects idealism, where some ahistorical element (such as philosophical method, or even the dogma of a material world existing independently of the subject) is posited as the fixed and certain foundation upon which the philosophical system can be constructed. Traditional conceptions of truth and foundational assumptions are rejected (including, it may be noted, Marxism's faith in the revolutionary potential of the proletariat). He therefore appears, superficially, to be committed to some form of relativism, such that critical theory is reduced to a sociology of knowledge, at best describing the material conditions within which knowledge claims are formulated. Yet Horkheimer retains a commitment to truth, not least because he needs some ground by which he can formulate and justify a criticism of contemporary society. He must therefore proceed negatively, which is to say that he forswears any positive idealist assertion of what is true, in favour of a recognition of falsehood. One may identify two interrelated strategies that Horkheimer adopts.

First, given that theorists are themselves cultural beings, the categories of their thought, however abstract, may be explicated in order to reveal a sedimented social content. Horkheimer thus argues that the contradictions found within **Kant**'s philosophy are not the result of subjective weakness upon his part, but result rather from the fact that in his very subjective strength, Kant is taking historically specific intellectual and cognitive resources to their limits. The contradictions in Kant's philosophy express the material contradictions of his society (Horkheimer 1972a, p. 204). Similarly, the ideas in which contemporary bourgeois society describes and justifies itself (such as free exchange, free competition and harmony of interests), may be revealed to be internally inconsistent, and as such indicative of the contradictions of bourgeois society (p. 215).

Second, Horkheimer's philosophy, in so far as it has a grounding, finds that grounding in the historical, embodied experiences of suffering, need and desire of concrete human individuals. The desire for happiness, Horkheimer claims, needs no justification (1972a, p. 45). In *The Dialectic of Enlightenment* (1944, 1947, co-authored with **Adorno**) and *Eclipse of Reason* (1947) he pursues something of this by exploring the subjective or instrumental reason that is dominant in contemporary capitalism, and that facilitates the domination and manipulation of nature (including human nature) to arbitrarily given ends. Such reason inhibits any critical examination of the ends to which it is employed (as is manifest most graphically in the Nazi's rational administration of the death camps) and as such allows partial and finite interests to be presented as absolute. Yet, for Horkheimer, 'nature' (again, including the repressed potential of human nature) may still revolt against such manipulation. In philosophy, myth and religion, and significantly in the 'dark' bourgeois authors such as De Sade and **Nietzsche**, or in the violent and brutal thoughts and activities of the insane and criminal, the currents of instrumental reason and its associated civilisation are denounced (Horkheimer 1947, pp. 92ff).

'Art and Mass Culture' (1972b, pp. 273ff) explores art's participation in this revolt and denunciation. Horkheimer is dismissive of any approach to culture that would measure aesthetic worth simply in terms of popularity. This would be an application of instrumental reason, administering art in the service of a superficial and ultimately repressive pleasure, and would treat it as any other commodity (e.g. Disney or the 'ball park'). Art retains a utopian potential precisely insofar as it rejects pleasure and easy comprehension. The modernist works of Joyce and Picasso (in opposition to the conventional narratives of Galsworthy's novels) pursue their own intrinsic logic, independently of any conventional expectations about how the art work is to be constructed, or how it is to communicate to an audience. As such they objectify despair. Precisely in failing to communicate, the art work exposes the conventionality of the dominant forms of communication that are serving to reproduce political tensions and suffering. Their very incomprehensibility is the incomprehensibility of real need and suffering by the ideas of bourgeois culture. As such art begins to expose the falsehood of the assumption that certain conventions are natural, or again, exposes the false presentation of finite interests as absolutes.

[AE]

Further reading: Benhabib *et al.* 1993; Wiggershaus 1994.

HUME, DAVID (1711–1776)

Scottish essayist (see Hume 1993), philosopher (1975, 1978) and historian (1983), whose critical examination of empiricism has been widely influential in the development of modern philosophy, not least through **Kant**'s reading of him. Hume is part of the Scottish Enlightenment, the flowering of intellectual activity, centring upon Glasgow and Hume's own Edinburgh, which occurred after the Act of Union in 1707. The emergence of a new professional class, as the Scottish legal, educational and religious institutions became independent of English control, created a new audience for informed writing on a broad range of topics. Hume writes for this audience, and his writing style develops – from the impetuous and youthful *Treatise*, through to the more measured *Essays* and *Enquiries* – cultivating a 'polite' style, modelled upon the English essays of Addison and Steele, that was considered appropriate to such an audience. Yet Edinburgh's polite society is also important as the model and source of the reflections upon culture that may be argued to underpin much of Hume's philosophy. It may be noted that while Hume's prose is typically vivid and elegant, a certain obscurity lends his philosophy to diverse and indeed contradictory interpretations. Any summary of Hume, including this one, is necessarily contentious.

Hume's *Treatise* and *Enquiries*, his principal philosophical statements, begin from the typical premises of an empiricist philosopher. He argues that all our knowledge comes from experience. The most primitive form of experience is an 'impression of sensation', which is to say the immediate, vivid and fleeting experience given to us by our five senses. The mind copies these impressions, as 'ideas of sensation', and it is these fainter ideas that continue to exist in the memory and intellect when the original sensuous stimuli have died away. Ideas are the raw material of our thought and imagination. Already this analysis raises two enormous problems. First, because we experience only impressions, we do not directly experience the external world. We therefore have no guarantee that the world that we experience is the real world. Second, the only thing that we can be sure about is what we are experiencing now. We can never be sure that the ideas stored in our memories are not corruptions of our original impressions. So, again, the world that we remember and think about need not be the world as it really is, or indeed as we experienced it.

These conundrums are the now rather clichéd basics of a certain form of philosophical inquiry. But it is what Hume does with them that is important. He has set up the problem that will run throughout his epistemology: how do we get from knowledge of what we do experience (impressions), to knowledge of what we cannot experience (the 'real' world, but also more concretely, how do we make sound predictions of what that world will be like in the future, or how do we establish what it was like in the historical past, before we were around to experience it)? He begins, seemingly like other philosophers before him, including **Descartes**, by striving to find a firm foundation to our knowledge of the world. Hume argues that we have two sources of knowledge. One is experience, and the other is reason. The problem with experience is that, as has already been suggested, we commonly make knowledge claims that exceed what experience alone could justify. Hume gives a telling example in his analysis of causality. I confidently judge that my skilfully struck cue ball caused the red ball to roll off into the pocket. The problem is that I do not actually perceive causality. Causality is not something that I see, hear or even smell. I see a white ball moving, I hear the sound of a collision, and I see the red ball moving. How do I know that the red ball would not have moved anyway? (This may seem an absurd question, but in complex causal relationships, such as the action of drugs upon a disease, it is a very real question. How do I know that the homeopathic remedy removed my hay fever symptoms? Might those symptoms have ceased of their own accord?) Hume turns to reason. Perhaps there is a necessary law of nature that billiards balls obey. But there are two problems here. First, evidence for a law of nature would itself be empirical, and to be cast iron, that would require empirical observation of every instance of the law applying. The point is that we want to use causal laws of nature to predict the future (that we cannot yet observe). Nothing in reason tells us that laws of nature apply indefinitely. Perhaps, using Hume's example, the sun, despite having risen everyday of our life so far, will not rise tomorrow. The second problem is the fallibility of reasoning. Mathematics may be rigorous, but mathematicians are fallible human beings. This is where Hume begins to make his major contribution to our understanding of these problems. He simply observes that a mathematician will become more confident in a new proof every time he checks it; but will be more confident still if his friends applaud it; and will be most confident when he receives 'the universal assent and applauses of the learned world' (Hume 1978, p. 180). The point is simple and radical: human beings are cultural animals. Even mathematicians work in a community, and the validity of their results comes through critical examination within a community. Here, then is the solution to the problem of causality, and indeed of all our knowledge claims. We make causal judgements, not simply through empirical experience or the application of reason, but because we have become habituated to see the world in a certain way. Causal judgements are matters of custom, not reason.

This conclusion has an important implications for both our scientific judgements and our moral judgements. In science, the laws we accept and work with might just be wrong. Descartes and other philosophers are appalled by this lack of certainty. Hume's point is that we live with it very well. We do not need certain knowledge. Maybe the sun will not rise tomorrow. If it does not, then we do not simply throw our hands up in despair, and we certainly do not declare a miracle. Rather, we go back and conservatively but critically revise our theories of planetary motion. Hume gives the example of a clock that stops. A 'peasant' can give no better account than to say that 'it does not go right'. The 'artisan' – who here is the model of a philosopher and a scientist – examines the mechanism, accepting that the same force of the spring will have the same influence on the wheels, but that perhaps a speck of dust has impeded the mechanism (Hume 1978, p. 132). In morality, much of what we think we know about other people comes not from experience, but from prejudice. Hume observes that liars will frequently come to believe their own lies if repeated often enough (just as we believe in a causal relationship, if experienced enough) (p. 86). More alarmingly, Hume remarks upon the resilience of prejudice: 'An *Irishman* cannot have wit, and a *Frenchman* cannot have solidity . . . tho' the conversation of the former in any instance be visibly very agreeable, and of the latter very judicious' (p. 99).

Hume, as is typical of an Enlightenment thinker, demands critical reflection to free us of the superstitions that cloud our scientific and moral judgement. Atypically, he finds no simple mechanism (be it reason or empirical observation) that can completely free us of superstition. Indeed, philosophical reflection, precisely because it cannot establish the existence of the external world or the necessity of causal relations, can become oppressive. The philosopher, in introverted reflection typical of Descartes, can quite rationally doubt the existence of the whole world. But, taking too seriously the issues such as the ones with which we began, for example the source of our sensory experiences, can but lead to madness: this is the fate of the sceptic, who fundamentally doubts the possibility of true knowledge. 'I am confounded with all these questions, and begin to fancy myself in the most deplorable condition imaginable, inviron'd with the deepest darkness, and utterly depriv'd of the use of every member and faculty' (p. 268). This oppression can be dispelled very simply. One enters polite society. 'I dine, I play a game of backgammon, I converse, and am merry with my friends'. After this, philosophical problems, pursued for their own sake and independently from the imperatives of activities of the professional and artisan classes, are 'cold', 'strained', and 'ridiculous' (p. 269). Philosophy for Hume is a vital tool of critical reflection, but ultimately it is to be led by the demands of a practical life.

Hume presents his *Treatise* as a 'science of man', and claims that such a science must ground all other sciences. The 'man' that he reveals is a social being. Indeed, he ridicules the idea that human beings could ever exist outside of society (p. 493). In his moral and political philosophy, this human being is revealed as a creature that is acutely sensitive to its existence alongside others: 'A violent cough in another gives us uneasiness; tho' in itself it does not in the least affect us. A man will be mortified, if you tell him he has stinking breath; tho' 'tis evidently no annoyance to himself' (p. 587). For Hume, we want to be agreeable to others, and there is little that is as disagreeable as 'the teller of long stories, or the pompous disclaimer' who spoils an otherwise enjoyable conversation (1975, p. 262). (Also, note that everyone hates a drinking companion who never forgets, for the 'follies of the last debauch should be buried in eternal oblivion, in order to give full scope to the follies of the next' (p. 209).) So thorough-going is this social existence, that my very self-identity may depend upon it. Personal identity cannot rest, as Descartes had suggested, upon some continuing 'soul substance', because Hume, the empiricist, turned to introspection and while he found 'some particular perception or other' in his mind, there is never any impression of a continuous self (1978, p. 252). The self, for Hume, may be little more than a function of such passions as pride and shame, that rest upon the judgement that others make of *my* possessions and characteristics: my 'beauty, strength, agility, good mien' and 'address in dancing' (p. 278). I am aware of myself in others' approval or disapproval of me.

Hume's philosophy of art struggles with humanity's social being, as he strives to find universal standards of artistic taste (1993). While he reinforces the idea of a canon of great works which can act as exemplars from which the artist and the audience alike can learn to appreciate good art, he is equally aware that not just different nations, but also different age groups will prefer and respond to different artists and styles of art. His bold assertion that Addison is a greater writer than Milton, and that this is as obvious as Tenerife being higher than a mole hill, strangely confirms his own argument. Addison *was* more important to eighteenth-century polite society. But just as one may use reason to recognise that a distant historical figure, such as Marcus Brutus, is more laudable than a close friend who naturally excites our sentiments of love (1978, p. 583) so, philosophically, one may reflect upon the habits and customs that serve to shape one's aesthetic prejudices and judgements. Yet, when Hume wrote, there was no pressing need to question the importance of Addison. Indeed, for Hume to question Addison's greatness might be as eccentric as the sceptic's questioning of the existence of the real world, and as equally futile a waste of one's philosophical energies.

[AE]

Further reading: Box 1990; Campbell and Skinner 1982; Chappell 1966; Hont and Ignatieff 1983; Livingston and King 1976; Morice 1977; Penelhum 1975; Stroud 1977.

HUSSERL, EDMUND (1859–1938)

Austro-German philosopher and principal figure in the early development of phenomenology. Husserl's intellectual career defies easy summary, not least because of his admirable habit of continually revising and developing his core arguments in the light of either the criticism of others or self-criticism. While there is a significant amount of scholarly debate about how distinctive the separate stages of Husserl's career are, it may be suggested that an increasingly radical engagement with the foundations of the natural sciences directs the development of his work.

In what is arguably his earliest mature work, the *Logical Investigations* (1900–1901), Husserl builds upon the thesis (proposed by the philosopher Franz Brentano) that consciousness is 'intentional'. This is to say that an act of consciousness (such as a belief, hope or wish) is always about some object (so that I always believe that such and such is the case, or I hope for a certain outcome). Crucially for Husserl, this does not entail that consciousness passively recognises or adopts a pre-existing external object. It is rather that the objects that we experience (phenomena) have the meaning that they have for us because consciousness constitutes them as such. A chair, for example, is not simply out there, waiting for me to recognise it. Rather, I actively construct a certain experience as that of a chair (and thus as something that I can use in a certain way). One consequence of this thesis is that the world of which I am conscious need not exist independently of my consciousness. Rather, the everyday world which I live in and experience is constituted through my presuppositions and expectations. It is a world that exists relative to me. More radically, the world that the natural sciences explore is similarly one that is constituted by a complex set of taken-for-granted assumptions, including the assumption that objects do exist independently of the observer, that Husserl calls the 'natural attitude'. Husserl's conclusion is then, that the results of science are uncertain. Precisely because it has not examined the assumptions upon which its particular world rests, science could be radically mistaken (and no refinement of scientific research methodologies could remedy that uncertainty).

Husserl's concern with uncertainty is inspired by a reading of the Enlightenment philosopher René **Descartes**. Descartes sought to rebuild our claims to knowledge on firm foundations. To find those foundations, he sought to doubt the veracity of every belief that it is logically possible to doubt. Ultimately, Descartes finds that he can doubt everything except his own (and his God's) existence. Husserl's approach is subtly different. Husserl does not doubt particular beliefs, but rather searches for something that is indubitable in the nature of belief itself. That is to say that he does not seek a particular belief or thesis from which he could rebuild knowledge, but, to put it a little

crudely, seeks an essential and invariable way of seeing (and constituting) the object of experience. Husserl therefore turns to each of our
acts of consciousness, and asks what aspects of them can be doubted.
Anything that we presuppose about the experience that could be
changed, without changing the experience as such, is put to one side.
We suspend judgement as to the truth or falsehood of the presupposition. Husserl calls this process 'bracketing': the suspension of judgement is an 'epoche'. Thus, for example, Husserl argues that it makes no
difference to the experience of, say, a tree, if I suspend the everyday
assumption of the existence of that tree. It is here that Husserl's project
is not merely more subtle than Descartes's, it is also more radical.
Descartes stopped with the thesis that he, at least, must exist. Husserl
goes further in order to suspend judgement as to the existence of the
particular person who is having the experience. The move, as strange as
it may seem, is important. The particular person is a product of historical, cultural and indeed physical factors. It is precisely these factors, in
all their suspect variability, of which Husserl is attempting to rid
experience. An indubitable experience cannot be the experience of a
historical individual, with all their prejudices and presuppositions.
Husserl therefore looks for certainty in the work of a pure and
unchanging subjectivity.

The problem with this project, which has its most complete
exposition in *Ideas* (1913), is that the heroic exertions of the philosopher, to strip away all uncertainty, do not obviously allow a way
back to the mundane, communally shared and taken-for-granted
world of the natural attitude. Philosophical reflections, however
exacting, are of little obvious use to the cultural world, and the project
of finding certain foundations for the sciences seems to have failed. In
his last works (including the unfinished *Crisis of European Sciences and
Transcendental Phenomenology*, 1938), Husserl pursues this problem. His
approach to the natural sciences becomes more critical. Specifically, he
is critical of the tendency that he finds in science since the time of
Galileo to reduce the natural world to mathematics (and to assume that
this is the correct or objective account of the world). He pits the
'theoretical' attitude of the sciences against a 'personalistic' attitude.
Building upon the earlier analysis of intentionality, Husserl can argue
that different attitudes constitute the world differently. An attitude is a
set of presuppositions that allows the human observer to recognise only
certain types of object. The concern of the natural sciences with causal
relations and quantification thus leaves them blind to the human
motivations, beliefs and desires recognised in the personalistic attitude.
Yet for Husserl, this is not a mere clash of two incompatible ways of

constituting the world. Rather, the personalistic attitude is that of what he calls the 'life-world', which is the historically achieved structure of beliefs and values that make up the taken-for-granted everyday world in which we all live. Science, for the later Husserl, rests upon this life-world, rather than aspiring to a condition of certain knowledge independent of it.

The trajectory of Husserl's work is significant, not least because it embodies much of the history of the approach to cultural theory of the twentieth century. Husserl begins with an Enlightenment aspiration to establish certain truth, stripped of all the corrupting vagaries of historical experience. Gradually, he turns to see humans as fundamentally historical and cultural beings that construct the world about them. The aspiration to reduce the world to exact, quantifiable mathematical terms is increasingly seen as a threat to that humanity. It is in this direction that **Heidegger**, **Merleau–Ponty** and **Schutz** take phenomenology.

[AE]

Further reading: D. Bell 1990; Macann 1993; B. Smith and Woodruff Smith 1995.

IRIGARAY, LUCE (1932–)

The work of the French philosopher, linguist and psychoanalyst Luce Irigaray explores the exclusion of women from patriarchal language, and thus attempts to find alternative forms of writing (an *écriture feminine*) that would allow women to represent themselves to themselves.

Her early research concerned the language of those suffering from delirium. *Speculum of the Other Woman* (1974) is, however, her first major theoretical work. (The 'speculum' of the title is a curved mirror, used to examine a woman's sexual organs.) The book is a challenge to psychoanalysis, and specifically to the way in which the mother–daughter relationship is accounted for in **Freud**ian and **Lacan**ian theory. Irigaray develops an analysis and criticism of Lacan's notion of the 'symbolic' – the sphere of language, law and thus culture. For Irigaray, the symbolic is exclusively masculine language and thought, and as such the analysis of the symbolic is merely the description of a patriarchal culture that excludes women. Anything that falls outside this symbolic or conceptual order can be thought about, communicated or analysed only if it is expressed in patriarchal language. As such it is falsified, for although it is the 'other' of that symbolic order, its representation within the order can only be as something that is the same as the order. Everything genuinely outside the order is left unidentified and unarticulated. (Thus, in an examination of the women, the speculum reflects the male observer.) This 'economy of the same' is seen to work in the formation of sexuality. Female sexuality, on the Freudian model, is accounted for as a divergence from the masculine norm, most precisely in the theory of penis envy. The woman is understood as lacking a penis (and thus is always placed in contrast to the 'fullness' of the male.) No positive value is given to the female sex organs, and female sexual pleasure in the clitoris is repressed as the woman takes on the role of the 'receptacle' of the penis. An implication of this is that any demand for female equality, however well motivated it may be by concern for the political and economic plight of women, capitulates to this patriarchal symbolic order, for it immediately assumes that women lack something that men already have.

The separation of the son from the mother entails the son entering the symbolic order. Language makes this separation possible for the son. Men can therefore know themselves through the symbolic order. Equally, men can know women, as objects, through that order. The first act of the son is to objectify the mother (and thus to understand the mother in terms of the prohibition of incest). In contrast, the daughter does not have the same medium to facilitate separation from the mother, and thus to achieve self-knowledge. The symbolic order, because it is patriarchal, remains foreign and inappropriate to women. The symbolic order presents women merely as potential mothers, and not as autonomous subjects. In being refused access to language (and thus access to society), women run a greater risk of psychosis (and a fall into a private language, that might yet be, Irigaray speculates, the language in which women can communicate with women).

This Sex Which is Not One (1977) explores these issues further. Feminine sexuality, sexual pleasure and desire are analysed. Female pleasure lies in touching, rather than in the masculine pleasure of looking (manifest in mirroring and representation). This touching is located in the woman's genitals, where the lips of the vagina are in continuous contact and caress. Hence, in contrast to male sexuality, sexual pleasure and subjectivity, that is defined in terms of a single site (the penis), the female is already double. In addition, recognition of the uterus, vulva and breasts allows Irigaray to assert (again in opposition to psychoanalysis) that women have 'sex organs more or less everywhere' (1985b, p. 28). The woman is plural, and as such is not confined within a masculine culture that is seen to counter everything in units. Female pleasure is therefore other to the patriarchal culture, and cannot be contained within its economy of looking that makes the woman passive. Unable to count or name female sexuality, psychoanalysis and patriarchal culture therefore ignore it, counting it as none (p. 26).

Irigaray's subsequent writing has explored the possibility of a feminine writing, through readings of the philosophical tradition that exposed what is repressed or passed over in silence (including the body, and the elements of water, earth, fire and air: Irigaray 1991) and the exploration of a 'feminine god' (of multiplicity and flow) that is outside the grasp of patriarchal religion and theology, but also is 'yet to come' (1986, p. 8).

[AE]

Further reading: Grosz 1989; Whitford 1991.

JAKOBSON, ROMAN (1896–1982)

The work of the Russian-born structural linguist, Roman Jakobson, covers a wide range of topics, including Slavic language and folklore, language acquisition and the breakdown of linguistic competence, poetry and phonology (i.e. the study of the sound system of language). His importance to cultural theory lies in his development of structuralism, from **Saussure**'s linguistics, and particularly in the application of structuralism to the criticism of poetry.

While influenced by Saussure's linguistics, and thus by an approach to language that emphasises meaning as being generated by the structural relationships between elements within a system (and not by the inherent meaningfulness of the elements), Jakobson does revise Saussure's approach. First, Jakobson is more interested in the inter-relationship between the underlying, static structure of language ('langue') and the concrete, historically changing utterances made by language users ('parole') than is Saussure. This is demonstrated in Jakobson's analysis of the ability of the language user to contextualise utterances. For example, in using personal pronouns ('I', 'you', 'we' . . .) and demonstratives ('here', 'this' . . .) the language user must at once be able to account for the place of the word in the structure (or code) governing the language (i.e. 'langue') and situate themselves and their message in a unique, historical context. This analysis of contextualisation is grounded in Jakobson's study of language acquisition and language loss (for example, in aphasia), which in addition extends out to analyses of metaphor and metonymy. The use of metaphor entails the speaker's ability to select and substitute meaningful elements, while use of metonymy (where a part – 'pen' – is used to refer to or stand for a whole – 'writer') entails the ability to combine and contextualise elements.

Jakobson extends Saussure's structural analysis of the relationship between signs within a linguistic system, into an analysis of the relationship between sounds. While Saussure recognises that the elements of a sign system acquire meaning through relationships of difference, Jakobson extends this to the language's sounds, or more properly its phonemes or 'distinctive features' (i.e. the set of simplest sounds that can be discriminated, and so used to distinguish words of unlike meaning). Thus, for Jakobson, the difference between 'tip' and 'dip' as meaningful words rests upon the minimal difference between /t/ and /p/. A language will therefore entail a series of contrasts, based on properties such as the aspiration and non-aspiration of sounds; sounds which are voiced and unvoiced; nasality; or the position of the tongue. (For contexts in which there is no chance of confusing two similar words, the contrast may not be marked by the speaker, and the words could be pronounced alike.) This concern with sound may be seen to emerge early on in Jakobson's sensitivity to poetry, and notably in his recognition that Russian and Czech poetry are distinguished in terms of the rhythms, and thus sound patterns, of the poems – rather than in the structure of metaphor or other aspects that might directly determine the expression of meaning in the poem.

In attempting to define poetry, and to determine what distinguishes poetic from non-poetic language, Jakobson identifies six functions of language (referential, poetic, emotive, conative, phatic and metalinguistic) that he claims are present in all verbal communication. While all may be present, one will dominate. In poetry, the poetic will dominate, leading to the aesthetisation of language, or a language of expression rather than communication – although it is never absent from other forms of communication, and works only in relation to the other functions (Jakobson 1987a). His structural criticism of poetry proceeds by attempting to establish an objective structure or pattern that underpins and organises the surface of the poem, and that facilitates expressive language. Certain elements of meaning and sound are seen to recur in precise structures (most importantly those of binary oppositions) throughout the poem. The aspiration to objectivity, and thus to establish a definitive and scientific reading of a poem, has been criticised, not least by post-structuralists. Jakobson only partially engages with the possibility that patterns are not discovered in poems, but are created in the process of reading. In general, his structuralist approach to communication makes a number of assumptions, not least of autonomous addressers or senders, and equally autonomous addressees or receivers, of messages, that are out of step with later structuralist and post-structuralist thinking on the possibility that the human subject, as addresser or addressee, are as much products of language as they are its users.

[AE]

Further reading: Bradford 1994; Sangster 1982; Waugh 1976.

JAMES, C. L. R. (CYRIL LIONEL ROBERT) (1901–1989)

Caribbean writer whose output includes works of fiction, journalism, **Marx**ist political theory, history, cultural commentary and literary criticism. James grew up in Trinidad; before leaving the island, he had published short stories and had written a novel, *Minty Alley* (1936). While he was steeped in English literature (and was especially influenced by the satire of Thackeray) James's own fiction is characterised by a sympathetic interest in the streetlife of ordinary Caribbean people. The theme of the relationship between the uniqueness of the individual and the vitality of their community recurs throughout his work. In 1932 he moved to England, where for a time he worked as the cricket correspondent for the *Manchester Guardian*. During this period his political philosophy began to take on its mature form, through an active participation in the Trotskyist movement (James 1937), and through an engagement with the concrete problems of West Indian independence and Mussolini's invasion of Ethiopia. Colonialism and the associated problems of revolutionary change were explored through his historical studies of Toussaint L'Ouverture, the eighteenth-century leader of a slave revolt in San Domingo (Haiti), published as *The Black Jacobins* (1938), but also explored in a drama, *Toussaint L'Ouverture* (later revised as *The Black Jacobins*, 1992b). Crucially, this study allowed James to question the assumption that Marxist revolution would occur first in the industrialised world, but also to question the role of political leadership by a party.

Between 1938 and 1956 James lived in the United States, which became crucial to his understanding of the development of the modern global order, and the cultural and political break from the 'old bourgeois civilisation' of Europe, and thus the direction in which the political and cultural development of the colonial nations should move. James's (1992c) study of *American Civilisation* embraced both popular culture and the literature of Walt Whitman and Herman Melville. He argued that cinema explored a new relationship between the individual and society. While the broad context of a global society was present, the mass of people could still find expression as individuals. The tension between individual and society is similarly seen in the work of Whitman and Melville. Both break from the European tradition (and crucially emerge at a moment of transition in American society, with the Civil War). Whitman finds a new idiom, in free verse, that celebrates American individuality and yet struggles vainly with the possibility of linking together those individuals into a Democratic community. Melville, in contrast, represents Whitman's individual in concrete social situations, such as the precisely described work routines of the crew of the *Pequod* in *Moby Dick* (Melville 1963). Yet Melville is equally aware of the destructive nature of the form of individuality that is arising in his America, and symbolises it in Ahab (who for James prefigures Hitler and the captains of capitalist industry in the twentieth century). Yet *Moby Dick*, in its depiction of the individual personality set against a broad backdrop of nature and cultural life, is seen by James to anticipate something of the structure of the greatest motion pictures, including Griffith's *Birth of a Nation*.

This cultural analysis of the relationship between individual and society, or more precisely of modern individualism and its thwarted aspiration to community, is complemented by the development of James's political theory. His concern specifically with the failure of the community to resist domination or fragmentation, as the crew of the *Pequod* fails to resist Ahab, leads him to develop a theory of state capitalism that is as critical of the Soviet Union as it is of Western capitalism (James *et al.* 1986). The Soviet Union is not seen to have transcended the conflict between capital and labour that is characteristic of capitalism, but rather to have transposed this conflict, through nationalisation, into the state. Similar tendencies are identified in the United States. At the core of this analysis is James's concern with the way in which individual freedom and creativity is compromised in contemporary societies through the increased centralisation of state bureaucracies. A crucial issue for James, explored as much in his political writings as in his cultural criticism, is the defence of the relationship between individual creativity and democracy.

James returned to the Caribbean in 1957, and continued to explore the nature of revolution and nationalism, specifically through reference to the independence movements in Africa, with the example of Ghana being pre-eminent. Yet James's most distinctive book of this final period is perhaps *Beyond a Boundary* (1963). Ostensibly a study of cricket, it combines elements of autobiography with philosophical, political and aesthetic reflection. It may not be an exaggeration to say that it is the greatest book ever written about sport. In developing James's lifelong themes of colonial politics, personal and national identity, popular and high culture, it justifies the importance of sport as a form of culture that facilitates the expression and self-articulation of the individual and the community, in all the complexity of their cultural and personal contradictions.

[AE]

Further reading: Buhle 1988; Cudjoe and Cain 1995; McLemee and LeBlanc 1994; Nielsen 1997.

JAMESON, FREDRIC (1934–)

American cultural critic, whose work is characterised by the breadth and subtlety with which he analyses postmodernism. In his earliest work, Jameson published important interpretations and translations of **Hegel**ian **Marx**ists. His study of **Sartre**'s Marxism (Jameson 1961) was followed by a wide-ranging analysis of the development of twentieth-century German Marxism (Jameson 1971) that served to introduce many English language readers to the work of **Lukács**, **Bloch**, **Benjamin** and **Adorno**. This interest in the Marxist tradition was complemented by close study of structuralist and post-structuralist responses to the problem of language (1972). His own theoretical position thus emerged from a fusion of a commitment to historical and political analysis grounded in Marxism, with a sensitivity to problems of language and narrative derived from structuralism (1991). This fusion allowed him to offer an analysis of postmodernism that was neither an unsympathetic rejection, nor yet an uncritical acceptance. Jameson recognised the appropriateness of characterising contemporary culture as postmodern, yet interpreted certain trends within postmodernism as leading to the undermining of effective political and moral thought.

In a series of essays published during the 1980s and 1990s, culminating in the book *Postmodernism, or, The Cultural Logic of Late Capitalism* (1991), Jameson developed this analysis. On one level, postmodern art is interpreted as a response to the crisis in modernism, as the great works of modernism cease to be shocking and oppositional (as was their original intention) and become incorporated as part of the cultural canon. Indeed, art is incorporated into capitalism, not least through the advertising and fashion industries. Further, the creativity of modernism, which gave rise to a plethora of distinctive individual styles, can no longer be matched. Within modernism everything has already been invented. On another level, Jameson understands post-modern culture as the expression of the logic of a new form of capital-ism. Following in part Ernest Mandel's account of *Late Capitalism* (1975) and his theory of economic cycles within capitalism, Jameson argues that postmodernism is the cultural paradigm corresponding to the form of capitalism that emerged after the Second World War. In broad terms, he argues that the individualism of nineteenth-century capitalism led to realist art, and the alienating bureaucratic capitalism of the early twentieth century led to the abstraction and subjectivism of high modernism. Late capitalism is characterised by new types of con-sumption grounded in the increased rate of change in fashion and style, the greater penetration of advertising and the mass media, improved communications, and the reduction of old tensions (such as that between city and countryside, centre and province) with increased universalisation and standardisation.

Postmodern culture, and thus the logic of late capitalism, is charac-terised by Jameson in terms of two characteristics: pastiche and schizo-phrenia. Both are explicated in terms of a fundamental change in the nature of subjectivity and language. The bourgeois subject of nineteenth-century capitalism has been exposed as a myth by post-structuralism (hence, for example, **Barthes**'s thesis of the death of the author). Yet more profoundly, language (and thus the linguistic and temporal grounding of the individual) has broken down. Modernism is characterised, for Jameson, by the analysis of the sign carried out in structuralist semiotics (for example of **Saussure**). The sign is divided into the signifier (the material noise or image) and the signified (the concept or meaning of the sign). The real object to which the sign might point is largely abandoned (for signs do not acquire sense by naming or pointing to the real world; they acquire sense through their relationship to other signs). Hence modernism can generate a series of languages or styles, unrestrained by the pull of any objective real world. Postmodernism takes a further step. If modernist invention is exhausted, as Jameson suggests, then one cannot originate new styles (which is to say, new systems of signs). One can only copy existing ones. Pastiche is thus a copying. Pastiche is, however, distinct from parody. The styles of individual modernist artists could still be par-odied, because the common language of bourgeois individualism remained, and one could make fun of modernism because of its deviation from that norm. Now the myth of the common language has been exposed, and so one has no grounds from which to be humorous. Pastiche is imitation without laughter. Postmodernism is thus an art about images, not about the real world (so that even photo-realism in painting is not a return to realism, for photo-realists paint photographs, i.e. images of reality, not reality itself). But more radically, Jameson turns to **Lacan**'s psychoanalysis in order to suggest that postmodern art is analogous to the condition of schizophrenia in no longer being able to accede to a public realm of speech and language. Signifiers are separated from signifieds. Language does not mean anything, and the postmodernist thus focuses upon the materiality of the sign as pure image, not upon its meaning, or crucially upon its historical positioning. Postmodern art thus reproduces an eternal present (in contrast to the narratives of realist and modern art, say in Balzac, Joyce or Proust).

Jameson's most recent work has sought to address his concerns about the political status of postmodernism. Modernist art, even if it is now exhausted, aspired to being critical of society, while postmodernism seems to acquiesce. He has turned again to Hegelian Marxism, and specifically to Adorno's negative dialectics, as a resource to revitalise critical thought within late capitalism (Jameson 1990a).

[AE]

Further reading: Hardt and Weeks 2000; Homer 1998.

JUNG, CARL GUSTAV (1875–1961)

Swiss psychologist, born in Kesswil. His early research, published while working at the Burgholzi, the university psychiatric clinic in Zurich, pioneered the theory of free association, using word association (and evaluation of delays before response and the appropriateness of the response word) to access emotionally charged ideas in the unconscious. In 1906 Jung published work on what was to become known as schizophrenia, and particularly on hallucinations. (He began here to take notice of the similarity between schizophrenic delusions and religious beliefs, so that the delusions are comparable to private theologies.) Jung sent a copy of this study, *The Psychology of Dementia Praecox* to **Freud**, thereby initiating a friendship and collaboration that lasted until 1913, and the publication of *The Psychology of the Unconscious* (1917). During this period Jung became president of psychoanalysis's International Association, and editor of its journal. It was during this period that Jung began sustained research into mythology, fairy-tales and religions. The break from Freud was brought about in part because of Jung's refusal to accept Freud's predominantly sexual interpretation of the libido. Jung's psychoanalysis was becoming increasingly concerned with the ways in which human existence, and the life of the individual, were given meaning. While Freud looked back to the childhood causes of behaviour and psychopathology, Jung looked forward, to the more or less romantically conceived struggle of the individuation of the mature person. (Jung saw Freud, and indeed Alfred Adler, as being concerned with problems faced during the process of maturation, while he looked to the crises of middle life of those who had achieved independence from their parents, sexual identity and economic independence.) The split from Freud initiated Jung's own mid-life crisis, and ironically led to the personal experience of the problems previously encountered at second hand in clinical practice. His personal habit, since childhood, of attempting to represent his own inner psychological state in talismen and other images, externalising the internal and thus making himself conscious of it, culminated in the drawing of abstract patterns (circular designs subdivided by four or by multiples of four) that he subsequently discovered corresponded to the mandalas used in Himalayan Buddhism. It was thus that the relationship between inner or personal imagery and public or cultural images (such as mythologies and religions) was further clarified, and the theory of the collective unconscious (the historically evolved propensity of archetypes to structure the form, rather than the content, of all such imagery) was posited. Culture, in Jungian terms, is therefore to be understood as an objectification of unconscious processes, giving conscious meaning to human existence. Jung's later work, while stimulating, is marred by self-indulgence and a lack of the rational discipline typical of Freud. (Indeed, it is tempting to perceive it as a Romantic reflection of **Lévi-Strauss**'s more rational and **Kant**ian project in *The Savage Mind*: Lévi-Strauss 1966.) Jung's final years were spent in private practice, living near Zurich, his lake-side house having been planned to symbolise his own psychological development.

[AE]

Further reading: De Laszlo 1992; Moreno 1974; Stevens 1994; Young-Eisendrath and Dawson 1997.

KANT, IMMANUEL (1724-1804)

German philosopher whose *Critique of Pure Reason* (1781, revised second edition 1787), often referred to as the first *Critique*, has exerted an important influence upon nineteenth- and twentieth- century philosophy. The first *Critique*, in conjunction with the second and third critiques – the *Critique of Practical Reason* (1788) and *The Critique of Judgment* (1790) – represents a systematic attempt to examine the scope and limits of human powers of reason in the theoretical, practical and aesthetic spheres of human activity. The first *Critique* lays down the basic principles that underpin Kant's thought. In that work he attempts to elucidate a path of analysis which avoids falling into deep scepticism with regard to the possibility of obtaining reliable knowledge concerning the world of human experience (a position exemplified for Kant by the empiricism of philosopher David **Hume**). This project involves the construction and justification of a reliable system of metaphysics. In Kant's terms, metaphysics involves the formulation of true judgements about the world which are nevertheless not reducible to experience. Such judgements Kant calls a priori judgements, that is, they can be arrived at independently of experience. In their purest form, such judgements are termed 'analytic', e.g. in thinking a subject, A, and a predicate, B, the predicate is contained within A as part of it. Analytic judgements are contrasted with synthetic judgements, in which the predicate, B, is external to the subject, A (*Critique of Pure Reason*, A7/B11). Synthetic judgements are thus those that involve an act of inference which goes beyond the scope of the concepts one has at one's disposal independently of experience (i.e. the empirical or external world). As such, all judgements concerning experience are synthetic judgements. The project which the first *Critique* sets itself is to establish a reliable basis for the act of making inferences about the world of experience. Thus, Kant argues that in order to know the world at all we must have within us concepts which are not merely reducible to experience or, in Humean terms, habit or custom. In this way, the scope and limits of theoretical reason are thus delineated.

In the second *Critique*, Kant lays out the formal conditions required for the exercise of reason in the field of practical action – principally in terms of the capacity reason has to impose moral obligations upon us through a priori principles which are then applicable to the domain of human practices. In this sense, reason is deemed to lay down the basis of freedom and moral law. In the same way, in the third *Critique* Kant applies himself to ascertaining what rational principles are at work in the domain of judgements of an aesthetic nature. Such judgements include judgements of taste about the nature of the beautiful and the sublime. With regard to the beautiful, the problem Kant addresses is: to what extent is it possible to make a subjective judgement (i.e. to construct a proposition which contains the predicate 'beautiful') about something, either in nature or in art, and at the same time assert that this judgement has universal validity? As with the first *Critique*, such judgements are held to involve the use of synthetic a priori propositions, and in this way are given universal validity.

In this context, Kant considers the nature of teleological judgements, i.e. those judgements which involve the attribution of purposiveness to things in nature. There are two types of purposiveness: first, extrinsic purposiveness, which includes those things which, although they cannot themselves be said to be organised in terms of a purpose, have one in relation to other things, e.g. earth, air, water, etc.; second, intrinsic purposiveness, which includes things about which one can ask such questions as 'What is it there for?' (*Critique of Judgment*, section 82). In asking the latter question one is presented with two possible answers: first, that the existence of the thing one asks about is not a matter of intentionality, but is a product of a mechanism of nature; second, that the thing has some intentional basis for its existence. If the second answer is the case, says Kant, then it is possible to conclude *either* that its purpose is to be understood in terms of itself, in which case it is 'not merely a purpose but also a final purpose' – a final purpose being 'a purpose that requires no other purpose as a condition of its possibility' (ibid., sections 82, 84) *or* that its purpose resides outside it and is, therefore, not a final purpose but a means. In the context of the world of nature (i.e. of the mechanisms which form the habitats of living creatures) Kant detects only the action of a mechanism. Humans, like other animals, are subject to this mechanism, and human understanding is obliged to think of the world in terms of such mechanisms. However, for Kant, human reason insists that the world around us needs to be comprehended in terms of laws which 'it can conceive of only as arising from purposes' (ibid.). As such, 'reason gives us sufficient grounds for judging man . . . to be not merely a natural purpose, which we may judge all organized beings to be, but also to be the ultimate purpose of nature here on earth, the purpose by reference to which all natural things constitute a system of purposes' (ibid., section 83).

What, in humanity, can be conceived of in terms of purposiveness is one of two things. The first of these is the human desire to attain happiness, and the second culture. The attainment of happiness is tied to the subjective, empirical purposes that individuals may set for themselves. Happiness is thus an idea which is so indistinct, and therefore implies a degree of diversity that renders it highly ambiguous. Hence, it cannot be said to be reflected in the world of nature, which 'is very far from having adopted him [i.e. humanity] as its special darling and benefited him in preference to the other animals, but has in fact spared him no more than any other animal from its destructive workings: plague, famine, flood, frost, or attacks from other animals large or small, and so on' (ibid.). Moreover, what Kant terms 'man's own natural predispositions' (i.e. the urge of one human to dominate over another, and the species' propensity to engage in acts of war, etc.) tend to contradict this view still further. For, even if nature were organised so that it satisfied all human needs, human behaviour itself would ensure that happiness was not a viable option for us to conceive of as our purpose. Humans, however, are distinguished by the fact that they are the only earthly beings which possess understanding, and hence the capacity to set themselves purposes. As such, humans have an instrumental relationship to nature, and can give it a purpose which is independent of it. Such a purpose would be self-sufficient, and hence a final one. Thus, if nature has a purpose it is by way of reference to humanity, and humanity gains the capacity to seek its ends through culture: 'Hence only culture can be the ultimate purpose that we have cause to attribute to nature with respect to the human species' (ibid.). Culture is thus the condition necessary for giving nature a purpose *through* the existence of humanity.

Culture, for Kant, can be divided into two crucial elements: skill, and discipline. The culture of skill consists in the development of practical ability, principally through the subjective capacities of individuals. This generally leads to the development of social inequalities, due to the fact that the majority of humans are required to spend their lives pursuing such skills, and thus providing the necessities which others who do not produce them need in order to survive. In consequence, society thus becomes divided into higher and lower classes. As culture develops, these divisions become more marked, and society more unstable. In order to limit this, rules which delineate the relationships between individuals are needed, i.e. laws which, taken as a whole, constitute civil society. Civil societies are in turn in need of being unified within a cosmopolitan 'system of all states that are in danger of affecting one another detrimentally' through war (ibid.). War is, however, a cause of the development of new abilities, and hence contributes to the culture of skill.

The culture of discipline is required, according to Kant, as a means of overcoming our natural, 'animal characteristics'. Such characteristics consist of 'inclinations [which] interfere very much with our human-ity' (ibid.) and are therefore in need of control. Discipline is itself, for Kant, an expression of what nature has given human beings, i.e. the capacity to overcome their animal natures. Nature itself, therefore, 'pursues the purpose of making room for the development of our humanity' through an appreciation of human achievements in the domain of the arts and sciences. The latter, it follows, serve to enable humans to overcome their animal nature: 'they make great headway against man's propensity to the senses, and so prepare him for a sover-eignty in which reason alone is to dominate' (ibid.). The domination of reason in humanity is hence the aim of culture, and this dominion is realised in the attainment of freedom, i.e. the capacity to make free and rational (and therefore, for Kant, moral) choices. It is this capacity which sets humans apart from nature. This is due to the fact that it is its freedom which enables humanity to be conceived as an end which requires no other justification than itself, as opposed to being a means to an end.

[PS]

Further reading: Bennett 1966, 1974; Chadwick and Cazeux 1992; Korner 1955; Lyotard 1994; Strawson 1966.

KRISTEVA, JULIA (1941–)

The Bulgarian-born literary theorist, linguist and psychoanalyst Julia Kristeva moved to Paris in 1965, becoming associated with Roland **Barthes**, and the group of writers and critics centring on the literary journal *Tel Quel*. She first came to academic attention as an inter-preter of the work of Mikhail **Bakhtin** and the Russian formalist approach to literary criticism (Kristeva 1986a). From Bakhtin's (1981) account of 'dialogism' – as the necessity of utterances being related to other utterances – she proposed the notion of intertextuality, indicat-ing that a text (such as a novel, poem or historical document) is not a self-contained or autonomous entity, but is produced from other texts. The interpretation that a particular reader generates from a text will then depend on the recognition of the relationship of the given text to other texts. Thus, for example, our understanding of a film adaptation of a novel will depend on our reading of that novel, or conversely our understanding of the novel is now framed by having seen the film. Intertextuality may be understood as the thesis that no text exists outside its continuing interpretation and reinterpretation. There can then never be a definitive reading of a text, that itself becomes part of the frame within which the original text is interpreted.

Séméiotiké: Recherches pour une sémanalyse (1969, 1986b) sees the emergence of a still more distinctive voice. Influenced by both **Marx**ism and **Saussure**'s semiotics, Kristeva's 'semanalysis' looks to the material aspect of language (and thus its sounds and rhythms) rather than to the communicative function that is emphasised by more orthodox approaches within semiotics. Kristeva argues that these material characteristics of language cannot be readily explained by scientific logic (in contrast to the communicative). Her analysis of the materiality of language brings to the fore language as process, and thus its heterogeneity to our ordinary understanding of the world. Poetry is then seen to be concerned with this material level, and to disrupt language as a vehicle of meaning and communication. (Mallarmé's poetry is exemplary in this respect, and this argument serves to indicate Kristeva's enduring commitment to avant-garde literature.) The distinction between communication and the material in language is further developed in terms of the distinction between that which is consciously apprehended and that which is available only to the unconscious. This in turn opens an account of subjectivity that parallels that of language. The conscious subject is something static and knowable. The unconscious yields a view of the subject as being in process (which is to say, subjectivity always entails an unspeakable or unnameable unconscious, that remains outside logical and conceptual understanding).

This analysis of subjectivity is developed, in the early 1970s, in *Revolution in Poetic Language* (1784). The 'symbolic' (derived from **Lacan**'s work), as the sphere of communicative language and culture, is set against '*le sémiotique*', the material level of language. 'Le sémiotique' is explicated through the concept of *chora*. While the term is ultimately derived from Plato, it refers to the undifferentiated bodily space occupied by the mother and child. It is unknowable (precisely because it is heterogeneous to – outside – the sphere of communication, and any attempt to name it or describe it would falsify it). It can, however, be glimpsed through the cracks that avant-garde poetry opens up in communicative language. (Kristeva is therefore concerned with the paradox of analysing that which cannot be analysed, and in demonstrating how that which cannot be analysed serves as a potential challenge to the political order that is manifest in the dominant culture and language of communication.) The *chora* is a non-patriarchal space (and so certain poets can be regarded as feminine, regardless of their actual gender). Taken further, poetry is seen to have links to the practices of the infant as she or he learns language. The poet uses a raw material of cries, singing, laughter and word-play offered by the child.

In her later work, Kristeva has offered more personal analyses of love (1987), melancholy (1989) and abjection (1982), nationalism and the experience of being a foreigner (1991). These analyses are grounded in her own experience and those of the patients of her psychoanalytic practice. They show a greater concern with the relationship of subjectivity to the symbolic, and thus to the need to separate from the mother, in order to enter successfully into culture. Melancholy, for example, occurs because the subject cannot form symbolic capacities. The melancholic is unable to love, remaining in a perpetual mourning for the mother, and as such (in an observation that puts an important twist on accounts of alienation) 'foreigners in their maternal tongue' (1989 p. 53).

[AE]

Further reading: Fletcher and Benjamin 1990; Grosz 1989; Lechte 1990; Lechte and Zournazi 1998; Moi 1986; A. Smith 1996, 1998.

KUHN, THOMAS S. (1922–1996)

An American historian of science and philosopher of science. Kuhn's most controversial attempt to contribute to our understanding of science came with the publication of his *The Structure of Scientific Revolutions* (1962). In this work he offers an account of the development of the sciences which runs contra to the accepted view of the sciences as intrinsically progressive. On this latter view science is seen as moving ever closer to a more accurate theoretical understanding of the world. However, according to Kuhn, this is a distorted model of how the sciences *actually* operate.

On Kuhn's view the sciences consist of a number of 'paradigms'. A paradigm is basically a system of beliefs and theories which scientists hold as currently true about the world. It thus supplies the scientists working within it with their conceptual schema for engaging with nature. The work of what Kuhn calls 'normal science' is to refine and integrate the theories and assumptions which comprise a paradigm. This activity Kuhn refers to as 'puzzle-solving'. Occasionally an anomaly arises, caused by a conflict between nature and a paradigm, which resists straightforward integration into a scientist's accepted theoretical framework. Usually such anomalies are 'solved' and the paradigm remains intact. Certain anomalies, however, resist easy solution by assimilation into the theoretical framework supplied by the paradigm. At times like this we move into a period of crisis that Kuhn calls 'extraordinary science'. During this period scientists are prepared to try ever more elaborate and 'ad hoc' adjustments to the theories within the paradigm in order to preserve its integrity. If the anomaly resists all of even the most extreme attempts at assimilation, we enter a period of 'scientific revolution'. At this stage the 'old' paradigm still exists, but it becomes increasingly unstable. Eventually, almost spontaneously, a 'new' paradigm emerges to replace the old one (1970, pp. 89–90) and the whole process begins again.

The truly revolutionary aspect of Kuhn's theory, however, is that once a new paradigm has emerged the scientists within it, he holds, 'work in a different world' (1970, p. 121). In other words, the new paradigm supplies the scientists with a new conceptual schema (see also under the entry for worldview) for contemplating the world which is wholly different to the one supplied by the old paradigm. The implication of this aspect of Kuhn's theory is that if scientists working within the old and new paradigms do not share the same assumptions about the world then they cannot communicate in any meaningful or rational way across the boundaries of these different paradigms. This being so, then there is no independent way of judging whether the new paradigm is a better or a more accurate measure of reality than the old one; the best we can claim is that they are just *different*. Thus, although progress may be possible within paradigms, i.e. during periods of normal science, we can makes no claims about progress between paradigms.

Unsurprisingly, this implication of Kuhn's theory, which has become known as the 'incommensurability problem', has met with much protest on the grounds that it seems to turn science into an irrational enterprise. It is also taken to have broader unacceptable social and political implications: 'unless men are disposed to approach one another's opinions in [a rational way], they cannot argue with one another, but only preach or hurl abuse' (Meynell 1975, p. 121). The net outcome, it is held, is an inevitable resort to violence. However, it has been suggested by others that this outcome depends on how one defines the incommensurability problem, thus it is by no means as inevitable as some insist. Indeed, recognising the radical implications of his earlier statement of his theory, Kuhn himself claims that not only is some form of translation possible between paradigms, it is also necessary (Kuhn 1970, p. 202).

[Stephen Horton]

Further reading: Bird 2000; Horwich 1993; Ziauddin 2000.

LACAN, JACQUES (1901–1981)

French psychoanalyst. Lacan is best know for his seminars which made psychoanalysis acceptable in France. Under the rubric of a 'return to **Freud**', he took on the French intellectual establishment and the International Psychoanalytic Association from which he was forced to resign because of his experiments with short analytic sessions instead of the prescribed fifty-minute hour. In 1964, he established the *Ecole Freudienne de Paris* and used it as his doctrinal platform until it was dissolved in 1980. Shortly before his death, he founded the *Ecole de la Cause Freudienne*, which is now headed by his son-in-law, Jacques-Alain Miller. Despite his critique of academic discourse, Lacan brought psychoanalysis to the university. A Department of Psychoanalysis was created in the University of Paris at Vincennes in 1969. The department at Vincennes was an attempt to reach out to scholars in the human sciences who were not analysts by training and remains controversial to this day.

Born in a Catholic family in 1901, Lacan received a Jesuit education following which he studied medicine. He then trained as a psychiatrist focusing on the study of paranoia. The horrific murder enacted by the Papin sisters was the subject of his doctoral thesis: *De la psychose paranoiaque dans ses rapports avec la personnalité* (1932) This case also fascinated the surrealists with whom Lacan was now in touch. His first major intervention in psychoanalysis was his theory of the 'mirror stage' in a speech, which he attempted to deliver, at the Marienbad Congress, in 1936. Lacan's development of the Imaginary as one of the fundamental cognitive coordinates of the subject was spelt out in the mythical invocation of the child held by a parent figure before the mirror. For the infant between the ages of 6 and 18 months, who is struggling in neuronal immaturity, the jubliant assumption of its body image serves an orthopaedic function: it promises the child the possibility of a unifying identity in the future. Lacan's theory of the mirror stage also drew upon the empirical work of James Baldwin, Charlotte Bühler and Henri Wallon. In 1938 Lacan also astutely summarised the work of

Karl Abraham and Melanie Klein in relation to the Oedipus complex in an encyclopedia article entitled 'La famille', where he argued that before the intervention of Oedipus, the infant is subjected to the phantasy of the fragmented body – an idea that reappears in the second version of the mirror stage in the *Écrits* (1966).

Lacan's theorisation of the Oedipus complex in relation to Claude **Lévi-Strauss**'s work on 'the elementary structures of kinship' and Ferdinand de **Saussure**'s theory of the signifer in his celebrated 'The function and field of speech of language in psychoanalysis' (Lacan 1977b) propelled him to theoretical stardom in France. Lacan's discourse focused on the function of the paternal metaphor (the so-called Name-of-the-Father) in mediating the child's access to the Symbolic realm. The Symbolic is the privileged term in this stage of Lacan's work: both neurosis and psychosis were understood through modes of exclusion from this order. The results of this inquiry into the role of the Real, the Imaginary and the Symbolic in the constitution of the subject was formalised in Schemas L and R – diagrammatic representations that are available in his paper 'On a Question Preliminary to any Possible Treatment of Psychosis', which was a result of a seminar conducted in 1955–1956 at the *École Normale Supérieure*. Later, realising the dangers of these Imaginary representations, Lacan began to toy with topological objects like the Möbius strip, the Klein bottle and the cross cap in order to model the subject's constitution through the fundamental orders (the Real, the Symbolic, the Imaginary and the *Sinthome*) that he had uncovered in order to facilitate a reading of the Freudian text. By implication, this also meant a reorientation of psychoanalysis along Lacanian lines, though he appears to have had some difficulty in explaining whether topology was a pedagogical convenience or a heuristic device.

Lacan's final seminars were an attempt to correlate the function of the Real in relation to the major motifs of psychoanalysis: sexuality, phantasy and death. In its ability to resist signification, the Real partakes of the primary process. Phantasy is no more just a private film which the subject watches obsessively in her head but a structuring process that seeks to mask the lack in the Symbolic Other. Unlike the psychoanalytic model of the 1950s, the later Lacan defines the therapeutic trajectory as a movement towards the Real rather than the Symbolic. The end of analysis is defined as 'death's death'. It is an attempt to come to terms with the fact that the Real always catches up with the subject. Lacan refers to this process as 'traversing the phantasy': in other words it is death that emerges as the real scandal of psychoanalysis and not sexuality, though it is the interimplication of these concepts in each other that propels the subject's phantasy. Lest this shift in emphasis from sexuality to death appear unnecessary in a 'return to Freud', we need but note Freud's own obsession with death in his later works like *Beyond the Pleasure Principle* (Freud 1991a). Therefore, unlike American ego psychology, Lacanian psychoanalysis does not promise the availability of the sexual relation. It is in the recognition of the non-existence of the sexual relation that the subject moves from the lure of the *objet a* to constituting its unique moment of truth in relation to its Symptom (what Lacan (1982) terms *Sinthome* in his reading of Jamès Joyce). Is it not his moment of truth then that Lacan isolates when he tells his followers: 'It is up to you to be Lacanians. As far as I am concerned, I am a Freudian'?

[Shiva Kumar Srininvassan]

Further reading: Clark 1988; Clement 1983; Leupin 1991; Marini 1992; Ragland-Sullivan 1986; Roudinesco 1990; Schneiderman 1983.

LEAVIS, F. R. (1895–1978)

Leavis's reputation as a cultural critic rests mainly on early works such as 'Mass Civilisation and Minority Culture' (Leavis 1933) and *Culture and Environment* (Leavis and Thompson 1933). Leavis argued that mass production had effectively destroyed a craft-based way of life. Instead of living and working in small communities, people now worked in large factories in big cities. Leavis was not opposed to mass production *per se*, on the contrary, in some fields he regarded it as 'essential' (Leavis and Thompson 1933, p. 32). What did concern him was the loss of tradition and whether there was a 'possible relation between the standardisation of commodities and standardisation of persons'.

Tradition, for Leavis, was 'spiritual, moral and emotional' (ibid., p. 81) and it 'preserv[ed] the "picked experience of ages" regarding the finer issues of life' (ibid.). Leavis used this notion of tradition to critique the factory system whose 'repetitive monotony' (ibid., p. 29), he believed, had dehumanising effects. A popular view at the time was that leisure compensated for the boredom of work but Leavis argued that 'such work unfits one for making the positive effort without which there can be no true recreation' (ibid., p. 100). For him, leisure was as dehumanising as work, particularly because leisure pursuits such as popular fiction debased language by appropriating it for wholly commercial ends.

Leavis believed that literary training would help people to resist the allurements of popular culture. The study of literature would help to keep alive that tradition of 'picked experiences' that was being eroded in the modern world. Furthermore, it would instil a sense of sensuous particularly in a world of increasing bureaucracy and abstract exchange.

One of the most interesting aspects of Leavis is the way he has been constructed in opposition to theory. Accordingly, he is presented as someone who has a naively mimetic view of literature. But this is simply inaccurate. Reality for Leavis was not something that was there, it was something that was created through language, '[i]n creating language, human beings create the world they live in' ('Thought Meaning and Sensibility: The Problem of Value Judgement', in *Valuation in Criticism and Other Essays*, 1986, p. 285). This brings him close to the post-structuralist idea of language as a system of internal differences that do not so much refer to reality as structure our concept of it.

Indeed, if theory is understood as the work of **Foucault**, **Lacan** and **Derrida** then there are certain overlaps between Leavis's thought and theirs. For example, Leavis, like Foucault, was concerned with the effects of discourse and this is evident in his observations about the institutions of leisure, psychology and standard English. Leavis was also highly critical of the Cartesian view of consciousness which 'must be exorcized' (1977, p. 31) in favour of a type of thought 'defy[ing] the rationality of either/or' (ibid., p. 37). Such remarks have a certain Derridean air. Similarly, the emphasis on consciousness in Leavis's work, the close relation between the development of consciousness and the recognition of a paternal line, and the importance of recognition in the dialogue of criticism opens his work to Lacanian reading.

Instead of rejecting Leavis, a more fruitful approach might be to develop the parallels between his work and that of theory. Another might be to examine the complex exchanges between the discourse of criticism and mass culture. For example, how the relations between text and reader, consumer and commodity stage, subvert and contain one another. Or again, how the image of the labourer at the heart of Leavis's criticism modulates, through an emphasis on discipline and training, into that of the efficient operative of scientific management. It is only by sifting through these relations and relations between criticism and mass culture that Leavis's legacy can receive the sort of detailed appraisal it still awaits.

[Gary Day]

Further reading: M. Bell 1988; Day 1996; Mulhern 1979.

LE CORBUSIER (1887–1965)

Pseudonym of Charles-Edouard Jenneret. (The pseudonym, derived from his great-grandmother's name, puns upon his appearance, as *le corbeau* or raven.) Born in southern France, his voluminous writings, including *Vers une architecture* (1923), *Urbanisme* (1925), *La Ville radieuse* (1933) and *Modulor* (1948), as well as plans and finished buildings, established Le Corbusier as one of the most influential theorists and practitioners of modernist architecture and urban planning. Even his early buildings demonstrate a modernist concern with the application of mass production techniques, and thus the possibilities of prefabrication. The inspiration of efficient, mass production techniques is encapsulated in the observation that a house is a machine for living in. Crucially, this does not commit Le Corbusier to the reduction of a house to a machine, or something that is purely functional. Indeed, many of the domestic dwellings he built demonstrate a great concern with luxurious interiors and outlooks. Rather, architecture is conceived as an exhaustively rational process. A number of his most important buildings and projects may be noted. The Maison Citrohan of 1922 is a model of a dwelling designed as a simple box, with pillars, typical of Le Corbusier's designs, raising it from the ground. The ideas behind this model were realised in a number of dwellings, including the Maison La Roche (1923) and Villa Sovoye at Poissy (1929–1931). His design for the League of Nations building in Geneva (1927), although never erected, brought him increased international fame. Large-scale commissions followed, including the Centrosoyons building in Moscow (1928) and the Pavillon Suisse for the Cité Universitaire, Paris (1930–1932), as well as buildings in Algiers and Rio de Janeiro. Le Corbusier's post-war work showed a continuing development. The Unité d'Habitation in Marseilles (1947–1952) is a single accommodation block, for 1,800 residents, and includes living units integrated with the provision of other requirements of everyday life (shopping, community services and a substantial recreational roof space). This building had a major influence on post-war mass housing. Le Corbusier's later works show a greater interest in the relationship between the building and its environment, so that they increasingly become unique buildings for particular sites. These include the church of Notre Dame-du-Haut at Ronchamp (1954), the monastery at Eveux-sur-l'Arbresle (1960) and major works in India (at Ahmedabad and Chandigard).

[AE]

Further reading: W. Curtis 1992.

LE DOEUFF, MICHÈLE (1948–)

The work of the French philosopher Michèle Le Doeuff is distinctive in its defence of philosophy, and its arguments that philosophy is a suitable vehicle of feminist thought. Other contemporary French feminist thinkers, such as **Irigaray** and **Kristeva**, present the rationality and order of philosophical thought as inherently patriarchal, and thus as incapable of conceptualising or communicating what it is to be female. In contrast, Le Doeuff argues in favour of the inherent openness of philosophy, such that it should always remain critical and above all self-critical, and the possibility of there being a plurality of rationalities within it. Philosophy therefore offers a model of autonomous thought that is valuable to feminism. Yet, while philosophy may be open in principle, Le Doeuff is equally aware that the actual historical practice of philosophy has been such as to limit it, closing off this openness and critical faculty, and as such has excluded or restricted the place of women philosophers, and has served to restrict the place of women in society in general. Actual philosophy is sexist. Le Doeuff's project may therefore be seen as the rescue of philosophy from its own practice.

The closure of philosophy may be identified at a number of points. A series of taken-for-granted and therefore unquestioned assumptions mark philosophical argument, and these typically work to exclude women. Thus, philosophy gives prominence to abstraction at the cost of concrete relevance, and restricts the potential 'wandering' of thought. Le Doeuff analyses this limitation through the role that images play in philosophy. While philosophy's self-understanding may be one of thorough-going rationality and self-reflection, in practice philosophical texts are seen to be structured through the presence of an imaginary level, that is specific to philosophy. The example of **Kant**'s description of the understanding as an island (a land of truth) is given. Such images are not, for Le Doeuff, mere metaphors, but are rather structures that serve to close off and limit philosophy's own self-critical nature. The image (most pertinently in that of an island surrounded by a stormy and dangerous ocean) surrounds the dogmatic assertions of philosophy, preventing them from being scrutinised or questioned. Questioning is inhibited precisely because such images fall outside the style of the usual philosophical argument, and will be bypassed by the reader as mere 'illustrations' (Le Doeuff 1986, p. 12). Thus, while philosophy aspires to omnipotence, and to be the foundation of all other inquiry, in practice is it limited. For Le Doeuff, such limitation is not merely the failure of philosophy, for it is also the point at which philosophy becomes most historically concrete and pertinent. The limitations, in effect, are the points at which an abstract philosophy touches and influences the real, historical world.

Philosophy's sexism is revealed in this context. On the one hand, a specific position for women within philosophy has been historically brought about. The woman is the disciple of the male philosopher. The woman thus marks the man as philosopher, as someone to whom others defer. Le Doeuff examines the relationship of the existentialist Jean-Paul **Sartre** to Simone De Beauvoir. While De Beauvoir presents herself as merely the disciple of Sartre, simply adopting his existentialist philosophy, in practice she is seen to transform it, most significantly as a moral philosophy, so as to speak with her own voice. On the other hand, a limited philosophy serves to define women. Philosophy's limited self-understanding, as thoroughly rational and abstract, defines the male position. The women is unsuited to such abstract reasoning, because of a practical and sensitive nature. The male is therefore defined in terms of reason, and the woman in terms of an unchanging sex. While analysing this argument in detail as it appears in the work of eighteenth century philosophers, Le Doeuff holds that it continues to inform philosophy and other forms of scientific enquiry (such as psychoanalysis). The very weakness of it as an argument marks philosophy's failure to reflect upon its own presuppositions, and thus to live to its own ideal. It is thus a self-evident limit of philosophy.

[AE]

Further reading: Grosz 1989.

LÉVINAS, EMMANUEL (1906–1995)

Lévinas was born of Jewish parents in Kovno, Lithuania. As a child he learned Russian and Hebrew, and his exposure to the moral dilemmas addressed by writers such as Dostoyevsky, Tolstoy and Gogol and the influence of Talmudic scholarship left indelible marks upon his mature thought. In 1923 Lévinas went to study philosophy in France, where he encountered Henri Bergson's writings. At this time he also established a friendship with the French writer and critic Maurice Blanchot. Lévinas attended Edmund **Husserl**'s lectures in Freiberg in the late 1920s, when he first encountered Martin **Heidegger**'s work. In 1930 Lévinas was awarded French citizenship. During the Second World War almost all of Lévinas's relatives in Lithuania were murdered by the

Nazis. From 1939 he served in the French forces as an interpreter until, in 1940, he was captured and made a prisoner of war. The immediate post-war years saw Lévinas become director of the Ecole Normale Israélite Orientale. He was also subsequently appointed to posts at the Universities of Poitiers and Paris-Nanterre, and held the chair in philosophy at the Sorbonne from 1973 until his retirement in 1976. Lévinas's works include *Existence and Existents* (1947), *Time and the Other* (1948), *Totality and Infinity* (1961) and *Otherwise than Being, or, Beyond Essence* (1974).

Lévinas's thought is in many ways indebted to the combined influence of Husserlian and Heideggerian phenomenology. For Lévinas, Heidegger's *Being and Time* (1927) can be counted as 'one of the finest books in the history of philosophy [. . .] One of the finest among four or five others' (Lévinas 1995a, p. 37). Lévinas regards the phenomenological approach espoused by Heidegger in this work as paying dividends in terms of the insights it yields. Indeed, he criticises the later Heidegger for abandoning important elements contained within this approach. At the same time, however, Lévinas does not cleave to Heidegger's project as it is outlined in *Being and Time*. Such a project aims to elaborate a fundamental ontology of human Being-in-the-world. In contrast, Lévinas asserts the primacy of ethics *over* ontology. This path is pursued through the outlining of what Lévinas argues to be the essential and cognitively irreducible relation between the self (which Lévinas refers to as 'the same') and the 'other'. For Lévinas, *Being and Time* offers an account of the nature of human existence (Dasein) that stresses its 'pre-theoretical' understanding of Being. A Heideggerian analysis of the other, therefore, can be developed only by way of an initial ontological investigation of Dasein's existential composition. Thus, Heideggerian ontology begins by asserting the individuated nature of Dasein – most famously exemplified by the claim that the Being of Dasein is in each and every case 'mine'. Against this view, Lévinas argues for recognition of the metaphysical preconditions of all ontology. Such preconditions at the same time precede and exceed the 'mineness' of Dasein's immediate self-awareness.

The word 'metaphysics', it should be clear, has specific connotations for Lévinas. 'Metaphysics', in Lévinas's sense, is conjoined essentially with the other, for it alludes to the tendency of thought to transcend the limits of its own particularity and seek out the other. Metaphysics 'is turned toward the "elsewhere" and the "otherwise" and the "other"' (Lévinas 1998b, p. 33). On such a view, human self-understanding is not grounded in a subjective self-awareness that is thing-like, as the Heideggerian model implies. We may be a kind of entity in that we live in a concrete world of experience, but we are entities who are driven, and indeed constituted, by our desire for the other. This desire is not akin to the desire we feel when we wish to consume food, enjoy music, or indulge in the pleasures of a walk in the countryside. Having desired and then found such things, one consumes or indulges in it, and in this way satisfaction is derived from desire. Encountering the other offers no such satisfactions, since the other cannot be grasped and consumed with a view to negating one's desire for it. In so far as one desires the other, one is subject to a metaphysical desire. 'The metaphysical desire has another intention; it desires beyond everything that can complete it. It is like goodness – the Desired does not fulfil it, but deepens it' (p. 34). The 'I' can never subsume the other, for it cannot be incorporated into an individual's self-consciousness. This is because the desire for the other is the expression of a kind of relation with something that, from a conceptual point of view, is neither given nor conforms to a pre-established idea. Thus, the metaphysical desire for the other can never be reduced to the 'I' of subjectivity. As such, one's sense of self is placed in question by and through one's own desire for the other. All humans have this desire because no one is a separate and autonomous being. Above all, the relationship between metaphysical desire and its object (the other) cannot be articulated in terms of the concept of totality. There is a simple reason for this: the desire for the other is a desire for infinity and what is infinite breaks open the bonds of totality.

Viewed from the standpoint of the self, the other is heterogeneous. Being a self (an 'I'), Lévinas argues, means having 'identity as one's content'. This does not mean that the self possesses an essence or core that remains the same throughout life. Rather, the self or 'I' continually recuperates its identity in the activity of living. For instance, a person endures a chronic illness. Such an experience necessitates that person reinterpreting their identity, which is understood differently from how it was understood before. By the same token, the meaning of that person's past is transformed: 'I was that person, now I am this person'. In this way, one's past identity is continually rethought in terms of who one 'is'. Likewise, who one 'will be', is also reinterpreted by way of this. The ability to engage in such self-interpretation, however, presupposes something enduring. Lévinas refers to this as 'the primal identity, the primordial work of identification. The I [that] is identical in its very alterations' (p. 34). The 'work of identification', which one can regard as a phenomenological process of self-identification wherein the I is thought as I, secures the other's incommensurability with regard to the self. The I remains 'the same' since, through all the alterations and resulting reinterpretations of identity that mark a person's life, the I nevertheless can never be other than 'the same': it is governed by the rule of identity.

With regard to the other, Lévinas states that what is 'absolutely other [*Autre*] is the Other [*Autrui*]' (Lévinas 1998b, p. 39). To put matters more simply, the domain of the other is not impersonal. What can be encountered as radically or 'absolutely' other with regard to the I are others. In this sense, the 'Other' is always already an individual, a 'you'. Because of this, the relationship between the self and the Other is neither a unity nor a totality, for it cannot be grasped in terms of the identity of the self. I have a relationship to the Other in so far as and in virtue of the fact that I cannot exert total control over them. The Other occupies a space that is radically different from mine, and the metaphysical desire for the other is concentrated upon the existence of a personal Other: a being who escapes the mastery of the self, and who is desired all the more because of that. Fundamentally different, standing in a relationship that can only be grasped in terms of heterogeneity, what self and Other have in common is the fact that neither can be defined by way of reference to notions of 'genus'.

The relationship between the self and the other is enacted through language. Lévinas writes of this in terms of 'conversation' or 'discourse'. When engaged in conversation, I speak with the Other. Yet the very enactment of speech assures the continuation of my distance from them. In conversation one necessarily acknowledges the other as having 'a *right* over' the self's 'egoism' (Lévinas 1998b, p. 40). The relationship that conversation engenders cannot be unified by way of the egoism of the self. In so far as one thinks in relation to the other one necessarily engages in speech, and because no totality can be deduced from this relation speech is always anti-systematic. Because of this, Lévinas tells us, we ought not to be deluded into believing that the self is the bastion of resistance to notions of system and totality. On the contrary, such resistance accords with the presence of the other, which overturns the totality and unity that the notion of the self (the 'I' that thinks) implies.

Lévinas's account effectively holds the relation between same and other to be an absolute, in so far as it is irreducible. The irreducible nature of this relationship takes precedence both with regard to concepts and representations and above all with regard to all ontology. Put another way, the self–other relation has priority over all possible attitudes that one may have toward 'things' that 'are'. In Lévinas's view, the Western metaphysical tradition has concerned itself primarily with articulating the existence of entities in terms of their relation to the assumed primacy of the self. In doing this ontology promotes freedom: through an ontological understanding of the world, I necessarily grasp my relationship with that world in terms of myself. Freedom is posited in the sense that the persisting identity of the self is able to recuperate the world to itself. However, Lévinas urges us to acknowledge the primacy of something that escapes this kind of conceptualisation, that remains stubbornly outside the domain of the self. Only through respecting the exteriority of the other do we attain insight into the primacy of a metaphysical relation that is at once more essential and fundamental than any ontological structure: this relation is that of ethics.

What Lévinas refers to as 'the welcoming of the other by the same' initiates an ethical relation. It is ethical because 'welcoming' of necessity challenges the autonomy and freedom of the self and thereby transcends it. This metaphysical transcendence is ethical because in order for it to be possible the self must allow itself to be challenged by the other in order even to acknowledge it. This recognition is the consequence of an engagement with the other. It is the concrete nature of this engagement that poses a challenge to the primacy of ontology within Western thought. In so far as Western philosophy pursues freedom it thinks in opposition to the ethical relation. Such a tendency, Lévinas argues, can be identified in Heidegger's thought. In *Being and Time*, the essence of what is human is located in a fundamental ontological relation with the existent. Heideggerian ontology, in other words, transforms the existent into property and possession. Against this Lévinas argues that the ontologically oriented belief that the other can be reduced to the same must be supplanted by the acknowledgement that the other precedes all possible ontology. This does not mean abandoning the ideal of truth that is celebrated by the Western metaphysical tradition. Rather, Lévinas argues that the intention of this ideal can be realised only by entering into discourse with the other, and thereby paying homage to its priority over the self.

The other, we have already noted, always involves a personal relation (the Other) and is always encountered by way of the face. In recognising the face of another we are compelled to affirm alternative standpoints. In contrast to traditional ontology, which thinks of the paradigmatic case of the relation of immediacy as being found in the relation between thinking subject and pondered object, Lévinas argues that immediacy, if properly understood, is encountered in this 'face to face' encounter. The self, however, is prevented from grasping the face with a view to wrapping a concept around it. This is because the face resists any language that privileges conceptual understanding. When gazing upon another's face I do not encounter a 'thing-like' entity that resists me in the way in which an immovable object resists me. The face is not like a rock that challenges my power over it by resisting being smashed to pieces. The presence such resistance would still allow me to affirm that I have some power – just not enough to break the rock. In contrast, the face's resistance questions the self's 'ability for power', i.e. the very notion of something called 'my power' that can be exercised over a passive 'thing'. The relation with the Other is a relation with a 'someone', and that someone cannot be 'possessed' in the fashion in which a thing can be. Naturally, one can seek power over others. For example, one can aim to annihilate what, in the other, is resistant to power (as in the act of murder). But annihilation, Lévinas argues, is not the same as possession: one commits murder only when one wishes for power over what is immune to power. Murder may negate the Other as a sensible being, since the one who is killed is no longer 'there', but murder does not negate the Other itself. This is simply because what is opposed to the mastery of the self is not some greater or lesser degree of power. What is opposed to the self is the infinity of the Other's transcendence. The desire for mastery that drives the murderer derives from the recognition that what is absolutely other poses an inviolable threat to the very mastery, possession and control that the murderer aims to establish through the act of killing.

Lévinas often remarks that the face is 'nude'. The Other speaks to me, and when this happens I am presented with a 'naked' face. The fact that a face turns towards one to speak involves a non-systematic presentation, a relation that cannot be reduced in its significance to a theory or system. Theories and systems alike are only possible because a relation with the Other precedes them. In this way, the face challenges systematic ontology. Such a view involves staking the important claim that individuated self-consciousness, the 'I' of traditional ontology, can no longer be regarded as primary. Likewise, because the face speaks one realises something essential about language: language cannot be reduced in significance to nothing more than an act or expression of behaviour (although it is also that). Language presents us with the coincidence of 'the revealer and the revealed' and it does so by way of the face. Through the Other's speech one is presented with a mode of 'pure experience' that shows a realm of objectivity concealed from self-introspection: the objectivity of the Other is announced when they speak, for at that moment they are revealed as being independent of every subjective moment. Such objectivity of the Other shows that coexistence is a presupposition of all human life. Only by way of language is the self-Other relation actualised. This, Lévinas holds, is essential to the social domain. In conversation or discourse what is continually registered is the fundamentally incommensurable nature of self and Other. Language actualises the relationship between the self and the other and through language the self is presented with what transcends it own individuated self-consciousness. The voice of the Other is the voice of the 'stranger' and hence remains forever exterior to the self. By acknowledging the Other, the self discovers that it is a social being. Thus, it is not, as ontology strives to show, our relation to 'things' that is of decisive import, but the always already established relation between the same and the other that constitutes the fundamental fact of human existence. From this it follows that, for Lévinas, metaphysics is not to be regarded as something abstract or empty. On the contrary, metaphysics is concretely acted out all the time in the ethical relation that forms the basic condition of human existence. Metaphysics, in this sense, is neither a conceptual grasping nor a representing of 'things', but characterises the fabric of human life itself by showing us that human existence is social, that the world is always a shared world.

Through the desire for the Other the primacy of the self is thereby called into question. However, the transcendence that characterises the Other is not to be understood simply in terms of 'exteriority'. For, the Other is not simple exteriority with regard to the I. The very language of 'outside' and 'inside' is challenged by Lévinas in that for him the Other approaches the self 'from above', i.e. from an unassailable height. The Other's transcendence resides in the implicit recognition that it lies 'above' the self, that it abides in a state of absolute separation that will not yield to the self's desire for mastery. The self is called into question by language, which manifests the Other concretely by way of the face. The Other, in this way, speaks from the vantage point of a transcendence that arises from language. This 'height' is designated by Lévinas as 'teaching' and what is taught in the transcendence of the I by the Other is ethics. Such teaching does not involve a violent imposition, for no will is imposed here. What is taught is revealed, and what is revealed is violence. Recognition of the Other teaches the self that, through the pursuit of its pleasures and enjoyments, it itself is potential violence. Through such teaching I realise that others are there, too, and that they too are beings endowed with a freedom like mine. The infinite distance that separates the self and the Other is neither bridged nor reconciled by this teaching. The self realises that the freedom of the Other is 'like mine', that the Other's purposes and enjoyments are incompatible with its own. On this basis, the self realises that the social relation it is situated in always consists of different interests. The social realm, enacted as language, therefore announces the essentially ethical character of all human life. Through this the Other is necessarily acknowledged as a condition of all human possibility. In the very act of recognition of the face what one 'sees' is itself a breaking open or rupture of 'being'. To this extent, and in contrast with the spirit of the Heideggerian ontology of *Being and Time*, what makes us human arises from our ability to 'stand out' from being. We stand out from Being (i.e. from an ontologically determined world composed of entities) because we are first and foremost ethical and cannot therefore be reduced in our significance to the status of entities. All human life depends upon the acknowledgement of an ethical prohibition that forbids violence, even if such prohibition cannot prevent it factually. The implicit recognition of this prohibition involves the acknowledgement of the Other. Lévinas's conception of ethics, therefore, can be characterised in terms of alterity. A Lévinasian ethics is an ethics of exteriority. It is also an anti-humanist ethics, or rather a 'humanism of the Other'. In this regard, and against traditional ontology, we can say that it is the Other who is the measure of the self, not vice versa. Lévinas's work has both influenced and been engaged with by a wide range of theorists, such as **Irigaray** who, while finding much value in his writings, has argued that Lévinas views woman as nothing more than as a negative image of man rather than as being truly Other. Jacques **Derrida** has also developed a similar line of argument (for some discussion of these issues see Davis 1996).

[PS]

Further reading: Bernasconi and Critchley 1991; Critchley 1999; Davis 1996; Peperzak 1997.

LÉVI-STRAUSS, CLAUDE (1908–)

The Belgian-born cultural anthropologist Lévi-Strauss has made a fundamental contribution to the development of structuralism, in large part through the use of techniques derived from the linguistics of **Saussure** and **Jakobson** in the study of various aspects of culture, including kinship, myth and art. As an anthropologist, his clearest influences are perhaps those of Emile **Durkheim**, and especially Durkheim's nephew and colleague, Marcel **Mauss**. Both look to the way in which human societies are structured. Mauss's essay on the gift (1925) is of greatest significance here. Mauss argues that relationships of gift exchange (or reciprocity) are to be found in various forms in all cultures, and crucially, that gift exchange is a total social fact – i.e. as a way of organising social behaviour and interaction, it has ramifications well beyond its obvious sphere of operation, so that the gift exchange could organise legal, political and religious life, as well as the economic. Lévi-Strauss himself picks up on the custom of southern France, of diners pouring the contents of small bottles of wine into their neighbour's glass (1969, pp. 58–60). Nobody comes out of this exchange with more or less wine than they would have had without the exchange. The exchange is purely a ritual of social contact. Lévi-Strauss is, like Mauss, concerned with the analysis of the structures that underpin and organise the surface phenomena of everyday life, and to recognise how these structures are manifest in diverse cultures. In effect, where much twentieth-century cultural anthropology has tended to emphasise the differences between human cultures (and ultimately the relativism of values and beliefs), Lévi-Strauss emphasises what humans have in common, and therefore also resists any temptation to place cultures in a hierarchy of cultural progress or complexity.

Lévi-Strauss's (1969) first major study, written in the United States during the Second World War, was of the structures of kinship. Marriage is understood as a system of exchange (with women being the medium of exchange). The incest taboo ensures that families must find marriage partners from other groups. Two structures of exchange are then identified. In restricted exchange, the exchange occurs between two groups, so that when a man from group X marries a woman from group Y, a man from group Y will marry a woman from group X. In generalised exchange, the marriage exchanges occur between an extended set of groups, so that a man from group A marries a woman from group B; a man from group B marries a woman from group C (not A); a man from group C marries a woman from group D; and a man from group D marries a woman from group A. *The Elementary Structures of Kinship* (1949) explores how these two basic structures are manifest in different cultures.

Lévi-Strauss's work on myth further extends the notion of structural analysis. He begins with mythologies as they have been collected in empirical fieldwork (and it is worth noting that for all his emphasis on explanation and analysis, Lévi-Strauss (1975) places great value on the importance of fieldwork in the training and development of an anthropologist). From these data, Lévi-Strauss is concerned not merely with uncovering the structure of particular myths, but also with revealing a structure that is common to a range of particular myths, often in widely different cultures. The myths as they are known to the member of the society (and as it might be recorded by an anthropologist or traveller) are but the manifestation or expression of the underlying (and unconscious) structure – and this structure is the real myth. A myth is therefore treated as a combination of meaningful elements (or symbols) that are combined together according to a limited set of laws (governing their combination and transformation). Lévi-Strauss's (1968b) own illustration is useful here. He breaks down the Oedipus myth into a sequence of eight elements. He then regroups these elements, breaking up the narrative order of the story, to suggest that certain elements are concerned with common themes. Thus, 'Cadmos seeks his sister, Europa, ravished by Zeus' 'Oedipus marries his mother Jocaster' and 'Antigone buries her brother Polynices, despite prohibition'; are all to do with incest (the overvaluing of blood relationships). Other elements undervalue blood relationships. The third and fourth groups respectively concern monsters being slain, and humans who are, to some degree monstrous. Put slightly differently, the third group concerns humanity denying its bestial origin, while group four acknowledges that origin. Thus, we find two 'binary oppositions', and note that group one stands to group two as group three stands to group four. These pairs come together in the opposition between the beliefs that the human species must have a non-human origin, and yet that all individual humans are born of the union of man and woman.

Lévi-Strauss draws a number of implications from this sort of analysis. As has already been suggested, this structure will be found in other myths. Similarly, different versions of the Oedipus myth will still reflect this same structure. From the centrality of binary oppositions, Lévi-Strauss suggests, first, that the wide, cross-cultural dispersal of myths (in the sense of the underlying, unconscious structure) is because myths are structured by the human mind (and the mind works by ordering the world in terms of binary oppositions). But further, myth in general is about these binary oppositions, or more precisely, it is about contradictions and paradoxes. Myth is an attempt to reconcile the irreconcilable: one and multiplicity; identity and difference; life and death; belief and reality. Because a myth is a 'logic model' attempting (vainly) to overcome these contradictions, it will generate ever more versions of itself.

[AE]

Further reading: Badcock 1975; Geertz 1973, 1988; Hayes and Hayes 1974; Leach 1970.

LUKÁCS, GYORGY (1885–1971)

The Hungarian philosopher and literary critic Gyorgy (or Georg) Lukács had an major influence on the development of Western **Marx**ism (that is to say, the largely **Hegel**ian Marxism developed in Western Europe), while also being the most sophisticated literary critic within the Soviet Union. His career can be divided into three phases. There is an initial non-Marxist phase; a transition to Marxism; and the application and development of a socialist realist literary criticism.

Lukács's *The Theory of the Novel* (1916), written during the final years before the First World War, is an approach to literature that is deeply indebted to Hegel, and especially Hegel's aesthetics. It is a pessimistic work, focusing on the way in which the novel deals with the meaninglessness of the contemporary social world. Lukács describes the social world as confronting its members as a 'second nature' of senseless conventions, so that they are, paradoxically, homeless in the world that should be their home. *The Theory of the Novel* is therefore, in all but name, a theorisation of alienation. The great novel copes with this, not by attempting to impose meaning upon a meaningless world, but by being an art form that is grounded in process (rather than the presentation of a finished product), so that the search for meaning comes to express the absence of meaning and the failure of that search.

If *The Theory of the Novel* laments the loss of a meaningful human community (represented by ancient Greece), or human society as a 'totality', Lukács's great work in Marxist philosophy, *History and Class Consciousness* (1922), finds this totality in the communist revolution. The communist revolution gives the world back to humanity. The world is once again meaningful, and the Communist Party is then credited with the task of leading the proletariat to its destiny as – in Hegelian terminology – the subject-object of history. That is to say that the proletariat, once fully conscious of their place in history, will be able to make history as they please, rather than being controlled by the external force of 'second nature'.

In addition to this theorisation of revolution, which gives it its optimism, the book also provides an analysis of the failures and contradictions of capitalism, most particularly the elaboration of Marx's theory of commodity fetishism alongside Max **Weber**'s account of bureaucracy, into a theory of reification (*Verdinglichung*) that provides an explanation of the economic and political mechanisms that underpin and generate second nature. Marx had provided an analysis of the process by which relationships between human beings (i.e. the meetings of human beings in commercial exchange in the market) take on the appearance of relationships between things (such that the relationships between humans come to be governed by the properties – and particularly the economic values – that appear to be inherent to the commodities exchanged). For Lukács this inversion is manifest in all social relations (and not merely in the economy), as in an increasingly rationalised and bureaucratic society, that which is qualitative, unique and subjective in human relationships is lost, as they are governed according to the purely quantitative concerns of the bureaucrat and the manager.

Finally, the book is also a rereading of the German idealist tradition in philosophy. The limitations and contradictions found in the work of **Kant** and Hegel, and not interpreted as the weaknesses of Kant and Hegel as individual thinkers, rather as Kant and Hegel taking the thought of their age to its limits (and thus to the point at which it breaks down). The thinker is thus seen as being conditioned by his or her age, and contradictions in thought reflect conditions in the economic base. Such an approach to intellectual and cultural products is of enormous influence on the analyses of art and culture carried out by other Western Marxists, such as **Horkheimer** and **Adorno**.

For the greater part of his life, Lukács lived and worked within the Soviet Union. His literary criticism worked largely within the restrictions imposed by the Soviet Communist Party (Lukács 1963, 1983). In various studies he articulated and defended a theory of realism, often in opposition to the modernism of capitalist culture. A realist novel (with Balzac being exemplary) expresses society as a totality that underpins the fragmentary surface that is encountered in everyday life. Lukács is thus critical of the naturalism of Zola or Flaubert, precisely because it remains a description of the surface. In contrast, the characters in Balzac's novels represent social forces. What is perhaps disappointing about Lukács's approach to literature, especially in contrast to the insightful materialist reading of philosophy in *History and Class Consciousness* (and even the literary criticism of his pre-Marxist work), is that he judges literature against a pre-existing model of society. He does not allow the novel to teach him what society is like. His debate with Ernst **Bloch** over expressionism is instructive (Bloch *et al.* 1977). For Lukács, expressionism is indicative of bourgeois decadence and irrationality – and thus the very inability of the bourgeoisie to grasp or acknowledge the totality of social forces – while for Bloch it is indicative of the fragmentary (or in his terminology, non-synchronous) nature of capitalism.

[AE]

Further reading: Arato 1979; Kadarkay 1995; Lichtheim 1970; Lunn 1982; Parkinson 1977; Pike 1985; Sim 1994.

LYOTARD, JEAN-FRANÇOIS (1925–1998)

A French philosopher of the post-structuralist school, Lyotard is perhaps best known for his book *The Postmodern Condition: A Report on Knowledge* (1979). In that work, Lyotard attempted to define the principle aspects of postmodernity in the wake of developing technology. Technology transforms knowledge:

> We can predict that anything in the constituted body of knowledge that is not translatable in this way will be abandoned . . . the direction of new research will be dictated by the possibility of its eventual results being translatable into computer language.
>
> (Lyotard 1979, p. 4)

Thought, then, becomes subject to 'the hegemony of computers', and the thinking subject is displaced by the inherently machinic tendencies of modern technology. Postmodernism fits into this scenario in that it embodies a critique of the subject, for whom knowledge, under the conditions dictated by technology, becomes externalised. Knowledge, transformed in this way, becomes linked to exchange value and the play of exterior forces. Lyotard thus defines the postmodern in relation to the immanent consequences of technical/scientific knowledge forms, but also in connection with alternative 'narrative knowledge' forms (1979, p. 7).

Scientific knowledge, Lyotard claims, is not a 'totality', but exists in relation to the larger domain of narrative knowledges, which it has a tendency to exclude. These latter, however, form the basis of social cohesion. Science requires one discursive practice in order to function, which relies on the assumed existence of criteria of evidence (the empirical level), and the belief that an empirical referent cannot provide two contradictory proofs. This, for Lyotard, is science's 'metaphysical' assumption, which it itself cannot prove. On the social level, however, this assumption, in excluding other knowledge forms, has the effect of splitting science off from the social order, and the relationship between knowledge and society 'becomes one of mutual exteriority' (pp. 24, 25). This, in turn, demonstrates that it is not possible to judge the validity of scientific claims by reference to narrative knowledge claims, or vice versa. Questions of legitimation stem from this tension, in so far as the development of 'postmodern science' (p. 60) has demonstrated the futility of trying to construct 'grand narratives' which seek to describe the totality of experience. Experience itself thus exceeds the limits of cognitive grasp. Postmodernism steps in at this point as a pragmatic response to the problem of legitimation which attempts to provide alternative narratives, but nevertheless spurns the pretension to universal knowledge claims.

Fragmentation is, however, a consequence of science itself. Lyotard notes that, in the same way that Nietzsche's diagnosis of European nihilism turned on the idea of science as having reached the point of realising that it itself did not match up to its own criteria for truth, so, too, the search for legitimation, which defines all knowledge forms, has a natural tendency to arrive at the point of delegitimation (p. 39). In other words, knowledge always finds itself to be rooted in unprovable assumptions. Hence the possibility of error is teleologically encoded into the project of knowledge. Thus, Lyotard concludes that the destruction of grand narratives is a result inherent in the search for knowledge itself. What he terms 'postmodern scientific knowledge' (p. 54) is therefore an immanent condition of all knowledge. Grand narratives are, in consequence, best replaced by 'little narrative[s]' oriented towards 'a multiplicity of finite meta-arguments' (pp. 60, 66).

In his later writings, principally in *The Differend: Phrases in Dispute* (1983), Lyotard adopted a rather different approach. In this text, he develops a conventionalist philosophy of language which works in terms of what he calls 'phrases' and 'genres'. A 'phrase' can be any form of utterance and is composed of four 'instances' (an addressor, an addressee, a sense and a referent) (section 25). It is not necessary that all of the instances be 'marked' (i.e. that there be a named addressor or addressee, a determined sense, or a designated referent) in order for a phrase to function. Every phrase presents a 'phrase universe', and determines the nature of each universe according to the way in which each of the four 'instances' that constitute it function in relation to one another (section 28). There are many different kinds of phrases, e.g. cognitive, aesthetic, ethical, political. Lyotard characterises each of these phrases as belonging to different 'phrase regimens'. Phrases belonging to different regimens are heterogeneous and, cannot therefore be translated into one another (section 178).

Genres of discourse differ from regimens in that they provide rules for linking phrases together in particular ways according to particular purposes (sections 179ff). Significantly, it is not possible to validate any genre of discourse from outside itself by way of resorting to a meta-language. It therefore follows that, just as the cognitive phrase regimen is one regimen among many, the cognitive genre is likewise merely one among many genres. The legitimation of genres is therefore a matter of internal consistency and cannot be deduced from any position external to them. Regimens, in contrast to genres, do not stipulate rules of linking. They are non-teleological and contain the 'rules of formation' whereby a phrase can be characterised as being cognitive, ostensive, etc. But these rules in no way prescribe which phrase from which regimen ought next to be linked onto the preceding phrase. Linking, it follows, is necessary; but how to link is contingent (section 136). It is hence impossible to assert legitimately from a position outside the cognitive genre that one ought to link on to a cognitive phrase with another compatible with the rules of that genre. In a manner akin to *The Postmodern Condition*, this argument precludes any establishment of meta-narratives external to the cultural conditions under which genres are formulated and put into practice.

What Lyotard does attempt to make room for, however, are those instances of phrases which cannot be voiced within a particular genre. Such phrases would be the phrases of victims who, because of the way in which genres operate, are silenced by them. These phrases Lyotard terms 'differends'. A differend is thus characterised as 'a damage accompanied by the loss of means to prove the damage' (section 7). Lyotard here gives the example of a French citizen who is a Martinican: such a person cannot complain about the possible wrongs they may suffer as a result of being a French citizen because the genre of French law, as the only genre in which such a complaint could be lodged, prevents the possibility of making it. A differend is thus 'the unstable state and instant of language wherein something which must be put into phrases cannot yet be' (section 22). In arguing that such phrases must be phrased (as a matter of principle), *The Differend* announces its ethical concerns – and these concerns are presented in terms of the proper goal of culture. 'Culture', Lyotard argues in a manner once again reminiscent of *The Postmodern Condition*, has come to mean 'the putting into circulation of information rather than the work that needs to be done in order to arrive at presenting what is not presentable under the circumstances' (1993, p. 260). With this statement one may conclude that Lyotard's later work, in so far as it establishes its own stakes in terms of arguing for the need to voice differends, conceives of right in terms of a view of culture voiced as far back as 1962, in the essay 'Dead Letter': 'Culture is lending an ear to what strives to be said, culture is giving a voice to those who do not have a voice and whom seek one' (1993, p. 33).

[PS]

Further reading: Bennington 1988; Readings 1991.

MACINTYRE, ALASDAIR (1929–)

Scottish-born philosopher, whose book *After Virtue* (1981) posed a major challenge to many more orthodox approaches to moral and political philosophy, and has stimulated a revival of virtue ethics. *After Virtue* begins with what MacIntyre calls a 'disquieting suggestion'. He imagines a society in which knowledge of science as a comprehensive system has been lost. All that remains are a few fragments of the old learning, but these are largely misunderstood precisely because the context that gave them their power and significance has been lost. He then asserts that this is the condition that our morality and moral language has fallen into since the Enlightenment. A moral language derived from Aristotle is being used, despite the fact that the concrete ground that gave sense to that language, the communal existence of the ancient Greek cities, has been lost. This leads all contemporary moral philosophies to collapse into forms of emotivism, where moral language can do nothing more than express the speaker's subjective feelings and preferences (so that 'Killing is wrong' simply means 'I do not approve of killing' or 'I am distressed by killing'). Moral argument would then be futile. MacIntyre therefore seeks to reinstate a Aristotelian ground to morality, specifically by raising the problem of the purpose (*telos*) of human life, and recognising how responses to that problem are based in communal life.

The concept of 'virtue' is central to MacIntyre's argument, and is analysed in terms of three components. First, a virtue is that quality which allows a person to enjoy the 'internal goods' of a 'practice'. A practice is a 'complex form of socially established' human behaviour. Baseball is a practice; merely throwing a ball is not. Internal goods are the things and experiences of value that one gets from participating in the practice. The money the baseball player earns is external to the practice, but the satisfaction from pitching a fast ball at tactically the right moment is unique and intrinsic to the game. MacIntyre's point, in large part, is that because practices are social and cultural activities, the goals that an individual human pursues are not crudely a matter of personal preference (as some forms of liberalism might claim), but come from the individual's involvement in society. The problem in contemporary society is that there is a plethora of competing practices. How is the individual to choose? Again, for MacIntyre, this question is not answered through subjective preference, but through the sort of story one wants to tell about one's life. It is not enough to say simply that I enjoy playing or watching baseball. I have to address deeper questions about the sort of practice baseball is, how it is to be played and developed, and how it relates to other activities and events (such as the pressures of commercialism). Thus one inquires into, and tells morally significant stories about, the sort of people who should be the heroes and heroines of the practice. Hence, the second element of virtue is narrative. Humans are seen as story-telling animals. The activities in which we engage are not intrinsically meaningful, but make sense only because of the broader context of life and culture within which they are performed. A virtuous person is thus on a quest to make sense of their lives, to bring some sort of unity to their participation in, and choice between, diverse practices. Ultimately one suggests (and tries to live) an answer to the question as to what the good life for a human being might be. The third element of virtue is tradition. Again, one's life is not lived or interpreted in isolation. Humans are historical beings, and the cultures in which they live furnish them with a complex web of resources, debts and expectations in accord with which they must make sense of their lives, and justify themselves to others. For MacIntyre tradition is not a dead weight that simply determines the preferences and goals of the members of the community, but is rather something vital, the future of which is being actively contested. What it means to be a baseball player (or a teacher, or a Scot) will be disputed, will draw upon different examples from, and different interpretations of, the past, and will develop in the search for new solutions to the challenges of the present. Virtue is the quality of honesty and courage in understanding oneself and one's community that sustains the vitality of a tradition.

MacIntyre's account has been accused of relativism, in the sense that what is virtuous (and thus morally good) seems to be relative to the particular tradition within which the question is posed. In subsequent books, especially *Whose Justice? Which Rationality?* (1988) and *Three Rival Versions of Moral Enquiry* (1990), he has tried to respond to this problem by exploring in much concrete detail the idea of the 'rationality of traditions', focusing upon the resources that a tradition has for calling itself into question, and for entering into dialogue with other traditions.

[AE]

Further reading: Horton and Mendus 1994; McMylor 1994.

MALRAUX, ANDRÉ (1901–1976)

In many respects the model of an engaged intellectual, Malraux's extraordinary life embraced adventure (collecting art works in Indochina), political struggle against colonialism, armed struggle (in the Spanish Civil War, French army and Resistance, for which he received the Légion d'honneur), and work as a minister in de Gaulle's post-war governments. His writings include a series of novels (Malraux 1934, 1938, 1952), semi-autobiographical reflections (1968, 1977) and studies of artists (1976) and art history (1949–1950, 1978). The theme that unifies this writing is a struggle to understand how a human should live – in an increasingly secular world after the 'death of God' – in the face of the absurd and meaningless contingencies of death, dependency and humiliation. The novels explore this basically existentialist theme through the possibilities of political commitment and human fraternity. The later writings present artistic creativity as humanity's self-affirmation in the face of its absurd destiny.

In *The Voices of Silence* (1951), Malraux ultimately confronts the problem of nihilism, but does so only after a complex and at times rhapsodic exploration of the global history of art. *Voices* has four parts. The first, 'Museum without Walls', examines the impact of photography on our understanding of art; 'The Metamorphosis of Apollo' and 'The Creative Process' examine the nature of change in art and the development of the individual artist respectively; while the final part, 'Aftermath of the Absolute', explores the fate of art after the European Enlightenment.

Modern photography has made possible the reproduction, and thus wide dissemination, of works of art. Malraux's argument is here indebted to **Benjamin**'s (1970b) analysis of the 'Work of Art in the Age of Mechanical Reproduction' (1936), although there is a difference in emphasis. Malraux is not concerned by the potential that photographic reproduction has to destroy the unique aura of the art work, but rather with the implications that reproduction has for the practice of the museum. In effect, the possibility of reproducing and juxtaposing diverse works of art amplifies what already occurs in museums. Museums collect and juxtapose art works created in different places and times. As such the museum is the foundation of art history, for it allows art works to be compared and classified. Now that process of comparison can be taken further, by juxtaposing mere photographs. That which is previously unavailable to public view is made available. But further, the photograph has an independence from its original, for by the devices of framing and selecting details of a work, lighting (for example of a sculpture or carving) and through the scale of the reproduction (so that miniatures can appear on the same scale as monumental bas-reliefs), the photograph effectively creates new art works. *Voices* is, of course, itself a prime example, with over 400 illustrations stretching from cave paintings to examples of twentieth-century modernism, and covering the products of six continents. (A merit of the 1978 Princeton edition is that it retains the distinctive 1950s reproductions, themselves now alien to our modern expectations of reproductive fidelity.)

Malraux's analysis is not merely of the museum, for the absorption of non-European art, folk and so-called primitive art is also characteristic of modern art. (Malraux was apprenticed to Daniel-Henry Kahnweiler, Picasso's art dealer and author of one of the first books on cubism.) Malraux thus presents the development of modern European art in terms of the explicit recognition, first by Goya, Hals and Rembrandt, that the plastic arts had their own language, in that painting was not the mere narration of external events, but is rather a matter of composition and the articulation of colour and line. Art thereby becomes conscious of its concern with style; with the way in which an object can be made into a painting or sculpture (by being reduced to two dimensions, or having its movement stilled). In this context, the career of the individual artist is not one of developing an innate talent to represent the external world. The artist rather has an impulse for art, and the young artist copies not the world, but other works of art. The artist's development comes as they recognise a conflict between the existing style of art and the art that they want to achieve. Art develops through a dissatisfaction with the past.

For Malraux the modern, post-Enlightenment age is one of agnosticism. The religious absolute has been replaced by scientific reason and new political freedoms. Art, however, challenges religion by presenting itself as absolute. The Romantic rebellion of the artist thus becomes a further precondition of the museum without walls, for it leads to the recognition of a continuum of art. Individual works and styles are stripped of their historical and cultural contexts, so that they may be juxtaposed, crucially without the antagonism that might be inherent, for example, in the religious or political value systems which they originally served. Other cultures are revealed not as rivals to our own, but rather as different visions of the same fundamental problem, that of the human condition. In his concluding reflections Malraux suggests that his humanism, fought for in the face of the threat of nihilism (that would see human cultures as of little more importance than a meadow ablaze with spring flowers), can be formulated thus: 'We have refused to do what the beast within us willed to do, and we wish to rediscover Man wherever we discover that which seeks to crush him to the dust' (Malraux 1978, p. 642). The fundamental value of art, revealed in modernism and in the global perspective of the museum without walls, is humanity's struggle against everything that would crush it to dust.

[AE]

Further reading: Lacouture 1975; Lyotard 1999; Madsen 1977; Thompson and Vigginai 1984.

MARX, KARL (1818–1883)

Political philosopher and social and economic analyst, whose work centres on a detailed analysis of capitalism, and particularly on the dynamics and class relationships within it. It may be seen as a fusion of German idealist philosophy (and especially that of **Hegel** and the Young Hegelians), British economics (for example, of Adam **Smith** and David Ricardo) and French socialism and positivism (including the work of Saint-Simon and Charles Fourier). His work has been of immense influence on global politics (so that by the 1980s, and prior to the disintegration of the Soviet bloc, some one-third of the world's population lived under a regime that claimed to be based upon his work).

Marx's philosophy may be initially characterised in terms of his understanding of what it is to be human. Human beings are labourers, which is to say that they are distinguished from all other animals in being self-conscious producers of their environments. Marx compares bees and architects (1976, p. 284). While a bee may produce a hive that is more elegant than the human architect's building, the best of bees is still inferior to the worst of architects, for the bee is driven purely by instinct, while the architect has constructed the building in their mind first. Human beings therefore have the potential to construct, not simply the physical environment, but the society of their choice. Humans, unlike other animals, can create themselves. Historical societies have failed to realise this ideal, partly because, as Marx argues, humans create history, but not under the conditions of their choosing (1973b, p. 146). Marx's philosophy is therefore devoted to analysing how existing historical conditions have come about, how they hinder the realisation of human potential, and how that potential can be realised.

As a materialist, Marx argues that human consciousness is ultimately a product of matter, which is to say, of the human engagement with the material world through labour. The very fact that humans are conscious, as well as the particular form which that consciousness takes, is a result of the state of economic production in a given society. Human history is therefore to be understood primarily in terms of changes in the economy. Early in his intellectual development, Marx uses a metaphor from architecture to characterise society. Just as the foundations (or base) restrict the sort of building (or superstructure) that can be constructed upon them, so the economy is the base of society (1975, pp. 424–428). The superstructure includes cultural activities (including the arts and religion), family life, aspects of the law and civil society.

The economy is analysed in terms of the contradiction existing between the 'forces of production' and the 'relations of production' (1975, pp. 424–426). The forces of production are composed of the technology available to the society. Thus, the only sources of power available to a feudal society are animals or other natural phenomena (such as wind and water). Capitalism has steam and other industrial power sources. Marx presupposes that there is a continual refinement of the forces of production, so that technological innovation gives society greater productive capacity. The relations of production are the relationships that exist between the producers and those who control production. After the earliest human societies ('primitive communism'), all societies have been divided in terms of two principal classes. An individual's class position is defined by their relationship to the economy. The subordinate class is composed of those who directly produce the society's goods and services. The dominant class does not itself produce, but lives by expropriating the products of the subordinate class's labour. The relationships between these classes will be determined by the potential of the forces of production. In feudalism the labourer is bound to the land, with the land being owned and controlled by the lord. A proportion of the feudal peasant's product is expropriated by the lord. In contrast, the capitalist forces of production allow new power sources to run many machines, which are brought together into the large productive units of the factory. Labour must therefore be freed from the land, and allowed to move freely to the (urban) factories. Feudal relations are therefore replaced by the capitalist labour market (where the proletariat sell their ability to labour to the highest capitalist bidder). While forces of production are dynamic, the relations of production are inflexible (not least because they enshrine the political interests of the existing dominant class). The transition from feudalism to capitalism therefore occurs violently. It requires a new class (the bourgeoisie or capitalists) to emerge to take control of the economy, imposing new relations of production that will allow the realisation of the productive potential that is present in the most advanced technology. Marx's contention is that with the development of capitalist industry in the nineteenth century, the forces of production have developed to such a degree that economic inequality and class exploitation is no longer necessary. The current subordinate class, the proletariat, can realise the equality and justice of a classless communist society, that such productivity makes possible. The goal of Marx's philosophy is therefore to facilitate the proletariat's revolutionary struggle to take control of the economy, and thus to transform it to fulfil the needs of all human beings.

The failings of capitalist society may be understood in terms of either exploitation or alienation. In his later work (1973a, 1976), Marx focuses upon the way in which exploitation is realised through commodity exchange. The labourer receives what appears to be a fair wage from a free labour market. However, the capitalist sells the finished product for more than the cost (including labour) of its production. The discrepancy between the value of the labour that is incorporated in the product, and the price that the capitalist receives is 'surplus-value'. Exploitation in capitalism is thus concealed behind the illusion of fair exchange, for both the labour market and the market for finished goods appear to be free and competitive. In his earlier writings Marx (1975) focuses on the way in which capitalism corrupts the potential for self-creation and the free transformation of the environment that is inherent in labour. The division of labour in capitalism entails that labour cannot be a fulfilling productive activity, for the labourer has no control over what they produce or what happens to that product. In addition, the fragmentation of the production process entails that the labourer never produces a complete product, or fully understands the production process in which they are employed.

All historical societies are characterised by class conflict, yet it is the nature of this conflict that is significant. While any given society may end in violent revolution, the class struggle prior to revolution is as much to do with culture as it is to do with the exercise of violence. The base–superstructure metaphor helps to articulate a theory of ideology. For Marx, an ideology is not merely a belief system. It is rather a set of beliefs that construe the world in a way that is in the interests of the ruling class. If the subordinate class accepts this view of the world, then it will accept the inevitability or legitimacy of the ruling class's dominance. (Thus, Marx observes, the ideas of the ruling class are the ruling ideas.) Hence, in feudalism, Christianity served to legitimise the existing social order by presenting it as God-given. The cultural activities of the superstructure, including religion, the arts and popular entertainment, and the educational system, may therefore simply be analysed as politically reactionary forces, a dominant ideology that maintains existing power structures. In his later writings, Marx suggests that in capitalism such ideologies are substituted, in large part, by the apparent fairness of commodity exchange, and more profoundly, by the phantasmagorical appearance of commodity exchange, such that seems to have an independence from the human labour that has gone into producing and sustaining it (Marx 1976, pp. 163–177). In calling this commodity fetishism, Marx is suggesting that in contemporary society human beings come to worship as divine and mysterious their own creations (just as supposedly primitive religions worship human images as gods).

Marx's earlier writings give a different account of ideology, that is expressed not least in his observation that religion is 'the opium of the masses' (1975, p. 244). Even in capitalism, religion serves to inhibit revolutionary activity, for example by promising the obedient poor compensation in the afterlife. More profoundly, however, Marx suggests that religion, like opium, is a stimulant to dreams (manifest in religious imagery and theology). The dreams are not mere delusions, but in their aspiration to a better life (for example, in the image of justice represented by the Christian idea of heaven), indicate something of what is at fault with existing society. Religion is the 'expression of real suffering and a protest against real suffering' (ibid.). Marx's point is that revolutionary action should not dismiss such dreams, but attempt to realise them in this world, rather than in the afterlife. (The meek inheriting the earth, for example, becomes a political imperative, not mere metaphysical yearning.) From this, it may be suggested that art, and indeed the cultural superstructure as a whole, in so far as it too is capable of expressing the real suffering, does not just function to maintain the existing political order, but is rather a site of struggle and a source of political motivation.

Marx writes little explicitly on art or culture. A short passage in his draft notes, *Grundrisse* (1857–1858), suggests that he saw art as having a problematic relationship to the economy. He observes, with reference to the ancient Greek epics and Greek tragic drama:

> Certain significant forms within the realm of the arts are possible only at an underdeveloped stage of artistic development. . . . . What chance has Vulcan against Roberts and Co., Jupiter against the lightning-rod and Hermes against the Crédit Mobilier? . . . Greek art presupposes Greek mythology, i.e. nature and the social forms already reworked in an unconsciously artistic way by the popular imagination.
>
> (Marx 1973a, p. 110)

The problem here is that while Greek art may, as the materialist would expect, bear marks of the economic and social formation within which it was produced, Marx cannot then account for the fact that modern humanity continues to derive pleasure and insight from this art.

[AE]

Further reading: Althusser 1969; Barrett 1980; Bottomore 1983; Carver 1991; G. Cohen 1978; Cunningham-Wood 1988; Giddens 1973; McLellan 1973; Mandel 1972; Mészáros 1986; R. Norman 1980; R. Williams 1977.

MAUSS, MARCEL (1872–1950)

French anthropologist whose work, built upon that of his uncle Emile **Durkheim**, played a major part in the development of the theory of cultural anthropology. Mauss influenced, among others, the structuralist anthropologist Claude **Lévi-Strauss** (1987).

A central concern of Mauss's is the impact that culture (as opposed to nature) has upon human development and behaviour. This is most graphically illustrated in his essay on the 'Techniques of the Body' (1935), which explores the differences in the way in which individuals of different cultures hold and use their bodies. That which is taken for granted in the mundane practices of standing, sitting and moving is revealed as being open to sociological explanation. It is not just a brute natural fact. Similarly, in an early essay on magic (1902–1903), Mauss (1972) identifies magic as a personal phenomenon (for the magician typically uses their powers for individual, rather than communal, benefit). Yet, further analysis demonstrates that magical powers are derived from socially recognised forms of religion and ritual, not least from the phenomenon known in the Pacific Islands as *mana*. *Mana*, although ultimately escaping definition, is broadly understood as the spiritual force recognised by the community. It can accumulate in individuals (giving them magical power, prestige or charisma), or even in objects. Thus for Mauss, a seemingly personal and natural phenomenon, such as an individual's charisma, is grounded in the rituals and beliefs that are facilitating the circulation of spiritual and emotional energy about the society.

The explanatory power of Mauss's essays tends to lie, not simply in the examination of the empirical details of a culture, but rather in the recognition of how diverse strands of social and psychological life are woven together through what he comes to call 'total social facts'. A total social fact is such that it informs and organises seemingly quite distinct practices and institutions. Mauss's most famous example of this is *The Gift* (1925). A gift is characterised by socially enforced obligations to give, to receive and to reciprocate, and as such grounds a form of exchange that is quite distinct from modern market exchanges. In the example of the *kula* rings of the Trobriand Islands, a trading party visiting a neighbouring island carries two types of goods. One type is the useful goods to be traded or bartered. A second type are ritual objects, imbued with great spiritual value (akin to *mana*). Only with the giving and acceptance of these ritual gifts are cordial relationships established, and the threat of violence dispelled, so that trading may then take place. Gifts are not kept though, but will be given, in turn, by the recipient as part of their own subsequent trading expeditions, thus moving the gifts about a circle of islands. Crucially, the gift relationship is therefore serving to underpin communal relationships between the islands, sustaining a trust and moral obligation that bartering or market exchange alone could not sustain. The 'big men' of the Pacific Islands and the *potlatch* of the Canadian Pacific Indians illustrate a further dimension of the gift. In giving a gift the receiver becomes obligated to the giver. The giver thus potentially gains status and political power through giving. If the recipient cannot reciprocate, and significantly cannot reciprocate with bigger gifts, status is lost in comparison to the original donor. Gifts may then be part of brutal and destructive competitions, that establish and challenge political hierarchies. Elsewhere gift relationships may be seen in the movement of women and dowries in marriage. In contemporary society, the rituals of exchange at Christmas and other festivals illustrate the continuing significance of gift exchange in maintaining communal relations.

[AE]

Further reading: Lévi-Strauss 1987.

MERLEAU–PONTY, MAURICE (1907–1961)

French philosopher and psychologist, who developed an approach to phenomenology that centred upon the embodied nature of human existence. Merleau-Ponty's work encompasses psychology (Merleau-Ponty 1963) and the attempt to articulate a humanist **Marx**ism (1964a, 1973a) as well as the philosophies of perception (1962), language and semiotics (1964b), aesthetics (1994) and ontology (1968). At the core of all this work is an aversion to Cartesian dualism. **Descartes** approached the problems of modern philosophy by defending the primacy and autonomy of the rational reflective individual human subject (the *cogito*). This subject's relation to the external world, including its own body, is principally one of rational understanding. It stands outside the world, and is capable of undistorted and certain knowledge of that world. Even in his first major work, *The Structure of Behaviour* (1942), Merleau-Ponty (1963) challenges this assumption. He argues that the world is not to be understood as a source of isolated stimuli (as behavioural psychology argues) that have pre-existing meanings in demanding determinate responses from the human subject. Rather individual stimuli are irreducibly part of a shifting structure of meanings and symbols, and the meaning of (and thus the subject's response to) any given stimulus depends upon the structure within which the stimulus occurs. The human subject thus responds to this world, not through the detached reflection of the Cartesian *cogito*, but through pre-reflective and practical participation within it. The subject is not independent of the world, but is as much a part of this structure as the stimulus itself. The meaningful relationship of the subject to its world is thus one that is primarily lived rather than rationally understood, and as such the subject is incapable of absolute and certain knowledge. What it knows, it knows because of what it is now.

This theme is developed in Merleau-Ponty's (1962) best known essay, *Phenomenology of Perception* (1945). The rejection of the Cartesian subject is here developed in a profound exploration of the 'lived-body'. Human existence is necessarily embodied. This is to say far more than the Cartesian might: that the mind is situated within a physical body. For Merleau-Ponty, a subject does not consciously pilot its body, as if it were a complex machine made up of muscles, nerves and bones. First, the parts of a body are not 'side-by-side' (as are the parts of a machine), but are interrelated. Each part of my body is expressive of the body as a whole, and thus I am in possession of this body as a whole. I am 'enveloped' in my body. This suggests that I do not primarily control my body through conscious deliberation. More significantly, my relationship to the world beyond my body is similarly pre-reflective. I am embedded in a bodily life of desires, habits and evaluations that are expressed through and entwined with a knowledge of the world that itself is embodied. The competent typist, for example, does not have to reflect consciously upon the position of each key. The knowledge of the keys' positions is 'in the hand'. The Cartesian *cogito*, 'I think', is thus displaced by what Merleau-Ponty calls a tacit *cogito*, 'I can' (1962, p. 137).

Just as he has rejected mechanistic and reductionist explanation in Cartesianism and behaviourist psychology, so too in his reflections on sexuality, Merleau-Ponty rejects the mechanistic implications found in **Freud**, whereby the manifest behaviour of the subject is reduced to an unconscious meaning. Freud's recognition of the meaningfulness of all behaviour is applauded, but there is, for Merleau-Ponty, no one universal trajectory of sexual development that allows for the unambiguous deciphering of that meaning. Rather, sexuality is one of the dimensions through which a human being's life comes to have a history. Sexuality is a projection of a person's being in the world, and thus of their particular 'style' as a person (pp. 158 and 150). But that history can always have different meanings, in response to shifts in the structure of inter-subjective meanings within which it is lived.

In his last works, including the unfinished *The Visible and the Invisible* (1964), Merleau-Ponty builds radically and critically upon his earlier work by arguing that it has still not completely shed the dualism to which it was opposed. The 'tacit cogito' is abandoned in favour of an analysis of 'Flesh' as the 'element' (as water, fire, earth and air are elements) of our being in the world (Merleau-Ponty 1968, p. 139). Already in *Phenomenology* Merleau-Ponty had begun to explore the complex relationship between inner and outer that emerges once dualism is abandoned. There cannot be an unproblematic inside (mind) set against an outside (body/world). Rather the inner and outer are 'reversible' (so that, for example, when left and right hands meet, the body is both touching and touched (1962, p. 93)). From a different perspective reversibility also emerges in the analysis of speech and language. In *Phenomenology* language is ultimately grounded in bodily gestures, expressing the emotional essence of one's community. But in learning our original language, we become enveloped in a (superficially external) tradition, so that we come to rely upon what has already been constituted outside us, in order to express our inner selves. In the later *Signs* (1960) it is Speech which says things, and Speech has us, rather than vice versa (1964 p. 19). In another context, Merleau-Ponty observes that the musician does not produce a sonata, but is 'at the service of the sonata' (1968 p. 153). This idea of reversibility is developed in the concept of 'chiasm' (that itself is regarded as being incarnate in Flesh). 'Chiasm' articulates this tension between inner and outer as the reversibility of self and world, so that, in the highly elusive imagery of *The Visible*, the seer is both vision and visible. However, Merleau-Ponty stresses that such reservability is never actually realised. Rather there remains a strife both within the self and between the self and the world, and this strife (or divergence) allows for an openness within Being. As throughout his work, Merleau-Ponty again stresses ambiguity and the impossibility of any definitive grounding to our judgements, for his ontology presupposes that Being is perpetually renewing itself.

[AE]

Further reading: Diprose 1994; Vasseleu 1998.

MILL, JOHN STUART (1806–1873)

English philosopher, social critic, political economist, civil servant and liberal. Mill was educated by his father. As Mill notes in his *Autobiography*, the latter handled his son's education by introducing him to a wide range of very difficult books from an early age. Thus, Mill started learning Greek at the age of 3 and he was familiar with half a dozen Platonic dialogues before the age of 10. As a youth Mill also became acquainted with the works of the utilitarian philosopher Jeremy Bentham (1748–1832), of whom his father James was perhaps the most prominent disciple, and the economic theories of David Ricardo. These figures are among those referred to as the 'Philosophical Radicals' of the nineteenth century and Mill himself came to be numbered among them. Mill's own work displays a critical attitude to utilitarianism, which he retains in a modified form. Utilitarianism, as propounded by Bentham, is the theory that holds that ethical actions can be evaluated by way of reference to the guiding principle of 'the greatest happiness of the greatest number'. This is also known as the principle of Utility. According to this principle one should, when presented with a moral problem, act in such a manner as to ensure that the consequences of one's action ensure the greatest happiness of the majority of people affected by it. For Bentham, it is human nature to avoid pain and pursue pleasure, and this principle is what also provides people with the basis for rules of conduct. Mill, in contrast, argues that although human conduct is dominated by the search for pleasure, it is also the case that there are higher and lower order pleasures. So, an educated person when faced with the choice of a lower order pleasure (e.g. indulging in alcohol) and a higher order pleasure (e.g. contemplating a work of art) will always choose the higher order one. Likewise, seeking the betterment of humanity as a whole is a higher order pleasure, as is the pursuit of a life of critical reflection. Mill's reputation rests upon a number of works: *System of Logic* (1843), *The Principles of Political Economy* (1848), *On Liberty* (1859), *Utilitarianism* (1863) and *The Subjection of Women* (1869). Of these, the most famous is *On Liberty*, which presents one of the most forceful arguments in defence of the individualistic philosophy of liberalism.

In *On Liberty* Mill's aim in the text is to explore 'the nature and limits' of society's power over the individual. The key issue of such power presents itself in the context of the 'struggle' between individual liberty and political authority. Although the tension between liberty and authority that concerns Mill is nothing new, in that it was also present in the Ancient world, modern society according to him is faced with a specific modulation of this problem. In short, modern society has undergone historical developments that have redefined the nature and terms of this struggle. In the past, Mill argues, the struggle over authority took the form of a contest between subjects and rulers. As such, this struggle centred on establishing the limits of the power of monarchies or aristocracies. In the modern era social provisions designed to satisfy the 'new demand for elective and temporary rulers' have led to the formation of institutions of representative democracy. This has raised a different problem. The rulers are now 'identified' with the ruled, and therefore the will of the government is also that of the people. However, with this comes a decisive increase in the power of collective opinion. For, a society in which the rulers are elected is also a society that can become subject to the power of majority opinion. This power Mill refers to as the 'tyranny of the majority'. By this term he is referring to the political condition in which 'society itself is the tyrant'. In Mill's view, then, modern society is characterised by way of the presence of a new type of conflict between two different forms of interest: those of the individual and those of society. Mill also refers to this in terms of a tension between 'collective opinion' and 'individual independence'.

Mill's approach, it should be clear, rests upon the endorsement of individualism. For him, the individual ought to be conceived above all as an independent entity. This entity has, according to him, an absolute right to independence with regard to the pursuit of his or her interests. Since society contains a diversity of individuals, it follows that such a society will also embody a diversity of interests. A society of this kind is the one that, for Mill, is the most progressive. For a culture to be designated progressive, therefore, means that it fosters individuality. By the same token, a culture that ceases to possess individual diversity ceases to be progressive. This is an important point for Mill, since a progressive society will, at the same time, be one that is presented with the possibility of conflict on a regular basis. This is because diversity brings with it the inevitable result that some individuals will exhibit interests and modes of behaviour that are 'antisocial' in the specific sense of having the potential for conflicting with the dominant norms that constitute public morality. In short, there is an ever present potential for disparity between collective forms of social organisation and individual interests simply because individuals can and will make choices that do not conform to the rule of convention. The individual, for Mill, most completely expresses their unique identity when they think and choose without direct reference to the force of custom. To choose something because it is the custom, it follows, is to make no choice at all, for it involves no more than the use of the 'ape-like' faculty of 'imitation' (Mill 1984, p. 123). To act in this way, in Mill's view, epitomises acceptance of the repressive power of the tyranny of the majority.

In the context of his diagnosis of the potential of modern society to dominate the individual by the force of popular opinion, Mill then attempts to set out the limits of public power. These limits depend largely on a contrast being drawn between the self-regarding and other-regarding aspects of human behaviour. For Mill, as long as an individual's beliefs or actions do not affect someone else (i.e. are self-regarding) they ought not to be the concern of society at large. An individual, in other words, ought to be free to choose the mode of living that suits them (one is free, it follows, to choose a style of living that is self-destructive). Likewise an individual should be entitled to freedom of thought and expression. The only limit set to these freedoms is that one person ought not to harm another. Of course, there is a problem with this view. It is, for example, very difficult to draw a line separating an individual's actions from their consequences for others. Equally, the expression of some opinions can be construed as being harmful to others. Mill's main point, though, is that respect for individuality, for different views and ways of living, is a precondition for a healthy culture. For, if 'free scope' is 'given to varieties of character' (Mill 1984, p. 120) this will have as its positive consequence the fullest possible realisation of human potential. Such diversity makes for the greater long-term benefit of society: 'In proportion to the development of his individuality, each person becomes more valuable to himself, and is, therefore, capable of being more valuable to others' (p. 127). Equally, the individual, for Mill, is the key to discovering 'new truths' necessary for society to continue to thrive in the future: 'There is always a need of persons not only to discover new truths and point out what were once truths are true no longer, but also to commence new practices and set the example of more enlightened conduct and better taste in human life' (p. 128). Individuality also presents itself as the highest possible object of aesthetic contemplation (p. 123) and exemplifies Mill's conception of a 'moral being' (p. 80).

The social and hence cultural role of the individual is thus of central importance to Mill's conception of the self. What is also notable is the fact that he situates his discussion in the context of a number of comments about other cultures. Thus, where European culture exemplifies individuality and historical development, Chinese culture is regarded as static and lacking individuality. Mill also draws a distinction between those who would be qualified to express their individuality in virtue of possessing maturity and those who would not. On one level this seems reasonable, in so far as children, to cite an obvious example, are often unable to make decisions about their fate in an informed manner. On the other hand, Mill also includes within this category 'those backward states of society in which the race itself may be considered in its non-age' (p. 69). For this reason, 'Despotism is a legitimate mode of government in dealing with barbarians, provided the end be their improvement and the means justified by actually effecting that end' (it should perhaps be borne in mind that Mill spent much of his life working for the British government of India). The word 'culture' for Mill, it follows, can be taken to signify European culture, for it is this that sets the standard whereby cultural development can be judged.

Mill was actively committed to furthering the rights of women in Victorian society. As a Member of Parliament he sought, in 1867, to amend the second Reform Bill in the House of Commons to include granting votes for women. In 1869 he published *The Subjection of Women*, a polemical pamphlet arguing against the view that the social inequalities experienced by women in the legal and political arenas could be justified by way of reference to any supposedly 'natural' differences between men and women. Thus, according to Mill, the so-called 'natural' incapacities of women are merely reflections of a male-dominated social order that needs, therefore, to be questioned. Women, he says, deserve equal access to educational opportunities. Likewise, Mill argues for the view that women are equally fit to undertake forms of work that are male dominated, and that in some respects they have superior abilities to them. For example, women have the ability to undertake a number of tasks at the same time and can gain rapid insight into situations, which Mill refers to as 'intuition'. At the same time, he is open to being criticised by feminists for his endorsement of the view that, in the last analysis, a woman's intuition stands in need of the guiding hand of a man's practical knowledge, or for claiming that an ill-educated woman will be a liability to an educated man. Mill is also open to being criticised for his humanism and liberal individualism. Thus, it could be argued, in placing so much emphasis upon the individual his thinking ignores the fact that individuality itself is a category that can be rendered open to various forms of critique, either from the **Marx**ist perspective of thinkers like **Althusser**, or the post-structuralist viewpoint espoused by figures such as **Lyotard**. Whether such criticisms blunt the force of Mill's liberalism is another matter however. For, on the one hand, it should be noted that his conception of individuality has historical and cultural aspects. Some cultures, after all, do not foster individuality according to Mill, which implies that social factors need to be taken into account when discussing it. Equally, Mill's claim that diversity is the highest expression of human potential has its parallels in a thinker like Lyotard's advocacy of a politics and ethics of cultural multiplicity.

[PS]

Further reading: Berger 1984; Halliday 1976; Ryan 1975; Skorupski 1989, 1998; J. Wood 1987.

NIETZSCHE, FRIEDRICH (1844–1900)

German philosopher whose work has exerted an important influence upon a wide range of philosophical, literary, cultural and political movements in the twentieth century. Nietzsche was born near the city of Leipzig, attended the famous Pforta School and subsequently studied at the universities of Bonn and Leipzig. At Leipzig he studied classical philosophy and first read the works of the German philosopher Schopenhauer. In 1869, at the age of 24, Nietzsche was appointed to a post at the University of Basel, Switzerland. A year later he was made a full professor of classical philology. Owing to ill health, he resigned from this post in 1879, and spent the remainder of his life living off the pension that the university had granted him. In January 1889, Nietzsche suffered a devastating mental collapse. Rendered a helpless invalid, Nietzsche was cared for by his mother and then by his sister until his death eleven years later.

In terms of published works, Nietzsche's creative life spanned the relatively brief period of 1872 to 1888. Although there are a marked differences in style and approach between the young and the mature Nietzsche, the books published during this time are marked by a consistent concern with the nature of culture. Thus, Nietzsche's first book, *The Birth of Tragedy* (1872) represents an attempt to interpret the cultural significance of Ancient Greek tragic art (e.g. the Oedipus plays of Sophocles). For the Nietzsche of *The Birth of Tragedy*, as for the later Nietzsche, Ancient Greek art represents one of the high points in the history of European culture. The question addressed by *The Birth of Tragedy* concerns how one is to make sense of this cultural achievement. The predominant interpretation of Greek culture espoused by figures such as J. J. Winckelmann (1717–1768) and subsequently Matthew **Arnold** (1822–1888) held that Greek culture was the expression of a calm and enlightened simplicity, epitomised by the harmony of design readily apparent in its sculpture and architecture. Against this Nietzsche argued for the view that the formal simplicity and beauty of such designs could only be accounted for by way of reference to something more subterranean and sinister. The formal harmony of such artistic works, Nietzsche argues, is in fact the sublimated expression of a violence that permeated Ancient Greek culture. In order to explain the nature of such violence, Nietzsche introduces two aesthetic categories: the Apollonian and the Dionysian. The Apollonian represents a formalised aesthetic of constraint, a channel or structure wherein artistic expression is rendered possible (the 'principle of individuation'). It is linked to the plastic art of sculpture. The Dionysian, in contrast linked to music and dance, represents violent and chaotic forces of becoming that embody a loss of the sense of self that characterises the Apollonian. In Greek tragedy Dionysian forces, Nietzsche argues, were harnessed by the Apollonian element, which provided a structural condition wherein the Dionysian could be given its fullest formal expression as art. In effect, Nietzsche's argument is that the great achievements of Greek culture were not the product of a harmonious rationality, but were in fact a direct consequence of the creative harnessing of inherently destructive forces present within the culture itself. Greek tragedy draws upon these Dionysian forces providing, by way of the chorus, the spectator with the metaphysical comfort

> that life is at the bottom of things, despite all the changes of appearances, indestructibly powerful and pleasurable [. . .] With this chorus the profound Hellene, uniquely susceptible to the tenderest and deepest suffering, comforts himself [. . .] Art saves him, and through art – life.
>
> (Nietzsche 1968a, section 7)

Thus, Greek art attained its heights of expression because of a need to make the terrible, destructive Dionysian reality of life bearable: art attains its greatest potential when it both serves and expresses the needs of life. Later in this text, Nietzsche links his argument to contemporary issues in German culture, arguing that Wagner's music can be understood as a means to 'a *rebirth of tragedy*' as providing the possibility for a rejuvenated German culture.

The Birth of Tragedy, it should be clear, is no work of philosophy. Indeed, the paradigmatic figure of philosophical reason, that of Socrates, is explicitly linked in the text to the destruction of the tragic form and the cultural decline of Ancient Greece. Nietzsche never abandons an ambivalent attitude toward Socratism and philosophy alike, but in his later work he does abandon his adherence to Wagner and to the Schopenhauerian elements evident in *The Birth of Tragedy*. Although two of the four *Utimely Meditations* (1873–1876) appear to celebrate these two men, it is possible to detect in the *Meditation* on Wagner the beginnings of Nietzsche's rejection of him. With the publication of *Human, All-Too-Human* in 1878 the break with Wagner is complete, and in this book Nietzsche also begins the process of distancing himself from Schopenhauer and from the German nationalism evident in *The Birth of Tragedy*. Likewise, a new direction to Nietzsche's thought is mooted in the form of a turn away from the aesthetic concerns of *The Birth of Tragedy* towards an interest in the nature of values. Thus, *Human, All-Too-Human* (1878) begins by making what seems to be a relatively trivial and general observation about the origins of important concepts: how can something originate in its opposite, such as truth in untruth, rationality in irrationality, or selflessness in selfishness? Nietzsche response to this question is twofold. First, he highlights the role of what he terms 'metaphysical philosophy' in the traditional understanding of these questions. In doing so Nietzsche initiates an approach to questions of metaphysics that he follows for the rest of his productive life. Metaphysical philosophy, it turns out, is committed to the view that oppositions are fixed in place – that reason cannot be derived from unreason, logic cannot have an illogical source, etc. This metaphysical view has been held because reason, truth and so forth have generally been attributed a 'miraculous source' underlying experience. Metaphysical philosophy thereby invokes what cannot be demonstrated by way of experience in order to justify its views. Equally, such philosophising effectively claims to have a supra-historical perspective. For metaphysical philosophy, Nietzsche argues, the word 'true' is taken to mean what cannot change.

Nietzsche's other response to his question involves opposing meta-physical thinking to what he terms 'historical philosophy'. According to Nietzsche's view, one ought to conceive of human knowledge in terms of a process of development whereby self-consciousness arises from the material conditions of life. One significant consequence of this process was to put in place assumptions that we are now unable to shake off. Thus, the manner in which we conceptualise our everyday experiences necessarily involves presuppositions that facilitate thought, and these presuppositions have their origin in the distant past of human development. Metaphysical philosophy is the uncritical inheritor of the assumption that the conditions of thought that govern us today are timeless structures upon which our knowledge of 'reality' rests. Meta-physical philosophers have taken these presuppositions as a 'given' starting point from which one then is able to embark upon the journey of inquiring into reality. In contrast, historical philosophy rejects this belief. Against such a view Nietzsche argues that reality is essentially characterised by change, that 'everything has become'. Hence, we can have knowledge only of empirical experience, that is, of so-called 'appearances', not of a timeless reality. Historical philosophy, in turn, looks for inspiration to the example of the 'natural sciences' and seeks thereby to provide us with a new account of the nature of thinking and valuing. What is needed, says Nietzsche,

> is a *chemistry* of the moral, religious and aesthetic conceptions and sensations, likewise of all the agitations we experience within ourselves in cultural and social intercourse, and indeed even when we are alone: what if this chemistry would end up by revealing that in this domain too the most glorious colours are derived from base, indeed from despised materials?
>
> (Nietzsche 1986, section 1)

As the chemical metaphor implies, what is in effect being proposed is a reductive account of the social domain of values. Values and feelings, like chemical compounds, may be susceptible to being broken down into their constituent parts by way of an analysis of their origins. The task of historical philosophy, therefore, is to provide us with an account of the basic building blocks from which the fabric of social life and thought is made. At the same time, this project involves abandoning the temptation to formulate universal knowledge claims about reality – all that historical philosophising can offer us is 'little unpretentious truths [. . .] discovered by means of rigorous method' (Nietzsche 1986, section 3).

The later Nietzsche departs to some degree with the views that are expressed at the beginning of *Human, All-Too-Human*. For one thing, his evident faith in the methodology of the natural sciences is tempered by an increasing scepticism with regard to their purportedly 'objective' status. As Nietzsche remarks in *Beyond Good and Evil* (1886), although we are often obliged to think of it as explaining reality, 'physics, too, is only an interpretation and exegesis of the world (to suit us, if I may say so!) and not a world explanation' (Nietzsche 1968a, section 14). The physical sciences can mislead us to the extent that we are inclined to believe that the concepts they employ designate states of 'things' and hence offer us explanations rather than interpretations. But even the notions of cause and effect, Nietzsche notes, are best understood as 'conventional fictions for the purpose of designation and communication [. . .] In the "in-itself" there is nothing of "causal connections", of "necessity" [. . .] there the effect does *not* follow the cause, there is no rule of "law"' (section 21). Science, it follows, does not offer us the 'truth' about the world. Rather, natural science offers one means among others of grasping our environment practically with a view to manipulating it. Nietzsche's mature advocacy of science, in the sense implied by the title of his book *The Gay Science* (*Die Fröhliche Wissenschaft*) (1882), implies rather more than the limited perspective denoted by the natural sciences. Science (*Wissenschaft*), as the later Nietzsche extols it, is as much a matter of sensibility as method (it is, to recall the title just mentioned, 'joyful' or 'gay'), and owes more to the notion of 'scholarship' or 'scholarly inquiry' than it does to the notion of a natural-scientific methodology.

The works Nietzsche wrote beginning in 1878 with *Human, All-Too-Human* and ending with the first four parts of *The Gay Science* (1882 – the fifth part was added in 1886) manifest other features that receive fuller expression in Nietzsche's later writings. Thus, there is an ever more pervasive scepticism concerning traditional forms of philosophical inquiry (such as epistemology or moral theory) and a developing interest in psychology, physiology and power. Most famously, *The Gay Science* announces the 'death of God' (Nietzsche 1974, section 125). This, as Nietzsche comments later in the book (section 344, added 1886) is the 'greatest modern event'. The event itself is characterised as a loss of faith in the Christian conception of God, and it marks the beginning of a period in modern European society wherein the moral 'certainties' that accompanied that faith must also, by the same token, be placed in question. It is this state of a loss of faith in moral values that Nietzsche baptises with the name 'nihilism'. Nietzsche's *Thus Spoke Zarathustra* (consisting of five parts, written between 1883 and 1892), a work that is both philosophical text and bible parody, represents a sustained and often rhapsodic engagement with the nihilistic implications of the death of God. Perhaps most notoriously, *Zarathustra* announces the need for the 'overman' as the supreme goal of human existence. The highest kind of cultural attainment possible, the overman is a being capable of a creative autonomy hitherto undreamed of by the average person, for he or she is a being able to live joyfully in a world devoid of the religious and moral metaphysical certainties that characterise Christian belief.

Nietzsche's rejection of Christian metaphysics entails for him not only a rejection of the moral tenets associated with that creed, but also a critical revaluation of the meaning of values as such. This revaluation is undertaken in the context of a developing theory of power. This theory holds that all identities are the product of relations of power (1968b, section 1067) and that life itself can, in turn, be understood in terms of the play of these relations. The term 'power' does not denote some kind of mysterious force that permeates independently existing 'things', but is in fact constitutive of entities as such. *On the Genealogy of Morals* (1887) provides ample evidence of Nietzsche putting the power theory to work. In this book, he takes his sustained critique of conventional religious and ethical systems one step further, and attempts both an analysis and critique of the genesis and lineage of ethical systems. Moral systems can, in Nietzsche's view, be divided into two distinct and contending camps: 'noble morality' and 'slave morality'. Each represents a different, and in the end incommensurable, realm of interests. Noble morality is an expression of the standpoint of aristocratic classes. It embodies the perspective of dominion and power and is affirmative in character in that it is rooted in the perspective of a dominant social grouping (that of nobles) which first affirms itself as 'good' and only then characterises those of a lower station as 'bad'. This Nietzsche terms the 'good–bad' ethical system of evaluation.

Slave morality, in contrast, is produced by those who encounter and evaluate the world from the perspective of the victim. The slave's identity is constituted in the wake of their being a victim of power, helpless in the face of dominant social forces, and therefore incapable of taking any practical steps to rectify their victim status. In an act of impotent revenge the slave labels his or her oppressor as 'evil'. It is only after this evaluative deed that the slave type affirms their own identity as 'good'. Slave morality therefore embodies a 'good–evil' ethical system of evaluation. The slave's conception of 'good' is a reactive response to the world, which first presupposes the identity of what is designated 'evil', as opposed to the active assertion of the 'good' made on the part of a noble or master (see Deleuze 1983). According to Nietzsche, Christian culture (with its roots located in the slave ethos of Judaism) is the prime example of slave morality, whereas the culture of Ancient Rome exemplifies noble morality. From this it is clear that Nietzsche regards the proper interpretation of the positing of values as a contextual issue. There are no 'true' values, since values as such have no meaning at all apart from the context of competing interests out of which they are articulated. In his late writings, such as *Twilight of the Idols* (1889), this viewpoint is developed ever more in a direction that implies an abandonment of the view that consciously held beliefs are autonomous 'causes' in any meaningful sense of the word. Here, Nietzsche proposes a 'symptomatic' reading of values, wherein they are to be read as 'signs' denoting a variety of attitudes to life. This approach is in line with an earlier argument presented in *Beyond Good and Evil*, which holds that there are no 'facts' of consciousness upon which it would be possible to erect an objective theory of values or knowledge. Thus, he tells us, any account of knowledge that begins with the nature of self-consciousness ignores the fact that it cannot itself explain what self-consciousness is:

> by far the greater part of conscious thinking must still be included among instinctive activities, and that goes even for philosophical thinking. We have to relearn here, as one has had to relearn about heredity and what is 'innate'. As the act of birth deserves no consideration in the whole process and procedure of heredity, so 'being conscious' is not in any decisive sense the opposite of what is instinctive.
>
> (Nietzsche 1968a, section 3)

In other words, we need to learn how to draw distinctions. The act of giving birth does not, of itself, confer heredity upon the one who is born, since important social and genetic factors do this. So, too, conscious thinking is not born of consciousness and nothing else. The genealogy of consciousness must also be understood in terms of its unconscious preconditions, for consciousness is something that emerges from unconscious conditions of thought. As Nietzsche puts it in a notebook entry dating from 1887–1888,

> 'Thinking', as epistemologists conceive it, simply does not exist: it is a quite arbitrary fiction, arrived at by selecting one element from the process and eliminating all the rest, an artificial arrangement for the purpose of intelligibility.
>
> (Nietzsche 1968b, section 477)

For Nietzsche, like **Hume**, we are instinctive or habitual animals. Most significantly, our habits are inseparable from the way in which humans use language. This is a view expressed as early as *Human, All-Too-Human* (see Nietzsche 1986, section 11). Language works by means of referring to our experiences, and because of this we fall prey to the belief that words actually refer to 'things' that exist independently of them. But, Nietzsche argues, even as we designate 'things' (and even the notion of a 'thing' is, after all, a kind of designation), we are actively imposing meaning upon our experiences by presupposing that there must be entities that correspond to the names we utter. It follows that we habitually understand words as representing in an unmediated manner the purportedly 'essential properties' of objects. Although this belief may be an essential precondition of language use, and to that extent is necessary as a precondition of such use, it does not follow that the belief is objectively true. Indeed, Nietzsche argues, names do not represent things (as metaphysical philosophy would assert). Rather, language expresses something essential about the relationship between humans and their environment: it is one of the ways in which we cope with our environment. A further implication of this view is that consciousness and language are intrinsically linked to one another. Thus, in *The Gay Science*, we are told that 'the development of language and the development of consciousness [. . .] go hand in hand' (Nietzsche 1974, section 354). Since we must think linguistically, our reason, too, is derived from the preconditions that facilitate language. Rationality, in other words, is a human achievement that springs from linguistic norms and practices (from human beings reacting in certain ways in relation to their environment). As with morality, therefore, the precise significance of reason needs, for Nietzsche, to be subject to a revaluation.

The culture of modernity is, for Nietzsche, bifurcated – it is caught between the two ethical systems he characterises in terms of nobles and slaves (although Nietzsche is clear on the point that the history of European culture, the prologue to modernity, is the history of the triumph of slave morality). Nietzsche's concern with modernity, which he takes to be the nihilistic outcome of the triumph of Christian doctrine, has led many commentators to identify him as a key figure in the discourse of postmodernism (see, for example, Vattimo (1988), who claims that with Nietzsche 'postmodernity is born'). Among thinkers associated in some way or another with postmodernism (and, by inference, the schools of structuralism and post-structuralism) Nietzsche's influence is evident in the work a variety of thinkers. Michel **Foucault**'s development of a variant of Nietzsche's power theory and 'genealogical method' forms the basis for much of his critical discourse on knowledge. Gilles **Deleuze** and co-writer Félix **Guattari** embrace a Nietzschean ontology of becoming, and regard Nietzsche as a prime instance of their favoured model of 'nomadic', anti-institutional thinking and, in *A Thousand Plateaus*, develop a psychological and physiological account of power relations in their attempt to provide a criticism of authoritarian discourse. Paul **de Man** and Jacques **Derrida** see in Nietzsche precursors of their own deconstructive approaches (although Derrida has come to view Nietzsche's legacy with an increasing suspicion – see *The Ear of the Other* (Derrida 1988a)). Nietzsche's work has also influenced the philosophers of the Frankfurt School, as is clear from **Horkheimer** and **Adorno**'s *Dialectic of Enlightenment* (1973). This work seeks to trace the development of the Enlightenment in the context of a struggle for power which, they argue, in its aim to destroy the pre-scientific mythological discourse of theological tradition creates its own mythological structure of rationalist dogma in its place. Adorno's later work – especially *Minima Moralia* (1978a) and *Against Epistemology* (1982) – often demonstrates very Nietzschean tendencies (an aphoristic style in the former, and a critical attitude to foundationalism in epistemology in the latter).

[PS]

Further reading: Adorno and Horkheimer 1973; Ansell-Pearson 1991; Deleuze 1983; de Man 1979; Derrida 1979, 1988a; Foucault 1977; Habermas 1988a; Hollingdale 1973; Kaufmann 1974; Magnus and Higgins 1996; Nietzsche 1968a, 1968b, 1974, 1982, 1983, 1986, 1995; Sedgwick 1995.

NUSSBAUM, MARTHA C. (1947–)

American classicist and feminist philosopher, whose writings demonstrate at once a commitment to rigorous argument and scholarship, and to the demand for engagement with the practical concerns of everyday political and moral life.

In her first publications Nussbaum established herself as a significant scholar of ancient Greek philosophy and literature. Yet her concerns were never purely philological. The Greek tragedies, the work of Plato and Aristotle (discussed in *The Fragility of Goodness*, 1986), as well as Hellenistic ethics (*The Therapy of Desire*, 1994), provided a resource to renew contemporary ethical and political theory. *Fragility* challenged the idea of an autonomous rational human individual that dominates modern ethics and liberal political theory. The assumption was that such an individual should be able to act independently of the contingency of luck, and that moral values themselves were immune to such contingency. Nussbaum offers a different vision of the human agent. Most movingly she borrows an image from the poet Pindar: 'But human excellence grows like a vine tree, fed by the green dew, raised up, among wise men and just, to the liquid sky' (Nussbaum 1986, p. 1). She glosses this as follows: 'I am an agent, but also a plant; . . . much that I did not make goes towards making me whatever I shall be praised or blamed for being' (ibid., p. 5). An adequate moral theory must therefore take account of the contingency of a human life that is at once embedded in a particular society and culture, and is embodied, where neither one's culture nor one's body can be chosen (and yet for which one is, to some degree, responsible). While **Plato**'s philosophy may be read as an attempt to understand human life in terms of its autonomy from contingency, the Greek tragedies (with their recognition of the possibility that fundamental moral values may come into irresolvable conflict), and subsequently **Aristotle**'s philosophy, give a clearer picture of the relationship that must be established between an acceptance of contingency and the force of human desire on the one hand, and the discipline of reason on the other.

Two themes may be seen to emerge from this work. First, Nussbaum is interested in literature as well as philosophy. She looks to literature, and particularly the modern novel, as a source of philosophical reflection and insight. In *Love's Knowledge* (1990) she reads writers such as Henry James, Dickens, Proust and Beckett as sharing Aristotelian concerns. They address the problem of how one should live one's life, and do this specifically by addressing the themes of the noncommensurability of valuable things; the priority of the particular (over universal reason); the ethical value of emotions; and the ethical relevance of uncontrolled happenings (Nussbaum 1990, pp. 35–44). In *Poetic Justice* (1995) this concern is taken further, to challenge the application of strict economic rationism to the realms of law and politics, and to defend the novel as a source of moral insight and stimulus to compassion. Crucially, however, Nussbaum never abandons reason in favour of an unchecked emotivism or sentimentalism. The task is rather to combine logic with compassion.

The second theme that may be extracted concerns the demand for philosophy to justify itself through practical engagement. The privilege of the philosopher, 'to be able to spend her life expressing her most serious thoughts and feelings about the problems that have moved and fascinated her most', must be set against the realisation that for most of the world's population such a life is 'a dream so distant that it can rarely be formed' (Nussbaum 1994, p. 3). Taking her model from Hellenistic ethics (Aristotle, the Epicureans, the Stoics), philosophy becomes a therapy for the soul, healing 'human diseases, diseases produced by false beliefs' (ibid., p. 14). Indeed, it is no exaggeration to say that reading an essay by Nussbaum can give the reader the sort of intellectual resources that serve to make some sense of life. (A surprisingly rare gift in a modern philosopher.) The demand for engagement has also led Nussbaum to address a wide range of political issues with acute sensitivity and originality. Her association with the World Institute for Development Economics Research (itself associated to the United Nations) has been articulated in work on quality of life (Nussbaum and Sen 1993), global development and the status of women (Nussbaum and Glover 1995) and sexuality and the rights of gays and lesbians (Nussbaum and Estlund 1997; Nussbaum and Olyan 1998; Nussbaum 1999).

[AE]

OAKESHOTT, MICHAEL (1901–1990)

British philosopher and political theorist. Oakeshott read for a history degree at Cambridge, but while doing so took courses in philosophy and political theory. In the 1920s he visited Germany, where he attended lectures in theology at Marburg and Tubingen. He lectured in modern history at Cambridge. In 1933 he published *Experience and its Modes*. This work, now regarded as a classic, was not well received (it took more than thirty years for the first edition to sell out). In the 1930s Oakeshott began to conduct research in political philosophy, concentrating on the writings of Thomas Hobbes (1588–1679). He was to become a renowned Hobbes scholar, and edited a highly regarded edition of Hobbes's *Leviathan*. After having served in the Second World War as the commander of a squadron of the intelligence gathering GHQ Liaison Regiment, Oakeshott resumed his academic career. In 1949 he was appointed Professor of Political Science at the London School of Economics. In 1962 he published a collection entitled *Rationalism in Politics and Other Essays*. Oakeshott retired in 1968. In 1975 he published *On Human Conduct*. Other works published by him include *On History and Other Essays* (1983) and *The Voice of Liberal Learning* (1989).

Of Oakeshott's works *Experience and its Modes* and *On Human Conduct* are probably the most important. Both are characterised by a critical attitude toward realist and rationalist philosophies, especially of the kind espoused by thinkers such as **Plato** and **Descartes**. Such a form of rationalism asserts the existence of a dichotomy between empirical experience and reality and claims, in turn, that reason is the privileged means of access to this reality. Against this view, Oakeshott's works endorse a version of philosophical Idealism (derived in part from the works of **Hegel**). According to this approach, experience and reality are one and the same thing; hence, there is no ultimate reality waiting for humans to discover it 'behind' the realm of experience. In *Experience and its Modes* Oakeshott (1933) argues that experience is the fundamental basis of reality. Experience is, in turn, characterised as constituting a unity in a constant state of flux. Equally, such reality can be comprehended by thought. Experience is disclosed, however, not as a totality but in the form of more or less stable parts or 'modes'. Although there are, Oakeshott argues, many possible modes of experience, *Experience and its Modes* concentrates upon just three. These are history, science and practice. These modes comprehend experience in distinct ways: in terms of the past (history), in terms of calculable relationships (science) and in terms of values and wants (practice). Nothing in experience, Oakeshott argues, can be grasped independently of a mode of experience. Equally, all concepts are specific to the mode in which they occur and are heterogeneous with regard to any mode (i.e. an idea has a meaning within one mode of experience that cannot be translated into another). Thus, there is a difference between a scientist referring to a chemical element called 'gold' and someone engaged in a practical form of activity talking of 'gold'. In each case, what is being referred to is not something that has a 'substance' that remains the same irrespective of context (mode), but two distinct 'things'. This is because all modes of experience are incommensurable with regard to one another. Since nothing in one mode can be translated into another, it follows that no knowledge claim (to give one example) can ever be said to be true of all modes. Equally, therefore, there is no superior tribunal to which one could appeal with regard to the aim of judging any mode of experience to be 'false' or 'true'.

Experience, Oakeshott contends, is a whole and there is only one concrete reality, but no single mode of experience has privileged access to that reality. Even philosophy, so beloved of the Western tradition, cannot claim that it has a greater ultimate purchase on reality than any other mode of understanding the world. Nevertheless, Oakeshott does give philosophy a special role in his thought. The role of philosophy is to expose the partial nature of all modes of experience. All modes of experience are abstractions and therefore lack concreteness, yet at the same time there is no thought that is not constituted within a mode of experience. Hence, Oakeshott argues, all we can ever do is acknowledge the relative and partial nature of our knowledge. Such acknowledgement is antithetical to every mode of experience since all modes have a tendency to present their partial view of reality as if it were the whole. Thus, the scientist no less than the practical person likes to believe that they have a privileged mode of access to reality as a whole. This is another way of saying that we all have a tendency to interpret experience in terms of our own needs and dispositions. Given Oakeshott's claim that all modes of experience are heterogeneous and bound by their own rules of validity, it follows that no mode ought to make claims that cannot be validated by way of reference to its own nature. For example, neither a scientist nor an historian is entitled to think they have the authority to pronounce on a political or ethical issue in his or her capacity as an expert in their particular field. Quite simply, neither have any special authority with regard to such issues in virtue of their status as historian or scientist.

The limits of modes of experience are shown, Oakeshott argues, by way of the fact that almost everyone is familiar with more than one. Thus, the scientist or the academic historian alike are also practical people who have everyday concerns. The logic of Oakeshott's position is further developed in his later writings. If there is an important development in his later thought it is to be found in the rejection of the **Hegel**ian sense Oakeshott gives to the term 'experience'. In his later writings the term ceases to signify a totality. In turn, the task of philosophy is modified: philosophy's role is to note the limitations of other forms of discourse (modes) not by way of reference to an ultimate but ultimately unconceptualisable whole, but with regard to one another. With this move away from the notion of totality Oakeshott's later work embraces an increasingly pluralistic viewpoint (see his essay, 'The Voice of Poetry in the Conversation of Mankind'; in Oakeshott 1991).

On Human Conduct represents Oakeshott's major attempt to present his theory of civil association. The work begins by arguing that any understanding of the nature of human conduct must be prefaced by an account of the nature of understanding. Understanding is an 'unsought condition' of human beings in so far as it is not something that we can choose to have or not have. We are just the kind of beings who have understanding. There are many levels or 'plateaux' of understanding. None is ultimately superior to any other but, Oakeshott argues, humans are characterised by a desire for greater understanding of their world. The notion of modes of experience in Oakeshott's earlier work is now replaced by an account that envisages the world in terms of events or 'goings-on'. Every act of understanding is regarded as an 'achievement'. But such achievements are not to be comprehended in terms of a progression towards the comprehension of an ultimate reality. Rather, every achievement of understanding is itself an invitation to further 'adventures' in understanding. Oakeshott argues that human conduct must be theorised in a manner appropriate to it. We ought not to think that behaviourist account of human relations is adequate for an account of the nature of civil association, for this would be to treat human activities as if they were processes. Human activity, Oakeshott argues, is to be understood not as a kind of process but as involving 'procedures', i.e. actions that are an exhibition of understanding and intelligence. Human conduct is therefore comprehensible only in terms of its being a form of activity undertaken by agents. The activities that humans perform include both practical actions and spoken ones. In turn, Oakeshott argues that every human performance is a 'self-disclosure' and humans discover their identity through performances. Thus, there is no universal model of human nature with regard to which all humans are defined. The self, in turn, is always embedded in a context and culture and hence has a history. However, there is no essential 'human nature' waiting to be discovered outside the historical and cultural conditions that constitute civil life. Equally, the history of human beings is neither an evolutionary nor goal-oriented process. To put it another way, according to Oakeshott there is no ultimate purpose to either history or culture since these are the spheres within which agents realise both their identities and pursue purposes. All human conduct consists of performances and all performances occur within the context of practices, which are 'by-products' of performances. An agent's relationship with others, Oakeshott contends, not determined by things like ties of blood, social systems or class divisions, but by way of practices. Practices are learned ways of doing things: they include things like customs, rules, and manners (e.g. to do something politely, scientifically, legally, etc.). Practices prescribe the conditions necessary for encounters with others, but they do not determine the choices that an agent may make when engaged in action. Oakeshott sees all human conduct as being composed of sets of various and, depending upon context, varying practices. Above all, a practice is a language of self-disclosure. Thus, agents realise who they are by doing things in specified ways. Practices are based in understanding. For example, one can have a 'neighbourly' relationship with someone. This implies a practice (being neighbourly) in respect of an understanding ('You, X, are my neighbour'). Primarily practices are linguistic: they are composed of a vocabulary and syntax that is continuously modified by use. All practices, in other words, are fluid.

From the notion of practice Oakeshott derives what he refers to as 'moral conduct'. Moral conduct concerns practices that are not concerned in any way with the successful outcomes of actions. Rather, they are those practices that are linked to principles of conduct. Crucially, all human conduct is moral, for Oakeshott, in so far as all forms of agency imply the acknowledgement of a moral practice. Morals are signs of human achievement, but they are not fixed. In common with all practices moral practices have developed and continue to develop. Every moral language/practice is learned, and they are signified by terms like 'right', 'wrong', 'proper', 'improper', 'obligation', etc. None pertains to a single meaning but is rather understood by way of specific contexts. Moral conduct is thus an 'idiom', i.e. a genre of speech wherein agents converse with, and thereby acknowledge, one another.

Oakeshott is not interested in offering a definition of human nature, since he regards any attempt at providing one as an essentially problematic undertaking. The term 'human being', he says, is simply 'indefinite'. But it does serve as a precondition of what he refers to as the 'civil relationship'. Quite simply, we have an ambiguous understanding of what it is that makes a human being a person. But this understanding is nevertheless presupposed in all consideration of social and cultural life. Again, what can be said of the civil relationship is that it implies an understanding of beings able to make choices that are expressions of intelligence. Within the realm of the 'civil relationship' Oakeshott identifies two key forms of human association. These are 'enterprise association' and 'civil association'. Enterprise association is a mode of civil relationship in which agents relate to one another as 'bargainers' or 'cives'. Cives are both seekers and providers of satisfactions. As such they may enter into a common pursuit, they can be allies linked together by dint of a common faith, or have some substantive goal in common. Enterprise association is thus a chosen form of relationship and any instance of this kind of relationship can be dissolved as easily as it is formed (e.g. if agents obtain their common goal then the reason for their mode of association vanishes). Relatively permanent forms of enterprise association will develop rules, the authority of which will depend upon their being fitted to realising the common purpose. Likewise, rules that do not serve the common purpose will not be adopted (a publicans' association, Oakeshott notes, is hardly likely to adopt a rule banning all of its members from contact with alcohol). Significantly, no set of rules is exclusively appropriate to any one purpose or form of enterprise association. Likewise, the particular decisions made within such a mode of association are only contingently connected to its purposes: an orchestra is a mode of enterprise association that has the common purpose of making music, but which music the orchestra plays on any given day is a contingent matter.

Oakeshott, however, is more interested in 'civil association'. This is because it is wrong to conclude that enterprise association is the sole mode of civil relationship. Human association does not occur merely in terms of a common purpose, but also in terms of a set of common practices. *Cives* are related not merely in terms of common goals but by the fact that they observe common ways of doing things. Such practices are not understood in terms of purposes but as sets of conditions that have no purpose extrinsic to them. Civil association, Oakeshott contends, is just such a practice. It is a mode of the enactment of human beings, and what is enacted and endlessly re-enacted is a language of civil understanding composed simply of rules. Speaking this language allows *cives* to consider themselves as moral agents, since the rules that constitute this understanding cannot be reduced to any particular agent's purposes or desires. Such rules are not themselves moral utterances, but form the basis of the possibility of engaging in moral talk. To live in the civil condition, then, is to live in accordance with the existence of rules that apply to all agents equally. Oakeshott refers to these rules as constituting '*lex*' or 'law'. *Lex* is produced by association according to rules, and these rules themselves constitute a system. Such rules 'create' the civic subject or self, and also make possible the adjudication between contending interests. Taken together, rules, *cives*, *lex* and other postulates of the civil condition make up '*respublica*', i.e. the realm of 'public concern' or civic life. *Respublica* is thus a 'manifold' of rules that are subscribed to by agents as a precondition of their pursuing substantive goals. One cannot approve or disapprove of such rules, but they can be held to be 'good' or 'bad', 'fair' or 'unfair', etc.

The acknowledgement of the authority of these rules, Oakeshott argues, constitutes the authority of *respublica*. Hence, authority and obligation in equal measure constitute the civil condition.

[PS]

Further reading: Franco 1990; Greenleaf 1966.

PARSONS, TALCOTT (1902–1979)

American sociologist who, as the principal exponent of what is known as structural functionalism, exerted an major influence over social theory in the middle part of the twentieth century. His work continues to have an impact in German sociology, specifically in debates over systems theory (Habermas 1987; Luhmann 1982).

At the core of Parsons's work one may situate the 'problem of order'. Social life is ordered. Meaningful interaction between social agents (what Parsons terms 'social action') has every appearance of stability, and the social institutions upon which agents rely typically behave in a predictable way. Shops and schools open and close at predictable times. Money keeps its value. The meanings of words do not change. Yet there is little that is self-evident about this order, for, as the seventeenth-century philosopher Hobbes had already suggested, the natural condition of humanity appears to be that of war, where selfish individualism is allowed to assert itself unconstrained. Less dramatically but more pertinently, nineteenth-century social scientists explored the tension that occurs in social life between that which is rational or predictable, and its non-rational ground (such as the religious values that for **Weber** underpin the rise of modern capitalism, or the traditional morality that for **Durkheim** makes the modern economic contract workable) (Parsons 1937).

Parsons wants to establish the conditions that make order possible, or in other words, to establish how the actions of individuals come to be co-ordinated into stable overarching structures. To do so he develops a complex theoretical model of social action, that abstracts from the contingencies of mundane life. The theory of social action can be seen to begin from a model of just two agents, A and B. If A and B are to interact, then A must base her action upon expectations as to what B will do, and vice versa. There is here what Parsons calls a 'double contingency', that suggests that, prima facie, stable social interaction is impossible, for an action presupposes knowledge of the way in which others will act in the as-yet unknown future. Here would be Hobbes's clash of mutually uncomprehending warriors. In responding to this problem, Parsons recognises that social agents are rarely if ever completely unknown to each other. One possibility is that A does not respond to B as a unique individual, but rather as to one who occupies a role (e.g. teacher, police officer, administrator, parent). Social roles come complete with precise normative expectations about how the occupant of the role will behave. Social order is established in part through the internalisation of roles, and the norms and values that serve to define them, by the agent, and the institutionalisation of these values throughout society (Parsons 1951).

Parsons develops this model by drawing upon a form of systems theory developed in cybernetics, but also from the functionalist social psychology of R. F. Bales (see Parsons and Bales 1955). A system may be understood, broadly, as a stable and organised structure that exists within an environment. It is argued that any system, if it is to maintain itself in a stable equilibrium, must satisfy four prerequisites. These are adaptation (i.e. the system must adapt itself to its environment); goal-attainment (i.e. setting and pursuing the specific objectives of the system); integration (i.e. keeping the system together as a whole); and pattern-maintenance (i.e. motivating the elements within the system to perform the tasks demanded of them). Any stable system of social action must therefore fulfil these four functions. It will do so through four distinct subsystems: the behavioural system (of the individual's physical interaction with the environment); the personality system; the social system; and the cultural system. Hence the set of roles – along with their associated norms and values – that may be found in a society are not to be understood as a contingent aggregation. The cultural system must generate values that control the norms and roles of the social system, and that are in turn internalised to control the motivation of the personality system (and so guide physical adaptation).

In Parsonian systems theory any given subsystem will itself be open to analysis in terms of its own subsystems (and conversely, any system may itself be a subsystem of some larger system). Hence, the social system, a subsystem of the general action system, may be analysed in terms of its own subsystems. The analysis of the relationship between society and the economy that Parsons developed with Smelser, treats the economy as its adaptive subsystem (Parsons and Smelser 1956). Parsons further proposes that the polity, constituted from public and private policy-making bodies, performs goal attainment; the community (the free association of agents, for example as citizens) performs integrative functions; while culture (including, for example, religious institutions, but also the professions) generates and maintains the value identity of the society as a whole. A final component of this analysis involves the 'media of interchange' that allow subsystems to communicate with each other within the system. The medium of the economy is money (facilitating exchange and measuring value). Power (coercing agents) is the medium of the polity, while influence allows the community to persuade agents. Culture requires value-commitments (which might be broadly understood as the agents' faith in the fundamental values that define their collective identity).

A frequent criticism of functionalist sociologies is their neglect of social change. Indeed, the above arguments have focused on the equilibrium and stability of social life. Parsons's dauntingly complex model of the social system does facilitate an account of social change (1977b). Appealing to a model of evolution, albeit one that recognises that social change does not inevitably move in a single direction, he suggests that societies evolve by becoming more highly differentiated (so that functional prerequisites are more precisely defined, and are fulfilled by increasingly specialised institutions or subsystems). A classic example of this is to be found in the history of the family in European society. Initially, the family was responsible for the biological rearing of children, for education, and for much economic activity. Today economic activities, as well as most educational and even some biological responsibilities, have been transferred to other, more specialised institutions.

[AE]

Further reading: Menzes 1977; Rocher 1974.

PEIRCE, CHARLES SANDERS (1839–1914)

American philosopher and founder of pragmatism. Peirce was born in Cambridge, Massachusetts; he graduated from Harvard in 1859, in 1863 was awarded the first ScB degree in chemistry given by that institution. Among other things, Peirce worked for a time carrying out research in astronomy, he also carried out experiments to determine the force of gravity (work which gained him an international reputation). Among his pupils were John **Dewey** and Josiah Royce.

Peirce is also famous for his conception of semiotics, which can be contrasted with the view implicit in the thinking of structuralism. On Peirce's model, a sign can be defined as that which 'stands for something in some respect of capacity'; additionally, signs can either (a) resemble in some manner what they stand for (Peirce calls these 'icons'), (b) have some causal connection with what they stand for ('indexes' – e.g. the symptoms of a disease are indexes of that disease), or (c) have no resemblance or causal link with what they stand for, but do so conventionally ('symbols'). All signs consist of a *representamen* and an *interpretant* (which can roughly be paralleled with **Saussure**'s distinction between *signifier* and *signified*). Significantly, however, Peirce includes an additional element within his view of the sign (in other words, signs are for him 'triadic'): all signs also have an *object*, which can be understood as the real in language. This should not be confused with a mind-independent 'physically real' referent. Although Peirce is a realist, in so far as (a) he is committed to the view that there is a world which exists independently of our ways of speaking about it (and that world can, indeed, resist them), and (b) he also holds that language can in the long term converge with that physical reality, he nevertheless argues that this is only possible in principle, *not* in practical terms. This is because we are finite and fallible beings. In turn, Peirce postulated a 'convergence theory', which argues that we can provide at best only approximations of the physically real world. Thus, inquirers engage in a process of investigation into their experiences, producing knowledge claims which are forever doomed to fall short of the absolute status of reference to which they aspire (i.e. truth).

On Peirce's model, inquiry is an activity in which every proposition asserted is understood in terms of other propositions, each subsequent one of which is capable of modifying those which came before it. It is thus emphatically not an activity that is marked out by a series of discontinuities, as with the account offered within the Saussurean fixed structure of *langue*. Translated into Saussure's terminology, from a Peircean standpoint *parole* is no longer subject to being marginalised by the primacy of *langue*. Instead, *parole* is located within a dialogical framework that is engaged in both constantly producing and modifying itself. In this sense, Peirce's work bears some similarities with that of **Bakhtin**. Like the Russian thinker, and unlike the structuralists, Perice's semiotics resists any tendency to reduce the production of meaning to a rigid bifurcation between the synchronic and diachronic planes, i.e. between system and process. In turn, Peirce's account is able to embrace change in a manner that others, e.g. structuralism, cannot.

[PS]

Further reading: Apel 1981; Merrell 1993; Murphey 1993.

PLATO (*c*.428–*c*.348 BC)

Ancient Greek philosopher. Plato was a pupil of Socrates (469/70–399 BC), a figure who, in virtue of his strong personality, appears to have exerted a powerful influence over many youthful aristocrats in Athens. Although Socrates himself wrote nothing, he is represented in many of Plato's writings, which form the basis for much of our knowledge of him. Few facts are known about Plato's own life. He was born a member of the Athenian aristocratic class and as a young man formed a close bond with Socrates. This friendship lasted right up until Socrates's execution at the hands of the Athenian authorities (he was charged with impiety and the corruption of youth, found guilty by the Athenian Assembly and sentenced to death by drinking hemlock). At around 40 years of age Plato left Athens for Sicily, where by way of Dion, the brother-in-law of the Sicilian monarch, he attempted (without success) to establish a form of state that accorded with the ideals of his philosophy. A subsequent visit to Sicily twenty years later, when Plato acted briefly as an adviser to Dion's nephew, the monarch Dionysius II, was equally unsuccessful. Upon returning to Athens from the first of his two visits to Sicily, Plato established the Academy, the most famous pupil of which was the philosopher **Aristotle**.

Plato's writings are the first philosophical texts of Ancient Greece that exist in complete form. All are written as dialogues, and well over twenty are known to have been authored by him. That said, the order in which the Platonic dialogues were written is by no means certain. Scholars generally divide Plato's corpus into three groups: first, what are probably the earliest dialogues (e.g. the *Laches*, the *Euthyphro* and the *Hippias Major*); second, the middle period dialogues (e.g. the *Phaedo*, the *Gorgias*, the *Protagoras* and most famously the *Republic*); third, the late dialogues (e.g. the *Theaetetus*, the *Sophist* and the *Laws*). The first group of dialogues usually presents the reader with a situation, initiated by a purportedly 'confused' Socrates, in which the person named in the title claims knowledge about some kind of virtue or other form of excellence (such as courage, piety, beauty). Socrates then proceeds to request ever more precise clarifications of the speaker's views, rejecting their offering of particular illustrations of a virtue or excellence and pressing them to provide instead a general definition of the issue at hand. Once offered, the speaker's views are subjected to interrogation by Socrates (often Socrates will make statements that demand a 'yes' or 'no' response from the other speaker) until finally he forces them into contradicting themselves. What is evidenced in these texts is the famous 'Socratic dialectic': a method that reveals the weaknesses of an argument by way of a conversation consisting of question and answer. The early Platonic works appear to endorse the view that one must be able to define what a virtue or technical ability is prior to being able to make any claim about it. Equally, the same rule applies when it comes to answering the question as to whether someone or some action epitomises a virtue or art. In these works, too, the view is put forward that people always act with a view to the good and that wrongdoing is consequently the result of lack of knowledge.

Plato's middle period dialogues present us with the figure of Socrates as a teacher refining his philosophical views and presenting them in systematic form. There is an increasing concern with ontological questions, e.g. the question as to whether there is a 'real' world apart from the world given to us by way of the testimony of the senses. This ontological concern is evidenced in the 'Theory of Ideas' or 'Theory of Forms', most famously expounded in the *Republic*. This theory holds that all particulars that have something in common do so because they are all instances of a universal Idea. Take three human beings: all are different in that they have different names, faces, personal histories and so forth. However, all three individuals are human. Thus, Plato argues, all three are connected in virtue of the fact that they are instances of the Idea 'human'. What links them together is the notion of the human itself. Equally, Plato argues that one can make the same point with regard to other notions, such as goodness, Being, beauty or justice. All particular occurrences of such properties can be defined as such because they are all instances of, say, 'the good in-itself' or 'the just in-itself'. In effect, what is being claimed is that in the realm of sensory experience no absolute judgements are possible. When, for example, we hold some particular state of affairs to be just or beautiful, it will always be possible to note that it falls short of absolute justice or absolute beauty in some manner or other. What we can aspire to with regard to the realm of the senses, it follows, amounts at best to attaining true beliefs that are correct (i.e. such and such *appears* to be the case). This can be contrasted with complete knowledge (which would entitle us to hold that such and such truly *is* the case). Hence, for Plato, knowledge and belief are different in kind from one another (see *Republic*, Book 5).

Plato's suspicion of the senses is most famously exemplified in Book 7 of the *Republic*. Here we are presented with the parable of the cave. Imagine people chained up in a cave in such a way that they are facing a bare wall. Behind them a fire burns, and objects are held in such a way that the light of the fire throws their shadows on to the wall. If the people in the cave had known no other life, Plato argues, would they not mistake these shadows for reality? Moreover, if one person escaped from the cave and returned to tell his comrades what he had seen, would they not laugh at him? The same goes for human life in general. Such life is lived in the welter of the senses and what underlies the realm of the senses (i.e. reality, as exemplified by the realm of Ideas) is concealed from us. In this way, Plato draws a distinction between not only appearance and reality, but characterises this distinction in a very specific manner. Whereas the senses show us a world that consists of things coming to be and passing away (a realm of ceaseless change or becoming), the reality that underlies this world has Being: it does not change but remains eternally what it is. The highest of the unchanging Forms or Ideas, which Plato holds to be the Idea of the Good, is like the sun: it illuminates the world and thereby makes objects 'visible' to us. In other words, the Idea of the Good endows human life with meaning by offering a standard whereby beliefs, actions, etc. can be judged. This is highest form of knowledge that can be attained and is called 'dialectic'. At the same time, and keeping with Plato's analogy, one cannot emerge from the cave of ignorance and fix one's gaze on the sun without being dazzled by it. The function of philosophy is to lead one, by way of abstract reflection on the nature of universals, away from the senses toward appreciation and understanding of the realm of Ideas and hence truth.

The *Republic* is a complex and ambitious work that sets itself the task of elucidating the basis for the best form of political organisation. Plato's conception of this involves a form of government that is organised according to objectively valid principles of justice. If they are to be objective such principles must not serve the interests of any particular group within the political community or city-state. Rulers who serve their own interests over and above those of others, for instance, represent a corrupt form of government. In order to be just, a ruler must serve the best interests of everybody, and in order to do this they must have access to moral truth. This, according to Plato, is achieved by way of philosophical study. A philosopher is someone whose personality is dominated by reason. As such, the philosopher is a lover of wisdom. He or she can therefore be contrasted with a person who loves their appetites (e.g. someone driven by the desires for wealth, sexual pleasure, food, or drink) or a person who desires above all else to be held in high esteem by others (e.g. someone who is interested in acquiring a good reputation by being honoured by others). The rulers of the Republic are therefore to be philosopher-kings. Such kings will have the ethical knowledge necessary to ensure that justice prevails within society.

Following the above tripartite distinction, Plato conceives of all those within the city-state as occupying one of three classes. First, there is the ruling or guardian-class (the philosopher-kings, whose love of justice entitles them to rule). These are selected from the second class of soldiers (both men and women, whose love of honour and esteem makes them fit for the task of defending the city). The third class is composed of artisans and farmers (whose love of wealth ensures the city's material welfare). These class divisions are not fixed in so far as individuals born into a class need not remain there if their 'soul' is composed of the 'metal' that defines membership of another class (gold, silver or bronze). This notion of different compositions of the soul is alluded to as a 'noble lie', a myth whereby social distinctions are naturalised so that the rulers' authority is accepted by the governed. Implicit within the acceptability of such a notion for Plato is his belief that all societies must of necessity be hierarchical: the key issue is which hierarchy is more acceptable – and we have already seen what Plato's response would be to this question. A key notion underlying the *Republic* is that of a harmony between rational desires, justice and happiness. To be a moral being means to pursue a rational mode of life that will at the same time make one a happy individual. The ideal city-state will reflect this harmonious structure in its social order. Everybody will have their place. Thus, it would be inappropriate for a member of one class to engage in activities not associated with that class. A cobbler ought not at the same time to be a leader, nor a farmer a juror, or a soldier a maker of money (Book 3). Equally, forms of behaviour ought to be regulated according to the same logic. It would be wrong, for example, for a guardian to indulge in drunkenness or idleness. By the same token, the aesthetic realm requires policing. Thus, in music, the 'relaxed' Ionian and Lydian modes are to be spurned in favour of more fitting harmonic forms that reflect courageous activity or self-control (i.e. the Dorian and Phrygian modes). In poetry and painting, too, regulation is necessary, for such arts are forms of imitation that operate several removes from the truth (Book 10). We can see the logic of Plato's argument here by recalling that truth, for him, means meditating on the eternal and unseen nature of Ideas or Forms, with the ethical Idea of the Good underpinning all the rest. If a craftsman, in contrast, makes tools that are copies of Ideas, artists in their turn make copies of copies, and are hence three removes from truth. To be a 'good' artist, it follows, requires nothing in the way of moral insight, merely opinion. Hence, artists ought to be barred from entry into the ideal city-state on account of their potentially corrupting influence.

From the above discussion it should be clear that, for Plato, social order and the characteristics that define it are mirrored in the individual. A person is an embodiment of the city or culture that produces him or her. In turn, Plato is happy to conceive of the differences between cultures as being exemplified by individual characteristics. Thracians, Scythians and other northeners possess 'spirit', those from Plato's Greece display 'love of learning', while Phoenicians and Egyptians are notable for their 'love of money' (Book 4). By the same token, a distinction is deployed which separates Greeks from non-Greeks or, to put it in Plato's terms, 'barbarians' from civilised men (Book 5). A sense of cultural identity thus pervades the *Republic*. Where 'the Greek race is its own and akin [. . .] barbarians', in contrast, 'are strange and foreign'. Civil war (i.e. war between Greeks) is an unnatural state and to be avoided at all costs, whereas war proper is conducted between Greeks and the 'natural enemies' who threaten to enslave them. Hence, the *Republic* conceives of the ideal city-state against a backdrop of cultural differences and articulates the rule of rationality and justice that determines the internal structure of the city in terms of the primacy of Greek identity. The ideal city's citizens will be Greek and for that reason 'good and civilized', occupying a shared realm of values (religious, ethical, political, etc.). Because of this they will treat each other with moderation when faced with disputes: 'they won't ravage the country or destroy the houses, and they'll continue their quarrel only to the point at which those who caused it are forced to pay the penalty by those who were its innocent victims'. Civil war will thereby be avoided and its methods reserved for the treatment of barbarians alone. Plato thereby demonstrates an awareness of cultural diversity, but is committed by his theories to its suppression.

Plato's late period dialogues are marked by some highly complex analyses of a wide range of issues. These include addressing problems with the Theory of Ideas (the *Parmenides*), engaging with the problem of knowledge in the context of the philosophies of becoming of Protagoras and Heraclitus (the *Theaetetus*), discussing the nature of pleasure (the *Philebus*) or the most suitable kind of government (the *Statesman*), offering a detailed cosmology in a manner that affirms the Theory of Ideas (the *Timaeus* – although there is some dispute as to whether this is a middle or late period work). In what is generally regarded as his last work, the *Laws*, Plato again returns to some of the themes that dominate the *Republic*, this time attempting to outline the legal structure of an imagined city-state.

The critical debate surrounding Plato's work and influence is so vast as to defy simple exegesis. Many of the key themes that dominate Western philosophy have their origins in Plato's thought: for example, arguments concerning the nature of knowledge, ethics, metaphysics and ontology, politics, and aesthetics. Equally, Western culture is pervaded by Platonic influences. This is evidenced not only and most obviously in various aspects of religious belief (although in the medieval period it should be noted that Christian doctrine was formalised by thinkers such as Aquinas under the predominant influence of Aristotle's works), but in diverse aspects of the arts (to take one less than obvious example, the aesthetics of a Soviet socialist realist theorist like A. A. Zhdanov has strong parallels with Plato's). That said, the central impact of Plato's writings is not necessarily evidenced in overt doctrinal adherence to his theories. Rather, important elements (such as the mathematical approach espoused in the later works, along with the Platonic emphasis on reason and harmony) find their expression in the thought of a wide range of figures. Thus, the astronomer Kepler (1571–1630), famous for his discovery of the elliptical orbits of the planets, was heavily influenced in his studies by the Platonic conception of the harmony of the spheres and espoused the view that mathematical principles were the most suited for astronomical work. More recently, philosophers such as **Nietzsche** have famously attacked Plato for setting in place the untenable and damaging conceptual opposition between the 'real' and 'apparent' worlds. For Nietzsche (writing in *Twilight of the Idols*, 1889), Plato's thought pays testimony to a crisis within Greek culture, wherein commonly held values have been overrun by an increasingly anarchic diversity of tastes. The Socratic/Platonic answer to this is, Nietzsche argues, to turn toward a conception of rationality that holds there to be an objective moral order as a means of regulating life. Following Nietzsche, twentieth-century philosophers such as **Heidegger** have sought to criticise the ontological distinction between sensible and intelligible that underlies Platonic and Aristotelian thought. For Heidegger this distinction constitutes the basis of Western metaphysics, which has in fact turned away from a genuine encounter with the problem of Being. Plato's thought has also come under attack from thinkers such as Karl Popper, who argues that texts like the *Republic* evidence totalitarian tendencies.

[PS]

Further reading: Hare 1982; Popper 1945; Reeve 1981.

POPPER, KARL (1902–1994)

British (although Austrian-born) philosopher of science and politics. Prior to Popper, the philosophers of science had generally sought to explain how scientific theories could be proven to be true. Popper, building upon the doubts expressed in the eighteenth century by David **Hume**, rejected the possibility of proof in the empirical sciences. While a scientific law could be formulated and tested through laboratory experiment and observations of the real world, no set of observations could exhaustively establish that the law held for all time and all space. It is impossible, for example, directly to observe occasions in the past when the law should have been in operation, or occasions in the future. Popper therefore argued that science proceeds, not by proving its hypotheses or explanations to be true, but by proving them to be false. The task of science is to formulate an explanation of phenomena (and typically phenomena that do not behave according to our pre-existing expectations of that behaviour). A good explanation will be such that it will entail certain predictions about future events, and that these events are observable. (Galileo hypothesised that the mass of an object will not influence the velocity with which it falls to the ground.) The explanation is then tested by observing whether the predicted events take place or not. (Galileo allegedly dropped two cannon balls of different mass simultaneously from the top of the Tower at Pisa. They landed together.) If the predicted events do occur, then the theory is corroborated (which is to say, that it can be accepted, for the moment, as if it were true). If they do not occur, then the theory is refuted. It has been proven to be false, and must be replaced by a better theory. Theories are continually under test, and as more or perhaps more subtle observations become possible, even a well-corroborated theory may eventually prove to be false. Popper uses this argument to distinguish between science and pseudo-science. Pseudo-science is such that it refuses to generate empirically testable predictions, or refuses to accept refutation of a theory when it occurs. For Popper both psychoanalysis and **Marx**ism are pseudo-sciences.

Science therefore thrives only when there is a continual testing of accepted theories. This model of science, and specifically of an open and mutually critical community of scientists, becomes the basis for Popper's political philosophy. His concept of the 'open society' entails that social decisions are not to be made by autocratic planners (and especially not those who, like certain crude Marxists, believe that they are working according to the iron laws of history), but rather through open and rational debate. Any member of the society must be free to criticise any policy proposal, and there must be a real possibility of new ideas being put into practice (and thus subject to empirical testing). For Popper such democratic openness is a precondition for economic growth. Open societies are economically more efficient than closed ones.

Popper's later work embraced a broad range of philosophical problems, and not least the relationship between his model of scientific inquiry and Darwinian accounts of evolution (in so far as both articulated an account of progress as problem-solving, with potential solutions being rigorously tested in terms of their practicality in the real world). Popper also offered an account of human culture, as what he termed 'World 3'. World 1 consists of objective and material reality (and thus physical things, animate and inanimate, in the environment). World 2 is composed of subjective, mental phenomena (thoughts, emotions, feelings). World 3 is both objective and mental. It is composed of the cultural products of human minds that gain an autonomy from any individual mind. Language, law, religion, art, science, ethics, the institutions of government and education are all examples of entities within World 3. One implication of this account is that while World 3 is a creation of the human mind, it is capable of having consequences and properties that are unintended by the creator. Popper gives the example of mathematics. The sequence of natural numbers is a human construction, yet, once this sequence exists, facts about it can be discovered, such as the difference between odd and even numbers or the properties of prime numbers. That these properties require discovery demonstrates the objectivity (in the sense of its autonomy from its creator) of World 3.

[AE]

Further reading: Magee 1973; O'Hear 1995.

RAWLS, JOHN (1921–)

American philosopher, whose defence of liberalism was responsible for the revitalisation of English-language political philosophy from the late 1960s onwards.

His philosophy, presented in *A Theory of Justice* (1972), draws its inspiration in large part from a renewal of the tradition of liberal social contract theory. Such accounts of political society, dating from the seventeenth century, saw society as being formed by the voluntary subscription of autonomous individuals to a contract that defines their reciprocal obligations and rights. While Rawls defines society as 'a cooperative venture for mutual advantage', he does not see society literally as a social contract. Rather, he suggests that *if* real society, with the freedoms that it guarantees to its members and its distribution of resources between individuals, was such that all its members would have freely signed up as if it were a contract, then it would be a just society. Everyone would feel that the freedoms and resources that society guarantees them were justified.

In order to develop this account, Rawls invites his readers to participate in a thought experiment. Imagine that you are in an 'original position' prior to society, and that you have the task of planning the society in which you will live. You are likely to plan a society that gives you, and people like you, a certain advantage. But this, for Rawls, would not be fair. It would treat certain people quite arbitrarily as more important or privileged than others. So, Rawls demands that the people planning the society know little about their personal characteristics and preferences. While you know some basic facts about what it is to be human and what motivates human action, you are placed behind a 'veil of ignorance' as to your own talents, intelligence and abilities, your gender, race, and health, and so on. When the veil is lifted you may find yourself to be intelligent, beautiful and healthy, or physically disabled, having learning difficulties, or just downright average. In effect, this thought experiment is designed to encourage the reader to empathise with the position of others, and thus to aspire to a certain objectivity in perceiving how society treats its members. (Imagine, Rawls suggests, that when you plan a society, that your worst enemy has the job of determining your place within it.) Rawls's point is that a just society is one that treats everyone appropriately. He argues that, from behind this veil of ignorance, you would accept two principles to organise your society. First, everyone has as extensive a set of equal liberties as is compatible with similar liberty for all. Such liberties would include the right to own property, to have freedom of speech and movement, to have a fair trial, and to participate in the political process. Second, a just society is a meritocratic one. There will be inequalities of wealth and income, but these inequalities are justified only in so far as they serve to encourage individuals to develop whatever abilities they have, and to employ them for the collective good. Ultimately, Rawls's measure of the justice of a society is the way in which it treats the least advantaged of its members. Rich capitalist entrepreneurs are justified, for example, only if their financial rewards are bringing about employment and the production of goods that are improving the life of people throughout society. In addition, if inequality comes about through the work one does, then it is also important that everyone has an equal opportunity to compete for all offices. This in turn presupposes that one has the opportunity, for example through the educational system, to recognise and develop one's talents. Hereditary inequalities are prima facie unjust.

Rawls has developed his position, not least in response to criticisms from communitarian philosophers (Sandel 1982). It was argued that his account of the original position failed to recognise the importance that communal and social resources play in allowing the individual to make decisions about justice. Different concrete communities will develop different traditions of what a just society is. In response, in *Political Liberalism* (1993), Rawls claims that he is addressing only readers who are already embedded within the Western liberal tradition. In the concept of the 'overlapping consensus' (Rawls 1987), he tries to account for the pluralism of contemporary liberal societies. Members of society will be committed to 'comprehensive doctrines' (such as religious, artistic and communal worldviews), that play a large role in constituting their self-understanding and sense of identity. In a just pluralist society, individuals will recognise that not everyone can be convinced of the truth of their own doctrine. They must then accept a degree of 'reasonable disagreement', so that their differences with others are never resolved. They must be tolerant of other comprehensive doctrines. Thus, in a just society, all 'reasonable comprehensive doctrines' will have a common overlapping ground of mutual toleration and commitment to the liberal principles detailed in *A Theory of Justice*. In effect, the citizen separates the complex self that is constituted through their comprehensive doctrines, from their participation as a political being in social structures that are shared with others, who come from often radically divergent communities.

[AE]

Further reading: Daniels 1978; Kukathas and Pettit 1990; Mulhall and Swift 1992.

RICOEUR, PAUL (1913–)

Paul Ricoeur is a philosopher of reflection. In other words, his writings are concerned, primarily, with human subjectivity: the way in which we think about ourselves. **Nietzsche** argued that we are 'strangers to ourselves' because our deepest motivations (drives) are hidden from us, and because we are constrained by moral values which we neither choose nor fully understand. **Freud** developed this self-estrangement into a theory which distinguished between the conscious 'ego' and the unconscious 'id'. **Marx** uncovered the ways in which what we think of as our own opinions, ideas, beliefs etc., usually turn out to be products of our socio-economic environment.

Ricoeur's response to this dilemma is to argue that consciousness can be inspected only indirectly, by means of the interpretation of its products: art, literature, music, ideology, institutions etc. But, since interpretation does not have any agreed rules, a 'conflict of interpretations' arises between competing explanations of human being: phenomenology, structuralism, psychoanalysis, Marxism, religious discourse and so on. Rather than opting for any one of these approaches at the expense of all the others, Ricoeur seeks out the most fruitful aspects of each, and attempts to bring them into meaningful dialogue. He considers it neither possible nor desirable that philosophy should arrive at any overarching synthesis which could count as a grand explanatory system; rather, he works 'to attain a certain point of unresolved tension' between competing claims, and retains 'an emphatic distrust of premature solutions'.

Such an approach is necessarily wide ranging. Ricoeur has written about philosophy, literature, theology, linguistics, politics and history, in a series of multidisciplinary explorations of the meaning of human being. His magnum opus, the three-volume *Time and Narrative* (1983–1985), stages 'a long and difficult threeway conversation between history, literary criticism, and phenomenological philosophy' from **Aristotle** to Thomas Mann. Comparing and contrasting a large number of such texts enables Ricoeur to explore in depth the set of problems which we encounter when we try to reconcile our internal consciousness of time with its measurement by means of calendars and clocks. He argues that narrative plays a vital role in our understanding, not only of time, but also of ourselves: our sense of identity is expressible only as a kind of story of temporal development. Some of the residual difficulties of *Time and Narrative* are addressed in *Oneself as Another* (1992).

Given the necessity of language to each and every kind of philosophical enterprise, it is possible, Ricoeur believes, to bring apparently remote, or even contradictory, ideas into meaningful contact by attending to their linguistic features and structures. This emphasis turns philosophy towards hermeneutics (interpretation theory).

Ricoeur's 'hermeneutics of suspicion' heeds the call of thinkers like Marx, Nietzsche and Freud to beware (and to unmask) false consciousness. But, not content to allow 'suspicious' approaches to dominate the field unchallenged, Ricoeur appeals to certain aspects of religious discourse to provide a balance. He argues that suspicion is necessarily limited by the trust which we are obliged to place in the language which we inherit and upon which we depend. On this basis, he speaks of a hermeneutics of the self which can claim to hold itself at an equal distance from the cogito exalted by **Descartes** and from the cogito that Nietzsche proclaimed forfeit.

[Kevin Mills]

Further reading: Hahn 1995.

RORTY, RICHARD (1931–)

American philosopher. Although trained within the so-called 'analytic' tradition, Rorty espouses an approach to philosophy that is generally referred to as 'neo-pragmatist'. Rorty draws heavily on the works of C. S. **Peirce**, William James and John **Dewey**, and also displays an enthusiasm for aspects of the writings of many 'continental' philosophers, such as **Nietzsche**, **Heidegger**, **Lyotard** and **Derrida**. In the early 1980s Rorty was happy to call his approach 'postmodern' (Rorty 1991a, pp. 60, 66). In other words, Rorty (like Lyotard) advocates an attitude toward philosophy that rejects 'meta-narratives'. Additionally, though, he links this attitude to a 'tradition' of philosophical practice that also includes thinkers such as **Hegel** and **Marx**. This tradition, Rorty argues, 'insists on thinking of morality as the interest of a historically conditioned community rather than "the common interest of humanity"' (Rorty 1991a, p. 198). In other words, Rorty endorses a rejection of a foundationalist approach to philosophy. According to Rorty, we need to overcome the temptation to seek out any foundations or first principles. Philosophers ought to abandon the idea that they can step outside the community and historical context in which they live and engage in a search for universals in the realm of knowledge or value. From the early 1990s Rorty ceases to refer to his approach as 'postmodern' because, he says, the word has become subject to such overuse that it ceases to signify anything particularly helpful. Instead, Rorty offers a range of new terms to summarise his position, for example 'post-Nietzschean philosophy'. The writings of Nietzsche, and post-Nietzschean European philosophy generally, Rorty holds, share common features with the American pragmatism.

There are, of course, differences between the European thinkers and pragmatists like James or Dewey, but they all share a critical attitude to the tradition of modern philosophy associated with **Descartes**, and can be described as 'anti-representationalists' and 'anti-essentialists'. Thus, Nietzsche, Rorty holds, is as devoted to analysing the practical effect of our beliefs on our conduct as Peirce or James.

Rorty's conception of pragmatism is well illustrated by turning to a central issue in the philosophy of language, especially as it has been dealt with by the Anglo-American tradition of analytic philosophy. Rorty argues that a neo-pragmatist position involves rejecting a 'representationalist' account of language. A representationalist, according to Rorty, is someone committed to the belief that there is a necessary connection between language and a mind-independent, non-linguistic reality. Representationalists are, it follows, 'realists'. The realist addresses questions of knowledge with the aim of providing an account of the relation between states of affairs and the correct (i.e. 'true') representation of them in language. The representationalist thereby assumes a world of relationships that exist independently of thought and language. Against this view, anti-representationalists like Dewey, James or Nietzsche, Rorty argues, 'deny [. . .] that truth is correspondence to reality' (Rorty 1998, p. 3). In other words, Rorty holds there to be no necessary connection between what we speak of and matters of fact because '*no* linguistic items represent *any* nonlinguistic items' (Rorty 1991a, p. 2). This does not entail a commitment to the view that our language has no relation to our environment. However, this relationship can be worked out in practical rather than universal and theoretical terms. Rorty's argument is that many of the concepts philosophers traditionally resort to, such as the notion of 'non-linguistic items' referred to by terms like 'fact of the matter', simply lack the kind of privileged explanatory role they have been claimed to possess. Rorty holds such notions to be unhelpful, since they get in the way of a genuine understanding of our relationship with our environment. This is because, in Rorty's view, language does not serve to 'represent' the world. It is, rather, a tool for coping with living in it.

Once representationalist pseudo-concepts are swept aside, Rorty claims, we will be in a position to address the issue of making claims about our experiences without being diverted by the fruitless temptation to search for a 'method' that requires justification by way of a supposedly 'real' world. The traditional primacy of 'theory of knowledge' must hence be abandoned. On Rorty's view, the activity of theorising about knowledge is nothing more than one (dispensable) form of discourse that is part of the larger ongoing conversation between communities of language-users. In other words, Rorty holds that the activity of asking questions about what we know involves issues that do not stand apart from the concerns that we, as language users, may have in virtue of our 'human peculiarities'. For the antirepresentationalist, like the later **Wittgenstein**, a knowledge claim is assessed according to the criteria of justification internal to language. Justifications, in other words, are given by way of the rules specific to a given 'language game'.

Rorty thereby advocates the abandonment of traditional philosophical questions, principally those allied with the **Plato**nic and Cartesian epistemological quests for 'foundations' upon which our knowledge can rest. Instead of such foundations Rorty proposes a conception of 'community' as serving to elucidate the relationship between humans and the world they inhabit. The contrast between this and the realist view is underlined by Rorty's use of the notion of 'solidarity'. By situating oneself within a community (be it imagined or actual) one acquires a sense of solidarity with others and hence develops a sense of individual identity. In turn, the pragmatist is able to hold that a truth-claim is meaningful only so far as it can be asserted by way of reference to the dominant belief of what 'true' is according to the norms of any specific community. From this it follows that we do not need to step outside the realm of the social and ethical paradigms of our own community when we engage in philosophy. This does not entitle us to hold that all forms of society or ethical views are as good as each other. But it does mean that 'we have to work out from the networks we are, from the communities with which we presently identify' (Rorty 1991a, p. 202). In Rorty's case, those 'networks' are associated with bourgeois, liberal democratic forms, which he is happy to endorse.

Rorty argues that what is needed is a transformation of our ideas about the value of philosophy. Such a transformation will be achieved only 'by a long slow process of cultural change – that is to say of change in common sense, changes in the institutions available for being pumped up by philosophical arguments'. Philosophical ideas, it follows, are culturally produced. Philosophy, in Rorty's view, is best understood as a form of 'therapy'. What we learn from the great philosophers is that many of the problems that preoccupied their predecessors were not really problems at all. So, Rorty tells us, Descartes offered a means of forgetting about the 'scholastic problems' of the medieval period, **Kant** found a way out of 'Cartesian problems', Hegel dispensed with the central 'Kantian problems', and Nietzsche and the pragmatists overcame the pitfalls of Hegelian metaphysics. 'Philosophical progress', it follows, does not involve getting nearer to an absolute truth. Rather, progress in Rorty's sense is about generating new ways of seeing our world. For this reason, philosophy cannot be thought of as a unified discipline with an ultimate purpose (i.e. discovering the fundamental nature of reality or moral truth). At best, philosophers are to be thought of as people who engage with the writings of figures like Plato, Kant or Hegel and engage in a critical manner with the issues they raise. In this way, philosophy is rendered no more than 'a kind of writing. It is delimited, as is any literary genre, not by form or matter, but by tradition' (Rorty 1982, p. 92). In other words, Rorty claims all human activities (philosophy included) are historically specific and cannot be understood properly apart from the culture in which they are embedded.

[PS]

Further reading: Brandom 2000; Kolenda 1990; Malachowski 1990.

ROSE, GILLIAN (1947–1995)

British social theorist, who through a profound reading of **Hegel** sought to navigate between the excesses and dangers of modernist absolutism and postmodernist relativism. Her work draws upon philosophy (not least in a close knowledge of the German tradition), sociology and theology, and embraces and draws together law, architecture, religion and literature.

Rose presents her project in terms of a choice between Athens – the tradition of rational philosophical argument that culminated in the Enlightenment and modernism, and that has its tragic denouement in Stalinism – and Jerusalem – an abandonment of reason in favour of love and community, and the recognition of otherness and the marginal, which is characteristic of a number of forms of postmodernism (Rose 1993, p. 1). While Rose situates herself within a Jewish tradition, she does not seek to replace Athens with Jerusalem, but rather to play the two traditions off against each other, so that any hubristic certainty in the truth of one's philosophical position is continually being undermined. Rose retains a faith in the possibility of (Athenian) truth, but only in the face of the risk of error, and in full consciousness of the violence that such error can unleash.

Rose's philosophy is 'speculative', in the sense of 'speculation' that is found in Hegel (Rose 1981). Speculation is thinking about thinking, and as such questions the tensions and incoherence that arise in the attempt to know, or to become conscious of the world. Rose argues that Hegel's philosophy (at least as expressed in his *Phenomenology of Spirit*, 1807) does not culminate in an absolute knowledge (where knowing subject and known object are at one – where the subject possesses the object completely). Rather, Hegel offers us an open-ended journey, during which the thinker may reflect upon the errors of one stage of consciousness and so move to another more adequate stage, but without ever ridding itself of error altogether. More precisely, the thinker is always embedded in social relations that inhibit truthful thought. The modernist denies this insight by trying to find a point of certainty from which they can begin to think, and thus rid their thinking of all error. The postmodernist may recognise his or her embeddedness in social relations, but uses that embeddedness as an excuse for abandoning the aspiration to truthful thought altogether. Both then unleash a violence: the modernist through the arrogant assertion of truth; the postmodernist through an inability to challenge effectively the violent misuse of power that characterises society.

Rose's magnum opus, the forbiddingly complex *Broken Middle* (1992), explores this problem of violence by addressing three themes: the anxiety of beginning, the equivocation of the ethical and the agon of authorship. The 'anxiety of beginning' refers to the problem of how one is to begin thinking or theorising if one is already subject to the violence of an unjust and oppressive society. Rose rejects the possibility of finding a starting point that is unsullied by such violence (e.g. the position of the oppressed as opposed to that of the oppressor). Indeed, she argues that what is fundamentally at fault with contemporary culture, and what makes violence disabling, is a loss in the sense of failure. Contemporary 'broken' culture (including philosophy) is unwilling or unable to take the risk of failure. It thus violently imposes its version of the truth upon its victims. Rose's 'equivocation of the ethical' responds by recognising that violence is enabling as well as disabling. One 'suspends' the ethical, by violently criticising contemporary society (and the philosophy and morality that legitimises it), and overthrowing its sense of certainty. The agent is constituted by the violence that is embedded in history and society, but the agent is thus constituted as an active being, and should not (as perhaps **Adorno** was: Rose 1993, pp. 53–64) be afraid of any political engagement, in case it leads to new violence. Violence will change society, but, because the agent will have misperceived the interests of others, the agent's criticism, once enacted as law or social policy, will indeed lead to a new imbalance of power. Yet, because the ethical has been only suspended and not abolished, the agent must still recognise that its own position is vulnerable. One proceeds, risking failure (just as Hegel's *Phenomenology of Spirit* progresses from one erroneous form of consciousness to the next). The 'agon of authorship' is thus the struggle to open oneself to others. To enter into dialogue with others is to renounce the self-assured, possessive subject that is the focus of Hegel's criticisms. One recognises one's failure, while declaring one's faith in the truth, and resisting any premature (and false) reconciliation of intellectual and political tensions.

Rose's philosophy is ultimately to be understood as a philosophy of history. In thinking about thinking, one reflects upon how thought has been embodied in and shaped by historical engagement. One struggles to understand history – to find principles by which history can be judged – and not to be numbed by the horror of the past (as **Benjamin**'s image of the angle of history, blown backwards over an unfolding landscape of catastrophe, suggests: Rose 1993, pp. 175–210). Only the struggle to understand can do justice to the victims of violence, and the voices of the oppressed and marginalised that have been silenced.

[AE]

Further reading: Tubbs 1997; R. Williams 1995.

ROUSSEAU, JEAN-JACQUES (1712–1778)

Geneva-born philosopher who was one of the key figures associated both with the Enlightenment and the birth of Romanticism. Rousseau was a political theorist, social critic, philosopher of education, novelist and moralist. He arrived in Paris in 1741 and established a friendship with the Enlightenment philosopher and co-editor of the *Encyclopédie*, Denis Diderot (1713–1784). The *Encyclopédie* was presented as a dictionary of the sciences and arts. In effect it was an Enlightenment manifesto which was assembled with the purpose of disseminating the radical ideas of the French *philosophes*. The *Encyclopédie* contains articles by figures such as Voltaire (1694–1778) which are generally characterised by a combination of anti-religious sentiment and the advocacy of tolerant and broadly 'liberal' politics grounded by a faith in the power of reason to produce a better society. Rousseau himself contributed articles to the *Encyclopédie* (on music and political economy). Among

Rousseau's most important works are *Discourse on Inequality* (1754), *Emile* (an essay on education: Rousseau 1991), *The Social Contract* (1762) and the *Confessions* (one of the most candid autobiographies ever written: Rousseau 1995).

Rousseau published the *Discourse on Inequality* in 1754. In this work he sets out the reasons of social inequality. Rousseau argues that there are two kinds of inequality. First, there is 'natural' inequality: some people are stronger than others, can run faster, etc. The other form of inequality is political or moral, and is the chief concern of Rousseau's *Discourse*. Political inequality derives from human actions and is rooted in social conditions. Rousseau deploys a 'state of nature' argument to investigate the origins of this form of inequality. On such a view, if we envisage humans existing in a state of nature, differentiated from one another only by natural inequalities, we can then ask what kinds of human action are responsible for social inequality. Rousseau envisages humans in the state of nature as solitary beings. They are non-linguistic and meet infrequently and contact between individuals is limited to casual encounters. Over time, however, humans abandon their solitary lifestyle, driven largely by material need. Language emerges as a result of this. The most primitive forms of society are thus envisaged by Rousseau as communities in which individuals live in proximity to one another bound by only the loosest of ties.

Such an epoch of human history Rousseau feels to be the happiest, for the 'noble savage' lives a simple life wherein the natural inequalities that distinguish people are of minimal importance. Social inequality only comes into existence with the institution of property, which brings the introduction of social differences rooted in inequality of possession. This kind of inequality characterises what Rousseau refers to as 'civil society'. As Rousseau says at the opening of Book 2 of the *Discourse*, 'The first man who, having enclosed a piece of land, thought of saying "This is mine" and found people simple enough to believe him was the true founder of civil society'. In the institution of property, therefore, Rousseau locates the origins of social inequality. The inequality of possession that is thereby created brings in its wake the founding of law, one of the cornerstones of modern civilised societies. Law itself is envisaged as being the creation of those with an interest in preserving the privilege that accompanies their possessions. Rousseau is thus opposed to the theories of the English liberal philosopher John Locke (1632–1704). Locke argued that civil society was instituted and consented to by individual in the state of nature because it was a means of arbitrating between the conflicting interests of individuals by offering the opportunity of equality before the law. For Rousseau, the opposite is the case. With the onset of private property, society becomes dominated by the interests of the wealthy and powerful, and equality before the law merely serves to preserve this situation. The 'consent' alluded to by Locke is in fact a confidence trick, for the have-nots in exchange for legal protection have repudiated their right to a share in the wealth of the rich. We could, of course, doubt the validity of any state of nature theory in so far as humans can be construed in their essence to be social creatures. But whether or not Rousseau's argument seems historically plausible is not really the most important question. What matters is that Rousseau's argument demonstrates the relationship between social inequality and the possession of property. In addition, Rousseau's argument also offers a means of accounting for the evils of human life without presupposing a corrupt or selfish human nature. In fact Rousseau takes the contrary view. Humans in their purportedly 'savage' state are for him essentially 'good', in that they are all equipped with 'natural compassion'. If human nature cannot be held responsible for the corruption that is present in modern society, then it follows that it is so-called 'civilisation' itself that ought to be regarded as the genuine cause of human misery.

Although Rousseau is a figure associated with the Enlightenment, the *Discourse* amply demonstrates the differences that separate Rousseau from a classical Enlightenment figure like Diderot. Whereas the latter conceives of rationality in liberating terms, in that the development of science and technology is taken to imply a progressive improvement in the conditions of human life, Rousseau does not. For Rousseau, on the contrary, science and the modern, civilised society that has produced it is retrograde in comparison with simpler ways of living. In 'unsophisticated' societies, Rousseau holds, virtue and happiness is a concrete and attainable reality rather than an abstract and unfulfilled possibility. Modern civil society, therefore, is corrupt and antithetical to genuine virtue.

There are similarities between the *Discourse* and Rousseau's famous treatise on politics, *The Social Contract* (1762) in so far as this text likewise indicates differences from the approach advocated by the *philosophes*. Whereas many *philosophes* espouse firm government (Voltaire, for example, argued that 'enlightened despotism' was among the more desirable forms of government) Rousseau does not. *The Social Contract* is a work that seeks to explore whether virtue is a concrete possibility once one has entered the realm of 'political society'. This text presents the reader with some important contrasts with the *Discourse*. For example, Rousseau now argues that civil society, properly understood, is the proper realm for the fullest attainment of human potential.

Likewise, he also claims that in the state of nature humans are really rather stupid and uninteresting. *The Social Contract* is an inquiry into the best form of government possible, and Rousseau now holds that if possible this kind of government would be synonymous with a moral life.

The Social Contract presents Rousseau's most radical contribution to the debate about the nature of government: his notion of the 'general will'. Whereas earlier thinkers, such as Thomas Hobbes (1588–1679) had argued that humans are faced with a stark choice between the free but insecure state of nature and a secure life fettered by governmental power, Rousseau rejects this dichotomy. The Hobbesian choice between freedom and servitude is not the only option, argues Rousseau, since it is also possible for people to rule themselves. Rousseau follows Hobbes and Locke in holding that civil society comes into being and receives its legitimacy by way of a social contract, i.e. a pact made between individuals. But for him a civil society can be envisaged that combines governmental power and freedom: all that is necessary is that the people themselves become the sovereign. This, for Rousseau, means that a society's citizens legislate with regard to their own laws. To be at liberty, on this view, is to be subject to laws that one has had a part in making oneself. An individual is therefore free to the extent that they are subject to a form of power that they can acknowledge as authoritative. The general will is the will of the whole community of citizens. This will, Rousseau argues, is an expression of a unity that also necessitates the protection of its constituent parts: no citizen can be injured without injury in effect being done to the whole. This relationship, of course, does not preclude conflicts arising between the sovereign will and the individual citizen, since private interests can always come into conflict with public ones. However, the general will, Rousseau argues, as the will of the whole must always take precedence over individuated interests. In a much-cited passage from *The Social Contract*, Rousseau says that dissenters from the general will 'shall be forced to be free'. Some commentators have made much of this statement, seeing in it a justification of totalitarianism. But this may be overstating Rousseau's position. For his argument is that the general will should be understood as the necessary condition of a just social life and that the overturning of this condition would thus be equivalent to the abandonment of justice. Private interests would be above the law, and this would render the very notion of law both corrupt and absurd.

With his advocacy of the general will Rousseau can be seen as an exponent of democratic power. To put the matter in a more subtle way, he is one of those thinkers who occupy the republican tradition (a tradition that includes such thinkers as **Aristotle**, Machiavelli and the English civil war thinker James Harrington). The key feature of this tradition is its argument that freedom and constraint (i.e. individual liberty and govermental power) are not opposed poles in the political arena. Against the liberal view espoused by thinkers such as **Mill**, who argues that individual liberty can only be properly comprehended by situating it in direct opposition to the normative force enshrined in law by popular government, Rousseau sees popular sovereignty and freedom as two sides of the same coin. There is, for him, no freedom without normative constraint.

A central theme in Rousseau's thought is to be found in assertion of a direct link between virtue and simplicity. This link is what allows him to condemn modern European culture as decadent. Simplicity is taken by Rousseau to be equivalent to such qualities as directness of utterance and honesty. Complexity, for instance in social manners, in aesthetics (the simplicity of melody versus the complexity of harmony in music) or in relation to forms of speech (see the *Essay on the Origins of Language*), is taken to imply falseness and deceit. This dichotomy has been analysed, among others, by **Derrida**, who has offered a deconstructive reading of Rousseau's claim that language arises from simple, 'primitive' cries that are direct expressions of emotions.

[PS]

Further reading: Dent 1988; J. Hall 1973; Merquior 1980.

SAID, EDWARD (1935–)

American literary critic, postcolonial theorist and political commentator who was born in the Middle East. In 1963 he was made Parr Professor of English and Comparative Literature, at Columbia University, New York, where he has remained to this day. Said's interests span the realms of cultural and critical theory and literary criticism. He has also actively engaged in contemporary political and cultural debates (for example, he has written about the historical roots of the dilemma of the Palestinian population – see *The Question of Palestine*, 1979).

In his book *Beginnings: Intention and Method* (1975), Said sought to draw a distinction between the mythical or divine attribution associated with the notion of 'origin' in classical thought (which carries with it implications of order, chronology and hierarchy) and the human and secular realm of 'beginning' (a word which has associations with modernity, and implies an overturning of classical hierarchy, and its replacement with heterogeneous and disparate forms). Beginnings arise out of existing traditions and transform them through an immanent process. They are exemplified by, for example, the novel form which, in its postmodern guise, can allow for the formulation of modes of language which transgress accepted conventions and hierarchies of meaning. In turn, Said formulates a view of meaning that emphasises the political and cultural dimensions of its production, drawing on the work of thinkers such as **Foucault** in order to outline his position. However, although he engages with their work in a positive manner, Said does not endorse uncritically attitudes common among exponents of poststructuralism, e.g. a tendency to view individual agency as a product of impersonal forces. Rather, for Said, the activity of interpretation should be regarded as a particularised and individual activity that takes the form of an engagement with traditional forms in order to question them in a communal context.

Equally, Said has criticised the attitudes of much post-structuralist inspired critical theory for abandoning its radical beginnings in the 1960s in favour of a view which emphasises 'undecidability' above all else, and reduces questions of the formulation of meaning to mere matters of the free play of 'textuality' (see *The World, the Text, and the Critic*, 1991). This reflects his commitment to a view of texts as being ensconced within concrete social and ideological constraints, the production of which is thus an engagement with these constraints. Texts are, in turn, not to be regarded as semantic structures open to interpretation solely in the light of the purported suspension of determinate meaning implicit in the view put forward by thinkers such as **Derrida**, but rather as systematically related to one another through their implication in a hierarchy of power relations. In turn, these power relations are also culturally located. From this it is clear that, for Said, textuality is a cultural matter, and questions of culture are also questions with a hierarchical dimension. Again drawing on Foucault, Said advocates a conception of culture which involves paying attention to the tendency of dominant forms to appropriate to themselves or pacify and thereby control other forms which lie outside them. This thesis is further developed in *Orientalism* (1978a), in which Said provides a critical analysis of the Western construction of 'oriental' culture in the guise of academic study. Said's thesis is that the conceptualisation of alien culture embodied by Orientalism is in fact a means of defining and thereby exercising control over it. Above all, Said, argues, although Orientalism ostensibly involves the description and definition of an alien culture, it in fact embodies a discourse through which European culture defined itself through providing a definition of the 'oriental' as exhibiting radically opposite tendencies ('irrational' as opposed to 'rational', etc.). This argument is further elaborated in Said's more recent work (see *Culture and Imperialism*, 1993), where he argues that the construction of African or Indian identity in, for example, the novelistic works of Jane Austen or Joseph Conrad, can be read as being implicated in the domination of colonial forms of power.

[PS]

Further reading: Sprinker 1992.

SARTRE, JEAN–PAUL (1905–1980)

French philosopher, novelist (Sartre 1947b, 1950, 1964a, 1968b) and playwright (1947a, 1962a), who was in many respects the model of a politically engaged intellectual (see 1984). In 1964 he was offered, but refused, the Nobel Prize for Literature. An indication of the esteem in which he was held is the fact that 50,000 people attended his funeral.

Sartre developed as a philosopher through his study of the phenomenology of **Husserl**, and particularly by developing Husserl's conception of the intentionality of consciousness. This entailed that human beings do not passively receive experiences of the external world, but actively give meaning to these experiences. Thus, in his earliest philosophical works (1956, 1957), Sartre began to explore the freedom that imagination gives the human individual in inventing their world. Sartre's great work, *Being and Nothingness* (1958), develops this account of human freedom into a full exposition of an existential philosophy. Sartre's existentialism is usefully summed up by the slogan from *Existentialism and Humanism* (1948), that 'existence precedes essence'. What this means is that human beings have no fixed essence. There is no human nature, and nor does the individual human being have any determining psychological traits. What any human being turns out to be is a result of their existence, which is to say, of the way in which they freely chose to live their lives. The depth of this freedom is delightfully illustrated in the example Sartre gives of a man who, while alone, is unhappy. Yet, when another person interrupts him, he freely changes his emotion, and at best promises his misery an appointment after his visitor has departed (Sartre 1958, p. 61).

Sartre's analyses freedom by constructing a complex terminology.

Human being is 'being-for-itself', in contrast to the 'being-in-itself' of all other entities (including other animals). An inkwell is an inkwell. It has no choice in the matter. In contrast, a human being cannot be summed up in any simple label or other description (a waiter, a lover, a gambler, a traitor), for humans always have the freedom to be something else. Beginning from the philosophy of consciousness, Sartre argues that there is always a space between the being-for-itself and the being-in-itself of which it is conscious. While I perceive the inkwell, I am also conscious that I am not the inkwell. The 'not' is crucial. Human beings bring nothingness into the world for we can recognise that something is not the case. Only in a world in which humans have the freedom to pursue diverse goals, and thus to make sense of that world in terms of the fulfilment and thwarting of those goals, could it be that Pierre is not in the café, or that my car engine does not work (1958, pp. 9–10). Being-in-itself is simply there; it is solid (*massif*). In contrast, being-for-itself is like a crescent moon. There is a gap, or nothingness, that is at once the source of human freedom and the potential that humans have to be something different. Consider this vignette (1958, pp. 32–33): a gambler, after a losing night, decides to give up gambling. He is confident in his resolution, and thus in the determining force of this principle by which he will live the rest of his life. Yet, on the following night, as he passes the casino, he realises that the resolution does not after all determine him. He must choose anew not to gamble. Even worse, for the rest of his life he must continue choosing not to be a gambler (just as previously he chose continually to be a gambler).

Our freedom is a burden. There is always a terrible suspicion that the choice that we have made is the wrong choice. We are haunted by the other possibilities that we have, even if momentarily, forgone. We thus flee from our freedom in acts of bad faith. At its simplest, we pretend that we have no choice in our occupation (as the waiter who appears like an automaton in his absorption in his tasks (1958, p. 59) or the criminal who blames his upbringing or his genes). More complex and disturbing forms of bad faith occur through relationships between human beings. On one level, the other person is a threat to our freedom, for when they look upon us, they define us, so that we are just an object in their world. The man caught spying at a keyhole is conscious of his very self as escaping him. He has his foundation outside of himself. He is a voyeur (1958, pp. 559–60). But on another level, this relationship can be exploited, in order to escape freedom. A man tries to become the whole world to his lover, which is to say, he relinquishes his own freedom, allowing himself to become an object that is freely defined by the love of the woman

(1958, p. 371). This works well, until the lover attempts to surrender her own freedom, and thus herself to become loved. Thus does love collapse into strife.

In his later works, Sartre engaged increasingly with **Marx**ism, and thus the tenor of his philosophy shifts from an overwhelming emphasis on the way in which the human subject determines the object, towards a recognition of the way in which the object conditions the subject. In his major work in Marxist theory, *Critique of Dialectical Reason* (1960), Sartre analyses the individual as a member of a number of social practices. Individuals act or inscribe themselves upon the world, but the inscribed matter (the 'practico-inert') takes on a life of its own and has power over the individual. The structures of the practico-inert confine the range of choices that the individual has. Freedom is now understood politically. Those individuals who share a common situation can become conscious of this commonality (in a 'we' that is composed of several 'myselves') (Sartre 1976, pp. 75–76) and then strive together to transform the alienating situation. The concern with the impact of the object upon the subject takes a different form in Sartre's studies of the life of the writers Jean Genet (Sartre 1963) and Gustave Flaubert (Sartre 1981–1993). Here the influence of childhood experience on character development is explored in exhaustive detail, so that the adult's freedom is seen only in the continual reinterpretation of the contradictions and tensions of his childhood character.

[AE]

Further reading: Danto 1975; Mészáros 1979; Poster 1979; Schilpp 1981; Warnock 1965.

SAUSSURE, FERDINAND DE (1857–1913)

The Swiss-born linguist Ferdinand de Saussure was responsible for the development of semiotics as a form of structural linguistics. As such, his work is of fundamental importance to structuralism (and influenced **Lévi-Strauss**, **Lacan**, **Jakobson** and the young **Barthes**) and remains of relevance to cultural studies, not least in that it provides one of the most powerful explanations of how human beings might ascribe meaning to the world in which they live. During his lifetime, Saussure was best known as a Sanskrit scholar. His reputation now rests upon a series of lectures given towards the end of his life, and published, from his notes and notes made by his students, as the *Course in General Linguistics*

(1916), that begin to articulate an alternative to the historically orientated linguistics of the nineteenth century.

Saussure challenges the idea that there is some intrinsic or historically emergent relationship between a word and its meaning. In order to analyse meaning, Saussure distinguishes between the signified and the signifier. The former is that to which language refers (which is a concept rather than a concrete object); the latter is that which does the referring (a word or sound pattern). While a sign is composed of these two elements, the relationship between them is held to be arbitrary, in the sense that it depends upon a cultural convention (and not upon some fixed point outside language and outside culture). Thus, it is merely a convention of the English language that the noise 'dog' refers to the concept of a domestic animal that barks. Saussure is not, however, concerned with the workings of a particular language (such as English or French), but with the rules that govern all languages. He thus distinguishes 'la parole' from 'la langue'. 'Parole' is composed of the concrete utterances of members of a language community. These concrete utterances are taken to manifest an underlying structure. This structure is 'langue'. In analysing 'langue', Saussure is treating language as a totality, which is to say that he recognises that the seemingly separate elements of a language are held together by a unifying structure. The elements within this structure therefore have meaning, not because they are inherently meaningful, or because they have some natural association with the external world, but because of the relationships in which that stand to each other, within the structure. These relationships are, Saussure argues, relations of difference; i.e. a sign has meaning because of its difference from other signs in the system. This is to argue that language does not map on to pre-existing differences out there in the world, but creates those differences. Hence, it is the English language that distinguishes dogs from cats, and from sheep, and from wolves, precisely because the meaning of 'dog' depends on it being 'not-cat', 'not-sheep', not-wolf' and so on.

Saussure's own analogy of a game of chess is instructive in elucidating his approach to language. In looking at a game in progress, all that matters is the current position of the pieces on the board. Nothing is gained by knowing how they got there. (If you know the rules of chess, you will be able to say which moves are now possible, and hopefully which are good and which bad.) Hence, the history of the particular game (or indeed the history of chess as such) is irrelevant. Saussure's approach is thus synchronic – i.e. concerned with language at a given moment in time. Further, the meaning of the pieces depends wholly upon their relationship to other pieces. There is nothing intrinsic to the king, as an object, that makes it a king. In an emergency it could be substituted by some other object (say a cigarette lighter) without disrupting the game. The meaning of the piece depends wholly upon its relationship to the meaning of the other pieces. It makes no sense to describe the moves permissible for a king, unless you know that the other pieces are allowed a different set of moves. A king is not a queen, pawn, knight, bishop or rook.

[AE]

Further reading: Culler 1986; Harris 1987, 1988; Holdcraft 1991.

SCHUTZ, ALFRED (1899–1959)

Austro-American philosopher and social theorist who developed a phenomenological sociology from the philosophy of **Husserl**. At the core of Schutz's social theory is the concept of 'life-world'. This is the world of natural things, other human beings and meaningful cultural entities (such as tools, languages and works of art) that we encounter on an everyday basis. The life-world, in effect, composes our mundane surroundings. Most of the time we take this world for granted, as it appears to us as something self-evidently coherent and meaningful. Schutz's major contention is, however, that this world cannot simply be given. We do not passively perceive what is there, external to us. Rather, as competent social agents we must actively construct and sustain this world in co-operation with others. The fact that the world appears to us to be self-evident is explained by the habitual manner in which we exercise our competences as social agents. If our activities in the world can proceed without hindrance, and we can carry on confidently, then we simply do not take note of the skills and stocks of knowledge that we are bringing to our social life. We remain in what Schutz calls, after Husserl, the 'natural attitude'. A shock of some sort is therefore required to disrupt the self-evidence of the life-world, and to force us to reflect upon it. For example, we leave rooms without conscious thought or reflection, because we habitually recognise doors and know how to turn door handles. We may fail to take notice of complex and important activities such as locking our front door, simply because it is such a routine action that we no longer need to think about it. It is only when the door resists our attempts to open it or to lock that we must reflect upon our actions, and question the external world and our skills: is the door jammed? Do we have the right key? Similarly, we routinely communicate successfully with other humans. It is only when communication breaks down that we become aware of the skills and stocks of knowledge that are needed in communication, and that the world is sustained reciprocally between social agents. It is precisely because I can assume that you are an agent who perceives the world much as I do (and thus shares in large part the interpretation of the world that I have inherited) that I can communicate and interact with you. Together we thus sustain our world. If we fail to communicate we must work to restore the common ground: Did you mishear me or misunderstand a word I used? Did you mistake my intentions and practical purposes? Does your world contain objects or tools that mine does not?

For Schutz particular cultures, with their distinctive histories, will give rise to different life-worlds. Thus, our immediate practical concerns, as well as the theoretical knowledge that we acquire from science, magic, or tradition will shift the meaning of the physical and social world. Certain objects and people will attain importance while others recede or are neglected altogether, and different practices will be drawn upon to exploit or interact with this environment successfully. However, Schutz's primary concern is not to describe the particular life-worlds of specific communities, but rather to explore the universal procedures and competences through which social life as such is made possible, and thus the social skills that underpin all life-worlds.

[AE]

Further reading: Berger and Luckmann 1966.

SIMMEL, GEORG (1858–1918)

A German philosopher and sociologist, Simmel is frequently cited as one of the founders of sociology. His work is at times impressionistic, covering a wide range of issues and ideas. His most consistent and rigorous development of a sociology is known as formal sociology. In it he studies the forms that govern diverse social relationships (such as triadic and dyadic relationships, or relationships of superordination and subordination). The study of forms extends to the examination of various types or roles under which humans are labelled and organise their actions (such as the stranger, the adventurer, the miser, the prostitute) and looks at diverse phenomena of contemporary social life, including fashion (Simmel 1957), the city (Simmel 1950b) and sexuality (Oakes 1984). Because many of his finest and most insightful writings are in essay form, rather than in the form of extended and rigorously defended treatises, his foundational position is more contested than that of **Marx**, **Weber** or **Durkheim**. Simmel has, however, much to offer, particularly in understanding the experience of the individual in contemporary society.

At the centre of his approach to sociology is the question: 'How is society possible?' (Simmel 1959). Society is made up of a large number of individuals, all pursuing their own interests and concerns, with minimal attention to the interests of others (beyond, perhaps, close friends and regular acquaintances). Yet, the result of all these individual actions is a stable, organised and generally quite predictable social whole. Simmel therefore wants to account for this stability. The philosopher **Kant** had posed the question 'How is nature possible?' in his *Critique of Pure Reason* (1781). His solution had involved arguing that nature is actually unified only by the human observer. In effect, all the diverse bits of nature are brought together into an ordered and predictable whole by the human mind. Simmel points out that the unity of society need not depend upon any external observer. Rather, society's unity depends upon the active participation of all its members. More concretely, he argues that the organisation of society is not the result of planning or of a conspiracy by some elite. Thus a bureaucracy, for example, is a very untypical form of social organisation. He observes that the elements that make up society (human beings) are conscious and creative beings. Human beings expect society to have order and stability, and even a predestination, as if society had been made especially for them. In addition, human beings come to social relationships armed with a wide range of skills and concepts (or types and forms) that allow them to find and create coherence in those situations. Humans therefore continually work hard – although perhaps without noticing it – in order to create and maintain at least an appearance of the order that they expect to be there.

Human beings do not have a grasp of society as a whole, but they are generally knowledgeable of the rules and conventions that govern their relationships with and behaviour towards others. He gives the example of a game of chess. To an outsider, unfamiliar with the rules, the movements of the players are mysterious. While seemingly co-ordinated and structured, they have no meaning. It could all be a strange ballet, choreographed by some third party. To the chess player, the movements are not simply meaningful, but are meaningful because each player is responding to his or her opponent's acts, through the common recognition of a set of rules. The players can anticipate and interpret the (immensely subtle) actions of their opponents. Simmel therefore anticipates much that comes to fruition in symbolic interactionism and phenomenological approaches to society.

For Simmel, human beings are not necessarily comfortable in the society in which they live and which they create. His most profound and moving writings concern what he calls the tragedy of culture (1968). The activities of human beings are initially subjective. They are full of the intentions and meanings that the individual subject ascribes to them. Yet, in giving public meaning to these actions (and thus in coordinating them with the actions of others), the subjective becomes solidified as objective. The products of human action (and thus culture in all is most diverse manifestations, from agriculture, through economic activity, to high and popular art) take on a momentum or logic of their own. The product of human action comes to confront and constrain the human being. Simmel gives an acutely disturbing illustration of this in his essay on 'The Stranger' (1950c). In the first stage of passion, erotic relations appear to those involved to be unique (and thus uniquely subjective, for what is more subjective than erotic passion?). 'A love such as this has never existed before.' Gradually, and for Simmel perhaps inevitably, this relationship becomes increasingly routine and humdrum. An estrangement sets in, and the relationship ceases to appear to be so unique. It is, after all, the general destiny of human beings to fall in love and marry (or at least, that is how our culture would portray matters). At this point, each partner realises that some other individual could have acquired exactly the same meaning for them. The unique, predestined and passionate relationship is merely an accident (to which we have ascribed its deep significance). In practice, we are all threatened by the thought that each of us is eminently replaceable, not just in contractual relationships, such as our work, but also in our most intimate and passionate relationships. Thus, for Simmel, as social beings, humans occupy roles, and while we imbue these roles with meaning and subjectivity, ultimately we are all fragments. Simmel's point is not simply that the potential of an individual can never be exhausted by the few roles that they play in life. It is rather that even in thinking of ourselves as 'individuals', individuality becomes one more type or role, and we become mere 'outlines', constrained by the limits of the culture within which we (must) live.

[AE]

Further reading: Frisby 1988, 1992a, 1992b, 1994; Frisby and Featherstone 1986.

SKINNER, B. F. (BURRHUS FREDERIC) (1904–1990)

American psychologist, who developed the behaviourist approach to the study of human behaviour, and had a major influence upon the application of psychology to everyday life through his account of 'behaviour modification'. Skinner's behaviourism may be characterised by its thoroughgoing rejection of any concern with the emotional or intellectual life of the subject (that is, he rejects 'mentalism'). He is therefore interested only in the correlations that can be established empirically between environmental stimuli and the observable behaviour of the animal or human. He is not interested in any mental events that might explain the correlation, such as for example, the pleasure or pain that the subject experiences, or the psychological drives that may have been promoted or inhibited. Skinner sees his behaviourism as entailing no theoretical framework or model of behaviour. He merely describes the correlations that do exist, and formulates laws of behaviour from those observations. There is, however, a very basic assumption grounding Skinner's work. It is that humans (and indeed other animals) are machines, in the sense that their behaviour is determinate, predictable and open to modification and control. This also entails the rejection of any consideration of instinctual patterns in behaviour that might exist prior to the animal's experience of its environment. He sees this assumption as falling in line with the tradition of Western science that arose with Galileo and Newton in the sixteenth and seventeenth centuries (Skinner 1953).

Skinner analyses behaviour in terms of 'operant conditioning'. While earlier behaviourist studies, such as those of Pavlov, had sought to establish the subject's response to a determinate stimulus (classically, dogs salivating in response to a stimulus that is associated with the delivery of food), Skinner allows his subjects to explore and manipulate an experimental environment. (This experimental environment is popularly known as a 'Skinner box', although Skinner's preferred term was 'operant conditioning apparatus'.) The subject is not given a stimulus, but rather the environment is such that certain types of behaviour (such as the pecking or touching of a button) will be rewarded (e.g. by food). The reward reinforces this selected pattern of behaviour, so that, according to Skinner's 'law of acquisition', the strength of the behaviour will vary according to when the reinforcing stimulus occurs. He proceeded to explore the way in which different 'schedules of reinforcement', i.e. differences in the intervals between the delivery of rewards, would affect behaviour. He argued that outside experimental conditions, reinforcements are typically delivered inconsistently, so that, for example, a worker is not necessarily paid immediately upon completing an item of work; a telephone call is not always answered; and a cooked meal does not always turn out as one expects. By varying the length of time that elapsed between reinforcements (so that, for example, a subject might be rewarded not every time that it performed the appropriate behaviour, but every one minute or every five minutes), Skinner established (perhaps unsurprisingly) that subjects learned more rapidly the more frequent the reinforcements. More interestingly, once a behaviour pattern is no longer reinforced, it is extinguished more rapidly if it had originally been reinforced continuously rather than intermittently. Reinforcement could also be varied according to the number of times that the subject had to perform an act before being rewarded. Again unsurprisingly, the more frequent and specific the reinforcement, the stronger the response. This result can be seen as having direct application to piece work payments to factory workers.

Significantly, Skinner (1957) argued that language was acquired according to the principles of operant conditioning. Language is understood as 'verbal behaviour', and children learn appropriate language use through its reinforcement by parents and others. The understanding of human beings as creatures that can be manipulated through operant conditioning, which underpins Skinner's account of language and other behaviour, allowed Skinnerian techniques to be applied to education, the working environment, health care and the penal system. 'Behaviour modification' worked by specifically rewarding desirable behaviour, rather than punishing undesirable behaviour. The parent therefore is expected to ignore a child's temper tantrums, but to ensure that rewards are clearly linked to desirable behaviour. It may be noted that in the context of mental health, this approach requires no knowledge of the workings of the patient's mind; merely the ability to link observable reinforcement to observable behaviour. In 1948 Skinner published his only novel, *Walden Two*. The title is an allusion to Thoreau's nineteenth-century evocation of an idyllic life of self-sufficiency, *Walden, or Life in the Woods*. Skinner presents an image of a utopian rural community that is ordered and regulated according to the principles of behaviour modification.

[AE]

Further reading: Modgil and Modgil 1987; Richelle 1995; Wiener 1996.

SMITH, ADAM (1723–1790)

Philosopher and political economist associated with the Scottish Enlightenment. Smith both studied and subsequently lectured at the University of Glasgow. His most famous publications were *The Theory of Moral Sentiments* (1759) and *The Wealth of Nations* (1776). The first of these works attempted to explain the basis of ethical judgements. Smith's preliminary answer to this issue is that, in spite of their generally selfish and acquisitive nature, humans have the capacity to feel 'sympathy' (i.e. empathy) for others. Sympathy, then, is our ability to identify with others; but it depends upon a number of other factors. Principally, our own judgement about another person's behaviour is dependent upon the appropriateness of their behaviour to their situation: if someone exhibits the emotion of terrible anger, and we do not know why, says Smith, we are likely to respond to them in a manner which is not sympathetic. Thus, before formulating a moral response to them we will await knowledge of why they are angry, and we will only feel sympathy if their anger appears warranted to us. In turn, the behaviour of others is governed by the sympathy principle: a person will moderate their behaviour to gain the sympathy of others because, Smith argues, we all are able to put ourselves in the position of spectators (i.e. ask the question 'How does my behaviour appear to this person?'). Consequently, out of self-interest, we modify our behaviour according to the expectations of others, and this is a mark of our social being. From this chain of reasoning, Smith develops the sympathy principle to account for the existence of moral sentiments: sympathy is the basis of our conduct towards others and thus forms the basis of the normative constraints that operate within a society. Indeed, Smith's is a view of ethics that thereby embraces the notion of normativity as being fundamental to human relations.

Smith also introduces the famous notion of the 'Invisible Hand' in *The Theory of Moral Sentiments*. We have, Smith says, God-given drives or instincts which take priority over our reasoning abilities. Humans are all prey to the promptings of powerful drives which they are compelled to obey blindly, without rational consideration. For instance, we are acquisitive beings; we are driven by greed. Smith gives the example of a pauper's child who hankers after the comforts of wealth. Subsequently, the child labours and becomes wealthy, and discovers only too late that enormous wealth is a 'mere trinket', of no real or lasting value. However, in the mean time, the effect of this labour has been beneficial to society because in the pursuit of wealth individuals develop the arts and sciences, learn how to cultivate the earth, build cities and, in short, improve the lot of human life. Thus, the greed of the individual has beneficial consequences which are of benefit to the whole of human society.

Smith's *The Wealth of Nations* develops this idea, and weaves it into an account of the emergence of modern civil society from the earlier feudal order of medieval Europe. Again, this modern form arises as a result of the selfish pursuits of individuals. *The Wealth* also analyses the role of civil government, instituted by the rich to secure their property rights against the poor, offers a comprehensive study of the nature of market forces, and advocates a conception of individual liberty which holds that the welfare of society depends upon the ability of the individual to pursue their own interests with the basic constraints of rules of justice. Again, the view is put forward that self-interested motives produce unintentional consequences which benefit humanity.

[PS]

Further reading: Morrow 1973; Raphael 1985; J. Wood 1984.

SONTAG, SUSAN (1933–)

American essayist and novelist (Sontag 1980, 1993, 2000), whose cultural analysis has covered such diverse topics as pornography, cinema, photography and health, as well as contemporary literature and literary criticism.

Sontag first came to wide public attention with the essays collected in *Against Interpretation* (1966). The title essay boldly challenges traditional ideas about the interpretation of works of art. She claims that interpretation that seeks to explicate the content of the art work has worked only to make art manageable or seemly. Such interpretation is found as much in ancient Stoic responses to Homer (where 'the rude features of Zeus and his boisterous clans' are allegorised away, thereby ensuring the morality of the gods) as in **Freud** (where, on the model of dream interpretation, a 'latent content' must be extracted from beneath the immediately experienced 'manifest content'). This, Sontag claims, is the revenge of the intellect upon art (1966, p. 17). Art's threat, crucially in its sensuality and immediacy, is defused, so that the art work can be appropriated within a pre-existing intellectual framework. Recognising that much modern art tries to avoid interpretation by shedding content (for example in the move to abstraction in painting or the triviality of the content of pop art), Sontag looks for approaches to interpretation that will focus upon form, not content. She laments that our models of form are spatial, and thus inadequate to temporal forms, such as the novel. A theory of narrative is required. That Sontag finds something of this in **Barthes** and **Benjamin**, long before they were the stock-in-trade of modern cultural criticism, is significant, not least in that an openness to continental thought has always been characteristic of her work (1982b). She complements formal approaches to interpretation with description, that would allow us 'to recover our senses. We must learn to *see* more, to *hear* more, to *feel* more', and that invites not interpretation, but 'an erotics of art' (p. 23).

'Notes on "Camp"', also collected in *Against Interpretation*, may be seen as an early, and highly influential, manifestation of much that is characteristic of postmodernism. Sontag turns away from high culture to a cultural form that, precisely in its apparent triviality, inverts the principles used to judge art. She explores the conditions under which the Camp statement, 'it's good *because* it's awful', can hold. These conditions include a sensitivity to ironic distance, to artifice and pastiche, and to the need to strive for the extraordinary and exaggerated.

On Photography (1973) draws together a series of reflections upon the social practice of photography. Two core themes might be identified in these essays: the all-persuasiveness of photography; and its moral ambiguity. With the transformation of photography into an industrial process, it becomes 'a social rite, a defense against anxiety, and a tool of power' (Sontag 1973, p. 8). The family is thus chronicled by the photograph, and the extended family today exists only in the photograph album. Similarly, photography mediates our confrontation with strange places, as we travel more. Tourism becomes the search for the photogenic (p. 9). The taking of photographs assuages our disorientation, and perhaps echoing the effect of interpretation on art, diffuses the threatening immediacy of sensual experience. Yet photographs are also a source of information, be this in scientific records or in the popular documents of photo-journalism. It is here that much of the moral ambiguity of photography occurs. Sontag records her own experience, at the age of 12, of coming across photographs of Bergen-Belsen and Dachau. 'Nothing I have seen . . . ever cut me as sharply, deeply, instantaneously. Indeed, it seems plausible to me to divide my life into two parts, before I saw those photographs . . . and after' (p. 20). Yet this profound moral impact is rare. She claims that photographs can at best foster nascent moral awareness in a population (so that photographs from Vietnam fuelled anti-war sentiments), but that the impact of the photograph soon wanes. Audiences were already immunised to the 1973 images of famine in sub-Saharan Africa (pp. 18–19). At root the photograph provides information without understanding (or, again echoing 'Against Interpretation', a moment in time as opposed to a narrative) (p. 23). The photograph cannot represent reality as it is, for in its all-persuasiveness, the photograph (or perhaps more precisely, the property of being photogenic) becomes the criterion upon which reality is judged (p. 87). 'Today,' Sontag concludes, 'everything exists to end in a photograph' (p. 24).

Illness as Metaphor (1979) and *AIDS and its Metaphors* (1989) pursue further the cultural construction of our perception of reality, however awful, through aesthetic and at times beautiful metaphors and images. Sontag is concerned with the way in which myths about illnesses can be resilient to the real suffering that the illness causes. Her analysis of tuberculosis (TB), for example, traces the way in which the appearance of the TB sufferer, by ignoring not least the stench of their breath, becomes fashionable in the nineteenth century, and is associated with poetic sensibility. Shelley could remark to Keats that 'this consumption is a disease particularly fond of people who write such good verses as you have done' (1979, ch. 4). The consumptive becomes interesting, as by confronting death, they are seen to explore their very individuality. The Romantic landscape is equally entwined with the experience of the consumptive, but also influences perceptions of how TB is to be cured. The consumptive, as a romantic figure, becomes a wanderer, a Bohemian and exile, seeking respite in such typically romantic land-scapes as mountains, Rome, and the Mediterranean and Pacific islands. Today, Sontag claims, the mythology of TB has been transferred to mental illness. While specific metaphorical images are taken over into the interpretation of mental illness (such as that of a voyage to enhanced consciousness; the need for exile in a sanatorium/asylum), again these images deny the real suffering of the disease.

[AE]

Further reading: Kennedy 1995; Sayres 1990.

TAYLOR, CHARLES (1931–)

Canadian philosopher who came to international prominence with work on **Hegel** (Taylor 1975) and on the philosophy of the social sciences (1985b). From this basis he has developed a powerful political theory, that has played a major part in the growing criticism of the liberal orthodoxy of Anglo-American philosophy. Taylor characterises human beings as 'self-interpreting animals' (1985d). In broad terms, this entails that humans, uniquely among the animal kingdom, must address the question of their self-identity. Humans have a sense of self, but as Taylor remarks, they do not possess a self in the way that they possess a liver or heart. The self is not a brute fact about the individual, but rather an interpretation that depends upon the linguistic resources that are available to the human being, and the way in which that language is used to make sense, not simply of oneself as a discrete being, but of the social and physical world around one, and of the one's relationship to that world. Taylor brings home his point by distinguishing between the emotions that a non-human (and thus non-language-using) animal could have, and the emotions that a human has. Humans can all feel certain emotions, such as fear or pleasure, in common with other animals, where there is an immediate response to a physical stimulus. However, Taylor suggests that an animal could not feel shame or pride. Such emotions are responses to culturally and communally defined situations, and centrally of oneself as a human subject within that situation. To be ashamed presupposes that one has some conception of the good to which humans should aspire, and of how one has fallen short of that ideal (and in addition, how others will perceive this fall). This conception of the good, and the resultant interpretation that it facilitates of human practices and situations, can be articulated only in human language. Human beings are thus situating themselves in what Taylor calls a moral space, and this moral space gives the individual the resources to make sense of their lives.

One important consequence of this account of human being is that it offers a profound account of moral argument (1985c). Taylor distinguishes our disagreements over matters of culinary taste from our moral disagreements. If you like sugar in your coffee and I do not, then there is nothing more to say. These are brute facts about our constitution, and it makes no sense to say that your taste is 'wrong' in any way. However, if you support capital punishment and I do not, this is not a matter of simple preference. Rather it involves what Taylor calls 'strong evaluation'. A person can legitimately be required to provide further explanation and justification of their moral judgements, and they will do this through appeal to more fundamental beliefs, specifically about their understanding of the dignity and worth of others, about their conceptions of the good life, and about their sense of their own dignity. Again, this is to appeal to a linguistically articulated moral space and one's awareness of one's place within that space. Taylor's core point, therefore, is that we do not come into the world equipped with moral preferences and the capacity to make moral judgement (as we might be equipped with a preference for sweet tastes). Rather, we acquire such evaluations from our culture. In turn, those evaluations serve to constitute our sense of self, for they articulate the goals after which we should strive, and the life stories that we will be able to tell about our success or failure in reaching those goals.

Evaluations are not static. While, for Taylor, it is only through our conversation with others within the community that we come, gradually, to learn what such terms as 'shame', 'pride' and 'love' mean, there is also scope for the transformation of value systems. Taylor is aware of the plurality of goods that confront members of contemporary societies. There will, Taylor argues, be 'hypergoods', or goals that are held to be of ultimate importance in determining the nature of human dignity, and that these hypergoods will serve to order the claims of other goods. Yet hypergoods are also a source of conflict. Different groups or communities may hold to fundamentally different hypergoods (and thus, what 'pride' or 'shame' means in different communities may be radically different). This conflict need not, for Taylor, result in an arid moral relativism (whereby debate between communities would be as pointless as debates over the merits of sweetened and unsweetened coffee). While Taylor rejects the possibility of electing one hypergood as absolutely good or true, he suggests that any given hypergood might be superior to another in the sense that it will provide for a more coherent and complex account of the world, and the agent's place in that world. Taylor can thus envisage an open-ended historical narrative, in which old hypergoods are replaced by new, richer ones (1989).

[AE]

Further reading: Mulhall and Swift 1992.

WEBER, MAX (1864–1920)

A German economist, historian and legal theorist, Max Weber is typically regarded as one of the founders of sociology. His work deals with issues that are fundamental to any comprehensive study of society and culture, including power, social stratification, bureaucracy, and the development and supremacy of modern capitalism.

At the centre of Weber's inquiries is the explanation of the origin of capitalism. What is perhaps Weber's best known essay, *The Protestant Ethic and the Spirit of Capitalism* (1904–1905) not only addresses this problem, but also serves as an illustration of much that is typical of Weberian sociology. Weber argues that one of the factors that is important as a precondition of the rise of capitalism in Western Europe is the Protestant (and especially Calvinist) faith. Weber therefore pits himself against the economic determinism that is characteristic of certain forms of Marxism. For Weber, economic factors (such as the development of the technology) are not sufficient to explain radical social change. Cultural factors, including the presence of appropriate religious beliefs, are also relevant. However, Weber never argues that an appropriate religious culture is the only precondition of capitalism. He suggests that a range of conditions need to be in place, from the simple presence of workable quantities of iron and coal, to the invention of efficient techniques of administration and accountancy. The Protestant Ethic thesis focuses, therefore, on one of the many preconditions of capitalism. Weber argues that, for capitalist development to take off, it is necessary for the profits of economic activity to be reinvested (rather than being used up in consumption). Protestantism provides the necessary motivation for this, through the doctrine of predestination. The Calvinist believes that his or her salvation or damnation is already decided. His or her actions, in this life, will not influence the outcome. The believers are therefore faced by a 'salvation panic'. Unable to influence their fate, they look for ways to mitigate the anxiety predestination causes them. There are two implications of this. On the one hand, they distract themselves through hard and continuous work. On the other hand, they look for signs that they might be saved. The very ability to work hard, and to work successfully, is one such sign. The Calvinist will therefore be inclined to reinvest profits, not to enjoy them. (It is important to note that Weber is arguing, not that Calvinists work hard in order to gain salvation, but rather, that through working hard, they reassure themselves that they are saved.) Weber supported this thesis through a series of studies of the world's major religions (Judaism, Hinduism, Confucianism and Islam). In each case, he was concerned to show that these religions did not have the same affinity with capitalism as did Protestantism, and therefore that the presence of these religions would inhibit the development of capitalism, even if other relevant conditions were present.

Weber's analysis of Protestantism further illustrates his approach to sociological explanation. He is concerned with the sense that social actors make of their historical situations, and how they respond to those situations. He distinguishes social action from behaviour. A bicycle accident is behaviour. Because it is an accident, the actors involved have not orientated their actions to each other. The arguments or apologies that follow the accident are social action, for now the actions have meaning. Each actor responds to the meaningful actions of the other. Sociological explanation therefore requires that we reconstruct, through empathy, the motivations that gave meaning to action in that particular social situation. Weber's analysis of Calvinism is therefore asking how a believer meaningfully responds to a deep and sincere faith in the doctrine of predestination.

The analysis of action goes further. Weber identifies four types of actions. These are, first, traditional action (where actors act in the way that they do, because that is how it has always been done); second, effective action (where the emphasis is upon the action being shaped through emotion, not rational planning); third, value-orientated action (where the action is motivated by the desire to realise some value, be it moral, political, religious or aesthetic, and is illustrated by the actions of the Calvinists); and fourth, goal-orientated action. The last of these is, in many respects, the most important. It is action governed by formal rules of instrumental efficiency. As such, it is action dominated by instrumental reason. This introduces another of Weber's great themes, that of rationalisation.

Weber is not concerned merely to explain the origin of capitalism. He wants also to explain why it becomes the dominant form of economic and social organisation throughout the world. The core of his explanation is to say that capitalism (and thus Western society, within which it emerged) is the most instrumentally rational, and therefore efficient, society ever to exist. Rationalisation has many subtle shades of meaning in Weber's writings, but already the four types of action, noted above, indicate something of its meaning. The types of actions are given in order of ascending rationality. Rationality therefore entails the ability to reflect upon one's action, to analyse its goals, and the ways in which you seek to achieve those goals. In traditional and effective action, that reflection is more or less inhibited. A society that employs instrumental rationality is therefore likely to be more flexible and dynamic than one in which action is traditional or effective.

Weber sees contemporary Western societies as thoroughly rational. Instrumental reason dominates not just the economy, but also law (as it comes to be based on systematic principles that are applied impersonally); science (as scientific research is disciplined by the controlled experiment and the demand for value-freedom, so that its results are not influenced by the personal preferences and beliefs of the scientist); and even architecture (where the gothic vault is seen to be more rational than any predecessor) and music (in the rise of the tempered scale, Western counterpoint and harmony, and the Western system of notation) (see Weber 1930, pp. 14–15). The exercise of power and therefore politics are also more rational in the West.

For Weber, one agent has power over another if the first can make the second do something that he, she or it would not otherwise have done. The exercise of power is not, for Weber, necessarily wrong or exploitative. One agent could exercise power over another, but in the other's real or perceived interest. Weber thus distinguishes power from authority, where authority is power that has legitimacy (which is to say that it is acceptable to those subject to the exercise of power). Weber identifies three sources of authority. The first, and least rational, is charismatic power. Here, the exercise of power depends upon the personality (or charisma) of the one holding power. (Weber identifies the great religious leaders, such as Christ and Muhammad, as charismatic leaders, and also great military leaders, such as Julius Caesar and Napoleon.) Traditional authority shifts the legitimacy of power from individual leaders, to the office which they hold. Authority therefore comes to depend upon social conventions and institutions. (Thus, for example, the authority of the medieval church is traditional authority.) Rational domination is characteristic of the modern state. Power is not simply invested in social institutions, but depends upon the rational organisation of those institutions. The modern state is therefore seen as an instrument of co-ordination, working through complex, bureaucratic administrative structures. Such structures are argued to be the most efficient in achieving given political ends, for they are not hampered by the whims of particular personalities (for they rely rather on trained bureaucrats acting impersonally according to the precisely defined rules of their offices), and the rules governing their procedures are the subject of rational reflection (not tradition or convention). Weber's account of bureaucracy is marked, however, by a profound melancholy. Rational domination suppresses individual freedom and spontaneity, and threatens to enclose society within an 'iron cage'. This aspect of Weber's work has had a significant impact on Marxists such as **Lukács** and **Adorno**.

A final point may be made about Weber's account of capitalism, power and rationality. There is a crucial ambiguity in Weber's analysis of rationality. It may be noted that Western science is deemed to be more rational than that found in other cultures, not least because it is value-free (separating moral and political issues as to the desirable state of the world, from purely factual issues about how the world actually is). This claim in itself justifies Weber's own sociology. Weber does not merely claim that his own work is value-free, but more profoundly situates it as the product of contemporary Western society. Such a society uniquely has the ability to look back on its own history, and reconstruct the rational development of its own position. Yet, Weber need not then be arguing that science in contemporary Western society has achieved some transcendent, ahistorical vantage point, from which it can see the social and natural world as it really is. Rather, scientific 'truth' lies in its power. It may be noted that an important influence on Weber, manifest clearly in his early career, was that of **Nietzsche**. In those early writings (see Weber 1994), he situates himself as a German intellectual, with the inevitable goal of defending German interests. This may readily be read as echoing Nietzsche's defence of German culture in *The Birth of Tragedy*. The later Weber may be seen to substitute his German identity with a Western European identity. Rationality is therefore associated, not with the achievement of objective truth, but with the achievement of the global influence of the Western economy. Western society is rational, not then according to some ahistorical criteria of reason, but because it is manifestly more powerful than any other form of reason. Knowledge for Weber, as for **Foucault** and Nietzsche, may therefore be intimately related to power.

[AE]

Further reading: Bendix 1960; Brubaker 1984; Freund 1998; Giddens 1971; Hamilton 1991; Mommsen 1974; Reinhard 1998; B. Turner 1981; Wolfgang 1992.

WILLIAMS, RAYMOND (1921–1988)

Welsh cultural critic, who was a major forerunner of contemporary cultural studies. Books such as *Culture and Society 1780–1950* (1958) and *The Long Revolution* (1961) served to map out much that is now taken as the basic subject area of cultural studies, as well as doing much to shape the understanding of culture that informs those studies. While Williams's work is therefore important to understanding the history of cultural studies, his work is in other respects somewhat marginal to the mainstream of the discipline. This is because his methods and techniques of analysis tended only gradually and partially to incorporate the insights of structuralism and semiotics that were fundamental to cultural studies in the 1970s and 1980s.

Culture and Society is an exercise in literary history, but explores literature by relating books and authors to the broader historical and social development of ideas, and to culture as a 'whole way of life', 'a mode of interpreting all our common experiences' (p. 18). Culture is therefore not the culture of an elite, but a culture that is embedded in everyday experience and activity. The culture that Williams is interested in is the culture that emerges as a complex criticism of industrial capitalism. Like his contemporary Richard **Hoggart**, Williams may however still be seen to be working in tension with the dominant **Leavis**ite approach to literature and culture, and thus the tension between an understanding of everyday culture as it is, and an attempt to evaluate parts of that culture more highly (or as more civilised) than others. *The Long Revolution* takes further the analysis of culture as a way of life. The revolution is that brought about by 'the progress and interaction of democracy and industry, and by the extension of communications' (p. 12), and the analysis concerns the way in which this affects all aspects of everyday life. A key (if not precisely defined) term introduced by Williams is that of 'structures of feeling': the lived experience of a particular moment in society and in history.

In the 1960s and early 1970s, Williams demonstrated a greater interest in the mass media. While in his early books he tends to present the mass media as a threat to the revolution of democracy and to the rise of a 'common culture', Williams gradually moves away from this position in *Communications* (1962) and in *Television: Technology and Cultural Form* (1974). While Williams therefore comes to examine a topic that is fundamental to cultural studies, his early approach is heavily marked by the influence of American media research, as to the more theoretical approaches that would come to the fore, for example, in the work of the Birmingham Centre for Contemporary Cultural Studies. Williams's description of his first encounter with American television (and thus the entwining of a film, advertisements and, crucially, trailers for films to be shown in the future), and thus the breakdown of a series of discrete programmes into a 'flow', has been widely cited (1974, p. 92).

Marxism and Literature (1977) marked a major development in Williams's work, as it represented his first thorough-going engagement with Marxism, and thus with a number of important theoretical resources for cultural studies, including **Althusser**'s conception of ideology and **Gramsci**'s concept of hegemony. Williams is unhappy with the uniformity suggested by orthodox Marxist accounts of historical epochs. He argues rather that any moment in history must be analysed in terms of the presence and interplay of dominant, residual and emergent cultures. This is to suggest, not merely that there are historically backward and forward looking elements within culture, but that culture is therefore a site of political contest, as groups express their incorporation within the dominant order and their resistance to it.

While Williams never offers a single formal presentation of his theoretical position (and indeed, that position develops and changes over Williams's career), his work may be characterised as a cultural materialism. His approach to culture is to recognise that it is entwined with (but not simply determined by) the economic and politic structures and experiences of life. At the heart of this is an exploration of the history, uses and political complexity of language, manifest elegantly in *Keywords* (1976, 1983) – which, of course, is a forerunner of Routledge's *Key Concepts* series.

[AE]

Further reading: Dixon 1990; Eagleton 1989; Prendergast 1995; Shepperson 1995; Tredell 1990.

WITTGENSTEIN, LUDWIG (1889–1951)

Austrian-born philosopher. Wittgenstein originally studied engineering. In 1912, he went to Cambridge and became a student of one of the founders of the analytic philosophy, Bertrand Russell (1872–1970). Wittgenstein served in the Austrian army during the First World War and subsequently gave up studying philosophy for ten years. In 1929 he became a research fellow at Cambridge, and subsequently Professor of Philosophy. Wittgenstein published only a single work during his lifetime, the *Tractatus Logico-Philosophicus* (1921). All of his other writings, including the *Philosophical Investigations* (1953), *Remarks on the Foundations of Mathematics* (1956), *The Blue and Brown Books* (1958) and *On Certainty* (1969) appeared posthumously.

The *Tractatus* is a work that concentrates primarily upon elucidating an account of language, which is conceived in terms of its representational function. Language is viewed by Wittgenstein as 'picturing' the world, and the aim of the text is to point out what must be true both of language and of the world alike in order for this picturing (representation) to be possible. The world, or reality, it is argued, is nothing more than the totality of 'facts' that can be asserted about it. There are, Wittgenstein holds, fundamental facts or 'atomic facts'. An atomic fact cannot be analysed down into constituent parts and is not dependent upon the existence of any other atomic fact. Language reflects this, in so far as it contains basic propositions that are likewise irreducible – 'atomic propositions'. It is these propositions that are regarded by Wittgenstein as picturing reality. Language, in other words, is fundamentally a medium that mirrors the world. Both language and the world are held to share a common structure. This structure is referred to as 'logical form'. When we assert complex propositions, Wittgenstein says, we are effectively combining various components of language in such a way that any proposition refers back to the fundamentally representational function that all atomic propositions share in common. Since all atomic propositions refer to the world they have a truth-value, i.e. they can be either true or false. Since all other propositions can be understood in terms of them, it follows that all propositions are functionally dependent upon the truth-values expressed in atomic propositions. Given that the aim of the *Tractatus* is to talk about the logical form of language, which grounds the possibility of its representational function and hence meaning, Wittgenstein is driven to admitting that it is strictly speaking impossible to talk about language in the way he is. This admission takes the form of the 'showing' and 'saying' distinction. According to this distinction, what can be shown cannot be said. In other words, the logical structure that language and the world share in common shows itself to us by way of the representational function of language. But since this structure makes meaningful talk possible it cannot actually be referred to in language. To put it another way, Wittgenstein claims it is impossible to stand 'outside' language, since language makes our world what it is. Famously, he tells us that the limits of our language constitute the limits of our world. Thus, what the *Tractatus* argues is, taken in rigorous terms, nonsense, for what the text is telling us about cannot strictly be said at all. The *Tractatus* ends with Wittgenstein telling us that the work itself should be treated like a 'ladder': once one has climbed this ladder it is best to cast it to one side.

A key problem that the *Tractatus* aims to address is the issue of how it is possible for language to represent reality. From the fact that Wittgenstein went on to abandon this view of language in his later writings it is clear that it has many problems. Fundamentally, the issue that must be broached for any representational theory to be persuasive is the question of how language and the world are conjoined. One has, in other words, to demonstrate how a 'fit' occurs between propositions and the world, i.e. how, as one eminent scholar put it, language and the world can be 'nailed' together. The problem with this is that in order to demonstrate this, one would have to stand outside of language and, as Wittgenstein argues, such a perspective is simply not available to us. Equally, a number of aspects of meaning do not seem to be linked to the referential function of language (see below). Wittgenstein's later writings effectively abandon this problem by turning instead to a different metaphor for language.

Instead of cleaving to the notion of representation, in the *Philosophical Investigations* Wittgenstein develops an approach that articulates questions of meaning in terms of 'language games'. One can, in simple terms, comprehend Wittgenstein's argument by asking how words have meaning. An advocate of the representational view of language might well answer in the following manner: words mean what they do because they denote objects or facts in the world of experience. On this view, one could envisage a situation in which a teacher is instructing a child about the meaning of words. In order to communicate the meaning of a word the teacher points to an object and utters the word, thus naming the object. This form of definition is referred to as 'ostensive definition'. In turn, the child repeats the name and so the word's meaning is communicated by referring to the thing that is named by way of ostensive definition. One central problem with this conception of how the meaning of words is secured centres on the question of how the child understands the meaning of pointing. In order for ostensive definition to be possible, the child must already know that the act of pointing is a way of indicating an object and that uttering a word while pointing means that the object is being named. Arguing that pointing is a means of establishing how the meaning of words is secured will not do since the meaning of pointing itself cannot be defined in this way. Wittgenstein's turn to language games is a means of avoiding this problem. He envisages the process of learning the meaning of words as being akin to the 'games by means of which children learn their native language' (Wittgenstein 1996, para. 7). Children learn language simply by playing games. Any game is composed of rules and conventions, and if we envisage a situation in which a child learns about the meaning of words by repeating them then what he or she is doing is acting according to conventions. The form of activity that occurs by way of the observation of conventions Wittgenstein calls a 'language game'. Language games consist of gestures, rules, customs, etc. Taken together, these constitute a structure of conventions. Such conventions always serve the purpose of the game. If we take this view, then a word's meaning will, in many instances, be definable by way of its role within a language game (para. 43). In turn, Wittgenstein notes, there are many possible sorts of language game. Since speaking language is always part of an activity, different activities can be grasped as instantiating different forms of life (para. 23). In turn, different language games represent instances of different 'forms of life'. If one speaks the same language as others then one is in effect observing a common set of conventions, and the collective observation of conventions implies that one thereby shares with others a common form of life. In this way, Wittgenstein effectively asserts that the practice of philosophy is not rooted in fundamental principles, such as the purportedly 'immediate' certainty of self-reflection (see **Descartes**). Rather, forms of life, since they constitute the basis upon which human activities are possible, cannot be questioned by philosophy and thus constitute its fundamental precondition.

Forms of life, however, are diverse. For example, flies and dogs are two species that represent fundamentally different forms of life. With regard to one another, such forms are incommensurable, i.e. the behaviour of one species cannot be translated into terms equivalent to the behaviour of another. Humans, too, are different from other animals. But humans can also inhabit very different worlds with regard to one another. Different cultures, for example, can be comprehended as different forms of life whose conventions are incommensurable with regard to one another. If someone from one culture were to be persuaded to accept the 'truths' (i.e. dominant beliefs) of another culture then it would not be the case that this would be achieved by their accepting the indubitable 'truth' of the assertions that constitute this web of beliefs (e.g. scientifically 'proven' beliefs). Such acceptance would merely indicate that this person had altered the way in which they look at the world: their 'world-view' would have changed. On this view, philosophy effectively becomes unwarranted nonsense if it displays any pretensions to endow life with an ultimate meaning. Rather, the role of philosophy is to note the differences that operate between different forms of life and thereby illuminate how misunderstandings can occur. Primarily, misunderstandings happen when we take the everyday conventions that go to make up a language game and start to use them to ask questions that are inappropriate to that game, i.e. questions that are not meaningful within the web of everyday activities that constitute that game.

[PS]

Further reading: Grayling 1988; Kenny 1993; Wright 1981.

GLOSSARY

Communitarianism

A political philosophy that argues for the primacy of the community over the individual. As a description of political life, communitarians argue that human beings are necessarily social animals, and that their sense of self-identity, their goals and values are constituted through their participation in a common culture and language. A more normative approach would argue in addition that there are certain goods that can be enjoyed only collectively, so that the proper task of politics is to reinforce and develop communal bonds and citizens' awareness of their dependence upon and duty to the community.

See Aristotle; Durkheim; MacIntyre; Oakeshott; Taylor.

Deconstruction

An approach to literary criticism and cultural analysis that is primarily derived from the work of Derrida. While Derrida insists that 'deconstruction' cannot be defined, so that it cannot be formulated in terms of a set of methodological rules independently of a particular analysis, at the heart of deconstruction one can identify a concern to challenge the certainties of structuralism. Where structuralism seeks to explicate the meaning of signs in terms of the opposition between two signs within a system (e.g. culture–nature; writing–speech; reason–emotion), deconstruction questions the priority or supposed superiority of one sign over the other, and thus seeks to demonstrate the instability of the opposition. Deconstruction thereby questions the very limits of language.

See De Man; Derrida.

Existentialism

Philosophy of human existence that stresses the irreducible freedom of the human individual. For the existentialist the individual human being has no pre-given nature (be this, for example, biological or genetic, or socially acquired through upbringing) that might determine or limit the ways in which they live their lives. The human individual is therefore continually confronted with the problem of how to live, and with a radical responsibility for all the decisions they make and actions they pursue. The individual can avoid the repressive burden of this responsibility by retreating into some form of 'bad faith' or 'inauthenticity', through which they would attempt to convince themselves that they in fact had no freedom.

See Heidegger; Malraux; Sartre.

Feminism

A group of political and social philosophies that begin from a recognition of the patriarchal (which is to say, male dominated) structure of contemporary society, and the role that culture plays in oppressing women, not least by presenting male interests, values and methods of reasoning as normal or natural. A genuine women's voice is thus marginalised or suppressed altogether. Different approaches to feminism will offer different analyses of the causes and nature of this oppression and thus of the possible solutions. A now rather hackneyed typology is to distinguish liberal feminists, who strive for substantial equality of the rights of women and men; socialist feminists, who argue that women's oppression is analogous to class exploitation; and radical feminists, who analyse patriarchy in terms of the oppression and manipulation of female sexuality. More recent debates in feminism have centred upon the problem of articulating female interests without essentialising female and male natures, and in recognising the white, Eurocentric bias of much feminist analysis.

See Cixous; Irigaray; Kristeva; Le Doeuff; Nussbaum.

Hermeneutics

The theory of textual interpretation and analysis. While hermeneutics has its origins in the interpretation of scriptural texts (and the task of distinguishing authentic and corrupt texts), and the interpretation of law, modern hermeneutics focuses upon the problems of interpretation in general, and the creation and recovery of meaning in written texts and in social life.

See Gadamer; Geertz; Heidegger; Ricoeur; Taylor.

Liberalism

An approach to political philosophy that is primarily concerned with the freedom of the individual within society. The individual, and not the collective (e.g. the community, nation or state) is the sole source of value, so that politics can be justified only in terms of the part they play in maintaining individual freedoms. The freedom of the individual is typically articulated in terms of a series of rights. Rights may enshrine either negative freedoms, such as the rights to life, free-speech and the ownership of property (where others have an obligation to leave the rights holder alone to pursue whatever goals they choose), or positive freedoms, such as the right to education or health care (where others, typically the state, have obligations to provide resources when the rights holder can best utilise them). A central concern of liberals is to demarcate the limits of state intervention in the private individual's life and so the degree to which the state can curtail individual freedom. Typically one is argued to be free until the pursuit of one's own freedom interferes with the freedom of others.

See Kant; Lyotard; Mill; Rawls; Rorty; Smith.

Marxism

A groups of approaches to social, economic and political analysis that derive their inspiration from the work of Karl Marx. While there is now a great diversity in Marxist philosophies, a core concern is recognition of the exploitative nature of social relations, typically understood in terms of a conflict between a dominant class that controls economic production (and benefits materially from that control), and a subordinate class that carries out the production of goods and services. The Marxist account of human social existence therefore stresses the determining influence of the economy over all other forms of social activity (although the precise nature and scope of this determination is highly disputed). As a political programme, Marxism aspires to the creation of a non-exploitative, communist society, typically through the revolutionary action of the subordinate capitalist class, the proletariat.

See Adorno; Bakhtin; Benjamin; Bloch; Brecht; Gramsci; Habermas; Hall; Horkheimer; James; Lukács; Marx; Sartre; Williams.

Modernism/modernity

While the precise meaning of these terms varies depending upon the context in which they are used, currently the dominant sense of 'modernity' refers to the nature of Western society from the seventeenth-century 'Enlightenment' onwards. Modernity is contrasted to previous forms of society, primarily in terms of the development of industry (associated initially with the exploitation of steam power), the growth of towns and cities, of capitalist markets, and the rise of industrial and governmental bureaucracies. Culturally, this development is grounded in the emergence of an empirical and rational science, and the associated challenge to superstition and religion, alongside increased democratic participation in political decision-making, which included the widespread questioning of traditional forms of authority (such as that of the church or aristocracy). Philosophically, the model of science leads to a belief in the possibility of attaining absolutely true knowledge (or at least solid and certain foundations from which scientific inquiry can proceed) and moral and political values that are valid for all cultures and all periods of history. In the arts, 'modernism' typically refers to the development in the late nineteenth century and beyond that involved a radical questioning of the conventions of painting and visual representation, of narrative and the use of language in the novel and poetry, and of tonality in music. Modernist art is thus highly self-reflective, at times formalist or abstract, and is defensive of its autonomy from everyday interests and concerns.

See Adorno; Benjamin; Bourdieu; Descartes; Durkheim; Elias; Freud;

Habermas; Hegel; Hume; Kant; Leavis; Le Corbusier; Marx; Parsons; Rousseau; Simmel; Weber.

Phenomenology

An approach to the theory of knowledge, derived from the work of Husserl, that focuses upon the way in which the world appears to human beings. The phenomenologist can be concerned with describing the world as it appears, rather than how we assume that it appears. This entails removing (or 'bracketing') all the prior expectations that we bring to our experience (such as a belief in the existence of a substantial world independent of its appearance in our consciousness). After Husserl, phenemenologists tended to focus more upon the way in which we give concrete meaning to the world – not least by paying attention to the fact that we engage with the world as embedded agents, and not as disembodied observers – or the way in which our expectations are used to constitute the world, and especially the social world, in which we live.

See Heidegger; Husserl; Merleau-Ponty; Sartre; Schutz.

Postmodernism

The term has many nuances of meaning, depending upon the context in which it is used. As part of an analysis of contemporary society, postmodernity is characterised by a shift away from the industrial forms of modernity, so that production is organised differently (typically by the geographical diffusion of the production process), with an increased dependence upon knowledge based industries. In philosophy the term is closely associated with the development of post-structuralism. Culturally, postmodernism entails a challenge to the ideals of the seventeenth-century European Enlightenment. A commitment to the possibility of absolute truth in scientific and philosophical inquiry, and the determination of ahistorical and universal standards of moral goodness and political justice, are replaced by a sympathy for relativism and pluralism, and at the extreme, the substitution of any concern with an independent physical or social reality by concern with reality as it is represented in the mass media. The postmodern arts, while in many respects building upon the radical self-reflection that is typically of modernism, tend to display greater interest in pastiche, surface effect (as opposed to formal rigour), irony and playfulness, and with a rejection of the modernist presupposition of a qualitative difference between the high and popular arts.

See Bataille; Baudrillard; Deleuze and Guattari; Foucault; Habermas; Jameson; Kuhn; Lyotard; Nietzsche; Rorty; Rose.

Post-structuralism

An approach to the analysis of the meaning of texts and other cultural artefacts and activities that developed from, and partially rejected aspects of, structuralism. Most importantly, post-structuralists tend to reject the aspiration to objective and definitive analyses of the structuralists. There is no post-structuralist methodology (in the sense of a set of rules of analysis that can be formulated independently of the object of inquiry). Post-structuralists are therefore generally freer and more idiosyncratic in their handling of issues. Orthodox notions of truth and morality are questioned. Post-structuralists typically espouse some form of cultural relativism, where knowledge claims and moral values are seen to have validity only within specific cultures or exercises of power.

See Barthes; Foucault; Lacan.

Pragmatism

An approach to philosophy, and especially to problems of meaning and truth, that has been developed in the United States since the late nineteenth century. While individual pragmatists diverge significantly in their philosophical positions, at the core of pragmatism is the recognition that the meaning of concepts (and thus it may be claimed, the truth or falsehood of propositions) is the concrete outcome of using those concepts. Thus, to use an example from C. S. Peirce, the meaning of the chemical formula of, say, sulphuric acid, is not the textbook definition but rather the practical implications that it has in terms of the experimental work that must be done, first, to establish that the substance I have before me is sulphuric acid, and second, the actions I must take to manufacture sulphuric acid. The truth of a proposition may then rest, not upon its correspondence to a reality that is independent of language, but rather upon what one seeks to achieve in uttering that proposition. In the context of a general knowledge quiz, the proposition 'There are nine planets in the solar system' is true (and will contribute to winning the quiz), regardless of any recent discoveries or debates as to the definition of 'planet' that may be current in astronomy.

See Dewey; Peirce; Rorty.

Semiology/semiotics

The theory of signs, and the way in which a study of signs and systems of signs can serve to explicate general problems of meaning and communication. While many approaches to semiology have their roots in the study of written and spoken language, all forms of meaningful human artefacts and actions can be treated as signs (including images and photographs, music, literature and myths). Semiology was the context within which structuralism was originally developed.

See Barthes; Jakobson; Saussure.

Structuralism

A method for analysing meaning that was developed in semiology, but came to be applied to a wide range of cultural artefacts and activities, and in such disciplines as anthropology, sociology, psychoanalysis, Marxism and literary criticism. Structuralism rests upon the assumption that the meaning of any sign (such as a word, an action within a story or myth, or an image) depends upon its relationship to other signs within the system (or structure). Crucially, meaning is not explained by an appeal to the historical development of the sign or system of sign. The concept of the binary opposition is central to structuralist approaches. It is argued that any given sign has meaning by its opposition to some other sign. Hence 'male' is not 'female'; 'culture' is not 'nature'. A cultural system can be seen to related binary oppositions according to the formula that a is to b as c is to d (e.g. male is to female as culture is to nature).

See Althusser; Barthes; Bourdieu; Chomsky; Eco; Jakobson; Lacan; Lévi-Strauss; Mauss; Saussure.

BIBLIOGRAPHY

Ackrill, J. L. (1981) *Aristotle the Philosopher*, Oxford: Oxford University Press.
Adorno, T. W. (1967) *(1955) Prisms*, London: Spearman.
——(1973a) *(1948) The Philosophy of Modern Music*, London: Sheed & Ward.
——(1973b) *(1966) Negative Dialectics*, London: Routledge & Kegan Paul.
——(1977) 'The Actuality of Philosophy', *Telos*, 31: 120–133.
——(1978a) *(1951) Minima Moralia: Reflections from Damaged Life*, London: New Left Books.
——(1978b) 'The Fetish Character of Hearing', in A. Arato and E. Gebhardt (eds) *The Essential Frankfurt School Reader*, Oxford: Blackwell.
——(1978c) 'On the Social Situation of Music', *Telos*, 33: 128–164.
——(1982) *(1956) Against Epistomology: Studies in Husserl and the Phenomenological Antinomies*, trans. W. Domingo, Oxford: Blackwell.
——(1984) *(1970) Aesthetic Theory*, London: Routledge.
——(1987) 'Late Capitalism or Industrial Society', in V. Meja, D. Misgeld and N. Stehr (eds) *Modern German Sociology*, New York: Columbia University Press.
——(1989) *(1933) Kierkegaard: Construction of the Aesthetic*, trans. R. Hullot-Kentor, Minneapolis, MN: Minneapolis University Press.
——(1991a) *The Culture Industry: Selected Essays on Mass Culture*, ed. J. M. Bernstein, London: Routledge.
——(1991b) *(1957–1963) Notes to Literature*, vol. 1, New York: Columbia University Press.
——(1991c) 'Trying to Understand Endgame', in his *Notes to Literature* volume 1, New York: Columbia University Press.
——(1991d) *(1968) Alban Berg: Master of the Smallest Link*, New York: Cambridge University Press.
——(1991e) *(1952) In Search of Wagner*, trans. R. Livingstone, London and New York: Verso.
——(1992a) *(1965–1974) Notes to Literature*, vol. 2, New York: Columbia University Press.
——(1992b) *(1963) Quasi una fantasia: Essays on Modern Music*, London: Verso.
——(1992c) *(1960) Mahler: A Musical Physiognomy*, trans. E. Jephcott, Chicago: University of Chicago Press.
——(1993) *(1963) Hegel: Three Studies*, Cambridge, MA: MIT Press.

Adorno, T. W. (1994a) *(1941)* 'On Popular Music', in J. Storey (ed.) *Cultural Theory and Popular Culture: A Reader*, London: Edward Arnold.

—— (1994b) *The Stars Down to Earth and Other Essays on the Irrational in Culture*, ed. S. Crook, New York: Routledge.

—— (1998a) *(1963–1969) Critical Models: Interventions and Catchwords*, New York: Columbia University Press.

—— (1998b) *Beethoven: The Philosophy of Music*, ed. R. Tiedemann, trans. E. Jephcott, Oxford: Polity.

—— (2000a) *The Psychological Technique of Martin Luther Thomas' Radio Addresses*, Stanford: CA: Stanford University Press.

—— (2000b) *Introduction to Sociology*, ed. C. Gödde, trans. E. Jephcott, Cambridge: Polity.

Adorno, T. W. and Horkheimer, M. (1973) *(1944) The Dialectic of Enlightenment*, trans. J. Cummings, London: Allen Lane.

Adorno, T. W., Frenkel-Brunswik, E. , Levinson, D. T. and Sanford, R. N. (1950) *The Authoritarian Personality*, New York: Harper.

Allen, N. J. , Pickering, W. S. F. , and Miller, W. W. (1998) *On Durkheim's Elementary Forms of Religious Life*, London and New York: Routledge.

Althusser, L. (1969) *(1959) For Marx*, trans. B. Brewster, London: New Left Books.

—— (1971) *Lenin and Philosophy and Other Essays*, London: New Left Books.

Althusser, L. and Balibar, E. (1970) *Reading Capital*, London: New Left Books.

Anderson, P. (1979) *Lineages of the Absolutist State*, London: Verso.

Ansell-Pearson, K. (1991) *Nietzsche contra Rousseau: A Study of Nietzsche's Moral and Political Thought*, Cambridge: Cambridge University Press.

Apel, K-O. (1976) 'The Transcendental Conception of Language Communication and the Idea of a First Philosophy', in H. Parret (ed.) *The History of Linguistic Thought and Contemporary Linguistics*, Berlin and New York: De Gruyter.

—— (1981) *Charles S. Peirce: From Pragmatism to Pragmaticism*, trans. J. M. Krois, Amherst, MA: University of Massachusetts Press.

Appleman, P. (ed.) (1970) *Darwin*, London: W. W. Norton.

Arato, A. (1979) *The Young Lukács and the Origins of Western Marxism*, London: Pluto.

Arato, A. and Gebhardt, E. (eds) (1978) *The Essential Frankfurt School Reader*, Oxford: Blackwell.

Arendt, Hanna (1951a) *The Burden of our Time*, London: Secker & Warburg.

—— (1951b) *The Origins of Totalitarianism*, New York: Harcourt Brace.

—— (1958a) *The Human Condition*, Chicago: University of Chicago Press.

—— (1958b) *Rahel Varnhagen: The Life of Jewish Women*, London: East and West Library.

—— (1963a) *Eichmann in Jerusalem: A Report on the Banality of Evil*, London: Faber & Faber.

—— (1963b) *On Revolution*, London: Faber & Faber.

—— (1968a) *Between Past and Future: Eight Exercises in Political Thought*, New York: Viking.

—— (1968b) *Men in Dark Times*, New York: Harcourt Brace.

—— (1970) *On Violence*, New York: Harcourt Brace.

—— (1973) *Crises of the Republic*, Harmondsworth: Penguin.

—— (1978a) *The Life of the Mind*, New York: Harcourt Brace.

—— (1978b) *The Jew as Pariah: Jewish Identity and Politics in the Modern Age*, ed. R. H. Feldman, New York: Grove.

—— (1982) *Lectures on Kant's Political Philosophy*, London: Harvester.

Arnold, M. (1993) *Culture and Anarchy and Other Writings*, ed. S. Collini, Cambridge: Cambridge University Press.

Austin, J. L. (1975) *(1955) How to Do Things with Words*, 2nd edn, Oxford: Oxford University Press.

Badcock, C. R. (1975) *Lévi-Strauss: Structuralism and Sociological Theory*, London: Hutchinson.

Baille, J. (2000) *Routledge Philosophy Guidebook to Hume on Morality*, London: Routledge.

Bakhtin, M. (1981) *The Dialogic Imagination: Four Essays by M. M. Bakhtin*, ed. M. Holquist, trans. C. Emerson and M. Holquist, Austin, TX: University of Texas Press.

—— (1984) *Rabelais and his World*, trans. H. Iswolsky, Bloomington, IN: Indiana University Press.

—— (1986) *Speech Genres and Other Late Essays*, ed. C. Emerson and M. Holquist, trans. V. McGee, Austin, TX: University of Texas Press.

Balibar, E. (1970) 'The Basic Concepts of Historical Materialism', in L. Althusser and E. Balibar, *Reading Capital*, London: New Left Books.

Barnes, J. (1982) *Aristotle*, Oxford: Oxford University Press.

—— (ed.) (1984) *The Complete Works of Aristotle*, 2 vols, Princeton, NJ: Princeton University Press.

Barrett, M. (1980) *Women's Oppression Today*, London: New Left Books.

Barsky, R. F. (1997) *Naom Chomsky: A Life of Dissent*, Cambridge, MA: MIT Press.

Barthes, R. (1967a) *(1953) Writing Degree Zero*, New York: Hill & Wang.

—— (1967b) *(1964) Elements of Semiology*, New York: Hill & Wang.

—— (1973) *(1957) Mythologies*, St Albans: Paladin.

—— (1974) *(1970) S/Z*, New York: Hill & Wang.

—— (1975) *(1973) The Pleasure of the Text*, New York: Hill & Wang.

—— (1977a) *Image, Music, Text*, trans. S. Heath, London: Fontana.

—— (1977b) 'Introduction to the Structural Analysis of Narratives', in his *Image, Music, Text*, London: Fontana.

—— (1977c) The Death of the Author, in his *Image, Music, Text*, London: Fontana.

—— (1977d) 'From Work to Text', in his *Image, Music, Text*, London: Fontana.

—— (1977e) *(1975) Barthes, R by Barthes, R*, New York: Hill & Wang.

—— (1977f) *On Racine*, trans. R. Howard, New York: Octagon.

—— (1977g) *Sade, Fourier, Loyola*, trans. R. Miller, London: Cape.

—— (1978) *(1977) A Lover's Discourse: Fragments*, New York: Hill & Wang.

—— (1981) *(1980) Camera Lucida: Reflections on Photography*, New York: Hill & Wang.

—— (1983) *Empire of Signs*, London: Cape.

—— (1985) *The Fashion System*, trans. M. Ward and R. Howard, London: Cape.

—— (1987) *(1966) Criticism and Truth*, Minneapolis, MN: University of Minnesota Press.

—— (1989) *Selected Writings*, ed. S. Sontag, London: Fontana.

Barthes, R. (1991) *The Responsibility of Forms: Critical Essays on Music, Art, and Representation*, trans. R. Howard, Berkeley, CA: University of California Press.

Bataille, G. (1985) *Visions of Excess: Selected Writings, 1927–1939*, trans. A. Stoekl *et al.*, Minneapolis, MN: University of Minnesota Press.

—— (1988) *(1949)The Accursed Share*, trans. R. Hurley, New York: Zone.

—— (1992) *On Nietzsche*, trans. B. Boone, London: Athlone.

—— (1994) *The Absence of Myth: Writings on Surrealism*, ed. and trans. M. Richardson, London: Verso.

Baudrillard, J. (1975) *(1973) The Mirror of Production*, trans. M. Poster, St Louis, MO: Telos.

—— (1981a) *Simulacra and Simulations*, trans. P. Foss, P. Patton and P. Beitchman, New York: Semiotext(e).

—— (1981b) *(1972) For a Critique of the political Economy of Signs*, trans. C. Levin, St Louis, MO: Telos.

——. (1988) *Selected Writings*, ed. M. Poster, Cambridge: Polity.

—— (1990a) *Revenge of the Crystal: Selected Writings on the Modern Object and its Destiny, 1968–1983*, London: Pluto.

—— (1990b) 'Mass Media Culture', in his *Revenge of the Crystal: Selected Writings on the Modern Object and its Destiny, 1968–1983*, London: Pluto.

—— (1990c) *Fatal Strategies*, London: Pluto.

—— (1991) 'The Reality Gulf', *Guardian*, 11 January.

—— (1993) *Symbolic Exchange and Death*, London: Sage.

Beiser, F. C. (1993) *The Cambridge Companion to Hegel*, Cambridge: Cambridge University Press.

Bell, D. (1990) *Husserl*, London: Routledge.

Bell, M. (1988) *F. R. Leavis*, London: Routledge.

Bendix, R. (1960) *Max Weber: An Intellectual Portrait*, Garden City, NY: Doubleday.

Benedict, R. (1935) *Patterns of Culture*, London: Routledge & Kegan Paul.

—— (1940) *Race: Science and Politics*, New York: Modern Age.

—— (1946) *The Chrysanthemum and the Sword: Patterns of Japanese Culture*, New York: Houghton Mifflin.

Benhabib, S. , Bonss, W. and McCole, J. (eds) (1993) *On Max Horkheimer: New Perspectives*, Cambridge, MA: MIT Press.

Benjamin, W. (1970a) *Illuminations*, ed. H. Arendt, London: Cape.

—— (1970b) *(1936)* 'The Work of Art in the Age of Mechanical Reproduction', in his *Illuminations*, London: Cape.

—— (1970c) *(1940)* 'Theses on the Philosophy of History', in his *Illuminations*, London: Jonathan Cape.

—— (1973a) *Charles Baudelaire: A Lyric Poet in the Era of High Capitalism*, London: New Left Books.

—— (1973b) *Understanding Brecht*, London: New Left Books.

—— (1977) *(1928) The Origin of German Tragic Drama*, trans. J. Osborne, London: New Left Books.

—— (1978a) *(1937)* 'Author as Producer', in: A. Arato and E. Gebhardt (eds) *The Essential Frankfurt School Reader*, Oxford: Blackwell.

—— (1978b) *Reflections*, trans. E. Jephcott, New York: Harcourt Brace Jovanovich.

—— (1979) *One-Way Street*, London: New Left Books.

—— (1986) *Moscow Diary*, trans. R. Sieburth, ed. G. Smith, Cambridge, MA: Harvard University Press.

—— (1994) *The Correspondence of Walter Benjamin*, trans. M. R. Jacobson, ed. G. Scholem and T. W. Adorno, Chicago: University of Chicago Press.

—— (1996a) *Selected Writings: Volume 1, 1913–1926*, Cambridge, MA: Belknap.

—— (1996b) (1972) *On Hashish*, trans. S. J. Thompson, Frankfurt: Suhrkamp.

—— (1999a) *Selected Writings: Volume 2, 1927–1934*, Cambridge, MA: Belknap.

—— (1999b) *The Complete Correspondence, 1928–1940*, Cambridge, MA: Harvard University Press.

—— (1999c) *The Arcades Project*, Cambridge, MA: Harvard University Press.

Bennett, J. (1966) *Kant's Analytic*, Cambridge: Cambridge University Press.

—— (1974) *Kant's Dialect*, London: Cambridge University Press.

Bennington, G. (1988) *Lyotard: Writing the Event*, New York: Columbia University Press.

Berger, F. R. (1984) *Happiness, Justice and Freedom: The Moral and Political Philosophy of John Stuart Mill*, Berkeley, CA: University of California Press.

Berger, P. L. and Luckmann, T. (1966) *The Social Construction of Reality: A Treatise in the Sociology of Knowledge*, London: Allen Lane.

Bernasconi, R. and Critchley, S. (eds.) (1991) *Re-reading Lévinas*, London: Athlone.

Bernstein, R. J. (ed.) (1985) *Habermas and Modernity*, Cambridge: Polity.

—— (1967) *John Dewey*, New York: Washington Square Press.

Bhabha, H. K. (1991) '"Race" time and the revision of modernity', *Oxford Literary Review*, 13.

—— (1994) *The Location of Culture*, London: Routledge

Bird, A. (2000) *Thomas Kuhn*, Chesham: Acumen.

Bloch, E. (1964) *(1918) Geist Der Utopia (Spirit of Utopia)* , Frankfurt: Suhrkamp.

—— (1970) *Man on his Own*, trans. E. B. Ashton, New York: Herder & Herder.

—— (1985) *Essays on the Philosophy of Music*, Cambridge: Cambridge University Press.

—— (1986a) *(1961) Natural Law and Dignity*, trans. D. J. Schmidt, Cambridge, MA: MIT Press.

—— (1986b) *(1959) The Principle of Hope*, 3 vols, Oxford: Blackwell.

—— (1988) *The Utopian Function of Art and Literature: Selected Essays*, London: MIT Press.

—— (1991) *(1962) The Heritage of our Times*, Oxford: Blackwell.

—— *et al.* (1977) *Aesthetics and Politics*, London: Verso.

Boggs, C. (1984) *The Two Revolutions: Antonio Gramsci and the Dilemmas of Western Marxism*, Boston, MA: South End Press.

Bogue, R. (1989) *Deluze and Guattari*, London and New York: Routledge.

Bottomore, T. (ed.) (1983) *A Dictionary of Marxist Thought*, Oxford: Blackwell.

Boundas, C. V. and Olkowski, D. (eds) (1994) *Gilles Deleuze and the Theater of Philosophy*, New York: Routledge.

Bourdieu, P. (1973) 'Cultural Reproduction and Social Reproduction', in R. Brown (ed.) *Knowledge, Education and Cultural Change*, London: Tavistock.

—— (1977a) *(1970) Reproduction in Education, Society and Culture*, trans. R. Nice, London: Sage.

Bourdieu, P. (1977b) *(1972) Outline of a Theory of Practice*, trans. R. Nice, Cambridge: Cambridge University Press.

——(1979) *Algeria 1960: Essays*, trans. R. Nice, Cambridge and New York: Cambridge University Press.

——(1984) *(1979) Distinction: A Social Critique of the Judgement of Taste*, trans. R. Nice, London: Routledge & Kegan Paul.

——(1985) 'The Genesis of the Concepts of Habitus and Field', *Sociocriticism, Theories and Perspectives II*, 2: 11–24.

——(1989) *(1984) Homo Academicus*, trans. P. Collier, Cambridge: Polity.

——(1990) *(1980) The Logic of Practice*, trans. R. Nice, Cambridge: Polity.

——(1991) *The Craft of Sociology: Epistemological Preliminaries*, ed. B. Krais, trans. R. Nice, Berlin and New York: Walter de Gruyter.

——(1993a) *The Field of Cultural Production*, Cambridge: Polity.

——(1993b) *(1987)* 'Manet and the Institutionalization of Anomie', trans. J. Parnell, in Bourdieu (1993a).

——(1994) *Academic Discourse: Linguistic Misunderstanding and Professional Power*, trans. R. Teese, Oxford: Polity.

——(1998) *Acts of Resistance: Against the New Myths of Our Time*, trans. R. Nice, Cambridge: Polity.

Box, M. A. (1990) *The Suasive Art of David Hume*, Princeton, NJ: Princeton University Press.

Boydston, J. A. (ed.) (1972) *Guide to the Works of John Dewey*, Carbondale, IL: Southern Illinois University Press.

Bradford, R. (1994) *Roman Jakobson: Life, Language, Art*, London and New York: Routledge.

Braidotti, R. (1994) *Radical Philosophies of Sexual difference: Luce Irigary*, London: Routledge.

Brandom, R. (2000) *Rorty and his Critics*, Malden, MA: Blackwell.

Brecht, B. (1941) *Mother Courage and her Children: A Chronicle of the Thirty Years' War*. trans. E. Bentley, New York: Grove.

——(1964) *Brecht on Theatre: The Development of an Aesthetic*, ed. and trans. J. Willett, New York: Hill & Wang.

——(1965) (1937–1951)*The Messingkauf Dialogues*, trans. J. Willett, London: Eyre Methuen.

——(1966a) *(1943) The Good Woman of Setzuan*. trans. E. Bentley, New York: Grove Press.

——(1966b) *(1948) The Caucasian Chalk Circle*, trans. E. Bentley, New York: Grove.

——(1966c) *(1943) The Life of Galileo*, trans. C. Laughton, New York: Grove.

Brecht, B. and Weill, K. (1963) *(1927–1929) The Rise and Fall of the City of Mahagonny*, Vienna: Universal.

Brecht, B. and Weill, K. (1964) *(1928) The Threepenny Opera*, trans. D. Vesey, New York: Grove.

Bronner, S. E. and Kellner, D. M. (eds) (1989) *Critical Theory and Society: A Reader*, London: Routledge.

Brubaker, R. (1984) *The Limits of Rationality: An Essay on the Social and Moral Thought of Max Weber*, London: Allen & Unwin.

——(1985) 'Rethinking Classical Theory: The Sociological Vision of Pierre Bourdieu', *Theory and Society*, 14: 723–744.

Bryant, C. G. A. and Jary, D. (eds) (1991) *Giddens' Theory of Structuration: A Critical Appreciation*, London and New York: Routledge.

Bryant, C. G. A. and Jary, D. (eds) (1996) *Anthony Giddens: Critical Assessments*, New York: Routledge.

Buck-Morss, S. (1977) *The Origin of Negative Dialectics: Theodor W. Adorno, Walter Benjamin, and the Frankfurt Institute*, New York: Free Press.

——(1991) *The Dialectics of Seeing: Walter Benjamin and the Arcades Project*, Cambridge, MA: MIT Press.

Buhle, P. (1988) *C. L. R. James: The Artist as Revolutionary*, London: Verso.

Burke, C. , Schor, N. and Whitford, M. (eds) (1994) *Engaging with Irigary*, New York: Columbia University Press.

Burke, P. and Van der Veken, J. (eds) (1993) *Merleau-Ponty in Contemporary Perspective*, Dordrecht and London: Kluwer Academic.

Burns, T. (1992) *Erving Goffman*, London: Routledge.

Caesar, M. (1999) *Umberto Eco: Philosophy, Semiotics and the Work of Fiction*, Oxford: Polity.

Caffrey, M. (1989) *Ruth Benedict: Stranger in this Land*, Austin, TX: University of Texas Press.

Calhoun, C. (ed.) (1992) *Habermas and the Public Sphere*, Cambridge, MA: MIT Press.

Calhoun, C., LiPuma, E. and Postone, M. (eds) (1993) *Bourdieu; Critical Perspectives*, Cambridge: Polity.

Campbell, R. H. and Skinner, A. (eds) (1982) *The Origins and Nature of the Scottish Enlightenment*, Edinburgh: J. Donald.

Canovan, M. (1974) *The Political Thought of Hannah Arendt*, London: Dent.

Capozzi, R. (ed.) (1997) *Reading Eco: An Anthology*, Bloomington, IN: Indiana University Press.

Carroll, D. (1987) *Paraesthetics: Foucault, Lyotard, Derrida*, New York and London: Methuen.

Carver, T. (ed.) (1991) *The Cambridge Companion to Marx*, Cambridge: Cambridge University Press.

Castoriadis, C. (1984) *Crossroads in the Labyrinth*, Cambridge, MA: MIT Press.

——(1987) *The Imaginary Institution of Society*, Oxford: Polity.

——(1988a) *Political and Social Writings Volume 1, 1946–1955: From the Critique of Bureaucracy to the Positive Content of Socialism*, Minneapolis, MN: University of Minnesota Press.

——(1988b) , *Political and Social Writings Volume 2, 1955–1960: From the Workers' Struggle against Bureaucracy to Revolution in the Age of Modern Capitalism*, Minneapolis, MN: University of Minnesota Press.

——(1991) *Philosophy, Politics, Autonomy*, Oxford: Oxford University Press.

——(1993) *Political and Social Writings Volume 3, 1961–1979: Recommencing the Revolution: From Socialism to the Autonomous Society*, Minneapolis, MN: University of Minnesota Press.

——(1997) *World in Fragments*, Stanford, CA: Stanford University Press.

Caygill, H. (1998) *Walter Benjamin: The Colour of Experience*, New York and London: Routledge.

Chadwick, R. F. and Cazeux, C. (eds) (1992) *Immanuel Kant: Critical Assessments*, London and New York: Routledge.

Chappell, V. (ed.) (1966) *Hume*, London: Macmillan.

Childs, P. and Williams, P. (1962) *An Introduction to Post-colonial Theory*, London and New York: Prentice Hall.

Chomsky, N. (1957) *Syntactic Structures*, The Hague: Mouton.

—— (1964a) 'Review of *Verbal Behaviour* by B. F. Skinner', *Language*, 35: 26–58.

—— (1964b) *Current Issues in Linguistic Theory*, The Hague: Mouton.

—— (1965) *Aspects of the Theory of Syntax*, Cambridge, MA: MIT Press.

—— (1966) *Cartesian Linguistics: A Chapter in the History of Rationalist Thought*, New York: Harper & Row.

—— (1969) *American Power and the New Mandarins*, Harmondsworth: Penguin.

—— (1972) *Studies on Semantics in Generative Grammar*, The Hague: Mouton.

—— (1973) *For Reasons of State*, New York: Pantheon.

—— (1975) *Reflections on Language*, New York: Pantheon.

—— (1983) *The Fateful Triangle: The United States, Israel and the Palestinians* London: Pluto.

—— (1986) *Knowledge of Language: Its Nature, Origin, and Use*, New York: Praeger.

—— (1988) *Language and the Problem of Knowledge: The Managua Lectures*, Cambridge, MA: MIT Press.

—— (1989) *Necessary Illusions: Thought Control in Democratic Societies*, London: Pluto.

—— (1991) *Deterring Democracy*, London: Vintage.

—— (1995) *The Minimalist Program*, Cambridge, MA: MIT Press.

Cixous, H. (1981) *(1975)* 'The Laugh of the Medusa', in E. Marks and I. de Courtivron (eds) *New French Feminisms*, Brighton: Harvester.

—— (1987) *The Newly Born Woman*, Manchester: Manchester University Press.

—— (1988) *Writing Differences: Readings from the Seminar of Helene Cixous*, ed. S. Sellers, Milton Keynes: Open University Press.

—— (1990) *Reading with Clarice Lispector*, ed. and trans. V. Andermatt Conley, London: Harvester Wheatsheaf.

—— (1992) *Readings: The Poetics of Blanchot, Joyce, Kafka, Kleist, Linspector, and Tsvetayeva*, ed. and trans. V. Andermatt Conley, New York and London: Harvester Wheatsheaf.

Cladis, M. S. (1992) *A Communitarian Defense of Liberalism: Emile Durkheim and Contemporary Social Theory*, Stanford, CA: Stanford University Press.

Clark, M. (1988) *Jaques Lacan: An Annotated Bibliography*, New York: Garland.

Clement, C. (1983) *(1981) The lives and Legends of Jaques Lacan*, trans. A. Goldhammer, New York: Columbia University Press.

Cohen, G. A. (1978) *Karl Marx's Theory of History*, Oxford: Clarendon.

Cohen, I. J. (1989) *Structuration Theory: Anthony Giddens and the Constitution of Social Life*, London: Macmillan.

Collini, S. (1988) *Arnold*, Oxford and New York: Oxford University Press.

Coltman, R. (1998) *The Language of Hermeneutics: Gadamer and Heidegger in Dialogue*, Albany, NY: State University of New York Press.

Connerton, P. (ed.) (1976) *Critical Sociology*, Harmondsworth: Penguin.

Cook, D. (1996) *The Culture Industry Revisited: Theodor W. Adorno on Mass Culture*, Lanham, MD: Rowman & Littlefield.

Cook, V. J. (1988) *Chomsky's Universal Grammar: An Introduction*, Oxford and New York: Blackwell.

Cottingham, J. (1986) *Descartes*, New York: Blackwell.

—— (1997) *Descartes' Philosophy of Mind*, London: Phoenix.

Craib, I. (1992) *Anthony Giddens*, London and New York: Routledge.

Critchley, S. (1999) *Ethics – Politics – Subjectivity: Essays on Derrida, Lévinas and Contemporary French Thought*, London: Verso.

Cudjoe, S. R. and Cain, W. E. (eds) (1995) *C. L. R. James: His Intellectual Legacies*, Amherst, MA: University of Massachusetts Press.

Culler, J. (1983) *Roland Barthes*, New York: Oxford University Press.

—— (1986) *Ferdinand de Saussure*, Ithaca, NY: Cornell University Press.

Cunningham-Wood, J. (ed.) (1988) *Karl Marx's Economics: Critical Assessments*, London: Croom Helm.

Curtis, D. A. (ed.) (1997) *The Castoriadis Reader*, Oxford: Blackwell.

Curtis, W. J. R. (1992) *Le Corbusier: Ideas and Forms*, London: Phaidon.

Daniel, J. O. and Moylan, T. (eds) (1997) *Not Yet: Reconsidering Ernst Bloch*, London and New York: Verso.

Daniels, N. (ed.) (1978) *Reading Rawls: Critical Studies on a Theory of Justice*, Oxford: Blackwell.

Danto, A. C. (1975) *Sartre*, London: Fontana.

—— (1981) *The Transfiguration of the Commonplace*, Cambridge, MA: Harvard University Press.

Davidson, A. (1977) *Antonio Gramsci: Towards an Intellectual Biography*, Atlantic Highlands, NJ: Humanities Press.

Davion, V. and Wolf, C. (eds) (2000) *The Idea of a Political Liberalism: Essays on Rawls*, Lanham, MD: Rowman & Littlefield.

Davis, C. (1996) *Lévinas: An Introduction*, Cambridge: Polity.

Day, G. (1996) *Re-Reading Leavis: Culture and Literary Criticism*, London: Macmillan.

Deflem, M. (1996) *Habermas, Modernity and Law*, London: Sage.

Deleuze, G. (1983) (1962) *Nietzsche and Philosophy*, London: Athlone.

—— (1990a) (*1969*) *The Logic of Sense*, trans. M. Lester with C. Stivale, London: Athlone.

—— (1990b) 'The Simulacrum and Ancient Philosophy', in his *The Logic of Sense*, London: Athlone.

—— (1991) *Cinema*, 2 vols, Minneapolis, MN: University of Minnesota Press.

Deleuze, G. and Guattari, F. (1977) (*1972*) *Anti-Oedipus: Capitalism and Schizophrenia*, trans. R. Hurley, M. Seem and H. R. Lane, New York: Viking.

Deleuze, G. and Guattari, F. (1987) (*1980*) *A Thousand Plateaus: Capitalism and Schizophrenia*, trans. B. Massumi, Minneapolis, MN: University of Minnesota Press.

de Man, P. (1978) 'The Epistemology of Metaphor', *Critical Inquiry*, 5: 13–30.

—— (1979) *Allegories of Reading*, New Haven, CT: Yale University Press.

—— (1983) (*1971*) *Blindness and Insight: Essays in the Rehtoric of Contemporary Criticism*, London: Methuen.

—— (1989) *Critical Writings, 1953–1978*, ed. L. Waters, Minneapolis, MN: University of Minnesota Press.

Dent, N. J. H (1988) *Rousseau: An Introduction to his Psychological, Social and Political Theory*, Oxford: Blackwell.

Derrida, J. (1973) '*Speech and Phenomena' and Other Essays on Husserl's Theory of Signs*, trans. D. B. Allison, Evanston, IL: Northwestern University Press.

Derrida, J. (1976) *(1967) Of Grammatology*, trans. G. Spivak, Baltimore, MD: Johns Hopkins University Press.

—— (1978) *(1967) Writing and Difference*, trans. A. Bass, London: Routledge & Kegan Paul.

—— (1979) *Spurs: Nietzsche's Styles*, trans. B. Harlow, Chicago: University of Chicago Press.

—— (1981) *Dissemination*, trans. B. Johnson, Chicago: University of Chicago Press.

—— (1982) *(1972) Margins of Philosophy*, trans. A. Bass, Chicago: University of Chicago Press.

—— (1987) *The Truth in Painting*, Chicago: University of Chicago Press.

—— (1988a) *(1982) The Ear of the Other: Otobiography, Transference, Translation Texts and Discussions with Jacques Derrida*, ed. C. McDonald, trans. P. Kamuf, Lincoln, NB: University of Nebraska Press.

—— (1988b) *Limited Inc.*, Evanston: IL: Northwestern University Press.

—— (1992) *Given Time: I. Counterfeit Money*, trans. P. Kamuf: Chicago and London: University of Chicago Press.

—— (1994) *Specters of Marx: The State of Debt, the Work of Mourning, and the New International*, tr. P. Kamuf: New York and London: Routledge.

—— (1996b) *Archive Fever: A Freudian Impression*, trans. E. Prenowitz, Chicago and London: University of Chicago Press.

Descartes, R. (1996a) *(1632) Le Monde*, ed. A. Bitbol-Hespériès and J-P. Verdet, Paris: Seuil.

—— (1999) *(1637, 1641) Discourse on Method and Meditations on First Philosophy*, trans. D. A. Cress, Indianapolis, IN: Hackett.

Dewey, J. (1891) *Outlines of a Criticial Theory of Ethics*, Ann Arbor, MI: Inland Press.

—— (1910) *How We Think*, New York: Heath.

—— (1916) *Democracy and Education: An Introduction to the Philosophy of Education*, New York: Macmillan.

—— (1959) *Dewey on Education: Selections*, ed. M. S. Dworkin, New York: Teachers College Press.

—— (1980) *Art as Experience*, New York: Perigee.

—— (1993) *The Political Writings*, eds D. Morris and I. Shapiro, Indianapolis, IN: Hackett.

—— (1997) *The Influence of Darwin on Philosophy and Other Essays*, New York: Prometheus.

Dews, P. (ed.) (1999) *Habermas: A Critical Reader*, Oxford: Blackwell.

Diprose, R. (1994) *The Bodies of Women: Ethics, Embodiment and Sexual Difference*, London: Routledge.

Dixon, M. J. (1990) *Raymond Williams: Culture and Materialism*, London: Pauper's Press.

Dowling, W. C. (1984) *Jameson, Althusser, Marx: An Introduction to 'The Political Unconscious'*, Ithaca, NY: Cornell University Press.

Drew, P. and Wootton, A. (eds) (1988) *Erving Goffman: Exploring the Interaction Order*, Boston, MA: Northeastern University Press.

Dreyfus, H. and Hall, H. (eds) (1992) *Heidegger: A Critical Reader*, Oxford: Blackwell.

Dreyfus, H. L. and Rabinow, P. (1982) *Michel Foucault: Beyond Structuralism and Hermeneutics*, Brighton: Harvester.

Durkheim, E. (1952) *(1897) Suicide: A Study in Sociology*, trans. J. A. Spaulding and G. Simpson, London: Routledge & Kegan Paul.

——(1976) *(1912) The Elementary Forms of the Religious Life: A Study in Religious Sociology*, London: Allen & Unwin.

——(1982) *(1895) The Rules of the Sociological Method*, London: Macmillan.

——(1984) *(1893) The Division of Labour in Society*, trans. W. D. Halls, London: Macmillan.

Durkheim, E. and Mauss, M. (1963) *(1903) Primitive Classification*, Chicago: University of Chicago Press.

Eagleton, T. (ed.) (1989) *Raymond Williams: Critical Perspectives*, Cambridge: Polity Press.

Eco, U. (1976) *A Theory of Semiotics*, London: Macmillan.

——(1983) *(1980) The Name of the Rose*, trans. W. Weaver, London: Secker & Warburg.

——(1984) *Semiotics and the Philosophy of Language*, London: Macmillan.

——(1990a) *The Limits of Interpretation*, Bloomington, IN: Indiana University Press.

——(1990b) *(1988) Foucault's Pendulum*, trans. W. Weaver, London: Pan.

——(1995) *(1986) Faith in Fakes: Travels in Hyperreality*, London: Minerva.

Elias, N. (1972) 'Theory of Science and History of Science: Comments on a Recent Discussion', *Economy and Society*, 1(2): 117–133.

—— (1974) 'The Sciences: Towards a Theory', in R. Whitley (ed.) *Social Processes of Scientific Development*, London: Routledge.

——(1978) *(1970) What is Sociology?*, London: Hutchinson.

——(1982) *(1939) The Civilising Process*, vol. 1, *The History of Manners*; vol. 2, *State Formation and Civilisation*, Oxford: Basil Blackwell.

——(1983) *(1935) The Court Society*, Oxford: Basil Blackwell.

——(1985) *The Loneliness of Dying*, Oxford: Basil Blackwell.

——(1987) *Involvement and Detachment*, Oxford: Basil Blackwell.

——(1991a) *The Symbol Theory*, London: Sage.

——(1991b) *(1987) The Society of Individuals*, Oxford: Basil Blackwell.

——(1992) *(1984) Time: An Essay*, Oxford: Basil Blackwell.

——(1994a) *Reflections on a Life*, trans. E. Jephcott, Cambridge: Polity.

——(1994b) *The Established and the Outsiders: A Sociological Enquiry into Community Problems*, London: Sage.

Elias, N. and Dunning, E. (1986) *Quest for Excitement: Sport and Leisure in the Civilising Process*, Oxford: Basil Blackwell.

Ellenberger, H. (1970) *The Discovery of the Unconscious: The History and Evolution of Dynamic Psychiatry*, London: Allen Lane.

Engels, F. (1970) *(1939) Anti-Duhring*, Moscow: Progress.

——(1973) *(1873–83) Dialectics of Nature*, trans. C. Dutt, New York: International.

Esslin, M. (1960) *Brecht: The Man and his Work*, New York: Doubleday.

Evans-Pritchard, E. E. (1951) *Kinship and Marriage among the Nuer*, Oxford: Clarendon.

Fanon, F. (1967) *(1961) The Wretched of the Earth*, trans. C. Farrington, Harmondsworth: Penguin.

——(1970) *(1964) Toward the African Revolution*, trans. H. Chevalier, Harmondsworth: Penguin.

Fanon, F. (1986) *(1952) Black Skin, White Masks,* trans. C. L. Markmann, London: Pluto.

Featherstone, M. (1987) 'Norbert Elias and Figurational Sociology', *Theory, Culture and Society,* 4(2–3): 197–211.

Fletcher, J. and Benjamin, A. (eds) (1990) *Abjection, Melancholia and Love: The Work of Julia Kristeva,* London and New York: Routledge.

Foucault, M. (1965) *Madness and Civilization,* New York: Pantheon.

—— (1970) *(1966) The Order of Things: An Archaeology of the Human Sciences,* London: Tavistock.

—— (1973) *(1963) The Birth of the Clinic,* New York: Pantheon.

—— (1977) 'Nietzsche, Genealogy, History', in D. F. Bouchard (ed.) *Language; Counter-Memory, Practice,* Oxford: Blackwell.

—— (1978) *(1976) The History of Sexuality,* vol. 1, *An Introduction,* Harmondsworth: Penguin.

—— (1979) *(1975) Discipline and Punish: The Birth and the Prison,* Harmondsworth: Penguin.

—— (1980) *Power/Knowledge: Selected Interviews and Other Writings 1972–1977,* ed. C. Gordon, trans. C. Gordon *et al.* London: Harvester Wheatsheaf.

—— (1985) *(1984) The History of Sexuality,* vol. 2, *The Uses of Pleasure,* Harmondsworth: Penguin.

—— (1986) *(1984) The History of Sexuality,* vol. 3, *The Care of the Self,* Harmondsworth: Penguin.

Fowler, B. (1997) *Pierre Bourdieu and Cultural Theory: Critical Investigations,* London: Sage.

Franco, P. (1990) *The Political Philosophy of Michael Oakeshott,* New Haven, CT: Yale University Press.

Freud, S. (1895) 'Project for a Scientific Psychology', in *The Standard Edition of the Complete Works of Sigmund Freud,* vol. 1, trans. J. Strachey, London: Hogarth Press and Institute of Psycho-Analysis.

—— (1908) 'On the Sexual Theories of Children', in *The Standard Edition of the Complete Works of Sigmund Freud,* vol. 9, trans. J. Strachey, London: Hogarth Press and Institute of Psycho-Analysis.

—— (1910) 'A Special Type of Choice of Object Made by Men', in *The Standard Edition of the Complete Works of Sigmund Freud,* vol. 11, trans. J. Strachey, London: Hogarth Press and Institute of Psycho-Analysis.

—— (1911) 'Formulation on the Two Principles of Mental Functioning', in: *The Standard Edition of the Complete Works of Sigmund Freud,* vol. 12, trans. J. Strachey, London: Hogarth Press and Institute of Psycho-Analysis (and Freud 1991a).

—— (1924) 'The Dissolution of the Oedipus Complex', in *The Standard Edition of the Complete Works of Sigmund Freud,* vol. 19, trans. J. Strachey, London: Hogarth Press and Institute of Psycho-Analysis.

—— (1953–1974) *The Standard Edition of the Complete Works of Sigmund Freud,* 24 vols, trans. J. Strachey, London: Hogarth Press and Institute of Psycho-Analysis.

—— (1973) *New Introductory Lectures on Psychoanalysis,* Harmondsworth: Penguin.

—— (1974a) *Introductory Lectures on Psychoanalysis,* Harmondsworth: Penguin.

—— (1974b) *(1895) Studies on Hysteria,* Harmondsworth: Penguin.

—— (1975) *(1901) The Psychopathology of Everyday Life*, Harmondsworth: Penguin.

—— (1976a) *(1900) The Interpretation of Dreams*, Harmondsworth: Penguin.

—— (1976b) *(1901) Jokes and their Relation to the Unconscious*, Harmondsworth: Penguin.

—— (1977a) *On Sexuality: Three Essays on the Theory of Sexuality and Other Works*, Harmondsworth: Penguin.

—— (1977b) *Case Histories I: Dora and Little Hans*, Harmondsworth: Penguin.

—— (1978) *Case Histories II: The Rat Man, The Wolf Man, A Case of Female Homosexuality*, Harmondsworth: Penguin.

—— (1979) *On Psychopathology*, Harmondsworth: Penguin.

—— (1985) *Art and Literature: Jensen's 'Gradiva', Leonardo da Vinci and Other Works*, Harmondsworth: Penguin.

—— (1990) *The Origins of Religion: Totem and Taboo, Moses and Monotheism, and Other Works*, Harmondsworth: Penguin.

—— (1991a) *On Metapsychology: Beyond the Pleasure Principle, The Ego and the Id and Other Works*, Harmondsworth: Penguin.

—— (1991b) *Civilization, Society and Religion: Group Psychology, Civilization and its Discontents and Other Works*, Harmondsworth: Penguin.

Freund, J. (1998) *The Sociology of Max Weber*, London: Routledge.

Frisby, D. (1988) *Fragments of Modernity*, Cambridge: Polity.

—— (1992a) *Simmel and Since: Essays on Georg Simmel's Social Theory*, London and New York: Routledge.

—— (1992b) *Sociological Impressionism: A Reassessment of Georg Simmel's Social Theory*, 2nd edn, London: Routledge.

—— (ed.) (1994) *Georg Simmel: Critical Assessments*, London: Routledge.

Frisby, D. and Featherstone, M. (1986) *Simmel on Culture: Selected Writings*, London: Sage.

Fuller, M. B. (1998) *Making Sense of MacIntyre*, Aldershot: Ashgate.

Gadamer, H-G. (1975) *(1960) Truth and Method*, London: Sheed & Ward.

—— (1977) *Philosophical Hermeneutics*, ed. D. E. Linge, Berkeley, CA: University of California Press.

—— (1992) *Hans-Georg Gadamer on Education, Poetry, and History: Applied Hermeneutics*, ed. D. Misgeld and G. Nicholson, trans. L. Schmidt and M. Reuss, Albany, NY: State University of New York Press.

—— (1994) *Heidegger's Ways*, trans. J. W. Stanley, Albany, NY: State University of New York Press.

Gay, J. (1969) *The Beggars Opera*, Lincoln, NB: University of Nebraska Press.

Gay, P. (1988) *The Enlightenment: An Interpretation*, 2 vols, London: Weidenfeld & Nicolson.

Geertz, C. (1956) *The Development of the Japanese Economy: A Socio-cultural Approach*, Cambridge, MA: Center for International Studies, Massachusetts, Institute of Technology.

—— (1960) *The Religion of Java*, Glencoe, NY: Free Press.

—— (1968) *Islam Observed: Religious Development in Morocco and Indonesia*, New Haven, CT: Yale University Press.

—— (1973) *The Interpretation of Cultures*, New York: Basic Books.

—— (1980) *Negara: The Theatre State in Nineteenth-Century Bali*, Princeton, NJ: Princeton University Press.

Geertz, C. (1983) *Local Knowledge: Further Essays in Interpretive Anthropology*, New York: Basic Books.

—— (1988) *Works and Lives: The Anthropologist as Author*, Cambridge: Polity.

—— (1995) *After the Fact: Two Countries, Four Decades, One Anthropologist*, Cambridge, MA: Harvard University Press.

—— (2000) *Available Light: Anthropological Reflections on Philosophical Topics*, Princeton, NJ: Princeton University Press.

Geoghegan, V. (1996) *Ernst Bloch*, London and New York: Routledge.

Gerson, L. P. (ed.) (1999) *Aristotle: Critical Assessments*, London: Routledge.

Giddens, A. (1971) *Capitalism and Modern Social Theory: An Analysis of the Writings of Marx, Durkheim and Max Weber*, London: Cambridge University Press.

—— (1973) *The Class Structure of the Advanced Societies*, London: Hutchinson.

—— (1977) *Studies in Social and Political Theory*, London: Hutchinson.

—— (1978) *Durkheim*, London: Fontana.

—— (1979) 'Agency, Structure', in his *Central Problems in Social Theory*, London: Macmillan.

—— (1982) *Profiles and Critiques in Social Theory*, Berkeley, CA: University of California Press.

—— (1984) *The Constitution of Society: Outline of the Theory of Structuration*, Cambridge: Polity.

—— (1987) *Social Theory and Modern Sociology*, Stanford, CA: Stanford University Press.

—— (1990) *The Consequences of Modernity*, Cambridge: Polity.

—— (1991) *Modernity and Self-Identity*, Cambridge: Polity.

—— (1992) *The Transformation of Intimacy: Sexuality, Love, and Eroticism in Modern Societies*, Cambridge: Polity.

—— (1993a) *New Rules of Sociological Method: A Positive Critique of Interpretative Sociologies*, 2nd edn, Stanford, CA: Stanford University Press.

—— (1993b) *The Giddens Reader*, ed. P. Cassell, Stanford, CA: Stanford University Press.

—— (1994) *Beyond Left and Right*, Cambridge: Polity.

—— (1995) *Politics, Sociology and Social Theory: Encounters with Classical and Contemporary Social Thought*, Stanford, CA: Stanford University Press.

—— (1996a) *In Defence of Sociology: Essays, Interpretations and Rejoinders*, Cambridge: Polity.

—— (1996b) *Introduction to Sociology*, New York: W. W. Norton.

—— (1997) *Sociology*, Cambridge: Polity.

—— (1998a) *Conversations with Anthony Giddens: Making Sense of Modernity*, Stanford, CA: Stanford University Press.

—— (1998b) *The Third Way: The Renewal of Social Democracy*, Cambridge: Polity.

Giddens, A. and Held, D. (eds) (1982) *Classes, Power and Conflict: Classical and Contemporary Debates*, London, Macmillan.

Gino, R. (1995) *Andre Malraux: Politics and the Temptation of Myth*, Aldershot: Avebury.

Goffman, E. (1956) 'Embarrassment and Social Organization', *American Journal of Sociology*, 62: 264–271.

—— (1959) *Presentation of Self in Everyday Life*, Harmondsworth: Penguin.

——(1961) *Asylums: Essays on the Social Situation of Mental Patients and Other Inmates*, New York: Doubleday.

——(1963) *Stigma: Notes of the Management of Spoiled Identity*, New York: Prentice Hall.

——(1967) *Interaction Ritual: Essays in Face-to-Face Behaviour*, Chicago: Aldine.

——(1974) *Frame Analysis*, New York: Harper & Row.

——(1979) *Gender Advertisements*, New York: Harper & Row.

——(1997) *The Goffman Reader*, ed. C. Lemert and A. Branaman, Oxford: Blackwell.

Goudsblom, J. (1987) 'The Sociology of Norbert Elias: Its Resonance and Significance', *Theory, Culture and Society*, 4(2–3): 326–329.

Goudsblom, J. and Mennell, S. (eds) (1998) *The Norbert Elias Reader: A Biographical Selection*, Oxford: Blackwell. .

Gramsci, A. (1971) *(1929–1935) Selections from Prison Notebooks*, London: Lawrence & Wishart.

——(1977) *Selections from Political Writings*, ed. Q. Hoare, trans. J. Mathews, London and New York: Lawrence & Wishart.

——(1985) *Selections from Cultural Writings*, ed. D. Forgacs and G. Nowell-Smith, trans. W. Boelhower, London: Lawrence & Wishart.

——(1989) *An Antonio Gramsci Reader: Selected Writings, 1916–1935*, ed. D. Forgacs, New York: Schoken.

——(1994) *Letters from Prison*, trans. R. Rosenthal, New York: Columbia University Press.

——(1995) *Further Selections from the Prison Notebooks*, trans. and ed. D. Boothman, London: Lawrence & Wishart.

Grayling, A. C. (1988) *Wittgenstein*, Oxford: Oxford University Press.

Greenleaf, W. H. (1966) *Oakeshott's Philosphical Politics*, London: Longman.

Grimshaw, A. (1991) *The C. L. R. James Archive: A Reader's Guide*, New York: C. L. R. James Institute.

Grosz, E. (1989) *Sexual Subversions: Three French Feminists: Julia Kristeva, Luce Irigaray, Michèle Le Doeuff*, Sydney: Allen & Unwin.

——(1994) *Volatile Bodies: Toward a Corporeal Feminism*, Bloomington and Indianapolis, IN: Indiana University Press.

Guerlac, S. (1993) 'Transgression in Theory in Ethics, Politics and Difference', in K. Oliver (ed.) *Ethics, Politics, and Difference in Julia Kristeva's Writings*, New York: Routledge.

Habermas, J. (1970a) 'On Systematically Distorted Communication', *Inquiry*, 13: 205–218.

——(1970b) 'Towards a Theory of Communicative Competence', *Inquiry*, 13: 360–375.

——(1971a) *(1968) Knowledge and Human Interests*, Boston, MA: Beacon.

——(1971b) *Toward a Rational Society: Student Protest, Science and Politics*, London: Heinemann.

——(1976a) *(1971) Theory and Practice*, Boston, MA: Beacon.

——(1976b) *(1973) Legitimation Crisis*, London: Heinemann.

——(1979) *(1976) Communication and the Evolution of Society*, Boston, MA: Beacon.

——(1983) *Philosophical-Political Profiles*, trans. F. G. Lawrence, London: Heinemann.

Habermas, J. 1984) *(1981) The Theory of Communicative Action*, vol. 1: *Reason and the Rationalisation of Society*, Cambridge: Polity.

—— (1987) *(1981) The Theory of Communicative Action*, vol. 2: *Lifeworld and System: A Critique of Functionalist Reason*, Cambridge: Polity.

—— (1988a) *(1985) The Philosophical Discourse of Modernity*, Cambridge, MA: MIT Press.

—— (1988b) *On the Logic of the Social Sciences*, trans. S. Weber Nicholsen and J. A. Stark, Cambridge: Polity.

—— (1989a) *(1962) The Structural Transformation of the Public Sphere: An Inquiry into a Category of Bourgeois Society*, Cambridge: Polity.

—— (1989b) *(1985) The New Conservatism: Cultural Criticism and the Historians' Debate*, Cambridge, MA: MIT Press.

—— (1990) *Moral Consciousness and Communicative Action*, Cambridge, MA: MIT Press.

—— (1992a) *Autonomy and Solidarity: Interviews with Jurgen Habermas*, ed. P. Dews, London and New York: Verso.

—— (1992b) *Postmetaphysical Thinking*, trans. W. M. Hohengarten, Cambridge, MA: MIT Press.

—— (1993) *Justification and Application: Remarks on Discourse Ethics*, trans. C. Cronin, Cambridge: Polity.

—— (1994) *The Past as Future*, ed. M. Pensk, Cambridge: Polity.

—— (1996) *Between Facts and Norms: Contributions to a Discourse Theory of Law and Democracy*, trans. W. Rehg, Oxford: Polity.

—— (1997) *A Berlin Republic: Writings on Germany*, trans. S. Rendall, Lincoln, NB: University of Nebraska Press.

—— (1998) *The Inclusion of the Other: Studies in Political Theory*, ed. C. Cronin and P. de Greiff, Cambridge, MA: MIT Press.

—— (1999) *On the Pragmatics of Communication*, ed. M. Cooke, Cambridge: Polity.

Hahn, L. (ed.) (1995) *The Philosophy of Paul Ricoeur*, Chicago: Open Court.

—— (ed.) (1997) *The Philosophy of Hans-Georg Gadamer*, Chicago: Open Court.

Hall, J. C. (1973) *Rousseau: An Introduction to his Political Philosophy*, London: Macmillan.

Hall, S. (1973) *Encoding and Decoding in Television Discourse'*, CCCS stencilled paper (see Hall 1980), Birmingham: Centre for Contemporary Cultural Studies.

—— (1975) *(1971) Television as a Medium and its Relation to Culture*, CCCS stencilled paper, no 34, Birmingham: Centre for Contemporary Cultural Studies.

—— (1980) 'Encoding/Decoding', in S. Hall, D. Hobson, A. Lowe and P. Willis (eds) *Culture, Media, Language*, London: Hutchinson.

—— (1982) 'The Recovery of "Ideology": The Return of the "Repressed" in Media Studies', in M. Gurevitch, T. Bennett, J. Curran and J. Woollacott (eds) *Culture, Society and the Media*, London: Methuen.

—— (1983) *The Politics of Thatcherism*, London: Lawrence & Wishart in association with *Marxism Today*.

—— (1985) 'The Toad in the Garden: Thatcherism amongst the Theorists', in C. Nelson and L. Grossberg (eds) *Marxism and the Interpretation of Culture*, Urbana, IL: University of Illinois Press.

—— (1996a) *Questions of Cultural Identity*, London: Sage.

—— (1996b) *Race, the Floating Signifier*, Northampton, MA: Media Education Foundation.

—— (1996c) *Critical Dialogues in Cultural Studies*, London and New York: Routledge.

—— (1997) *Representation: Cultural Representations and Signifying Practices*, London: Sage.

Hall, S. and Jefferson, T. (eds) (1976) *Resistance through Rituals: Youth Subcultures in Post-War Britain*, London: Hutchinson.

Hall, S. and Whannel, P. (1964) *The Popular Arts*, London: Hutchinson.

Hall, S., Critcher, C., Jefferson, T., Clarke, J. and Roberts, B. (eds) (1978) *Policing the Crisis: Mugging, the State and Law and Order*, London: Macmillan.

Hall, S., Hobson, D., Lowe, A. and Willis, P. (eds) (1992) *Culture, Media, Language: Working Papers in Cultural Studies, 1972–79*, London: Hutchinson.

Halliday, R. (1976) *John Stuart Mill*, London: Allen & Unwin.

Hamilton, P. (1983) *Talcott Parsons*, Chichester: Horwood.

—— (ed.) (1991) *Max Weber: Critical Assessments*, London: Routledge.

—— (ed.) (1993) *Talcott Parsons: Critical Assessments*, London: Routledge.

—— (ed.) (1995) *Emile Durkheim: Critical Assessments*, London and New York: Routledge.

Hamilton, W. D. (1964) 'The Genetic Evolution of Social Behaviour', *Journal of Theoretical Biology*, 7: 1–52.

Hardt, M. and Weeks, K. (eds) (2000) *The Jameson Reader*, Oxford: Blackwell.

Hare, R. M. (1982) *Plato*, Oxford: Oxford University Press.

Harker, R. *et al.* (eds) (1990) *An Introduction to the Work of Bourdieu: The Practice of Theory*, London: Macmillan.

Harris, H. S. (1972) *Hegel's Development: Toward the Sunlight 1770–1801*, Oxford: Clarendon.

Harris, R. (1987) *Reading Saussure: A Critical Commentary on the Cours de Linguistique Générale*, London: Duckworth.

—— (1988) *Language, Saussure and Wittgenstein: How to Play Games with Words*, London: Routledge.

Hartmann, G. (ed.) (1979) *Deconstruction and Criticism*, New Haven, CT: Yale University Press.

Hayes, E. and Hayes, T. (eds) (1974) *Claude Lévi-Strauss: The Anthropologist as Hero*, Cambridge, MA: MIT Press.

Hegel, G. W. F. (1931) *(1807) The Phenomenology of Mind*, trans. J. B. Baille, London: Allen & Unwin.

—— (1942) *(1821) The Philosophy of Right*, Oxford: Clarendon.

—— (1948) *Early Theological Writings*, trans. T. M. Knox, Philadelphia, PA: University of Pennsylvania Press.

—— (1969) *Science of Logic*, trans. A. V. Miller, London: Allen & Unwin.

—— (1970) *(1817) Philosophy of Nature*, Oxford: Clarendon.

—— (1971) *(1817) Philosophy of Mind*, Oxford: Clarendon.

—— (1975a) *(1817) Hegel's Logic*, trans. W. Wallace, Oxford: Clarendon.

—— (1975b) *Lectures on the Philosophy of World History*, trans. H. B. Nisbet, Cambridge: Cambridge University Press.

—— (1975c) *Lectures on the History of Philosophy*, trans. E. S. Haldane, Lincoln, NB: University of Nebraska Press.

Hegel, G. W. F. (1975d) *Hegel's Aesthetics*, 2 vols, trans. T. M. Knox, Oxford: Clarendon.

——(1977) *(1807) The Phenomenology of Spirit*, trans. A. V. Miller, Oxford: Clarendon.

——(1988a) *Introduction to the Philosophy of History*, trans. L. Rauch, Indianapolis, IN: Hackett.

——(1988b) *(1827) Lectures on the Philosophy of Religion*, Berkeley, CA: University of California Press.

——(1991a) *(1817) The Encyclopaedic Logic, with the Zusatze*, trans. T. F. Geraets, W. A. Suchting and H. S. Harris, Indianapolis, IN: Hackett.

——(1991b) *(1821) Elements of the Philosophy of Right*, trans. H. B. Nisbett, ed. A. Wood, Cambridge: Cambridge University Press.

——(1998) *The Hegel Reader*, ed. S. Houlgate, Oxford and Malden, MA: Blackwell.

——(1999) *Hegel: Political Writings*, ed. L. Dickey and H. B. Nisbet, Cambridge: Cambridge University Press.

Heidegger, M. (1962) *(1927) Being and Time*, trans. J. Macquarrie and E. Robinson, Oxford: Blackwell.

——(1993) 'What is Metaphysics?' *(1929)*, 'On the Essence of Truth', 2nd edn (1949), 'Building, Dwelling and Thinking' (1951) and 'The Question Concerning Technology' (1953), all in his *Basic Writings: Revised and Expanded Edition*, ed. D. F. Krell, London: Routledge.

Held, D. (1980) *Introduction to Critical Theory: Horkheimer to Habermas*, London: Hutchinson.

Held, D. and Thompson, J. (eds) (1990) *Social Theory of Modern Society: Anthony Giddens and his Critics*, Cambridge: Cambridge University Press.

Hill, M. A. (ed.) (1979) *Hannah Arendt: The Recovery of the Public World*, New York: St Martin's Press.

Hiorth, F. (1974) *Naom Chomsky, Linguistics and Philosophy*, Oslo: Universitetsforlaget.

Hoggart, R. (1957) *Uses of Literacy*, London: Chatto & Windus.

——(1967) *The Literary Imagination and the Study of Society*, Birmingham: Centre for Contemporary Cultural Studies.

——(1969) *Contemporary Cultural Studies: An Approach to the Study of Literature and Society*, Birmingham: University of Birmingham Press.

——(1970) *Speaking to Each Other: Essays*, London: Chatto & Windus.

——(1982) *An English Temper: Essays on Education, Culture and Communications*, London: Chatto & Windus.

——(1988) *Life and Times*, 3 vols, London: Chatto & Windus.

Holdcraft, D. (1991) *Saussure: Signs, System and Arbitrariness*, Cambridge: Cambridge University Press.

Hollingdale, R. J. (1973) *Nietzsche*, London: Routledge & Kegan Paul.

Holmwood, J. (1996) *Founding Sociology? Talcott Parsons and the Idea of General Theory*, London and New York: Longman.

Hoiquist, M. (1990) *Dialogism: Bakhtin and his World*, London: Routledge.

Holub, R. (1992) *Antonio Gramsci: Beyond Marxism and Postmodernism*, London and New York: Routledge.

Homer, S. (1998) *Fredric Jameson: Marxism, Hermeneutics, Postmodernism*, Cambridge: Polity.

Hont, I. and Ignatieff, M. (eds) (1983) *Wealth and Virtue: The Shaping of Political Economy in the Scottish Enlightenment*, Cambridge: Cambridge University Press.

Horkheimer, M. (1947) *Eclipse of Reason*, New York: Oxford University Press.

—— (1972a) 'Traditional and Critical Theory', in his *Critical Theory: Selected Essays*, trans. M. O'Connell, New York: Continuum.

—— (1972b) 'Art and Mass Culture', in his *Critical Theory: Selected Essays*, trans. M. O'Connell, New York: Continuum.

—— (1974) *Critique of Instrumental Reason*, trans. M. O'Connell *et al.*, New York: Continuum.

—— (1978) *Dawn and Decline: Notes 1926–1931 and 1950–1969*, New York: Seabury.

—— (1980) *(1960)* 'Schopenhauer Today', in M. Fox (ed.) *Schopenhauer: His Philosophical Achievement*, Hassocks: Harvester.

—— (1989) *(1931)* 'The State of Contemporary Social Philosophy and the Tasks of an Institute for Social Research', in S. E. Bronner and D. M. Kellner (eds) *Critical Theory and Society: A Reader*, London: Routledge.

—— (1993) *Between Philosophy and Social Science: Selected Early Writings*, trans. G. F. Hunter *et al.*, Cambridge, MA: MIT Press.

Horkheimer, M. and Adorno, T. W. (1973) *(1947)* *The Dialectic of Enlightenment*, London: Allen Lane.

Horton, J. and Mendus, S. (eds) (1994) *After MacIntyre: Critical Perspectives on the Work of Alisdair MacIntyre*, Cambridge: Polity.

Horwich, P. (1993) *World Changes: Thomas Kuhn and the Nature of Science*, Cambridge, MA and London: MIT Press.

Houlgate, S. (1991) *Freedom, Truth and History: An Introduction to Hegel's Philosophy*, London and New York: Routledge.

How, A. (1995) *The Habermas–Gadamer Debate and the Nature of the Social: Back to Bedrock*, Aldershot: Avebury.

Hoy, D. C. (ed.) (1986) *Foucault: A Critical Reader*, Oxford: Blackwell.

Huck, G. J. (1995) *Ideology and Linguistic Theory: Naom Chomsky and the Deep Structure Debates*, London and New York: Routledge.

Hudson, W. (1982) *The Marxist Philosophy of Ernst Bloch*, London: Macmillan.

Hume, D. (1975) *(1748 and 1751) Enquiries*, ed. L. A. Selby-Brigg and P. H. Nidditch, Oxford: Oxford University Press.

—— (1978) *(1740) A Treatise of Human Nature*, ed L. A. Selby-Brigg and P. H. Nidditch, Oxford: Oxford University Press.

—— (1980) *Dialogues Concerning Natural Religion*, ed. R. H. Popkin, Indianapolis, IN: Hackett.

—— (1983) *(1778) The History of England*, 6 vols, Indianapolis, IN: Liberty Classics.

—— (1985) *(1757)* 'Of the Standard of Taste', in his *Essays: Moral, Political and Literary*, ed. E. F. Miller, Indianapolis, IN: Liberty.

—— (1993) *Selected Essays*, ed S. Copley and A. Edgar, Oxford: Oxford University Press.

—— (1997) *(1779) Natural History of Religion*, ed. N. K. Smith, London: Macmillan.

Husserl, E. (1954) *(1938) The Crisis of European Sciences and Transcendental Phenomenology*, Evanston, IL: Northwestern University Press.

—— (1962) *(1913) Ideas*, New York: Collier.

Husserl, E. (1964) *On the Phenomenology of the Consciousness of Internal Time (1893–1917)*, Bloomington, IN: Indiana University Press.

——(1970) *(1900–1901) Logical Investigations*, trans. J. N. Findlay, London: Routledge & Kegan Paul, and New York: Humanities Press.

——(1982a) *Ideas Pertaining to a Pure Phenomenology and to a Phenomenological Philosophy, First Book: General Introduction to a Pure Phenomenology*, trans. F. Kersten, The Hague: Martinus Nijhoff.

——(1982b) *Ideas Pertaining to a Pure Phenomenology and to a Phenomenological Philosophy Book 2: Studies in the Phenomenology of Constitution*, trans. R. Rojcewicz and A. Schuwer, Dordrecht and Boston, MA: Kluwer.

——(1995) *Cartesian Meditations: An Introduction to Phenomenology*, trans. D. Cairns, Dordrecht and Boston, MA: Kluwer.

——(1999) *The Essential Husserl: Basic Writings in Transcendental Phenomenology*, ed. D. Welton, Bloomington, IN: Indiana University Press.

Inglis, F. (2000) *Clifford Geertz: Culture, Custom, and Ethics*, Cambridge: Polity.

Inwood, M. (1983) *Hegel*, London: Routledge & Kegan Paul.

——(ed.) (1985) *Hegel*, Oxford: Oxford University Press.

——(1992) *A Hegel Dictionary*, Oxford: Blackwell.

Irigaray, L. (1985a) *(1974) Speculum of the Other Woman*, Ithaca, NY: Cornell University Press.

——(1985b) *(1977) This Sex Which is Not One*, Ithaca, NY: Cornell University Press.

——(1986) *Divine Women*, Sydney: Local Consumption.

——(1991) *(1980) Marine Lover of Friedrich Nietzsche*, New York: Columbia University Press.

——(1992a) *Elemental Passions*, trans. J. Collie and J. Still, New York: Routledge.

——(1992b) *(1990) Culture of Difference*, New York: Routledge.

——(1993a) *(1984) An Ethics of Sexual Difference*, New York: Cornell University Press.

——(1993b) *(1990) Je, tu, nous: Towards a Culture of Difference*, London: Routledge.

——(1993c) *Sexes and Genealogies*, trans. G. C. Gill, Ithaca, NY: Cornell University Press.

——(1994) *Thinking the Difference: For a Peaceful Revolution*, trans. K. Montin, New York: Routledge.

——(1996) *I Love to You: Sketch of a Possible Felicity in History*, trans. A. Martin, New York: Routledge.

Irwin T. and Fine, G. (eds) (1995) *Aristotle: Selections*, Indianapolis, IN: Hackett.

Jakobson, R. (1955) *Slavic Languages: A Condensed Survey*, 2nd edn, London and New York: King's Crown Press.

——(1970) *Shakespeare's Verbal Art in Th'expence of Spirit*, The Hague: Mouton.

——(1971) *Studies on Child Language and Aphasia*, The Hague: Mouton.

——(1971–1985) *Selected Writings*, vols 1–6, The Hague: Mouton.

——(1973) *Main Trends in the Science of Language*, London: Allen & Unwin.

——(1978) *Six Lectures on Sound and Meaning*, trans. J. Mepham, Hassocks: Harvester.

——(1983) *Dialogues*, Cambridge: Cambridge University Press.

——(1987a) 'Linguistics and Poetics', in K. Pomorska and S. Rudy (eds) *Language and Literature*, Cambridge, MA: Harvard University Press.

—— (1987b) *The Sound Shape of Language*, 2nd edn, Berlin: Mouton de Gruyter.

—— (1990) *On Language*, Cambridge, MA: Harvard University Press.

James, C. L. R. (1936) *Minty Alley*, London: Secker & Warburg.

—— (1937) *World Revolution 1917–1936: The Rise and Fall of the Communist International*, London: Secker & Warburg.

—— (1963) *Beyond a Boundary*, London: Hutchinson.

—— (1978) *(1952) Mariners, Renegades and Castaways: The Story of Hermann Melville and the World We Live In*, Detroit, MI: Bewick.

—— (1980) (1948) *Notes on Dialects: Hegel, Marx and Lenin*, London: Allison and Busby.

—— (1992a) *The CLR James Reader*, ed. A. Grimshaw, Oxford: Blackwell.

—— (1992b) *(1938) The Black Jacobins*, in James (1992a).

—— (1992c) *American Civilisation*, Oxford: Blackwell.

James C. L. R. , Dunayevskaya, R. and Briggs, G. (1986) *(1950) State Capitalism and World Revolution*, Chicago: Charles H. Kerr.

Jameson, F. (1961) *Sartre: The Origins of a Style*, New Haven, CT: Yale University Press.

—— (1971) *Marxism and Form*, Princeton, NJ: Princeton University Press.

—— (1972) *The Prison House of Language*, Princeton, NJ: Princeton University Press.

—— (1978) *Fables of Aggression*, Berkeley, CA: University of California Press.

—— (1982) *The Political Unconscious*, Ithaca, NY: Cornell University Press.

—— (1990a) *Late Marxism: Adorno, or the Persistence of the Dialect*, London: Verso.

—— (1990b) *Signatures of the Visible*, New York and London: Routledge.

—— (1991) *Postmodernism, or, The Cultural Logic of Late Capitalism*, London: Verso.

—— (1994) *The Seeds of Time*, New York: Columbia University Press.

Jarvis, S. (1998) *Adorno: A Critical Introduction*, Oxford: Polity.

Jay, M. (1984) *Adorno*, Cambridge, MA: Harvard University Press.

Jenkins, R. (1992) *Pierre Bourdieu*, London: Routledge.

Johnson, L. (1979) *The Cultural Critics: From Matthew Arnold to Raymond Williams*, London: Routledge & Kegan Paul.

Jones, E. (1964) *The Life and Work of Sigmund Freud*, Harmondsworth: Penguin.

Jung, C. G. (1959) *The Collected Works of C. G. Jung, vol. 91, Archetypes and the Collective Unconscious*, London: Routledge & Kegan Paul.

—— (1993) *(1917) The Psychology of the Unconscious: A Study of the Transformations and Symbolism of the Libido*, London: Routledge.

—— (1998) *Symbolic Life: Miscellaneous Writings (Collected Works of C. G. Jung, vol. 18)* ed. W. McGuire, trans. R. F. Hull, London: Routledge.

Kadarkay, A. (ed.) (1995) *The Lukács Reader*, Oxford and Cambridge: MA: Blackwell.

Kant, I. (1952a) *(1790) The Critique of Judgement*, Oxford: Oxford University Press.

—— (1952b) *(1790) The Critique of Practical Reason and Other Writings in Moral Philosophy*, trans. and ed. L. White Beck, New York: Garland.

—— (1964) *(1781) Critique of Pure Reason*, trans. N. Kemp Smith, London: Macmillan.

—— (1970) *Political Writings*, ed. by H. Reiss, Cambridge: Cambridge University Press.

Kant, I. (1976) (*1788*) *Critique of Practical Reason, and Other Writings in Moral Philosophy*, tr. and ed. L. White Beck, New York: Garland.

—— (1983) *(1786)* 'Speculative Beginning of Human History', in his *Perpetual Peace and Other Essays*, trans. T. Humphrey, Indianapolis, IN: Hackett.

—— (1987) *(1790) The Critique of Judgement*, trans. W. S. Pluhar, Indianapolis, IN: Hackett; (1952) Oxford: Oxford University Press.

Kaplan, G. and Kessler, C. (eds) (1989) *Hannah Arendt: Thinking, Judging, Freedom*, Sydney: Allen & Unwin.

Kaplan, E. A. and Sprinker, M. (1993) *The Aithusserian Legacy*, London: Verso.

Kaspersen, L. (2000) *Anthony Giddens: An Introduction to a Social Theorist*, trans. S. Sampson, Malden, MA: Blackwell.

Kateb, G. (1984) *Hannah Arendt: Politics, Consciousness, Evil*, Totowa, NJ: Rowman & Allanheld.

Kaufmann, W. (1974) *Nietzsche: Philosopher, Psychologist, Antichrist*, Princeton, NJ: Princeton University Press.

Kellner, D. (ed.) (1989) *Postmodernism/Jameson/Critique*, Washington, DC: Maisonneuve Press.

Kennedy, L. (1995) *Susan Sontag: Mind as Passion*, Manchester: Manchester University Press.

Kenny, A. (1992) *Aristotle on the Perfect Life*, Oxford: Clarendon.

—— (1993) *Wittgenstein*, Harmondsworth: Penguin.

Kojeve, A. (1969) *Introduction to the Reading of Hegel*, ed. A. Bloom, trans. J. H. Nichols, New York: Routledge.

Kolenda, K. (1990) *Rorty's Humanistic Pragmatism: Philosophy Democratized*, Tampa, FL: University of South Florida Press.

Korner, S. (1955) *Kant*, Harmondsworth: Penguin.

Krieken, R. van (1998) *Norbert Elias*, London: Routledge.

Kristeva, J. (1969) *Séméiotiké. Recherches pour une sémanalyse*, Paris: Seuil.

—— (1980) *Desire in Language*, New York: Columbia University Press.

—— (1982) *(1980) Powers of Horror: An Essay on Abjection*, New York: Columbia University Press.

—— (1984) *(1974) Revolution in Poetic Language*, New York: Columbia University Press.

—— (1986a) 'Word, Dialogue and Novel', in T. Moi (ed.) *The Kristeva Reader*, Oxford: Blackwell.

—— (1986b) 'The System and the Speaking Subject', in T. Moi (ed.) *The Kristeva Reader*, Oxford: Blackwell.

—— (1987) *(1983) Tales of Love*, New York: Columbia University Press.

—— (1989) *Black Sun*, New York: Columbia University Press.

—— (1991) *(1988) Strangers to Ourselves*, New York: Columbia University Press.

—— (1994) 'Psychoanalysts in Times of Distress', in S. Shamdasani (ed.) *Speculations after Freud*, New York: Routledge.

Kruks, S. (1994) *The Political Philosophy of Merleau-Ponty*, Aldershot: Gregg Revivals.

Kuhn, T. S. (1970) *The Structure of Scientific Revolutions*, 2nd edn, Chicago: University of Chicago Press.

Kukathas, C. and Pettit, P. (1990) *Rawls: A Theory of Justice and its Critics*, Cambridge: Polity.

Lacan, J. (1975) *(1932) De la psychose paranoiaque dans ses rapports avec la personnalité*, Paris: Seuil.

——(1977a) *(1973) Four Fundamental Concepts of Psychoanalysis*, London: Hogarth.

——(1977b) *(1966) écrits: A Selection*, trans. A. Sheridan, ed. J-A. Miller, London: Routledge.

——(1982) *(1979)* 'Joyce, *le Symptôme Actes du 5ème Symposium James Joyce*', *L'Ane*, 6.

Lacouture, J. (1975) *Andre Malraux*, trans. A. Sheridan, London: André Deutsch.

Laszlo, V. S. de (ed.) (1992) *The Basic Writings of C. G. Jung*, London: Routledge.

Lavers, A. (1982) *Roland Barthes: Structuralism and After*, Cambridge, MA: Harvard University Press.

Leach, E. (1970) *Lévi-Strauss*, London: Fontana.

Leavis, F. R. (1933) *Mass Civilization and Minority Culture*, Cambridge: Cambridge University Press.

——(1972) *Nor Shall My Sword: Discourses on Pluralism, Compassion and Social Hope*, London: Chatto & Windus.

——(1977) *The Living Principle: 'English' as a Discipline of Thought*, London: Chatto & Windus.

——(1979) *(1933) For Continuity*, London: Norwood.

——(1986) *Valuation in Criticism and Other Essays*, ed. G. Singh, Cambridge: Cambridge University Press.

Leavis, F. R. and Thompson, D. (1933) *Culture and Environment*, London: Chatto & Windus.

Lechte, J. (1990) *Julia Kristeva*, London: Routledge.

Lechte, J. and Zournazi, M. (1998) *After the Revolution: On Kristeva*, Sydney: Artspace.

Le Corbusier (1983) *(1925) Urbanisme*, London: Garland.

——(1954) *(1948) The Modulor: A Harmonious Measure to the Human Scale Universally Applicable to Architecture and Mechanics*, London: Faber & Faber.

——(1958) *(1955) Modulor II*, London: Faber & Faber.

——(1967) *(1933) The Radiant City: Elements of a Doctrine of Urbanism to be Used as the Basis of our Machine-Age Civilization*, London: Faber & Faber.

——(1987a) *(1923) Towards a New Architecture*, London: Architectural Press.

——(1987b) *(1924) The City of Tomorrow and its Planning*, London: Architectural Press.

Lecourt, D. (1975) *Marxism and Epistemology: Bachelard, Canguilhem and Foucault*, trans. B. Brewster, London: New Left Books.

Le Doeuff, M. (1982) 'Utopias: Scholarly', *Social Research*, 49(2).

——(1986) *(1980) The Philosophical Imaginary*, Stanford, CA: Stanford University Press.

——(1987) 'Ants and Women, or Philosophy without Borders', *Philosophy*, 21: 41–54.

——(1989) *Hipparchia's Choice: An Essay Concerning Women, Philosophy etc.*, Oxford: Blackwell.

——(1995) 'Simone de Beauvoir: Falling into (Ambiguous) Line', in M. Simons (ed.) *Feminist Interpretations of Simone de Beauvoir*, University Park, PA: Pensylvania State University Press.

Lehmann, J. M. (1994) *(1956) Durkheim and Women*, Lincoln, NB: University of Nebraska Press.

Leupin, A. (ed.) (1991) *Lacan and the Human Sciences*, Lincoln, NB and London: University of Nebraska Press.

Lévinas, E. (1987) *(1948) Time and the Other , and Additional Essays*, trans. R. A. Cohen, Pittsburgh, PA: Duquesne University Press.

——(1989) *The Lévinas Reader*, ed. S. Hand, Oxford: Blackwell.

——(1995a) *Ethics and Infinity: Conversations with Philippe Nemo*, trans. R. A. Cohen, Pittsburgh, PA: Duquesne University Press.

——(1995b) *(1947) Existence and Existents*, trans. A. Lingis, The Hague: Kluwer.

——(1998a) *(1991) Entre Nous: Thinking-of-the-other*, trans. M. Smith and B. Harshav, London: Athlone.

——(1998b) *(1961) Totality and Infinity: An Essay on Exteriority*, trans. A. Lingis, Pittsburgh, PA: Duquesne University Press.

——(1998c) *(1974) Otherwise than Being, or, Beyond Essence*, trans. A. Lingis, Pittsburgh, PA: Duquesne University Press.

Lévi-Strauss, C. (1966) *(1962) The Savage Mind*, London: Weidenfeld & Nicolson.

——(1968a) *(1958) Structural Anthropology*, Harmondsworth: Penguin.

——(1968b) 'The Structural Study of Myth', in his *Structural Anthropology*, Harmondsworth: Penguin.

——(1969) *(1949) The Elementary Structures of Kinship*, London: Eyre and Spottiswoode.

——(1970) *(1964) The Raw and the Cooked: Introduction to a Science of Mythology*, vol. 1, London: Cape.

——(1973) *(1967) From Honey to Ashes: Introduction to a Science of Mythology*, vol. 2, London: Cape.

——(1975) *(1955) Tristes Tropiques*, New York: Atheneum.

——(1977) *(1973) Structural Anthropology*, vol. 2, Harmondsworth: Penguin.

——(1978) *(1968) The Origin of Table Manners: Introduction to a Science of Mythology*, vol. 3, London: Cape.

——(1981) *(1971) The Naked Man: Introduction to a Science of Mythology*, vol. 4, London: Cape.

——(1987) *(1950) Introduction to the Work of Marcel Mauss*, trans. F. Baker, London: Routledge & Kegan Paul.

Lichtheim, G. (1970) *Lukács*, London: Fontana.

Livingston, D. W. and King, J. T. (eds) (1976) *Hume: A Re-Evaluation*, New York: Fordham University Press.

Lodge, D. (1990) *After Bakhtin: Essays on Fiction and Criticism*, London: Routledge.

Luhmann, N. (1982) *The Differentiation of Society*, New York: Columbia University Press.

Lukács, G. (1963) *(1958) The Meaning of Contemporary Realism*, London: Merlin.

——(1964) *Essays on Thomas Mann*, trans. S. Mitchell, London: Merlin.

——(1970) *Lenin: A Study on the Unity of his Thought*, trans. N. Jacobs, London: New Left Books.

——(1971) *(1922) History and Class Consciousness: Studies in Marxist Dialectics*, trans. R. Livingstone, London: Merlin.

——(1972a) *Studies in European Realism*, London: Merlin.

——(1972b) *Tactics and Ethics: Political Writings 1919–1929*, trans. M. McColgan, London: New Left Books.

——(1975) *The Young Hegel: Studies in the Relations between Dialects and Economics*, trans. R. Livingstone, London: Merlin.

——(1978a) *(1916) The Theory of the Novel*, London: Merlin.

——(1978b) *The Ontology of Social Being*, vol. 1, *Hegel's False and his Genuine Ontology*, tr. D. Fernbach, London: Merlin.

——(1980) *The Destruction of Reason*, trans. P. Palmer, London: Merlin.

——(1981) *Essays on Realism*, ed. R. Livingstone, Cambridge, MA: MIT Press.

——(1983) *(1937) The Historical Novel*, Lincoln, NB and London: University of Nebraska Press.

——(1995) *The Lukács Reader*, ed. A. Kadarkay, Oxford: Blackwell Publishers.

——(1991) *The Process of Democratisation*, trans. S. Bernhardt and N. Levine, Albany, NY: State University of New York Press.

——(1993) *German Realists in the Nineteenth Century*, trans. J. Gaines and P. Keast, Cambridge, MA: MIT Press.

——(1995) *The Lukács Reader*, ed. A. Kadarkay, Oxford: Blackwell.

——(2000) *A Defence of History and Class Consciousness: Tailism and the Dialect*, trans. E. Leslie, London and New York: Verso.

Lukes, S. (1973) *Emile Durkheim*, London: Allen Lane.

Lunn, E. (1982) *Marxism and Modernism: An Historical Study of Lukács, Brecht, Benjamin and Adorno*, Berkeley, CA: University of California Press.

Lyons, J. (1991) *Chomsky*, London: Fontana.

Lyotard, J-F. (1979) *The Postmodern Condition: A Report on Knowledge*, Manchester: Manchester University Press.

——(1988) *(1983) The Differend: Phrases in Dispute*, trans. G. van den Abeele, Manchester: Manchester University Press.

——(1991) *The Inhuman: Reflections on Time*, trans. G. Bennington and R. Bowlby, Cambridge: Polity.

——(1993) *Political Writings*, trans. B. Readings and K. P. Geiman, London: UCL Press.

——(1994) *Lessons on the Analytic of the Sublime: Kant's Critique of Judgment, sections 23–29*, trans. E. Rottenberg, Stanford, CA: Stanford University Press.

——(1999) *(1996) Signed, Malraux*, trans. R. Harvey, Minneapolis, MN: University of Minnesota Press.

Macann, C. (1993) *Four Phenomenological Philosophers: Husserl, Heidegger, Sartre, Merleau-Ponty*, London and New York: Routledge.

McCarthy, T. (1978) *The Critical Theory of Jürgen Habermas*, London: Hutchinson.

MacIntyre, A. (1958) *The Unconscious: A Conceptual Analysis*, London: Routledge & Kegan Paul.

——(1967) *Secularisation and Moral Change: The Ridell Memorial Lectures*, London: Oxford University Press.

——(1969) *The Religious Significance of Atheism*, New York: Columbia University Press.

——(1970) *Marcuse*, London: Fontana.

——(1981) *After Virtue: A Study in Moral Theory*, 2nd edn, London: Duckworth.

——(1988) *Whose Justice? Which Rationality?*, London: Duckworth.

MacIntyre, A. (1990a) *First Principles, Final Ends and Contemporary Philosophical Issues*, Milwaukee, WI: Marquette University Press.

—— (1990b) *Three Rival Versions of Moral Enquiry*, London: Duckworth.

—— (1998a) *A Short History of Ethics*, London: Routledge.

—— (1998b) *The MacIntyre Reader*, ed. K. Knight, Oxford: Polity.

—— (1999) *Dependent Rational Animals: Why Human Beings Need the Virtues*, London: Duckworth.

McLellan, D. (1973) *Karl Marx: His Life and Works*, New York: Harper & Row.

—— (1995) *Karl Marx: A Biography*, London: Papermac.

McLemee, S. and Le Blanc, P. (eds) (1994) *C. L. R. James and Revolutionary Marxism: Selected Writings of C. L. R. James 1939–1949*, Atlantic Highlands, NJ: Humanities Press.

McMylor, P. (1994) *Alasdair MacIntyre: Critic of Modernity*, London and New York: Routledge.

Madsen, A. (1977) *Malraux: A Bibliography*, London: W. H. Allen.

Magee, B. (1973) *Popper*, London: Fontana.

Magnus, B. and Higgins, K. M. (eds) (1996) *The Cambridge Companion to Nietzsche*, Cambridge: Cambridge University Press.

Mahon, M. (1992) *Foucault's Nietzschean Genealogy: Truth, Power, and the Subject*, Albany, NY: State University of New York Press.

Malachowski, A. R. (ed.) (1990) *Reading Rorty: Critical Responses to Philosophy and the Mirror of Nature (and Beyond)*, Oxford and Cambridge, MA: Blackwell.

Malraux, A. (1934) *(1933) Man's Fate*, trans. H. M. Chevalier, New York: Random House.

—— (1938) *(1937) Man's Hope*, trans. S. Gilbert and A. MacDonald, New York: Random House.

—— (1949–1950) *The Psychology of Art*, 3 vols, New York: Pantheon.

—— (1952) *(1943) The Walnut Trees of Altenburg*, trans. A. W. Fielding, Chicago: University of Chicago Press.

—— (1968) *(1967) Anti-memoirs*, trans. T. Kilmartin, New York: Holt, Rinehart & Winston.

—— (1976) *(1974) Picasso's Mask*, trans. J. Guicharnaud and J. Guicharnaud, New York: Holt, Rinehart & Winston.

—— (1977) *(1974) Lazarus*, trans. T. Kilmartin, New York: Holt, Rinehart & Winston.

—— (1978) *(1951) The Voices of Silence*, trans. S. Gilbert, Princeton, NJ: Princeton University Press.

Mandel, E. (1972) *Marxist Economic Theory*, London: Merlin.

—— (1975) *Late Capitalism*, London: Verso.

Marchionatti, R. (ed.) (1998) *Karl Marx: Critical Responses*, London: Routledge.

Marini, M. (1992) *Jacques Lacan: The French Context*, trans. A. Tomiche, New Brunswick, NJ: Rutgers University Press.

Marx, K. (1968) *(1852) The Eighteenth Brumaire of Louis Bonaparte*, in *Karl Marx and Fredrich Engels: Selected Works*, London: Lawrence & Wishart.

—— (1971) *(1859) A Contribution to the Critique of Political Economy*, London: Lawrence & Wishart.

—— (1973a) *(1857–1858) Grundrisse*, Harmondsworth: Penguin.

—— (1973b) 'The Eighteenth Brumier of Louis Bonaparte', in his *Surveys from Exile*, ed. D. Fernbach, Harmondsworth: Penguin.

—— (1975) *Early Writings*, trans. R. Livingstone and G. Benton, intro. L. Colletti, Harmondsworth: Penguin.

—— (1976) *(1867) Capital: A Critique of Political Economy*, vol. 1, trans. B. Fowkes, Harmondsworth: Penguin.

Marx, K. and Engels, F. (1970) *(1845–1846) The German Ideology*, London: Lawrence & Wishart.

Marx, K. and Engels, F. (1985) *(1848) The Communist Manifesto*, Harmondsworth: Penguin.

—— (1963) *Primitive Classification*, trans. R. Needham, London: Cohen & West.

—— (1966) *(1925) The Gift: Forms and Functions of Exchange in Archaic Societies*, London: Routledge & Kegan Paul.

Mauss, M. (1963) *Primitive Classification*, trans. R. Needham, London: Cohen & West.

—— (1966) *(1925) The Gift: Forms and Functions of Exchange in Archaic Societies*, London: Routledge & Kegan Paul.

—— (1972) *(1902–1903) A General Theory of Magic*, trans. R. Brain, London: Routledge.

—— (1973) (1935) 'Techniques of the Body', trans. B. Brewster, *Economy and Society*, 2(1): 70–88.

Mauss, M. and Herbert, H. (1981) *(1899) Sacrifice: Its Nature and Function*, trans. W. D. Halls, Chicago: University of Chicago Press.

May, D. (1986) *Hannah Arendt*, Harmondsworth: Penguin.

McLemee, S. and Le Blanc, P. (eds) (1994) *C. L. R. James and Revolutionary Marxism: Selected Writings of C. L. R. James 1939–1949*, Atlantic Highlands, NJ: Humanities Press.

Mead, M. (1959) *An Anthropologist at Work: Writings of Ruth Benedict*, Boston, MA: Houghton Mifflin.

—— (1974) *Ruth Benedict*, New York: Columbia University Press.

Melville, H. (1963) *Moby-Dick, or, the Whale*, in *The Works of Herman Melville, vols 7-8*, New York: Russell & Russell.

Mennell, S. (1989) *Norbert Elias: Civilisation and the Human Self Image*, Oxford: Basil Blackwell.

—— and Goudsblom, J. (eds) (1998) *Norbert Elias: On Civilisation, Power and Knowledge*, Chicago: University of Chicago Press.

Menzes, K. (1977) *Talcott Parsons and the Social Image of Man*, London: Routledge & Kegan Paul.

Merleau–Ponty, M. (1962) *(1945) Phenomenology of Perception*, London: Routledge & Kegan Paul.

—— (1963) *(1942) The Structure of Behaviour*, trans. A. L. Fisher, Boston, MA: Beacon.

—— (1964a) *(1947) Humanism and Terror*, trans. J. O'Neill, Boston, MA: Beacon.

—— (1964b) *(1960) Signs*, trans. R. C. McCleary, Evanston, IL: Northwestern University Press.

—— (1968) *(1964) The Visible and the Invisible*, trans. A. Lingis, Evanston, IL: Northwestern University Press.

—— (1973a) *(1955) Adventures of the Dialect*, trans. J. Bien, Evanston, IL: Northwestern University Press.

—— (1973b) *(1969) Prose of the World*, trans. J. O'Neill, Evanston, IL: Northwestern University Press.

Merleau-Ponty, M. (1992) *Texts and Dialogues*, ed. H. J. Silverman, and J. Barry, London: Humanities Press.

—— (1994) *The Merleau-Ponty Aesthetics Reader*, ed. G. A. Johnson, Evanston, IL: Northwestern University Press.

Merquior, J. G. (1980) *Rousseau and Weber: Two Studies in the Theory of Legitimacy*, London: Routledge & Kegan Paul.

—— (1991) *Foucault*, London: Fontana.

Merrell, F. (1993) *Sign, Intertextuality, World*, Bloomington, IN: Indiana University Press.

Mészáros, I. (1979) *The Work of Sartre*, vol. 1, *Search for Freedom*, Hassocks: Harvester.

—— (1986) *Marx's Theory of Alienation*, 4th edn, London: Merlin.

Meynell, H. (1975) 'Science, the Truth, and Thomas Kuhn', *Mind*, 84: 79-93.

Miguel-Alphonso, R. and Caporale-Bizzini, S. (eds) (1994) *Reconstructing Foucault: Essays in the Wake of the 80s*, Amsterdam: Rodopi.

Mill, J.S. (1900) *(1848) Principles of Political Economy, with some of their Applications to Social Philosophy*, London: Longmans, Green.

—— (1984) *(1859) On Liberty*, ed. G. Himmelfarb, Harmondsworth: Penguin.

—— *(1985) (1863) Utilitarianism: On Liberty*, London: Fontana.

—— (1986) *(1969) The Subjection of Women*, New York: Prometheus.

—— (1996) *(1843) System of Logic*, in J. S. Mill and J. M. Robson, *Collected Works of John Stuart Mill, VIP System of Logic: Ratiocinative and Inductive*, London: Routledge.

Mintz, S. (1984) 'Ruth Benedict', in S. Silverman (ed.) *Totems and Teachers*, New York: Columbia University Press.

Modell, J. (1983) *Ruth Benedict: Patterns of a Life*, Philadelphia, PA: Pennsylvania University Press.

Modgil, S. and Modgil, C. (eds) (1987) *B. F. Skinner: Consensus and Controversy; Reflections by B. F. Skinner*, New York and London: Falmer.

Moi T. (ed.) (1986) *The Kristeva Reader*, Oxford: Blackwell.

Moltmann, J. (1967) *The Theology of Hope*, London: SCM Press.

Mommsen, W. J. (1974) *The Age of Bureaucracy: Perspectives on the Political Sociology of Max Weber*, Oxford: Blackwell.

Moravcsik, J. M. E. (ed.) (1968) *Aristotle: A Collection of Critical Essays*, London: Macmillan.

Moreno, A. O. P. (1974) *Jung, Gods and Modern Man*, London: Sheldon.

Moriarty, M. (1991) *Roland Barthes*, Cambridge: Polity.

Morice, G. P. (ed.) (1977) *David Hume: Bicentenary Papers*, Edinburgh: Edinburgh University Press.

Morrow, G. R. (1973) *The Ethical and Economic Theories of Adam Smith*, Clifton, NJ: A. M. Kelly.

Mortley, R. (1991) *French Philosophers in Conversation: Lévinas, Schneider, Serres, Irigary, Le Doeff, Derrida*, New York: Routledge.

Mulhall, S. (1996) *Heidegger and Being and Time*, London: Routledge.

Mulhall, S. and Swift, A. (1992) *Liberals and Communitarians*, Oxford: Blackwell.

Mulhern, F. (1979) *The Moment of Scrutiny*, London: New Left Books.

—— (1995) 'Culture and Authority', *Critical Quarterly*, 37(1): 77-89.

Murphey, M. G. (1993) *The Development of Peirce's Philosophy*, Indianapolis, IN: Hackett.

Nielsen, A. L. (1997) *C. L. R. James: A Critical Introduction*, Jackson, MS: University Press of Mississippi.

Nietzsche, F. W. (1968a) *Basic Writings of Nietzsche* (including *The Birth of Tragedy*, *1872*; *Beyond Good and Evil, 1886*; *On the Genealogy of Morals, 1887*) ed. and trans. W. Kaufmann, New York: Basic Books.

——(1968b) *The Will to Power*, trans. W. Kaufmann and R. J. Hollingdale, New York: Viking.

——(1974) *(1882) The Gay Science*, trans. W. Kaufmann, New York: Vintage.

——(1982) *(1881) Daybreak*, trans. R. J. Hollingdale, Cambridge: Cambridge University Press.

——(1983) *(1873–1876) Untimely Meditations*, trans. R. J. Hollingdale, Cambridge: Cambridge University Press.

——(1986) *(1878) Human, All-Too-Human*, trans. R. J. Hollingdale Cambridge: Cambridge University Press.

——(1995) *The Portable Nietzsche* (including *Thus Spoke Zarathustra*, *1883–1892*; *Twilight of the Idols, 1889*; *The Antichrist, 1888/1895*) ed. and trans. W. Kaufmann, New York: Penguin.

Nordquist, J. (1997) *Pierre Bourdieu: A Bibliography*, Santa Cruz, CA: Reference and Research Services.

Norman, H. (1999) *Routledge Philosophy Guidebook to Hume on Knowledge*, London: Routledge.

Norman, R. (1980) *Hegel, Marx and Dialectic*, Hassocks: Harvester.

Norris, C. (1987) *Derrida*, London: Fontana.

——(1988) *Paul de Man: Deconstruction and the Critique of Aesthetic Ideology*, London: Routledge.

Noys, B. (2000) *Georges Bataille: A Critical Introduction*, London: Pluto.

Nussbaum, M. C. (1986) *The Fragility of Goodness: Luck and Ethics in Greek Tragedy and Philosophy*, Cambridge: Cambridge University Press.

——(1990) *Love's Knowledge: Essays on Philosophy and Literature*, New York and Oxford: Oxford University Press.

——(1994) *The Therapy of Desire: Theory and Practice in Hellenistic Ethics*, Princeton, NJ and Chichester: Princeton University Press.

——(1995) *Poetic Justice: The Literary Imagination and Public Life*, Boston, MA: Beacon.

——(1999) *Sex and Social Justice*, New York and Oxford: Oxford University Press.

Nussbaum, M. C. and Estlund, D. M. (1997) *Sex, Preference and Family*, Oxford: Oxford University Press.

Nussbaum, M. C. and Glover, J. (eds) (1995) *Women, Culture and Development*, Oxford University Press.

Nussbaum, M. C. and Olyan, S. M. (eds) (1998) *Sexual Orientation and Human Rights in American Religious Discourse*, New York and Oxford: Oxford University Press.

Nussbaum, M. C. and Sen, A. (eds) (1993) *Quality of Life*, Oxford: Oxford University Press.

Oakes, G. (ed.) (1984) *Georg Simmel: On Women, Sexuality and Love*, New Haven, CT: Yale University Press.

Oakeshott, M. (1933) *Experience and its Modes*, Cambridge: Cambridge University Press.

Oakeshott, M. (1975a) *Hobbes on Civil Association*, Oxford: Blackwell.

—— (1975b) *On Human Conduct*, Oxford: Clarendon.

—— (1983) *On History and Other Essays*, Oxford: Blackwell.

—— (1989) *The Voice of Liberal Learning: Michael Oakeshott on Education*, ed. T. Fuller, New Haven, CT: Yale University Press.

—— (1991) *Rationalism in Politics and Other Essays*, Indianapolis, IN: Liberty Fund.

O'Connor, B. (ed.) (2000) *The Adorno Reader*, Oxford: Blackwell.

O'Hear, A. (1995) *Karl Popper, Philosophy and Problems*, Cambridge: Cambridge University Press.

O'Neill, M. (ed.) (1999) *Adorno, Culture and Feminism*, London: Sage.

Ortner, S. B. (1999) *The Fate of 'Culture': Geertz and Beyond*, Berkeley, CA: University of California Press.

Outhwaite, W. (1994) *Habermas: A Critical Introduction*, Oxford: Polity.

—— (ed.) (1996) *The Habermas Reader* Oxford: Polity.

Parkinson, G. H. R. (1977) *Georg Lukács*, London: Routledge & Kegan Paul.

Parsons, T. (1937) *The Structure of Social Action*, New York: McGraw-Hill.

—— (1951) *The Social System*, Glencoe, IL: Free Press.

—— (1954) *Essays in Sociological Theory*, New York: Free Press.

—— (1967) *Social Theory and Modern Society*, New York: Free Press.

—— (1977a) *Social Systems and the Evolution of Action Theory*, New York: Free Press.

—— (1977b) *The Evolution of Societies*, Englewood Cliffs, NJ: Prentice Hall.

—— (1978) *Action Theory and the Human Condition*, New York: Free Press.

Parsons, T. and Bales, R. F. (1955) *Family: Socialisation and Interaction Process*, New York: Free Press.

Parsons, T. and Smelser, N. J. (1956) *Economy and Society*, New York: Free Press.

Passerin d'Entreves, M. and Benhabib, S. (1996) *Habermas and the Unfinished Project of Modernity: Critical Essays on the Philosophical Discourse of Modernity*, Cambridge: Polity.

Payne, M. (1993) *Reading Theory: An Introduction to Lacan, Derrida, and Kristeva*, Cambridge: Blackwell.

Pearce, F. (1989) *The Radical Durkheim*, London: Unwin Hyman.

Pefanis, J. (1991) *Heterology and the Postmodern: Bataille Baudrillard, and Lyotard*, Durham, NC: Duke University Press.

Penelhum, T. (1975) *Hume*, London: Macmillan.

Peperzak, A. (1997) *Beyond: The Philosophy of Emmanuel Lévinas*, Evanston, IL: Northwestern University Press.

Pickering, W. S. F. (ed.) (2000) *Durkheim and Representations*, London and New York: Routledge.

Pike, D. (1985) *Lukács and Brecht*, Chapel Hill, NC: University of North Carolina Press.

Pippin, R. B. (1989) *Hegel's Idealism: The Satisfaction of Self-Consciousness*, New York: Cambridge University Press.

Plato (1993) *The Last Days of Socrates: Euthyphro, Apology, Crito, Phaedo*, trans. H. Tredennick and H. Tarrant, Harmondsworth: Penguin.

—— (1997) *Complete Works*, ed. J. M. Cooper, Indianapolis, IN: Hackett.

—— (1999) *Republic*, trans. G. M. A. Grube, Indianapolis, IN: Hackett.

Pogge, T. W. (1989) *Realizing Rawls*, Ithaca, NY: Cornell University Press.

Popper, K. (1945) *The Open Society and its Enemies*, London: Routledge & Kegan Paul.

—— (1957) *The Poverty of Historicism*, London: Routledge & Kegan Paul.

—— (1959) *The Logic of Scientific Discovery*, London: Hutchinson.

—— (1963) *Conjectures and Refutations*, New York: Harper & Row.

—— (1972a) 'Conjectural Knowledge: My Solution to the Problem of Induction', in his *Objective Knowledge*, Oxford: Oxford University Press.

—— (1972b) *Objective Knowledge: An Evolutionary Approach*, Oxford: Oxford University Press.

—— (1974) *The Philosophy of Karl Popper*, ed. P. A. Schilpp, LaSalle, IL: Open Court.

—— (1977) *The Self and its Brain*, Berlin: Springer.

—— (1992) *Unended Quest: An Intellectual Autobiography*, London: Routledge.

Poster, M. (1979) *Sartre's Marxism*, London: Pluto.

Prendergast, C. (ed.) (1995) *Cultural Materialism: On Raymond Williams*, Minneapolis, MN: University of Minnesota Press.

Priest, S. (1998) *Merleau-Ponty*, London: Routledge. Quinton, A. (1999) *Hume*, London: Routledge.

Quinton, A. (1999) *Hume*, London: Routledge.

Radcliffe-Brown, A. R. (1952) *Structure and Function in Primitive Society*, New York: Free Press.

—— (1977) *The Social Anthropology of Radcliffe-Brown*, ed. A. Kuper, London: Routledge & Kegan Paul.

Ragland-Sullivan, E. (1986) *Jacques Lacan and the Philosophy of Psychoanalysis*, London and Canberra: Croom Helm.

Ransome, P. (1992) *Antonio Gramsci: A New Introduction*, New York: Harvester.

Raphael, D. D. (1985) *Adam Smith*, Oxford: Oxford University Press.

Rawls, J. (1972) *A Theory of Justice*, Oxford: Clarendon.

—— (1987) 'The Idea of an Overlapping Consensus', *Oxford Journal of Legal Studies*, 7(1): 1–25.

—— (1993) *Political Liberalism*, New York: Columbia University Press.

—— (1999a) *Collected Papers*, Cambridge, MA: Harvard University Press.

—— (1999b) *The Law of Peoples; with, The Idea of Public Reason Re-Visited*, Cambridge, MA: Harvard University Press.

Readings, B. (1991) *Introducing Lyotard: Art and Politics*, London and New York: Routledge.

Rée, J. (1974) *Descartes*, London: Allen Lane.

Reeve, C. D. C. (1981) *Philosopher-Kings*, Princeton, NJ: Princeton University Press.

Reinhard, B. (1998) *Max Weber: An Intellectual Portrait*, London: Routledge.

Richardson, H. S. (ed.) (1999) *Development and Main Outlines of Rawls's Theory of Justice*, New York: Garland.

Richardson, M. (1994) *Georges Bataille*, London: Routledge.

Richelle, M. N. (1995) *B. F. Skinner: A Reappraisal*, New York: Lawrence Erlbaum.

Ricoeur, P. (1974) *The Conflict of Interpretations: Essays in Hermeneutics*, Evanston, IL: Northwestern University Press.

—— (1981) *Hermeneutics and the Human Sciences*, ed. J. B. Thompson, Cambridge: Cambridge University Press.

Ricoeur, P. (1984–1988) *(1983–1985) Time and Narrative*, 3 vols, Chicago: University of Chicago Press.

—— (1992) *Oneself as Another*, trans. K. Blamey, Chicago: University of Chicago Press.

Robbins, D. (1991) *The Work of Pierre Bourdieu: Recognizing Society*, Buckingham: Open University Press.

Roberts, J. (1982) *Walter Benjamin*, London: Macmillan.

Robertson, R. and Turner, B. S. (1991) *Talcott Parsons: Theorist of Modernity*, London: Sage.

Rocher, G. (1974) *Talcott Parsons and American Sociology*, London: Nelson.

Rorty, R. (1972) 'The World Well Lost', *Journal of Philosophy*, 69: 649–665.

—— (1978) 'Philosophy as a Kind of Writing: An Essay on Derrida', *New Literary History*, 10.

—— (1982) *Consequences of Pragmatism: Essays, 1972–1980*, Brighton: Harvester.

—— (1991a) *Objectivity, Relativism, and Truth: Philosophical Papers*, vol. 1, Cambridge: Cambridge University Press.

—— (1991b) *Essays on Heidegger and Others: Philosophical Papers*, vol. 2, Cambridge: Cambridge University Press.

—— (1998) *Truth and Progress: Philosophical Papers*, vol. 3, Cambridge: Cambridge University Press.

—— (1999) *Philosophy and Social Hope*, Harmondsworth: Penguin.

Rose, G. (1978) *The Melancholy Science: An Introduction to the Thought of Theodor W. Adorno*, London: Macmillan.

—— (1981) *Hegel Contra Sociology*, London: Athlone.

—— (1984) *Dialect of Nihilism: Post Structuralism and Law*, Oxford: Blackwell.

—— (1992) *The Broken Middle: Out of our Ancient Society*, Oxford: Blackwell.

—— (1993) 'Architecture to Philosophy – the Post-Modern Complicity', in her *Judaism and Modernity: Philosophical Essays*, Oxford: Blackwell.

—— (1995) *Love's Work*, London: Chatto & Windus.

—— (1996) *Mourning Becomes the Law: Philosophy and Representation*, Cambridge: Cambridge University Press.

Rosenfeld, M. and Arato, A. (1998) *Habermas on Law and Democracy: Critical Exchanges*, Berkeley, CA: University of California Press.

Roudinesco, E. (1990) *Jacques Lacan & Co.: A History of Psychoanalysis in France 1925-1985*, trans. J. Mehlman, Chicago: University of Chicago Press.

Rousseau, J-J. (1968) *(1762) The Social Contract*, trans. M. Cranston, Harmondsworth: Penguin.

—— (1984) *(1754) A Discourse on Inequality*, trans. M. Cranston, Harmondsworth: Penguin.

—— (1986) *(1781) On the Origin of Language*, trans. J. H. Moran & A. Gode, Chicago: University of Chicago Press.

—— (1991) *On Education*, Harmondsworth: Penguin.

—— (1995) *The Confessions: and, Correspondence, including the Letters to Malesherbes*, Hanover, NH: University Press of New England.

Ryan, A. (1975) *J. S. Mill*, London: Routledge.

Said, E. (1975) *Beginnings: Intention and Method*, New York: Columbia University Press.

—— (1978a) *Orientalism*, New York: Random House.

—— (1978b) 'The Problem of Textuality: Two Exemplary Positions', *Critical Inquiry*, 4: 673–714.

—— (1991) *The World, the Text, and the Critic*, London: Vintage.

—— (1992a) *Musical Elaborations*, London: Vintage.

—— (1992b) *(1979) The Question of Palestine*, London: Vintage.

—— (1993) *Culture and Imperialism*, London: Chatto & Windus.

—— (2000) *The Edward Said Reader*, ed. M. Bayoumi and A. Rubin, New York: Vintage.

Said, E. and Mohr, J. (1993) *After the Last Sky: Palestinian Lives*, London: Vintage.

Sandel, M. (1982) *Liberalism and the Limits of Justice*, Cambridge: Cambridge University Press.

Sangster, R. B. (1982) *Roman Jakobson and Beyond: Language as a System of Signs; the Quest for the Ultimate Invariants in Language*, Berlin and New York: Mouton Publishers.

Sartre, J. P. (1947a) *Theatre, Les Mouches; Huis Clos; Morts sans sepulture; La Putain respectueueuse*, Paris: Gallimard.

—— (1947b) *The Reprieve*, trans. E. Sutton, London: Hamish Hamilton.

—— (1948) *Existentialism and Humanism*, trans. P. Mairet, London: Eyre Methuen.

—— (1949) *Intimacy and Other Stories*, trans. L. Alexander, London and New York: N. Spearman.

—— (1949–1950) *(1947) What is Literature?* trans. B. Frechtman, New York: Philosophical Library.

—— (1950) *Iron in the Soul*, trans. G. Hopkins, London: Hamish Hamilton.

—— (1956) *(1940) The Psychology of Imagination*, trans. B. Frechtman, New York: Washington Square Press.

—— (1957) *(1936) The Transcendence of the Ego*, trans. F. Williams and R. Kirkpatrick, New York: Noonday.

—— (1958) *(1943) Being and Nothingness*, trans. H. Barnes, London: Methuen.

—— (1962a) *Altona, Men without Shadows, The Flies*, Harmondsworth: Penguin.

—— (1962b) *(1936) Imagination: A Psychological Critique*, trans. F. Williams, Ann Arbor, MI: University of Michigan Press.

—— (1963) *(1952) Saint Genet, Actor and Martyr*, trans. B. Frechtman, New York: Braziller.

—— (1964a) *(1938) Nausea*, trans. L. Alexander, New York: New Directions.

—— (1964b) *The Problem of Method*, trans. H. E. Barnes, London: Methuen.

—— (1964c) *(1963) The Words*, trans. B. Frechtman, New York: Braziller.

—— (1965) *Situations*, trans. B. Eisler, London: Hamilton.

—— (1968a) *(1957) Search for a Method*, trans. H. Barnes, New York: Vintage.

—— (1968b) *(1947) The Age of Reason*, trans. E. Sutton, London: Hamish Hamilton.

—— (1971) *Sketch for a Theory of the Emotions*, trans. P. Mairet, London: Methuen.

—— (1976) *(1960) Critique of Dialectical Reason*, trans. A. Sheridan-Smith, London: New Left Books.

—— (1981–1993) *(1971–1972) The Idiot of the Family*, 5 vols, trans. C. Cosman, Chicago: University of Chicago Press.

—— (1984) *War Diaries: Notebooks from a Phoney War, November 1939–March 1940*, trans. Q. Hoar, London: Verso.

Sartre, J. P. (1992) *(1983) Notebooks for an Ethics*, trans. D. Pellauer, Chicago: University of Chicago Press.

Sassoon, A. S. (1987) *Gramsci's Politics*, 2nd edn, London: Hutchinson.

Saussure, F. de (1974) *(1916) Course in General Linguistics*, trans. W. Baskin, Glasgow: Fontana.

—— (1983) *(1916) Course in General Linguistics*, trans. R. Harris, London: Duckworth.

Sayres, S. (ed.) (1990) *Susan Sontag: The Elegiac Modernist*, New York and London: Routledge.

Schilpp, P. A. (1943) *The Origin of Dewey's Instrumentalism*, New York: Columbia University Press.

Schilpp, P. (ed.) (1981) *The Philosophy of Jean-Paul Sartre*, LaSalle, IL: Open Court.

Schneiderman, S. (1983) *Jacques Lacan: The Death of an Intellectual Hero*, Cambridge, MA and London: Harvard University Press.

Scholem, G. (1981) *Walter Benjamin: The Story of a Friendship*, trans. H. Zohn, New York: Schoken Press.

Schutz, A. (1962) *Collected Papers*, vol. 1, The Hague: Martinus Nijhoff.

—— (1964) *Collected Papers*, vol. 2, The Hague: Martinus Nijhoff.

—— (1967) *(1932) The Phenomenology of the Social World*, London: Heinemann.

Schutz, A. and Luckmann, T. (1974) *The Structures of the Lifeworld*, London: Heinemann.

Searle, J. (1969) *Speech Acts*, Cambridge: Cambridge University Press.

Sedgwick, P. (ed.) (1995) *Nietzsche: A Critical Reader*, Oxford: Blackwell.

Shearmur, J. (1996) *The Political Thought of Karl Popper*, London: Routledge.

Shepperson, A. (1995) 'On the Social Interpretation of Cultural Experience: Reflections on Raymond Williams's Early Cultural Writings 1958–1961', MA thesis, University of Natal, Durban, South Africa.

Sheridan, A. (1980) *Michel Foucault: The Will to Truth*, London: Tavistock.

Sherman, N. (ed.) (1999) *Aristotle's Ethics: Critical Essays*, Lanham, MD: Rowman & Littlefield.

Shiach, M. (1991) *Helene Cixous: A Politics No Writing*, London: Routledge.

Silverman, H. J. (ed.) (1991) *Gadamer and Hermeneutics*, New York: Routledge, Chapman & Hall.

Sim, S. (1994) *Georg Lukács*, New York and London: Harvester Wheatsheaf.

Simmel, G. (1950a) *The Sociology of Georg Simmel*, New York: Free Press.

—— (1950b) *(1903)* 'The Metropolis and Mental Life', in *The Sociology of Georg Simmel*, ed. and trans. K. H. Wolff, Glencoe, IL: Free Press.

—— (1950c) *(1908)* 'The Stranger', in *The Sociology of Georg Simmel*, ed. and trans. K. H. Wolff, Glencoe, IL: Free Press.

—— (1957) 'Fashion', *American Journal of Sociology*, 62(6): 541–558.

—— (1959) *(1908)* 'How is Society Possible?', in *Georg Simmel 1858–1918: A Collection of Essays with Translations and a Bibliography*, ed. K. H. Wolff, Columbus, OH: Ohio University Press.

—— (1968) *(1911)* 'On the Concept and Tragedy of Culture', in his *Conflict in Modern Culture and Other Essays*, New York: Teachers College Press.

—— (1971) *On Individuality and Social Forms: Selected Writings*, ed. D. Levine, Chicago: University of Chicago Press.

—— (1978) *(1907) The Philosophy of Money*, London: Routledge & Kegan Paul.

Skinner, B. F. (1953) *Science and Human Behaviour*, New York: Macmillan.

—— (1957) *Verbal Behaviour*, New York: Appleton Century Crofts.

—— (1973) *Beyond Freedom and Dignity*, Harmondsworth: Penguin.

—— (1974) *About Behaviourism*, London: Cape.

—— (1976) *(1948) Waldon Two*, London: Macmillan.

—— (1978) *Reflections on Behaviourism and Society*, Englewood Cliffs, NJ: Prentice Hall.

—— (1985) 'Cognitive Science and Behaviourism', *British Journal of Psychology*, 76(3): 291–301.

—— (1988) 'The Operant Side of Behaviour Therapy', *Journal of Behavioural Therapy and Experimental Psychiatry*, 19(3): 171–179.

—— (1989) *Recent Issues in the Analysis of Behaviour*, Columbus, OH: Merrill.

Skorupski, J. (1989) *John Stuart Mill*, London: Routledge.

—— (ed.) (1998) *The Cambridge Companion to Mill*, Cambridge: Cambridge University Press.

Smart, B. (1983) *Foucault, Marxism and Critique*, London: Routledge & Kegan Paul.

Smith, A. (1976a) *(1759) The Theory of Moral Sentiments*, ed. D. D. Raphael, and A. L. Macfie, Oxford: Clarendon.

—— (1976b) *(1776) The Wealth of Nations*, ed. R. H. Campbell, A. S. Skinner and W. B. Todd, Oxford: Clarendon.

—— (1996) *Julia Kristeva: Readings of Exile and Estrangement*, New York: St Martin's Press.

—— (1998) *Julia Kristeva: Speaking the Unspeakable*, London: Pluto.

Smith, B. and Woodruff Smith, D. (1995) *The Cambridge Companion to Husserl*, Cambridge and New York: Cambridge University Press.

Smith, G. (ed.) (1988) *On Walter Benjamin: Critical Essays and Recollections*, Cambridge, MA: MIT Press.

—— (ed.) (1999) *Goffman and Social Organisation: Studies in a Sociological Legacy*, London and New York: Routledge.

Smith, S. (1984) *Reading Althusser: An Essay on Structural Marxism*, Ithaca, NY: Cornell University Press.

Sontag, S. (1966) *Against Interpretation, and Other Essays*, New York: Dell.

—— (1973) *On Photography*, New York: Farrar, Giroux.

—— (1979) *Illness as Metaphor*, London: Allen Lane.

—— (1980) *Under the Sign of Saturn*, London: Writers & Readers.

—— (1982a) *A Sontag Reader*, Harmondsworth: Penguin.

—— (ed.) (1982b) *A Barthes Reader*, London: Cape.

—— (1983) *The Benefactor*, London: Writers & Readers.

—— (1989) *AIDS and its Metaphors*, London: Allen Lane.

—— (1993) *The Volcano Lover: A Romance*, London: Vintage.

—— (1994) *Styles of Radical Will*, London: Vintage.

—— (2000) *In America*, London: Cape.

Sorell, T. (1987) *Descartes*, Oxford: Oxford University Press.

Sprinker, M. (ed.) (1992) *Edward Said: A Critical Reader*, Oxford: Blackwell.

Stevens, A. (1994) *Jung*, Oxford: Oxford University Press.

Strawson, P. (1966) *The Bounds of Sense: An Essay on Kant's Critique of Pure Reason*, London: Methuen.

Stroud, B. (1977) *Hume*, London: Routledge.

Swartz, D. (1997) *Culture and Power: The Sociology of Pierre Bourdieu*, Chicago: University of Chicago Press.

Taylor, C. (1975) *Hegel*, Cambridge: Cambridge University Press.

—— (1979) *Hegel and Modern Society*, Cambridge: Cambridge University Press.

—— (1985a) *Human Agency and Language: Philosophical Papers I*, Cambridge: Cambridge University Press.

—— (1985b) *Philosophy and the Human Sciences: Philosophical Papers II*, Cambridge: Cambridge University Press.

—— (1985c) 'What is Human Agency?', in Taylor (1985a) .

—— (1985d) 'Self-Interpreting Animals', in Taylor (1985a) .

—— (1989) *Sources of the Self*, Cambridge: Cambridge University Press.

—— (1995) *Philosophical Arguments*, Cambridge, MA: Harvard University Press.

Thayer, H. S. (1981) *Meaning and Action: A Critical History of Pragmatism*, Indianapolis, IN: Hackett.

—— (ed.) (1989) *Pragmatism: The Classic Writings*, Indianapolis, IN: Hackett.

Thibault, P. (1997) *Re-Reading Saussure: The Dynamics of Signs in Social Life*, London and New York: Routledge.

Thompson, B. and Vigginai, C. A. (eds) (1984) *Witnessing Andre Malraux: Visions and Re-Visions*, Middletown, CT: Wesleyan University Press.

Thomson, P. and Sacks, G. (eds) (1993) *The Cambridge Companion to Brecht*, Cambridge: Cambridge University Press.

Tredell, N. (1990) *Uncancelled Challenge: The Work of Raymond Williams*, London: Pauper's Press.

Tubbs, N. (1997) *Contradiction of Enlightenment: Hegel and the Broken Middle*, Aldershot: Ashgate.

Tully, J. (ed.) (1994) *Philosophy in an Age of Pluralism: The Philosophy of Charles Taylor in Question*, Cambridge: Cambridge University Press.

Turner, B. S. (1981) *For Weber: Essays on the Sociology of Fate*, London: Routledge & Kegan Paul.

Turner, G. (1996) *British Cultural Studies*, 2nd edn, London: Routledge.

Various (1993) Special issue on Pierre Bourdieu, *French Cultural Studies*, 4(3).

Vasseleu, C. (1998) *Textures of Light: Vision and Touch in Irigary, Lévinas and Merleau-Ponty*, London: Routledge.

Vattimo, G. (1988) *The End of Modernity: Nihilism and Hermeneutics in Postmodern Culture*, trans. J. R. Snyder, Cambridge: Polity.

Voloshinov, V. N. (1973) *(1929) Marxism and the Philosophy of Language*, New York: Seminar Press.

Warnke, G. (1987) *Gadamer: Hermeneutics, Tradition, and Reason*, Cambridge: Polity.

Warnock, M. (1965) *The Philosophy of Sartre*, London: Hutchinson.

Waugh, L. (1976) *Roman Jakobson's Science of Language*, Bloomington, IN: P. de Ridder.

Weber, M. (1930) *(1904–1905) The Protestant Ethic and the Spirit of Capitalism*, London: George Allen & Unwin.

—— (1946a) *From Max Weber: Essays in Sociology*, ed. H. H. Gerth and C. W. Mills, London: Routledge & Kegan Paul.

—— (1946b) *(1921)* 'Bureaucracy', in his *From Max Weber: Essays in Sociology*, London: Routledge & Kegan Paul.

——(1946c) *(1921)* 'Class, Status, Party', in his *From Max Weber: Essays in Sociology*, London: Routledge & Kegan Paul.

——(1946d) 'India: The Brahman and the Castes', in his *From Max Weber: Essays in Sociology*, London: Routledge & Kegan Paul.

——(1964) *(1922) The Theory of Social and Economic Organisation*, trans. A. M. Henderson and T. Parsons, New York: Free Press.

——(1978) *(1921) Economy and Society*, ed R. Guenther and C. Wittich, Berkeley, CA and London: University of California Press.

——(1979) *(1923) General Economic History*, New Brunswick, NJ: Transaction.

——(1994) 'The Freiberg Address', in his *Political Writings*, Cambridge: Cambridge University Press.

Weinsheimer, J. (1985) *Gadamer's Hermeneutics: A Reading of* Truth and Method, New Haven, CT: Yale University Press.

White, S. K. (1988) *The Recent Work of Jürgen Habermas: Reason, Justice and Modernity*, Cambridge: Cambridge University Press.

Whitfield, S. J. (1980) *Into the Dark: Hannah Arendt and Totalitarianism*, Philadelphia, PA: Temple University Press.

Whitford, M. (1991) *Luce Irigaray: Philosophy in the Feminine*, London: Routledge.

Wiener, D. N. (1996) *B. F. Skinner: Benign Anarchist*, Boston, MA: Allyn & Bacon.

Wiggershaus, R. (1994) *The Frankfurt School: Its History, Theories and Political Significance*, trans. M. Robinson, Cambridge: Polity.

Wilcox, H. (ed.) (1990) *The Body and the Text: Hélène Cixous, Reading and Teaching*, Hemel Hempstead: Harvester.

Willett, J. (1984) *Brecht in Context: Comparative Approaches*, London: Methuen.

Williams, D. (1989) *Truth, Hope, and Power: The Thought of Karl Popper*, Toronto and London: University of Toronto Press.

Williams, R. (1958) *Culture and Society 1780–1950*, London: Chatto & Windus.

——(1961) *The Long Revolution*, London: Chatto & Windus.

——(1962) *Communications*, Harmondsworth: Penguin.

——(1968) *Drama from Ibsen to Brecht*, rev. edn, London: Chatto & Windus.

——(1973) *The Country and the City*, London: Chatto & Windus.

——(1974) *Television: Technology and Cultural Form*, London: Fontana.

——(1976) *Keywords*, London: Fontana.

——(1977) *Marxism and Literature*, Oxford: Oxford University Press.

——(1983) *Keywords*, 2nd edn, London: Fontana.

——(1986) *Culture*, London: Fontana.

——(1989a) *Resources of Hope: Culture, Democracy, Socialism*, London: Verso.

——(1989b) *The Politics of Modernism: Against the New Conformists*, London: Verso.

——(1991) *Writing in Society*, London: Verso.

——(1995) 'Between Politics and Metaphysics: Reflections in the Wake of Gillian Rose', *Modern Theology*, 11(1): 3–22.

Winch, P. (1958) *The Idea of a Social Science and its Relation to Philosophy*, London: Routledge & Kegan Paul.

Wittgenstein, L. (1956) *Remarks on the Foundations of Mathematics*, trans. G. E. M. Anscombe, Oxford: Blackwell.

——(1958) *Philosophical Investigations*, 2nd edn, trans. G. E. M. Anscombe, Oxford: Basil Blackwell.

Wittgenstein, L. (1967) *Remarks on the Foundations of Mathematics*, ed G. H. von Wright, R. Rhees and G. E. M. Anscombe, trans. G. E. M. Anscombe, Oxford: Blackwell.

—— (1974) *(1921) Tractatus Logico-Philosophicus*, trans. D. F. Pears and B. F. McGuinness, London: Routledge & Kegan Paul.

—— (1981) *Zettel*, ed. G. E. M. Anscombe and G. H. von Wright; trans. G. E. M. Anscombe, Oxford: Blackwell.

—— (1994a) *(1969) On Certainty*, trans. D. Paul and G. E. M. Anscombe, Oxford: Blackwell.

—— (1994b) *The Wittgenstein Reader*, ed. A. Kenny, Oxford: Blackwell.

—— (1996) *(1953) Philosophical Investigations*, trans. G. E. M. Anscombe, Oxford: Blackwell.

Wokler, R. (1995) *Rousseau*, Oxford: Oxford University Press.

Wolfgang, J. M. (1992) *The Political and Social Theory of Max Weber: Collected Essays*, Cambridge: Polity.

Wolin, R. (1994) *Walter Benjamin: An Aesthetic of Redemption*, Berkeley, CA: University of California Press.

Wood, A. W. (1990) *Hegel's Ethical Thought*, Cambridge: Cambridge University Press.

Wood, J. C. (ed.) (1984) *Adam Smith: Critical Assessments*, London: Croom Helm.

Wood, J. C. (ed.) (1987) *John Stuart Mill: Critical Assessments*, London: Croom Helm.

Wright, G. H. von (1982) *Wittgenstein*, Oxford: Basil Blackwell.

Young, R. (1990) *White Mythologies: Writing, History and the West*, London and New York: Routledge.

—— (1995) *Colonial Desire*, London: Routledge.

Young-Eisendrath, P. and Dawson, T. (eds) (1997) *The Cambridge Companion to Jung*, Cambridge: Cambridge University Press.

Ziauddin, S. (2000) *Thomas Kuhn and the Science Wars*, Duxford: Icon.

Zuidervaart, L. (1991) *Adorno's Aesthetic Theory: The Redemption of Illusion*, Cambridge, MA and London: MIT Press.

INDEX

Note: Page numbering in **bold type** indicates the subject's main entry.